STARDUST MELODIES

PANTHEON BOOKS
60 YEARS OF PUBLISHING

WILL FRIEDWALD

STARDUST

MELODIES

*The Biography of Twelve
of America's Most Popular Songs*

PANTHEON BOOKS, NEW YORK

Library of Congress Cataloging-in-Publication Data

Friedwald, Will, 1961–
Stardust melodies: the biography of twelve of America's most popular songs / Will Friedwald.
p. cm.
Contents: Star dust — St. Louis blues — Ol' man river — Mack the knife — Body and soul — I got rhythm — As time goes by — Night and day — Stormy weather — Summertime — My funny valentine — Lush life.
ISBN 0-375-42089-4
1. Popular music—United States—History and criticism. I. Title.

ML3477 .F75 2002
782.42164'0973—dc21   2001036514

www.pantheonbooks.com

Book design by M. Kristen Bearse

Printed in the United States of America
First Edition
2 4 6 8 9 7 5 3 1

IN MEMORY OF

HERB FRIEDWALD

1935–1997

N+

AND FOR

BEAUTIFUL

FOR FILLING MY LIFE WITH JOY

All right, you cats been talkin' 'bout you got rhythm.
You got this and you got that. *I* got rhythm!
I'm gonna see what you all got.

—LOUIS ARMSTRONG,
his spoken intro to "I Got Rhythm"

Singing is the lowest form of communication.

—HOMER SIMPSON

There are three kinds of songs—
happy songs, sad songs, and songs for teenagers
who like things like 'Tweedle-Dee-Dee.'

—FRED FLINTSTONE

CONTENTS

INTRODUCTION
AND ACKNOWLEDGMENTS

IN 1970 THE GREAT CHOREOGRAPHER George Balanchine put together a ballet entitled *Who Cares?,* a work based on seventeen of George Gershwin's most famous songs. Clive Barnes, in reviewing the work for the *New York Times,* quoted one of Noel Coward's best-known bromides, "How potent cheap music is." I don't know if Sir Noel, who was alive and active at the time, ever read this review, but he had already lived more than long enough to see this line of his not necessarily misquoted but misused time and time again. The line appears in Coward's play *Private Lives,* in a scene in which the actor-playwright-composer, upon hearing one of his own songs, makes an in-joke at his own expense. Coward never intended it in the spirit in which Barnes and other commentators have used it, as a sweeping indictment of the whole of twentieth-century colloquial music. It was one thing for Coward to display a charming touch of self-deprecation, but it's unlikely that anyone, up to and including Sir Noel, actually regarded his songs, or those of Gershwin, Porter, or Kern, as "cheap music."

Nonetheless, potent they are. The potency of pop music derives from its immediacy and intimacy, empowering this music to move us on a deep level, and in a way that few other artistic mediums can. The history of classic American pop (which is to say, the kind that flourished before and even during the coming of rock-and-roll, and which continues to survive in spite of it) is the story of singers, bandleaders, instrumentalists, jazz improvisers, Broadway shows, and Hollywood films.

Yet one element persists above all, and that is the songs themselves. Astronomers can trace the birth, life, and death of a star, but there has never been a serious attempt to chart the biographies of the most important of the Great American Popular Songs.

The central thesis of this book is that the classic American song is the most flexible form of music: it's conceivable that one could take a tune by

Bob Dylan and play it as a waltz, a cha-cha, or a swing flag-waver, but why would you want to? Nothing would be gained by reinterpreting that particular piece of material. Likewise, it would be wrong to deviate very far from the tempos Mozart indicated for his Jupiter symphony. However, the first four bars of that symphony bear a mysterious resemblance to "For All We Know" by Sam Lewis and J. Fred Coots, and one can interpret that 1934 number—like all pop songs—in any tempo, in any time signature, in any style. The American Popular Song is like a car full of clowns at the circus: from the outside it looks small and unassuming, yet you can't believe how much is contained inside. As Mel Tormé put it mildly, "Popular songs are subject to constant interpretation."

When I mentioned the idea behind this book to people over the year or so it took me to write it, their question was always the same: How did you come up with your list of songs? I generally avoided answering by saying that it was actually my editor, Bob Gottlieb, who came up with the list (which is at least half true, since there's not a single item on it that he and I didn't discuss in detail and agree to).

This list is not intended as our choice of the twelve greatest songs of all time, nor is it a list of the twelve most popular or most recorded songs of all time. It's merely a list of twelve great songs, each of which has enough of a history, a long enough list of recordings, and a wide enough variety of interpretations in many different styles.

We considered a number of songs that are widely heard in jazz, such as "Cherokee," "How High the Moon," and "Tiger Rag," but although all of them have lyrics that have been recorded, they primarily exist as jazz instrumentals and are only infrequently sung—people remember "Moon" less for its original text than for Ella Fitzgerald's scat solo on it. I also had the idea of including, to use a long-extinct term, a "novelty" song—something like "Three Little Fishes" or "Civilization" would give me the opportunity to discuss a whole other genre of popular music. But I quickly realized that no one novelty can be considered representative of that entire genre, nor could I find one that lends itself to a variety of interesting interpretations.

Readers will no doubt be puzzled by the absence of even one song by Irving Berlin. Both my editor and I feel that Berlin was probably the greatest songwriter of all time (hardly a minority opinion), but I also found it impossible to pick any individual song of his that stood out from the others. Certainly "White Christmas" is Berlin's single best-known work, yet it didn't meet our criteria for inclusion: it's been heard in different styles for nearly sixty years, but its form and content demand a certain consistency to the interpretations. "White Christmas" is almost always heard as a sober, seasonal song no matter if it's being done by Bing Crosby, Elvis Presley, the Drifters, Charlie Parker, or even Anita O'Day. We considered many of Berlin's finest songs, particularly "Blue Skies" and "How Deep Is the Ocean?" but neither of them really stood out from the others the way that, say, "Night and Day" stands out as Cole Porter's single most notable song. In a way, it would have been easier to do a book of twelve Berlin songs than to choose just one.

The same can almost be said for Harold Arlen and "Stormy Weather." At one point we did consider "Over the Rainbow," but that's a clear-cut case of a song that's going to live from here to eternity linked "with an umbilical cord made of piano wire" (to quote Sheridan Whiteside) to a single performer. Others have sung it besides Judy Garland—Frank Sinatra, Ella Fitzgerald, and Tony Bennett are hardly slouches—but I think it's fair to say that all performances by all other singers were pretty much given in reaction to Garland and her lifelong association with the song.

LIKE EVERY OTHER AUTHOR, I have a list of acknowledgments—you know, friends who looked over the manuscript or even just talked it over with me and made suggestions, additions, and corrections. I must, however, begin with the names of two associates who made this book possible. Without Bob Gottlieb as editor and chief "inspirator" (as Louis Armstrong would say), there's no chance I would have written this book. Even the idea for the project came out of informal discussions and a long friendship with Bob. He had already edited, extracurricularly, my *Sinatra! The Song Is You,* for which he performed what amounted to an eleventh-hour rescue job. This time Bob helped me shape the whole work from the beginning, and was instrumental not only in determining the list of songs to be included but in deciding what each chapter would include.

Extra-special thanks also to Mitch Zlokower (aka Zak Mitchell). Mitch is a professional pianist, singer, conductor, composer, and orchestrator whom I met through my lifelong chum Eric Comstock about ten years ago (it turns out that Mitch and I both went to Edward R. Murrow High

School, although he turned up there about a decade after me). It's appropriate that Mitch plays the piano, because he serves the same function for me that a pianist does for a singer: because he understands music so deeply and intimately, he was able to help me get inside the songs the way a writer and fan (and, I proudly declare it, a really dreadful amateur saxophonist) never could. Mitch's understanding of harmony was particularly useful. Of course, all mistakes and errors of judgment remain strictly mine.

Not long ago, I happened to be sitting next to a friend of mine and his eleven-year-old daughter at an awards show. After we had heard several dozen winners get up and make long, overwrought acceptance speeches, his little girl said, in a voice loud enough for everybody to hear, "Gee, Daddy, is it really such a big deal?" The great thing about the acknowledgments in a book, perhaps the literary equivalent of an awards-show acceptance speech, is that no one forces you to read them.

Having said that, it's now time for that customary list of associates who put in their two cents and made this book a better place to live in: Helen Green, Cindy Bitterman, Dan Morgenstern, Mike Peters, Maria Carcidi, Eric Comstock, Ivan Santiago, Scott Schecter, Roger Sturtevant, Ken Bloom, George Avakian, Dick Hyman, Jim Maher, Bob "Snix" Sixsmith, Roger Schore, Heather Gilchriest, Dave Weiner, Dan Levinson, Gary and Lea Giddins, Richard Sudhalter, Joan Bender, Adam Thorburn, David Carey, Dave Wondrich, Dr. Demento (aka Mr. Barry Hansen), Al Simmons, John Leifert, Mike Kieffer, Don McGlynn, Richard Ehrenzeller, Andrew Homzy, Glenn Simensky, David Ostwald, Joe Lauro, Chuck Granata, Wodehouse scholar David McDonough, Berthe Schuchat, Mickey Clark, Jonathan Cohen, Vince Giordano, Jon Zeiderman, Al Simmons and the Toast Group, David "PegHead" Torreson and the songbirds list (songbirds@yahoogroups.com), Sherwin Dunner, Leonard Maltin, Bruce Goldstein, Ron Hutchinson and the Vitaphone Project, Stephanie Cooper, Tim Brooks, Bonnie Schiff-Glenn, Rich Markow, and Jeff Healey. My agent, William Clark, deserves special thanks for helping to make this book a reality. Did I forget to thank the Creator?

I also want especially to thank Peter Mintun for providing me with many cheerful facts, quite a few of which completely contradict the written record about Herman Hupfeld and, even more so, Johnny Green. And to Loren Schoenberg, for spending hours with the manuscript and doing some serious kibbitzing with regard to the more technical matters.

These people were all extraordinarily generous with their record collections, their knowledge, and their selves, and this work is all the richer for them.

CAPE COD DISC JOCKEY Dick Golden, a longtime friend of Tony Bennett's, recently had the opportunity to talk about music with a group of young people. He started by asking them if they could name the tune that won the most recent Grammy as the best song of the year. They couldn't. Then he asked if they could name the number-one hit the year before. Again, they couldn't. Lastly, he asked if they'd heard of "Body and Soul," "Summertime," or "My Funny Valentine." And all of them had. Now, to be fair, they probably would also know at least a few songs by the Beatles, but it's remarkable to me that they know more songs by George Gershwin than they do by Bob Dylan, even though Dylan wrote his best songs far more recently and works in a genre that is allegedly much closer to home for millennial youth. Obviously, the songs by Gershwin and his interwar and mid-century contemporaries have a particular currency that is not to be found in the pop music of the last forty years. This book is an attempt to examine the qualities these writers brought to their art, and to discuss how they play themselves out in different ways in different songs.

WILL FRIEDWALD
February 2001

STAR DUST (1927)

music by Hoagy Carmichael

words by Mitchell Parish

L UCY IS HOLDING A SAXOPHONE. It turns out, as she informs friend Ethel Mertz, she's an amateur musician. Who knew? Lucy then blows into the mouthpiece and produces a few dyspeptic squawks. "It kind of sounds like 'Star Dust,' " says Ethel, diplomatically. "Yeah," Lucy responds, "everything I play sounds like 'Star Dust.' "

Somehow this least expected of testimonials to "Star Dust" resonates particularly loudly. By the mid-1950s, when *I Love Lucy* was the most popular show in America (and therefore, one assumes, a credible barometer of national taste), "Star Dust" had already been around for twenty-five years and was long established as the most popular of popular songs. Ten years later, it was estimated that Hoagy Carmichael's classic had been recorded at least five hundred different times and its lyric translated into forty languages. (Although over the years, on record labels and in various other places, it has sometimes been spelled as a single word, the correct title is given as two words, "Star Dust.")

Long before *Lucy*, "Star Dust" had also become archetypal Tin Pan Alley: its dreamy, somewhat meandering melody had inspired thousands of other tunes, its metaphor lyric had launched God knows how many other reveries of love and loss. Small wonder that everything Lucy played should remind her of the song. Yet long after its canonization, "Star Dust" remains a maverick: its construction, its history, and its unique place in the celestial firmament of essential American music stamp it as a song like no other.

The song's melody and lyric are both uncommonly introspective for a popular song. The tune, especially intricate, but without being fussy, is almost delicate in the way it unfolds, yet at the same time, it's masculine enough to withstand extremely tough treatment at the hands of such macho, hell-for-leather improvisers as Coleman Hawkins and Roy Eldridge. Mitchell Parish's words are, if not as urbane as some by Cole Porter or Lorenz Hart, sensitive in a way that few pop songs are. Yet what makes all this sensitivity unique is the long association of "Star Dust" with male performers, especially boy singers and jazz musicians. Although a number of women have sung it, the major recordings are predominantly by men (with the unlikely exception of Ella Fitzgerald).

"Star Dust," it would seem, is a love song made for men to express the way they feel about women. That's how Ben Webster played it, as a solo feature with Duke Ellington's orchestra. Up until 1940, Webster had been known primarily as one of the hardest-hitting tenormen in jazz, noted for his rough-and-tumble up-tempo playing and his gritty blues technique. (Off the bandstand, as well, Webster had a reputation for settling disagreements with his fists, and did not restrict himself to exercising them only on members of his own sex.) It was at the Ellington orchestra's famous 1940 dance in Fargo, North Dakota (famous primarily for being an early example of a remote concert recording) that Webster's rhapsodically romantic treatment of "Star Dust" was first documented. The song became a staple of his repertoire for years after he had departed the Ellington ranks, and Webster would periodically prevail upon Jack Towers, the engineer who had recorded the Fargo concert, to cut him a few 45-rpm acetate pressings to hand out to friends.

According to legend, composer Carmichael (1899–1981) was thinking about a girl when the melody of "Star Dust" first hit him, around 1926. Until then, he had regarded the making of music, whether as performer or composer, strictly as a sideline. His piano playing had supported him through law school (Indiana University), but on graduating he gave up practicing the piano to practice law ("and be a real success") with a firm in Miami. It didn't last. By 1927, Carmichael was back in Indiana, and back to music.

If Hollywood had ever filmed Carmichael's life (Gary Cooper would have gotten the role, and Hoagy himself would have played his own fictitious sidekick, named "Cricket" or "Smoke" or something), the scene of "Star Dust"'s creation would have been shot against a painted backdrop of a nocturnal sky rich with starlight. Our hero, while paying a nostalgic visit to his alma mater, happens to pass the campus's lover's lane, or "spooning wall" as it was known, and begins thinking about all the girls he'd loved and lost in his college days. While pondering one old school romance in particular, the kernel of a melody just pops into his head. A frantic Carmichael dashes in search of a piano and locates one in the campus coffee house—a cozy little joint called the "Book Nook"—where, oblivious to all else, our hero works the melody out and gets it down on paper. Shortly afterward, he plays it for a friend and former classmate named Stu Gorrell, who remarks that it reminds him "of the dust from the stars drifting down through a summer night." From there comes the title "Star Dust." "I had no idea what the title meant," Carmichael later said, "but I thought it was gorgeous."

The legend, as is often the case, probably isn't true: according to Richard Sudhalter, currently in the process of finishing the first serious biography of Carmichael, Hoagy had been working on the tune at least since early 1926, possibly while still in Miami. Thus the whole story about the spooning wall and the Book Nook may have been a later invention, although the wall notion would later find its way into the lyric.

Carmichael introduced "Star Dust" on records in a session for Gennett Records, the number-one label for jazz and blues in the Midwest, on Halloween, 1927. He recruited a symphathetic band of friends who usually played under the leadership of pianist Emil Seidel, although in this case they were credited on the original label as "Hoagy Carmichael and His Pals." The verse is introduced by trumpeter Byron Smart, following which the main melody is laid out by one of the alto players (Gene Woods or Dick Kent). Then Carmichael plays a one-chorus piano solo (a true solo, as he is completely unaccompanied) that immediately sets up a brilliant set of variations on the song. The arrangement is in D natural (two sharps), which, as Sudhalter observes, must have been the key Carmichael felt best suited his piano solo. He certainly wasn't doing the horns any favors by throwing them into "sharp-infested waters."

The original 1927 tempo of "Star Dust" is considerably faster than we're accustomed to hearing, especially in the wake of Nat King Cole and Frank Sinatra. This has misled many historians to describe "Star Dust" as having originally been a "stomp" or a "ragtime" number. Although the melody has the feel of a jazz improvisation, particularly one by Hoagy's hero Bix Beiderbecke, make no mistake: "Star Dust" was always essentially a reflective, contemplative tone poem. Indeed, back at the beginning, Carmichael even wrote a set of love lyrics to the tune. But love songs, like every other kind of music then, were also meant for dancing, and the idea of a band or a jazz-influenced pop singer doing a number in slow rubato (really slow out-of-tempo balladeering, as we know it today, was not heard in pop music until the coming of Sinatra, decades later) was all but unknown. Carmichael's 1927 disc of "Star Dust" moves along at a comparatively fast clip, yet it's slower than most other recordings by Carmichael's compadre Emil Seidel or by any other band of the era.

It has also been widely reported (by Alec Wilder, among others) that the verse was added only later, at about the time Mitchell Parish wrote his famous lyric. But the verse is there on the 1927 premiere recording by Hoagy and pals. Just listen: the disc opens with a guitar intro (the instrument was just beginning to be widely heard in the new age of electrical recordings; banjos had dominated in the acoustic era) before the trumpet takes the now famous verse, which can be heard on virtually all the early "jazz" versions of the tune. The apocryphal story of the verse being written later on was to work against Carmichael: for years a rumor persisted that the verse wasn't written by Carmichael at all but by Don Redman, a composer and arranger who worked for Carmichael's publisher, Irving Mills. As with the persistent gossip that Fats Waller actually wrote some of Jimmy McHugh's songs, there's nothing to back it up.

Although Redman didn't write the verse, that pioneering jazz orchestrator (also saxophonist, bandleader, and novelty vocalist) does play an important role in the career of "Star Dust." Redman, who had spent the earlier part of the twenties as musical director for Fletcher Henderson's band, was by then the leader of McKinney's Cotton Pickers. The McKinney's band, based in Detroit, seems to have been the first to record "Star Dust" after Carmichael, working under the pseudonym of "The Chocolate Dandies." (This was in October of 1928, nearly a year after Carmichael had recorded the entire song, verse included.) Carmichael brought his own chart to Detroit and met with Redman, who, according to Sudhalter, "filled it out and corrected the voicings," although he left it in Carmichael's key, D major.

Apart from the evidence of the verse existing on the original Gennett recording, there's the evidence of one's own ears. A single hearing of its melody, which is even more meandering and ruminative than the chorus's, should be enough to convince anyone that the verse is by the same hand that penned the central chorus melody. The chord changes in the verse are slightly more conventional than they are in the chorus, as we'll see, but the melody of the verse is either the work of the same mind—it uses the same kind of range and intervals—or the mind of a darn clever forger.

There's one particularly lovely record of "Star Dust" from 1987 by avant-garde jazzman Archie Shepp, most of whose career can be regarded as a rebellion against the traditional musical values that "Star Dust" had come to stand for. What we find here, however, is a romantic tenor treatment of the great love song in the best Ben Webster tradition, done as a duet with the remarkable expatriate pianist Horace Parlan. The oddest thing about this recording is that the CD booklet credits the song to "Carmichael-Redman," inserting Don Redman's name and omitting poor Mitchell Parish entirely.

Paradoxically, in its time, "Star Dust" was hardly a traditional song. Compared to most pop songs of the late twenties, "Star Dust" is conventional in certain aspects but in many others it's rather daringly different, for its day or any other. It consists of a thirty-two-bar chorus that can be broken down into four eight-bar sections, as well as a sixteen-bar verse, something that can be said of about ninety percent of the items in what we consider to be the Great American Songbook. The current edition of the published sheet music is in C. The melody moves primarily in thirds. Sometimes these are major thirds (as C to E) and sometimes minor thirds (as B to D). While this is uncommon, Sudhalter notes, there are are other songs of the period that do use these bigger intervals as organically as "Star Dust" does, among them "Coquette," "Make Believe," "I'll Get By," and "All of Me."

"Star Dust" also has an uncommonly wide range. And while other songs do this, too—"Night and Day" covers an octave and a fifth whereas "Star Dust" travels only an octave and a third—these other songs generally use their high and low notes as a means of heightening the drama. "Night and Day" saves its low G for a climactic moment, but "Star Dust" uses its widely polarized high-highs and low-lows as an integral aspect of its basic melody. At the start of the second bar we're on a low D ("spend") and exactly four beats later we're holding a high E for a whole measure, and a bar after that we're back down at low D. As I say, this is no special effect; it's simply the bread and butter of the "Star Dust" melody. The song never stops jumping high and then stooping low.

When we talk about the structure and the harmony of any given song, we're usually talking about two separate, if interrelated, issues. With "Star Dust," however, it's impossible to discuss one without the other. As we've noted, the song is thirty-two bars in length, but it's not laid out in typical *A-A-B-A* form. With most songs, it's immediately apparent where the eight-bar sections begin and end; with "Star Dust," the start of the B section is more ambiguous. The form is *A-B-A-C,* but even that isn't clearly spelled out, and each section is eight bars long.

In many songs—"I'm in the Mood for Love," for instance—we get a recurrence of the tonic chord at either the beginning or end, or both, of each eight-bar section. This doesn't happen on "Star Dust." The tonic normally helps serve notice that one section is ending and a new one is beginning, but in "Star Dust" the chords keep progressing right through the start of the new segment. And the lyric matches this movement: rather than stop a sentence and start a new one, lyricist Mitchell Parish pins an ongoing thought to this passage, which just continues uninterrupted. The B section melody begins at the start of bar nine, on the last three words of the line, "when our *love was new.*" Those words fall on the V chord (the fifth, which in C major is G), and in fact this is the only time in the chorus when Carmichael gives us the same note (G) three times in a row. Instead of the tonic (C), we linger on the unresolved dominant and don't get to the tonic again for another two measures.

The song starts on the IV (F) chord in major, then shifts, in bar 3, to minor (Fm+7); we don't spend any time to speak of on the tonic until bar 5, where it arrives, appropriately, on the word "melody." Traveling through the circle of fifths, we pass through the iii (Em7), the VI (A7), the ii (Dm7), and hit the iv (Fm+7) again. The harmonies of the opening section are reminiscent of the 1918 "After You've Gone" and anticipate Gerald Marks's 1931 jazz classic "All of Me," among many other songs. The difference is that those other two songs employ some of the same chords in a more conventional fashion. In "Star Dust," the subdominant (Dm7) leads to the dominant (G) at the start of the B section, expressed in two bars of variations on the dominant chord (G7, Gdim7, G7 again, and then G7 with an augmented 5th to correspond with a D-sharp on the word "*in*-spir-a-tion"). The B section also dwells on the II chord ("But that was long ago . . ."), either a D9 or a D7.

The return to the A section is in itself striking. As noted, the transition from A to B is so subtle that we don't even notice we're changing sections.

The shift back from *B* to *A* is more pronounced, and jarring in fact, because it brings us back to *A* before we've really registered it mentally that we've left *A* to begin with. This second *A* section, which begins with the words "Beside a garden wall," is identical to the first melodically and harmonically (only the lyric is different), the only time anything is repeated in the song. The chords of the final section, *C*, are, for the most part, solidly major. This not only provides the song with a strong and unambiguous resolution, but gives the last eight bars a decidedly anthemic feel. The sixteen-bar verse that precedes the chorus begins and ends in C but has many of the characteristics of the refrain (including a melody that travels primarily in thirds). The third bar of each A section ("night" and "bright") is truly a long, sustained E note against the Fm+7 (IV) chord. This is an amazing dissonant note probably not found in any other song of the period.

IRVING MILLS HAD BEEN publishing Carmichael's compositions at least since "Washboard Blues" in 1926. By 1930, Mills had solidified his reputation as a music publisher and band agent specializing in black and jazz-oriented talent—most famously Duke Ellington (whom he represented as both a performing artist and a composer). Thus "Star Dust" quickly began to circulate in black and jazz circles, although, as we have seen, the first group to record the song after Carmichael was not one of Mills's East Coast charges but the Detroit-based McKinney's Cotton Pickers (aka the Chocolate Dandies). Coincidentally, however, both of the group's principal arrangers, Will Hudson and Don Redman (McKinney's musical director), would eventually join Mills's staff.

Mills himself would produce recordings of "Star Dust" by at least four different bands, the first in November 1928, with a studio unit, the personnel of which is still unknown, credited on the label as "Mills' Merry Makers." A low-register clarinet splits the first chorus of the melody with a nimble-fingered trombonist; a no less nimble altoist plays the verse. Most interestingly, the tempo is the slowest the tune has yet been heard in (on record), and the key is a half-tone up (E flat) from Carmichael's. By contrast, the next Mills version, made in September 1929 (back in D), is a more rough and ready affair with vigorous solos from trumpeter Manny Klein and altoist Jimmy Dorsey and the familiar faster tempo, as well as a piano solo that recalls the composer's Gennett effort. In an imaginative jazz switch, the original Carmichael piano solo appears as a sax trio statement. The impresario seems to have put this date together to feature Carmichael and his songs (all three on the session are his) and, in one case, even his singing. Though Hoagy was front and center, the results were still released as by "Irving Mills and His Hotsy-Totsy Gang."

By 1929, the tune had caught on solidly among jazzmen, but it wasn't known at all to the general public. That would change when Mills decided to have a lyric written for it. In his autobiography, Carmichael disavowed the notion of "Star Dust" serving as a love song with lyrics. "It didn't seem a part of me," Carmichael recalled thinking when he finally heard the finished work. Yet, as we've seen, Carmichael had written his own words to it back at the very beginning, words that were considerably more sugary than the 1929 text to "Star Dust" that the world has come to know. This lyric was the work of Mitchell Parish (1900–1993), a Mills staff member who, like Carmichael, worked in the legal profession. Unlike Carmichael, however, Parish continued to labor as a law clerk through most of the thirties, even though he was already responsible for some of the most profitable songs of the era. A year younger than Carmichael, Parish, who (according to some sources) was born in Shreveport, Louisiana, but grew up with all the other songwriters on Manhattan's Lower East Side, had been writing professionally since 1920. He had been associated with Mills at least since 1922, when "Waltz of India" was published as credited to Parish (who wrote the words), Jimmy McHugh (who wrote the music), and Mills (who probably did nothing, but often cut himself in as a co-composer in order to pocket an even larger chunk of the proceeds).

Like Mills, Parish would make a specialty of songs with jazz associations—his first notable success was "Sweet Lorraine." (It could be that Art Tatum was acknowledging Parish when he quoted "Sweet Lorraine" in the middle of his "Star Dust"; and perhaps it's no coincidence that Nat King Cole recorded definitive versions of both songs.) In 1930, Parish would anonymously write the lyrics to "Dreamy Blues" and help transform it into "Mood Indigo," thereby beginning a long association with Duke Ellington. Parish would eventually broaden his scope from jazz instrumentals to all manner of works that required lyrics in English, including Leroy Anderson's "pops" pieces (e.g., "Sleigh Ride") and foreign songs (e.g., "All My Love").

The final lyric for "Star Dust" seems to be a crystallization of ideas by Parish, Stu Gorrell, and Carmichael himself (who had used the phrase "Star Dust melody" in his original), and the story told in the lyric is consistent with Carmichael's tale of how the tune happened to come to him. It can be summed up in a single sentence: a fellow alone at night gazes up at the stars and, reflecting on a past love, hums a song in his head. Toward the end of the first *A* section, we learn that the song is being sung to the absent lover. As he does with much else in the lyric, Parish sneaks this fact in somewhat cagily, with his rhetorical shift from the first to the second person: ". . . and I am once again with you." In a Tin Pan Alley kind of a way, the idea is almost Proustian—that just one listen could inspire so much reminiscin'. It's also important to note that the text was written in 1929, the year that Wall Street laid an egg, and that its popularity blossomed over the course of the Great Depression. "Star Dust" is hardly a Depression song in the same sense as "Brother, Can You Spare a Dime?" or "The Gold Diggers Song (We're in the Money)," but it makes sense that the basic conceit of the song—fond recollections of a recent bygone time when things were better—must have been especially welcome in the early thirties.

The chorus opens with the well-known phrase "Sometimes I wonder . . . ," which, as a construction, is as awkward as it is beautiful. Carmichael used it as the title of his second autobiography (1965), supposedly at the suggestion of Peggy Lee. (His first memoir, from 1946, also had a relevant title, *The Star Dust Road*.) Yet sometimes one wonders exactly what purpose is served by that opening phrase. Before the protagonist can get to the moonlit reverie, he must first contemplate the nature of the reverie itself. Perhaps it goes with the masculine slant of the song: men don't want to deal with their feelings and can't come out with their emotions directly. What he really wants to tell us is that he spends "the lonely nights dreaming of a song," but first he feels obliged to justify all that dreaming. It's all a bit rhetorical—after all, if he really doesn't know why he spends the lonely nights dreaming of a song, he's dumber than he looks—but Parish gets the job done with the high standard of professionalism that was his stock-in-trade.

The verse, if florid in the traditional Tin Pan Alley way, is especially effective: by opening with the word "And," he instills the feeling that the story has started even before the song commences, that we're merely tuning in to a game already in progress. Carmichael's rough 1926 lyric uses the phrase "star dust" over and over, but Parish is more economical with it. The reference, in the verse, to "the purple dust ["dusk" in some versions] of twilight times" might lead some to accuse him of writing purple prose, but it does start to set up the idea of "dust" as something other than a household inconvenience—a substance that could indeed have cosmic, even romantic, significance. The term "star dust" itself appears only twice in the text, and both times it's worked into a triple metaphor of love, the cosmos, and music—near the end of the verse ("the star dust of a song") and the chorus ("my star dust melody"). Parish also throws in a reference to a "garden wall" (and he would come up with "sleepy garden walls" for "Deep Purple," a very star-dusty number from 1939). Perhaps this "garden wall" is a manifestation of the "spooning wall" that allegedly inspired Carmichael in the first place: the song has now become part of its own mythology.

Thus, "Star Dust" was complete, with verse and chorus and lyrics, by 1929. It was only in May 1930, however, that the first "pop" version—albeit instrumentally—of the song was recorded. The term "pop" is here in quotes because this was Isham Jones's band, which was only slightly less of a jazz organization than those led by Mills or even Don Redman. (Jones even plays the song in two sharps, the familiar key of the earlier jazz versions.) In addition to being a bandleader, Jones was himself a composer and arranger, and his band would launch the careers of two other composer-arranger-bandleaders, Victor Young and Gordon Jenkins, both of whom would figure prominently in the evolution of "Star Dust."

Jones, who wrote a few all-time standards himself ("It Had to Be You," "I'll See You in My Dreams"), led one of the premier dance bands of all time. It is perhaps an oversimplification to say that he and Young, who arranged this chart, deserve full credit for carrying "Star Dust" over from jazz original into pop folklore. In David Ewen's *American Popular Song,* Jimmy Dale, another gifted arranger of the immediate pre-swing era, is credited with the innovation of playing "Star Dust" in a "slower tempo and in a sentimental style," although this was, as we've seen, the direction the song was headed in from the beginning. Still, while the Jones-Young "Star Dust" of 1930 is only slightly slower than the 1928 Mills Merry Makers version, it is indisputedly the first pop performance of the song, including, among other elements, a small string section with the melody stated by Young himself on violin. There's no doubt that the Jones record was the first to introduce "Star Dust" to the mass audience.

"Star Dust" was among the final selections that Young would orches-
trate for Isham Jones; in 1931 Young became a house conductor for the
American Recording Corporation (ARC) and launched a series of dance-
band sides under his own name on the Brunswick label. One of the earli-
est of these (May 1931), by the newly christened "Victor Young and His
Orchestra," was a twelve-inch concert treatment of "Star Dust." Though
Young's orchestra was the principal attraction on this side, it featured the
Boswell Sisters, a vocal group from New Orleans that ARC's head, Jack
Kapp, had also only recently signed.

"The Bozzies," as they were nicknamed, were notorious among song
pluggers for recasting and altering the melodies of songs in a completely
original and very jazzy way, and this particular "Star Dust" takes a lot of
liberties with Carmichael's tune. Some of these variations sound as if they
were the work of the sisters themselves, but others sound as if they originated as part of Young's idea for transforming the tune into an extra-long
concert work. There's a generally grandiose approach throughout, and
several symphonic-style tempo changes. In this case, the biggest departure from the written melody is an original intro which goes "I am always
dreaming of the 'Star Dust' " and then reappears as "My poor heart is
broken and I'm lonely / Always dreaming of the sweet star dust." From
that point on, the Boswells sing it close to straight, very slowly with only
sustained strings. When they get to the second half ("beside a garden
wall . . .") the vocal trio goes briefly into swingtime but slows down
again for the coda. The piece winds up with a big concerto finish in which
the Boswells reappear briefly. One can't finally rate this as either a classic
Boswell Sisters record or a classic version of "Star Dust," but it's a fascinating four and a half minutes. (The best vocal group version is probably
the Mills Brothers' Decca single of 1939, which is one of the last to spotlight the brothers' penchant for vocal imitations of instrumentation, a
major factor in their early thirties sides.)

We don't know what recording of the song first included the lyric,
although the Ben Selvin version of April 22, 1931 (featuring Benny
Goodman and Tommy Dorsey in the sections and a vocal by Smith
Ballew), has to be among the first. Then there is Ted Wallace and His
Campus Boys from a month later. In the Selvin track, trumpeter Mannie
Klein plays the verse (and Ballew sings one of the words on a wrong
note); in the Wallace recording the vocal is handled by the gifted but

insane trumpeter Jack Purvis. However, for all intents and purposes the Mitchell Parish text became part of American musical history with two breakthrough recordings in 1931 by Bing Crosby (August) and by Louis Armstrong (November). These were the two performances that gave "Star Dust" pop and jazz immortality, respectively. Crosby and Armstrong further testify to the close connection between these two forms, in that "Star Dust" can be both things at once—sentimental love song and hot jazz stomp.

Crosby doesn't only croon his version in a sweet romantic style, he scats and he whistles and at various points improvises on the melody, even exchanging phrases with alto soloist Jimmy Dorsey (who'd already played the tune on the '29 Mills version). This Crosby version (in C major) closes with a few notes on the celeste, as if to suggest stars twinkling in heaven's firmament. Its accompaniment was directed by Victor Young, then Brunswick's chief house conductor, in his third recording of the song in less than eighteen months. The orchestration, presumably by Young, slows the tempo down still further—it's definitely a ballad by now—but it's still considerably faster than it would be in the post-Sinatra era. Crosby's reading of the verse is particularly masterful; this is surely the definitive early vocal version of the song. The only real contender wouldn't come along until the the classic Nat Cole–Gordon Jenkins version twenty-five years later.

Crosby had known Carmichael at least since 1927; Carmichael's idol had been the greatest of all midwestern jazzmen, Bix Beiderbecke, and Crosby had worked with that legendary cornetist in Paul Whiteman's orchestra. As historians such as Duncan Schiedt and Richard Sudhalter have shown, there was indeed an Indiana-Iowa school of jazz in the mid-twenties, and Beiderbecke was its greatest son. Bix's influence is palpable on such Carmichael classics as "Star Dust," "Blue Orchids," and, especially, "Skylark."

Carmichael's relationship with the other great trumpeter of the era—indeed of all time—Louis Armstrong hasn't been investigated as thoroughly as it deserves to be. In 1929 and '31 Armstrong recorded three of Carmichael's early classics, "Star Dust," "Rockin' Chair" (with Hoagy himself in duet), and "(Up a) Lazy River." In *The Faber Companion to 20th Century Pop Music,* the editors claim that "Star Dust" quotes from Armstrong's 1927 "Potato Head Blues." Sudhalter points out that bars 3 and 4 of Armstrong's "Potato" solo are echoed in the stop-time portion, bars 25 and 26, of Armstrong's "Star Dust" solo. But this occurs in Armstrong's version only, not in "Star Dust" as written. Loren Schoenberg adds that this particular "lick" also turns up in a lot of classical music and isn't necessarily something Carmichael would have gotten only from Armstrong.

All three songs became staples of Armstrong's repertoire, particularly the latter two, and he would record more than a dozen of Carmichael's songs over the years, giving him more attention than any other composer. The jewel of the whole batch, however, is Armstrong's 1931 "Star Dust" (in D flat), which survives in two takes. As Louis glorifies the melody, with both a stellar trumpet solo and his vocalizing, his energetic paraphrase is irresistible. In Armstrong's treatment, the last lines become the exclamation "Oh memory! Oh memory!" (not heard in the alternate take), itself a veritable rallying cry for "Star Dust."

And musicians were indeed rallied by it. Among Armstrong's trumpet progeny who took it on were Louis Prima—who was still very much under Armstrong's sway when he was featured playing it on a 1934 big-band date for Associated transcriptions led by Joe Venuti—and the cockney Nat Gonella, who recorded it both in 1935 and 1940. (Other Pops-influenced players who had something outstanding to say with "Star Dust" include Yank Lawson, with Bob Wilber, and Ruby Braff.) Coleman Hawkins, the next great soloist in jazz after Armstrong, made two recordings of it during his European sojourn, in 1935 and 1937.

Also in '38 it was performed by the team of Chu Berry and Roy Eldridge, who in that year could have been described as "Hawkins and Armstrong: The Next Generation." Eldridge did even better by Hoagy's tune six years later in a bravura treatment with his big band. That 1943 disc is a strong and forceful yet tasteful performance, open-belled and beautiful, which clearly shows what "Star Dust" was all about. "Star Dust" was also grist for the mill of many virtuoso soloists, starting with pianists Art Tatum (1934), Garnet Clark (1935), and Fats Waller (1937).

Thus, by 1931 the song was up and running. Irving Mills recorded it yet again, now with lyrics, with virtually all his bands (nearly all of which, by now, were black), including the Mills Blue Rhythm Band (1931) and Cab Calloway (1931), both of which succeeded Ellington at the Cotton Club at various times. White arranger Will Hudson, leading his own Mills unit, recorded it in 1936, and non-Mills black bands were doing it, as well: Fletcher Henderson (1931), Jimmie Lunceford (another Cotton Club band, 1934), and Edgar Hayes (1938).

Lunceford's record is both elegant and disappointing. The melody is stated by lush, opulent reeds, just the way the song ought to be heard— no problem there, except that the second half is dominated by a vocal from trombonist Henry Wells, who, like most black band singers of the thirties, seems strangely indebted to the white falsettos and tenors of a decade earlier, although there's something of the Crosby-Armstrong tradition in his phrasing. He's not bad, but he's not special, either, and the space should have been used for something more interesting.

The last of the Mills charges to capitulate was his number one band, Duke Ellington. Ellington may well have been playing "Star Dust" live for years, but there's no written or recorded evidence that it was in the band's book until around the time he was parting company with Mills in 1940; the Maestro would occasionally return to the tune for many years thereafter.

BY THE TIME BENNY GOODMAN ignited the big-band boom in 1935, "Star Dust" was recognized as the most played staple of the swing era, a perfect vehicle for a large jazz ensemble that wanted to play something a little more introspective than "Bugle Call Rag." Not coincidentally, all four of the major white swing bands on Victor—Benny Goodman, Tommy Dorsey, Glenn Miller, and Artie Shaw—cut the tune for the corporation between 1936 and 1940. "Star Dust" was a major part of the swing vocabulary, and virtually every band had its own interpretation of it. It was a ballad that wasn't excessively sentimental and a jazz original that wasn't based in the blues.

Both Goodman and Tommy Dorsey had long and involved relationships with the song, starting with the 1931 Ben Selvin version, on which both were present, Goodman playing alto. The classic Goodman Victor version of 1936, arranged by Fletcher Henderson, was a classic of the early swing era. It had roots in two sources, the first being the 1931 version by Henderson's own orchestra. A lot has been said about white bands of the period taking black bands as models; the Henderson orchestra recording is a clear-cut case of a black group being inspired by the white, midwestern school of Carmichael, Bix Beiderbecke, and the Jean Gold-kette band. As Bill Challis, who arranged the Henderson version, told Phil Schaap in 1985, the leader was deliberately trying to evoke the sound of the Beiderbecke–Frank Trumbauer ensembles, with cornetist Rex Stewart doing Bix. Stewart aside, it's not a very successful attempt; Henderson's band, abandoning their own glorious idiom, sounds sloppy and underprepared. (Their homage to Bix and Tram on "Singin' the Blues" came off better.)

In June 1935, two months before his Palomar Ballroom "break-through," Goodman recorded a noncommercial version of "Star Dust" for Thesaurus, RCA Victor's transcription service. This three-and-a-half-minute treatment is quite nice, opening with the melody on the muted trumpets, except for the second A (bars 16–24), which is given over to like-muted trombones. The second chorus is a pip: it's all Goodman, again except for the second A, taken by altoist Toots Mondello. These particular solos are more typical examples of white musicians relying on black role models, since Mondello is in a Benny Carter bag here and Goodman, in his last eight, brings to mind the jumping between high and low that Armstrong did on "Alligator Crawl."

The transcription, released as by "The Rhythm Makers Dance Orches-tra," is a semi-slow number for dancing. The tempo picks up considerably with the 1936 Henderson chart, which is still a dance number, but one that makes the dancers work harder. It's much more of a piece with the swing era; the only soloist of note here is the leader, and he doesn't reuse any of the ideas from the Rhythm Makers record. The glory is in the ensemble and in the swinging fashion in which they phrase Carmichael's now classic melody. One almost wishes that the leader and the orchestrator had set things up so that Goodman played all the way through, which would make this close enough to a concerto for clarinet to scare the hell out of Artie Shaw.

Conversely, Goodman's 1939 sextet record of "Star Dust" is all solos, principally by Goodman, who takes the opening melody; once again he turns over the second A to another soloist, this time to vibraphonist Lionel Hampton, who does so well with it that BG lets him walk off with the ending C section as well. The other star player in the sextet is BG's newly hired virtuoso electric guitarist Charlie Christian in his first session with the clarinetist's small group. Goodman's own solo is surely one of the most beautiful documents of any jazzman playing Carmichael's most famous melody, or for that matter, any jazz musician playing a melodic improvisation. Goodman plays slowly and rhapsodically, squeezing every note, every delicious sound, that can be wrung out of it.

It's also one of the few Goodman records in which a sideman gets more solo space than the leader—Christian takes a full chorus, whereas Goodman grabs only half of one for himself. When Christian enters, he plays everything but Carmichael's tune, playing instead a new melody he had already composed based on Carmichael's chord sequence and detouring through Tony Jackson's 1916 hit "Pretty Baby." The ending is inspired: there's nothing better in the entire universe than Goodman playing the melody and Christian jamming on the harmony, and for a few lines in the final C section they do this simultaneously before heading into the coda.

Incidentally, although Christian lived only twenty-three years, he managed to record "Star Dust" twice, returning to it in 1940 for a small group session organized by John Hammond to provide surprisingly jazzy backing for Eddy Howard, an emerging pop vocalist not otherwise associated with jazz. Les Paul recorded a treatment with his guitar-piano-bass trio that shows his debt to Christian as well as to the King Cole Trio's Oscar Moore, the guitarist with that legendary combo.

Hampton gets just as much room as Goodman—and he's prominent behind the leader at both the beginning and end. When the vibraphonist-showman formed his own orchestra, "Star Dust" eventually became one of his big numbers; in fact, along with "Moonglow" and "Midnight Sun," "Star Dust" was one of Hampton's best-known ballad features in the six-decade history of his band. With Hampton, however, the term "ballad" is relative: although he played "Star Dust" at a tempo considerably slower than "Flying Home" or "Cobb's Idea," with him a ballad is no less a vehicle for extrovert crowd-pleasing than some killer-diller flag-waver. Of all the hundreds of times Hamp played "Star Dust," there are at least a handful of exceptional live recordings, in several of which one can hear the crowd breathing along with him and not missing a beat: gasping every time he takes a breathtaking run and guffawing everytime he interjects an unlikely quote.

Best of all is the 1954 Apollo Theatre concert album, in which in the middle of "Star Dust" Hampton throws in "Pretty Baby" as a (possibly) spontaneous homage to Charlie Christian and his own role in the classic 1939 Goodman-Christian "Star Dust." When it was appropriate, Hampton could also play a truly intimate love song, most notably on his long series of quintet recordings with Oscar Peterson for Norman Granz in the mid-fifties; their ten-minute discourse on "Star Dust" set a new standard for introversion for both the vibraphonist and the pianist. A few years later, Hampton recorded yet another outstanding "Star Dust," this one on his own label, Who's Who, with an all-star cast including trombonist J. J. Johnson (who gets the opening melody statement), Coleman Hawkins (in the last of four times he would record it), Clark Terry, and Hamp himself, who finishes it off.

Tommy Dorsey cut the tune three times in 1931 alone: with Selvin (April), with Victor Young on his concert version with the Boswell Sisters (May), and with Bing Crosby and Young (August). What's surprising about the later 1936 Victor recording by Dorsey's own orchestra is that, unlike virtually every other swing-band treatment of the period, it features a one-chorus vocal refrain. Sad to say, it's that vocal, by Edythe Wright, that prevents this from being one of the superior versions of the song. Paul Weston's arrangement starts out predictably but superbly with TD himself playing the tune in his best semi-slow (you notice I didn't say "half-fast") ballad. It's a tough spot for any singer to be in, having to follow one of the great voices of popular song—a brass voice operated via slide that was more expressive than most human voices—on one of the greatest melodies of all time. Over the years, Dorsey would employ a number of singers who could have pulled this off—Sinatra, Jo Stafford, Dick Haymes, maybe even Bob Allen or Connie Haines—but Wright isn't up to it. She's not a bad singer, and hers is a welcome presence on the majority of her many sides with TD, but it would take a great one to follow Dorsey here, and this she is not. One dreams in vain that her chorus had been given to tenor-sax aristocrat Bud Freeman, who joined the band just in time for this session.

Still, the 1936 Dorsey version is a music-industry milestone in that it may well be the only time when a major record label released a disc with the same song, in two very different interpretations, on each side: one side had Goodman's 1936 "Star Dust," the other side had Dorsey's. Four years later, Victor could have rereleased the Dorsey track backed with another version of the same song by the same bandleader. In 1940, Dorsey redid "Star Dust" as a vehicle for what he called his "Sentimentalists," a combination of solo vocalist Frank Sinatra, the Pied Pipers vocal quartet, and the Dorsey orchestra rhythm section (featuring drummer

Buddy Rich and Joe Bushkin on celeste). This was the same format with which the Dorsey crew had recorded "I'll Never Smile Again," their blockbuster hit of a few months earlier, and "Star Dust" must have seemed a likely follow-up. (It also uses the tinkling celeste to suggest twinkling stars, à la the classic 1931 Bing Crosby version.)

Just as the melody seemed a natural for Goodman's clarinet and Dorsey's trombone, it was inevitable that it would be exalted in the best fashion of the overall ensemble sound of Glenn Miller's orchestra. Miller may not have had the swing of Goodman or the gentle sentiment of Dorsey, but his orchestra was one of the great romantic sounds in recorded music. Miller's 1940 "Star Dust," with its shimmering reeds and a tempo that screams for close dancing of the most intimate kind, also features brief solos by trumpeter Clyde Hurley (in an especially Armstrongian vein), clarinetist Willie Schwartz, and two spots by tenorist Tex Beneke. (Miller did the tune again around 1944 in a special performance with his Army Air Force Orchestra and guest vocalist Dinah Shore.) Given that Miller and Artie Shaw cut the tune within a few months of each other, and that both recorded extra-length versions (well over three minutes), it seems possible that RCA may have been considering a new, two-sided twelve-inch disc of "Star Dust." As far as I know, this never happened.

Artie Shaw is also responsible for two very different versions of "Star Dust": in December 1938, he played it with his standard big band in an arrangement that survives only as an aircheck (first released commercially in 1954); two years later, in October 1940, he waxed his more famous Victor recording, using his large, West Coast–based orchestra with strings. This is widely considered one of the highlights of the entire big-band era. With characteristic modesty, the clarinetist-leader himself has described it as "*the* definitive big band record of 'Star Dust.' " Maybe so, and although it was voted the greatest record of all time in *Billboard* disc jockey polls, it doesn't seem to me any more of a masterpiece than either of Goodman's two commercial recordings from the period. And Shaw himself has suggested that he likes the 1938 version just as much. Maybe I'm hearing too much in it when I suggest that New York–based, theater-based composers (Gershwin, Rodgers, Kern) were more Shaw's meat than midwesterners; perhaps the Chicago-nurtured Goodman, who had spent more time with such proto-cool jazzers as Beiderbecke, Trumbauer, and Red Nichols, had an advantage here.

Still, Shaw's record is indisputably a classic. Shaw made a point to include trombonist Jack Jenney, who had recorded the song in 1938, in a treatment spotlighting his own trombone that can be described as one of—if not *the*—definitive big band versions. The orchestration is all the more inspired because it consists, essentially, of nothing more than a string setting for two choruses and three solos: trumpeter Billy Butterfield (who plays the opening melody open-belled), Shaw himself (sixteen bars), and Jenney (eight bars); the band plays the final eight. Such an arrangement can work only if the soloists are outstanding, and they are considerably more than that. The clarinet solo is one of the greatest ever performed; only half a chorus long (Shaw takes a full chorus on the '38 track and returns for a tag at the end), it is stunningly conceived, balanced, and executed, particularly the triplets in bar 10 and the way Shaw manages to capture the sweep of Carmichael's tune, the rapid movement from high to low. (Surprisingly, although the record is otherwise in D flat, Shaw's own half-chorus is in F.) Jack Jenney gets just eight bars to knock us out, and he more than succeeds with a statement that sounds amazingly smooth even when he zooms up to a fifth that, in the words of Meredith Willson, is a whole octave higher than the score.

In these years, "Star Dust" was also swung by Les Brown, Glen Gray and the Casa Loma Orchestra, and Benny Carter, among many others. (Comparatively few sweet bands essayed it, apart from Wayne King in 1931, Jan Garber in 1937, and Eddy Duchin in 1938.)

Pianists, saxes, and trumpets aside, the tune was played by virtuosi on all manner of unusual jazz axes: vibraphone (Adrian Rollini, 1938); harmonica (Larry Adler, 1937, and, later, Borah Minevitch and his Harmonica Rascals, and, still later, Jerry Murad and the Harmonicats); and accordion (Phil Green, 1937). Although no one would have assumed that the song was proper washboard band material, the Washboard Rhythm Kings cut a corker of a version fairly early in the game, back in July 1931: rollicking pianist Eddie Miles doubles as featured singer and choir leader, liberally reshaping the melody in a manner halfway between Armstrong and Billie Holiday.

The idea of a washboard "Star Dust" will surely amuse turn-of-the-millennium listeners but it wouldn't have caused any great stir in 1931. Nevertheless, two of the undeniably great versions of the song were done on instruments that would have surprised its composer—the harmonica, then a novelty instrument, taken seriously by few, and the bass. Where

Adler was a classical mouth-organ virtuoso and Minevitch, that harmonica rascal, a vaudeville act, Toots Thielemans wins hands down as
the greatest "serious" jazz soloist on the instrument. At times he's the
Stephane Grappelli of the harmonica, at other moments he's its Ben Webster. The Belgian multi-instrumentalist recorded "Star Dust" live in 1986
with an American rhythm section led by pianist Fred Hersch. This is
the saddest of all "Star Dust"s; the mood is minor throughout, and while
one keeps expecting the tempo to brighten and the spirits to lift, it never
happens.

The other major "Star Dust"—heard on an instrument barely in use in
jazz when the song was written, and then almost never as a solo instrument—is a recording by bassist Oscar Pettiford. A pioneering player
from roughly the same generation as Jimmy Blanton, Pettiford was part
of the evolution of the bass from strictly a timekeeping functionary into a
solo voice. His "Star Dust," from his 1956 album *Another One* (on the
Bethlehem label), more than makes the case. Pettiford plays verse, then
chorus, then improvises on the changes in a masterful way that plays second fiddle to no horn player.

In thirties Europe, the tune served as a virtual theme song for jazz
itself, being recorded by local London acts like the Six Swingers (1935),
the Ballyhooligans (1938), British reed virtuoso Freddy Gardner, and
Buddy Featherstonhaugh (1943), and Joe Daniels and His Hotshots in
Drumnastics (1937), in addition to Nat Gonella. In Paris, it was played by
Americans like black bandleader Willie Lewis (1936), while Django
Reinhardt cut it with both Coleman Hawkins and Garnet Clark, and the
French crooner Jean Sablon sang it as "Cette Melodie." "Star Dust" also
turns up in North Carolina (Jimmy Gunn and His Orchestra, 1936) and
New Orleans (Joe Derbigny and His Orchestra, actually a quartet, in
1940, and the West Brothers Trio, which consisted of mandolin, guitar,
and bass, 1935). By far the most extreme version of "Star Dust" was by
Charlie and His Orchestra, a German dance band sponsored by the Nazi
government that, as we shall see with other songs, specialized in retooling
American popular standards with anti-Allied and anti-Semitic lyrics for
propaganda purposes.

IT'S SAFE TO SAY that by 1940, "Star Dust" was a song known by everybody, although it was principally the property of jazz and jazzmen; up

through the big band era, it was played far more often than it was sung. By the late 1940s and fifties, "Star Dust" is heard in equal parts from swing and "mainstream" players (there's a classic treatment by Lester Young and Oscar Peterson), modernists, and both male and female vocalists. Before 1945, jazzmen treated it as a piece of material from their own tradition, much the way they would something by Duke Ellington or "Tiger Rag." As far as the jazz world was concerned, "Star Dust" and Carmichael were local boys who had made good. In the bop era and beyond, "Star Dust" no longer seemed the personal property of the improvising musician; now it was just another great song, and its jazz origins had lost their relevance.

Still, there was no dearth of outstanding versions. Paul Desmond, Roland Hanna, and Gerry Mulligan are examples of modern jazzmen who liked the tune well enough to record it more than once and in widely varying contexts. If Armstrong and Roy Eldridge did much to make the tune seem attractive to trumpeters of the thirties and forties, Clifford Brown did the same for trumpeters of the fifties and sixties. Howard McGhee, a player who bridged the gap between swing and bop, cut it at the time of the transition with Coleman Hawkins's sextet in 1945 (Maggie played the verse, Hawk played the chorus), and may have been the first modernist to play it.

But in terms of pure melody, the treatment on *Clifford Brown with Strings* (1955) is at the top of list. Brown's playing here is stark and spare—this from a firebrand of a player who could blast out a million notes a minute when called for. His statement, both in the melody and in a brief improvisation, makes for fine contrast with the string background. Trumpeter Donald Byrd (on the 1960 *Motor City Jazz Scene*) and flügelhornist Wilbur Harden (with John Coltrane, on a 1958 date released variously as *Star Dust* and *The Star Dust Session*) both seem inspired by Clifford Brown, as does Coltrane himself. Lou Donaldson states the melody rapturously in front of a well-orchestrated chamber-style accompaniment that arranger Duke Pearson makes sound bigger than it actually is. It's on an obscure album not issued until decades after it was recorded, eventually released as both *Sweet Slumber* and *Lush Life,* even though "Lush Life" isn't on it, and it's still not available on a domestic CD.

The Byrd is more typical of modern-era album ballads in that a single soloist out of the collective dominates the song, although pianist Tommy Flanagan also gets a piece of the action. The Coltrane-Harden track is unusual in that virtually everybody in the group (essentially the Miles

Davis Quintet with Harden in place of Davis) gets to solo. As a gathering of entirely standard ballads, the session is a forerunner of such later masterpieces as *John Coltrane Ballads* and *John Coltrane–Johnny Hartman*, although it doesn't feature Coltrane improvising at length on the changes. He paraphrases the melody beautifully, and then lets Harden, pianist Red Garland, and bassist Paul Chambers take over.

One of the best trumpet treatments of the tune is the two-horn rendition by the then very old (ninety-one) Doc Cheatham and the then very young Nicholas Payton. Cheatham states the opening melody. We forgive his missing the occasional note—how amazing to be hitting notes at all at that age—for he plays with an elegance and a lilt that must have taken him decades of seasoning to acquire. Released shortly before the veteran brassman's death in 1997, at age ninety-two, this is undoubtedly the last recording of the song by a member of Carmichael's own generation.

The improvisations of Mulligan and Desmond are also of considerable merit. Both of Mulligan's recordings find the baritone saxophonist spinning the most intricate harmonic variations imaginable, which seems even more remarkable when one realizes that neither peformance includes a chordal instrument other than the bass. Mulligan was one of the jazzmen most committed to sitting in with other groups and teaming up with other titans of various instruments, thus it's not surprising that both of his "Star Dust"s should be collaborations. The first comes from his 1957 reunion with soft-toned trumpeter Chet Baker, the second from an inspired teaming with Paul Desmond in 1962 (*Two of a Mind*). The individual solos by both Mulligan and Baker, the first reminiscent of Artie Shaw, are outstanding, but the interplay between the two horns is even more so.

As good as his playing on the 1957 is, Mulligan sounds even more inspired following Desmond in '62: Baker may complement Mulligan, but Desmond challenges the baritonist in a mysteriously nonaggressive fashion. At least three documents exist of Desmond playing the tune with the Dave Brubeck Quartet, from 1952, '53, and '55. If the Desmond-Mulligan uses no piano at all, the Desmond-Brubeck features the light-toned altoist with the potentially heaviest piano player this side of Oscar Peterson. Yet Brubeck's playing here is outstanding for the way he stays out of Desmond's path and supports him without his characteristic semiclassical pounding. Brubeck comps amiably behind Desmond's twisty-turny solo and then does fine on his own. One admires any leader who has the good sense and inner security to so completely showcase a talented sideman.

Even if the two Mulligan "Star Dust"s didn't employ a piano, the song found its way into the hands of plenty of keyboardists in the postwar era, particularly Roland Hanna and Erroll Garner, each of whom recorded it on multiple occasions. Hanna laid down a lovely, inwardly directed reading on his 1982 *Gershwin, Carmichael, Cats,* and another distinguished reading six years later on *The Bar,* which offers a hint of Fats Waller's "Jitterbug Waltz" at the start. Erroll Garner cut it in 1945, 1962, and 1964, and each time he incorporates many of his classic trademarks, including the long, out-of-left-field intro (if you hadn't heard it before you would have no idea what tune he was about to play), introducing the melody with a gigantic arpeggio that seems to cover the entire keyboard in a single motion, and then revving into tempo and rendering the tune in showers of notes, cascades of notes, buckets and barrels of notes.

Yet no keyboard player could compete with that preeminent virtuoso of the keyboard, the great Jonathan Edwards. There are conspiracy-theorists out there who persist in the claim that "Jonathan Edwards" was an alter ego and alias for composer-orchestrator-producer Paul Weston, who (with his wife, Jo Stafford, as "Darlene Edwards") made these records as a means of parodying incompetence in the pop-music industry. Some will even insist that Mr. Edwards, with his heavy-handed piano pounding, overdramatic approach, complete lack of rhythm, and frequent employment of wrong notes, sounds like Liberace on some forerunner of Prozac. Other pop pianists, like Peter Nero and Liberace himself, essayed "Star Dust," but needless to say, none could compare to the amazing Jonathan.

AS SINGERS GRADUALLY TOOK OVER the show on the pop side of the fence, more vocal versions of "Star Dust" began to appear. Crosby returned to it in 1939 in a far more relaxed reading (minus the verse) than he had rendered eight years earlier, and would re-reprise it in 1954 as part of his *Musical Autobiography.*

Leslie Hutchinson, England's well-known singer–pianist–bon vivant–

superstar, sang "Star Dust" in 1942. He begins, ingeniously, with the final phrase ("though I dream in vain . . ."), then, rather than going back to the beginning, cuts to the second half of the verse ("you wander down the lane . . ."), before finally making it to the chorus proper ("Sometimes I wonder . . ."). He's accompanied just by his own piano until the refrain, at which point he's joined by a small string orchestra. Hutch's voice is rich and full, as is his piano technique, which manages to seem simultaneously grandiose and ragtimey. Even when he sounds somewhat affected he's still lovable, and even when his attempts at sounding conversational are contrived, they're charmingly so. In the end, it's all about his voice and his mannerisms; he is the singer for whose sound the term "fruity" could have been invented.

Although there were more than a few male vocal versions, like those by Tony Martin and Billy Eckstine, by the 1950s this male sensitivity piece was more usually sung by female singers (sometimes they did the verse, even though women generally aren't obliged to wonder why they wonder why). Tony Martin (on an album with the made-for-parody title *Mr. Song Man*) sings it completely straight, and while it's not as deep as Jo Stafford's "straight" reading, it's still a lovely treatment. Billy Eckstine sang it beautifully on a 1950 single, but for once Eckstine's accompaniment isn't quite right. Buddy Baker's arrangement is kind of Martian and otherworldly-sounding, as if the only place to properly observe the dust from the stars is from outer space. In the end, the arrangement doesn't completely suit either the singer or the song.

Starting with the war, "Star Dust" seems to have brought out the best in all manner of female singers. There's a superior treatment by Dinah Shore with Glenn Miller's Army Air Force wartime band (one of the only times the distinctive Miller sound is heard behind a star vocalist), who also cut it later with John Williams during the album era. Anita Ellis, early in her career, when she sounded somewhat like Shore, cut it on a commercial transcription; the voice is lovely but the performance isn't as strong as she would have accomplished later on.

Ginny Simms, the MGM starlet and onetime Kay Kyser vocalist, recorded a superior "Star Dust," as did Kay Starr, who produced an inspired, hot jazzy version at the very start of her career as a solo chirp. One of Starr's chief influences, Connie Boswell—or, as she then spelled it, "Connee"—came back to the song in 1956, sans sisters but with a tinkly celeste background. The voice sounds darker and heavier than when

Boswell was at her prime in the 1930s, but she gives it all she's got and delivers a fine, no-nonsense performance.

Jo Stafford and Sarah Vaughan set new standards for Carmichael's standard: the first for singing it more or less exactly as written, the second for leaving Hoagy's melody behind in the dust. What Vaughan does with the tune is gloriously musical. She starts with something I don't think I've ever heard elsewhere—a scat paraphrase of the verse. From the chorus on she sings the lyrics but continues to improvise and continually reshape the melody. Included in her 1958 *No Count Sarah* (featuring members of the Basie band but not the Count himself), it's a one-chorus gem and a treatment of the melody that's as well constructed as the best of Clifford Brown, Paul Desmond, or Gerry Mulligan. Where Vaughan dances all over the place with "Star Dust," Stafford (1950) makes it sound great without so much as dotting a note or flatting a fifth. Both Stafford's and Vaughan's "Star Dust"s are surprisingly slow, sensual, and even funky, and are firmly rooted in the big-band tradition, emphasizing reeds and a steady four-four pulse rather than strings and rubato time.

WE TEND TO THINK of Ernestine Anderson as a hot jazz singer and Keely Smith as a stone-faced torch singer. Yet for their "Star Dust"s the two artistes seems to have undergone transfusions from each other. Smith's 1959 version, with Nelson Riddle, turns out to be surprisingly jazzy. Following a slow verse opening, she changes grooves abruptly and launches into medium swing tempo on "melody haunts . . ."; then, at the coda, she repeats "the memory of love's . . ." three times before slowing down and easing into the last word, "refrain." Anderson's five-minute treatment, from 1958, is also a stunner. Using an arrangement by Pete Rugolo, she begins with the chorus, drops back to the verse, and then returns to the end of the melody of love's refrain. Anderson is at once soulful and introspective, capturing the mood of the song perfectly. (Incidentally, Carmichael happened to catch Louis Prima and Keely in Las Vegas once and heard her version of "Star Dust." Before leaving the room, he let the couple know in no uncertain terms that he thought their treatment of his song was without question the worst he'd ever heard.)

Doris Day's "Dust," like that of Anita Ellis, was recorded for a transcription and made available to the public only decades later. Too often identified exclusively with sunshine and optimism (not that there's anything *wrong* with those qualities), Day shows in this performance with the Page Cavanaugh Trio that she can deal with the darker emotions as well. The song is also something of a departure for the bop-influenced vocal duo of Jackie and Roy—the performance they turn in is unusually straight for them. The pair does the verse ad lib and the chorus slightly faster in tempo, but this could be any first-rate jazz singer with a solid rhythm section; good as it is, there's nothing Jackie and Roy–ish about it. Etta Jones's version, on her *Save Your Love for Me* album, is entirely satisfying, particularly her Billie Holiday–like twist at the end of the verse ("gone *by*") and her interaction with pianist Cedar Walton and tenor champ Houston Person.

The major female singer who made a career staple out of the "Star Dust" melody was Ella Fitzgerald. One of the great false notions concerning the supreme jazz singer was that she undervalued lyrics and at times acted as if she didn't even know what she was singing about. Fitzgerald put the lie to that accusation most decisively in a series of twenty tracks done in 1950 and 1954 (collected on CD as *Pure Ella*), in which she's accompanied only by the supersensitive pianist Ellis Larkins. "Star Dust," which no less than Fitzgerald herself, belonged to both the jazz and pop worlds, was an inspired choice. Taking it slowly yet with unmistakable jazz feeling, Fitzgerald eschews the verse but leaves little doubt as to why she was known as the First Lady of Song. She would return to the Carmichael classic three more times on record: an as-yet-unissued live version from Mr. Kelly's (the Chicago jazz club) in 1958; a bossa nova single reflecting the Brazilian craze of 1962; another studio reading, on her only album for the Stateside label, in 1966. In 1973, trumpeter Roy Eldridge played the song in tribute to Fitzgerald as part of a concert issued by Columbia as *Ella Fitzgerald: Newport Jazz Festival Live at Carnegie Hall*.

Before Eldridge played his solo feature on that evening, Ellis Larkins appeared with Fitzgerald on three numbers, but, unfortunately, "Star Dust" wasn't one of them. It would seem that despite her three fine issued versions, Eldridge was probably one of the few people who associated the song with Fitzgerald. By contrast, Nat King Cole recorded the song only once, that track consisting of a single straight-through rendition of the verse and chorus. But that was all he needed to establish "Star Dust" as one of the major classics of the Cole canon. (Oddly enough, although several Cole concerts survive, and though he was starring in a weekly TV program around this time, no other recording of his doing the tune is known to exist.)

Taped on December 19, 1956, the song is the second track on *Love Is the Thing,* the first of three classic albums Cole made with Gordon Jenkins, that most grandiosely sentimental of all pop arranger-conductors. By now, both Cole (once one of the hottest pianists of the swing era and beyond) and the song had left their jazz roots behind. Like much of Jenkins's orchestrations, the writing is so gloriously schmaltzy that it becomes a statement about the nature of art and schmaltz. ("If this guy were Jewish," Frank Sinatra once said, "he'd be unbearable.") Cole's vocal is typically reserved, letting the background and the images suggested by the lyric put forth most of the emotion: unlike Jenkins (and like Bing Crosby), Cole likes to imply a feeling, to suggest and hint at it more than directly state it. Then again, Cole couldn't be doing what he was doing so effectively were Jenkins not doing what *he* was doing so effectively.

The American musical idiom, jazz and the best pop, is much too idiosyncratic for anyone to name favorites; whether one likes Ella Fitzgerald's version of a song better than Sinatra's is generally a matter of whether one prefers Fitzgerald or Sinatra, and much of the time it's an apples-and-oranges comparison. But if forced to pick one single version of "Star Dust," I would have to go with the Cole-Jenkins (or possibly Armstrong . . . or possibly Crosby . . . you see what I mean).

The Nat Cole recording also provided "Star Dust" with its greatest cinematic expression. In 1940, the song had inspired the title of a Twentieth Century Fox film, *Stardust,* a B-level programmer concerning behind-the-screen doings in Hollywood. It was perhaps the first time that the "star" in "Star Dust" was used to indicate movie stars. In 1943, the song turned up in another "B," *Hi Buddy,* a Universal musical starring Harriet Hilliard Nelson, of *Ozzie and Harriet* fame. Over the years, the phrase was used in the titles of westerns (*Stardust on the Sage,* 1942, with Gene Autry) and science fiction (*Mission: Stardust,* in 1968). Perhaps inspired by the 1957 hit single of the tune by Billy Ward and the Dominoes, the expression was also briefly embraced by cinematic rock-and-rollers in the 1975 *Stardust* (about a fictitious but Beatle-esque pop band) and the 1983 *Ziggy Stardust and the Spiders from Mars* (David Bowie in concert). Directors Woody Allen (*Stardust Memories,* 1980) and Richard Benjamin (*My Favorite Year,* 1982) adroitly tied all the song's associations—memories of past days, old loves, old melodies, and even old movie stars—into one tidy package. Allen used the 1931 Louis Armstrong over the end titles, and Benjamin and producer Art Levinson opened even more effectively by placing the 1956 Nat Cole–Jenkins over the main title. Even before the credits were over, a mood had been established, a scene set.

Frank Sinatra wasn't known to be intimidated by so-called "definitive" performances of songs by his fellow singers. However, the two singers he apparently regarded as his keenest competition were Cole and Fitzgerald. For instance, as we'll see, after attempting to record Billy Strayhorn's "Lush Life" in 1958, Sinatra announces to the engineers and musicians present that he'd rather leave that one for Nat Cole. Yet he had a long history with "Star Dust": in 1940 he did it with Tommy Dorsey, and while his is the featured voice, he is only one of five singers on the record, and is only heard emerging from the ensemble for key lines here and there. Later in the forties Sinatra occasionally sang "Star Dust" on radio, but generally only did excerpts from the song as part of a longer medley. There's a short film of him singing it for a minute and a half in the context of radio's *Your Hit Parade* in 1943, but so far neither the video nor the audio component of this has been available to the public, even in a bootleg. There was never to be a definitive, mature Sinatra reading of the complete text.

Yet in 1961 Sinatra conceived one of the most unusual readings of "Star Dust" ever. On *Sinatra and Strings,* there's a long, semi-symphonic introduction by orchestrator Don Costa (which contains a new countermelody all Costa's own, that could be described as a verse to the verse) and then we hear Sinatra open with the familiar verse ("And now the purple dusk . . ."). It's sixteen bars of classic Sinatra, with his customary perfect balance of emotion and reserve. Then, when we get to the end of the verse ("music of the years gone by . . ."), the Costa countermelody swirls up again in the flutes, answered by violins, and the whole ensemble goes into the coda. And that's it. No "Sometimes I wonder . . ."; no nightingale and fairy tale; no garden walls, sleepy or otherwise; no chorus whatsoever. For two minutes and forty seconds, Sinatra and Costa have treated us to the most gorgeous reading of the verse, then left it at that. It must be noted that Sinatra achieved his aim, no matter whether it was to come up with a "Star Dust" that was distinctly different or to prove that the verse could exist as an independent entity. He proved his point, but it would be a stretch to describe the 1961 version as satisfying: one still yearns for him to come back to "Star Dust" and sing the complete enchilada.

Sinatra's most persuasive reading of "Star Dust" is both his first and his last—that is to say, the earliest known version, which is also the most recent to be released. This is a 1939 aircheck of the young singer doing the song with Harry James and His Orchestra, issued commercially in 1995. The treatment is simplicity itself: after a single piano plink, the first chorus is Sinatra, singing the refrain all the way through. Then there's a whole chorus by the reed section, dancing up and down in a manner that recalls Benny Carter's writing. The leader himself takes over for the last chorus, which, in the best Armstrong tradition, is hot and lusty, climaxing in stop-time cadenzas around where the bridge would be and building to a socko finish. The reeds are pretty much the only section audible behind Sinatra, and they get a chorus all to themselves, but near the end of James's solo the brass starts charging in and makes the thing even more exciting. The four-minute track is not only my candidate for the best of all existing Sinatra "Star Dust"s but one of the tune's finest big-band moments.

IT MAY WELL BE THAT there's no better microcosm of the "Star Dust" experience in jazz and popular music than the many ways in which the song was heard within the universe of Ellingtonia, and in particular the many treatments by one of the greatest denizens of the Ducal domain, Ben Webster. On one level, it's one of the most played tunes in Ellington's repertoire, although the band made only one commercial recording of it. However, beginning in 1940, Ellington never left it out of his band book for very long. It survives on what, in recent decades, have proved to be the two most popular live documents of the Ellington orchestra, the 1940 Fargo, North Dakota, appearance and the 1957 stop in Carrolltown, Pennsylvania, released as *All Star Road Band*. Whereas both of those were dance dates, "Star Dust" also played a part in Ellington's most celebrated series of concert appearances, his annual run of shows at Carnegie Hall from 1943 on. ("Star Dust" was played at Ellington's December '43 show, one of the only Carnegie concerts that has not been issued commercially.) Recordings also exist from Birdland in New York (1954), Wiesbaden, Germany (1963), an air force base in Sacramento (1960), and Caesar's Palace in Las Vegas (1969), not to mention the Steak Pit in Paramus, New Jersey (1971), and the Covered Wagon Inn in Wayne, Pennsylvania (1972).

As mentioned earlier, Ellington first documented an arrangement of "Star Dust" around the time that he parted company with Irving Mills, the song's publisher. In fall 1940, he introduced two arrangements, one (listed in W. E. Timner's *Ellingtonia*) with a vocal by Herb Jeffries, and then the famous Fargo version, spotlighting Ben Webster. The 1943 Carnegie Hall version, arranged for the band by Mary Lou Williams, initiated a tradition of using "Star Dust" to feature Ellington's trumpeters, starting with Williams's then-husband, Harold "Shorty" Baker. The 1953 Capitol commercial recording continues in that same mode, featuring Willie Cook, who had more or less taken over Baker's role of "soft" trumpet in the Ellington brass section, backed by reeds reminiscent of Glenn Miller (or rather, that part of the Ellington tonal universe that in fact anticipated the Miller sound). By the time of the Carrolltown dance in 1957, Baker is back in the band, and "Star Dust" is his property once again. There are also recordings slightly outside the Ducal domain by trumpeters Rex Stewart (with Larry Adler in 1944; the harmonica virtuoso having also recorded it in England six years earlier) and Clark Terry (on *Serenade to a Bus Seat,* 1957).

Saxophonically speaking, the Carmichael classic shows up on Paul Gonsalves's 1963 encounter with Sonny Stitt. There's also a 1961 Ellington spinoff record starring Johnny Hodges with the orchestra conducted by Billy Strayhorn (who also played piano on a 1950 version by singer Al Hibbler with a group listed as "The Ellingtonians"). This 1961 version, though released under the names of Hodges and Strayhorn, is actually a feature for trombonist Lawrence Brown, if that makes any sense. It's one of the more soulful renditions of Carmichael's tune, managing to be smooth like Tommy Dorsey and mournfully bluesy like Jack Teagarden at the same time.

To hear Hodges himself playing the "Star Dust" melody, though, one must turn to the altoist's rather surprising 1966 album as guest soloist with Lawrence Welk (you read that correctly)—not exactly what you'd call a Ducal context. One can only guess what the greatest of all jazz alto saxophonists must have thought when the offer came in to do an album with Welk. The notes quote the saxist as saying "I never played 'Star Dust' before in my life." True enough. The Lawrence Welk–Johnny Hodges album is more a curiosity than a mediocrity. The bandleader-mogul, to his credit, sought to produce an album of Hodges ballads with string orchestra, and even though he bills himself on the cover (which undoubtedly served to boost sales, the proceeds of which benefited Hodges), he does not back the great saxist with his famous "champagne music" orchestra. Rather, it's all Hodges playing over a rather nondescript studio orchestra, with charts by Los Angeles journeymen like Benny Carter and Pete King, who arranged the album's "Star Dust." It's not especially inspired, but it's far from bad.

When Ben Webster first began playing "Star Dust" with Ellington, as on the 1940 Fargo, it was just a year or so after Coleman Hawkins's breakthrough improvisation on "Body and Soul." Webster's extended solo on "Star Dust" has a lot of the same feeling as Hawkins's extended solo— the same intensity, the same dynamics, the same mounting excitement and drama. But if the song was a statement of Webster's intensity in 1940, by the 1950s it was a statement of his emerging mellowness, the big plush sound that he employed on love songs. Webster cut several spectacular takes in 1951 with the Johnny Otis Orchestra—a rather fanciful name for a rhythm section with vibraphone—one of which commences with a vibes intro reminiscent of the celeste intro on the 1940 Dorsey-Sinatra version. Webster is fierce yet intimate, making the familiar melody of "Star Dust" sound as if it's moving up and down in chromatic half-steps rather than thirds. He returned to the tune several more times on record: among them, in 1959 with pianist Gerald Wiggins in Los Angeles, in '65 in Copenhagen, and again in Scandinavia in '69. But the best of the subsequent Webster "Star Dust"s is his honey-tinged reading on the 1964 *See You at the Fair* LP on the Impulse! label. Never before has this song about the stars seemed so fundamentally down to earth.

OBVIOUSLY, WE CAN'T ANATOMIZE every version of "Star Dust" here, not even every outstanding one. But we'll mention a few more. Mel Tormé used it as a tantalizing kind of show-off piece for his amazing chops, and had been singing it for at least a decade before he finally recorded it, on what turned out to be his last album (*Live at the Disney Institute,* 1996). Slow and soulful in the best Ben Webster manner, the piece ends as Tormé ascends telescopically, half-step by half-step, up to a stellar high note.

Apart from Armstrong, Carmichael probably most enjoyed the performances of the song by such associates as Jack Teagarden (who played a doozy of a feature of it with Armstrong's All-Stars in a California concert in 1951) and Joe Venuti, who nearly forty years after his big-band transcription returned to it in a stunning duet with Marian McPartland in 1973.

The composer himself returned to his most famous tune repeatedly over the decades: there's a beautiful version for Decca in 1942, in which he approaches the melody not as its composer, who would, presumably, want to preserve it as written, but as a jazzman, whose mission is to personalize it and, if need be, rewrite it, paraphrase, even recompose it if necessary (he drops an octave lower than we expect him to at one point). Sadly, he left it off *Hoagy Sings Carmichael,* a 1957 album taped in Hollywood, in which he is accompanied by the cream of "cool school" West Coast jazzmen of the period. However, it is included on *In Hoagland,* the last album the composer-pianist-singer would appear on, taped in 1981, the last year of his life, when he was pushing eighty-two. No matter that it is not performed by the Hoagster himself here—Annie Ross and Georgie Fame are deputized for the occasion—the important thing is that Carmichael chose it to be part of his musical last will and testament. Decades earlier, he had written: "This melody was bigger than I. Maybe I hadn't written it at all. It didn't sound familiar even. To lay back my claims, I wanted to shout back at it, 'Maybe I didn't write you, but I found you!' " Its inclusion on his final statement signifies that Carmichael had at last made peace with his composition.

By that time, "Star Dust" had long since become a self-fulfilling prophecy. Whenever one wonders about a melody that haunts one's reverie, that song is more than likely, after seventy years, to be "Star Dust" itself.

BONUS TRACKS

"Star Dust" Goes to Minton's; or, the Least-Known "Star Dust"s That You Do Want to Hear

There are several live, location recordings taken down in 1941 on a portable disc recorder at Minton's, Harlem's legendary after-hours club and ground zero for the bebop revolution. The more famous is a feature for emerging savant Dizzy Gillespie. Indeed, this is the earliest recorded extended ballad masterpiece for the great trumpeter. Thelonious Monk, then the house piano player for the joint, is heard briefly on the other, as is Joe Guy, a decent trumpeter (unfortunately, best remembered by posterity for his mutually nonbeneficial relationship with Billie Holiday); the two stars here, however, are singer Helen Humes and tenor saxist Don Byas. Humes sings two choruses in the classic Ethel Waters mold: the first comparatively straight but with considerable swing feeling, the second more jazzy and playful, and each is a model of clarity and intimacy. Then Byas solos, and the discrepancy between Humes's sweet-girly voice and his big-tone tenor is startling at first. But Byas, too, is a warm and personal player. He also gets two choruses of variations, one in which he plays on the melody, the other in which he rhapsodizes on the chords. Joe Guy then splits the difference between the two for sixteen bars, and Humes and Byas finish it out together. Although Byas recorded the song commercially in Paris in 1950, in a treatment similar to his second chorus from the Minton's disc, there's no "Star Dust" quite like this one. Even for a song that's enjoyed hundreds of excellent performances by jazz and pop royalty, this version—heard on *Don Byas: Midnight at Minton's*—is a standout.

"Star Dust" Goes to Mars; or, the Least-Known "Star Dust" That You Don't Want to Hear

The oddest treatment I've ever encountered is one by cabaret entertainer Nan Blackstone, recorded in Chicago in 1936. Blackstone was a singer-pianist who specialized in double-entendre comedy songs of the most risqué sort. She was a female contemporary of such licentious, gender-bending boîte lizards as Dwight Fiske and Rae Bourbon, and a predecessor to Ruth Wallis, Ava Williams, and other off-color lady singers who made the kind of under-the-counter LPs that your parents hid behind the bookcase. Blackstone's very rare 1936 Decca disc of "Star Dust" is the only completely straight, G-rated ballad I've ever heard her sing, although "straight" may not be the right word. On one level, she does seem to want to be taken seriously as a balladeer. On another, she can't resist throwing in little asides ("Though I dream in vain . . . I dream in vain, my baby baby . . .") much the way she does on her more off-color ventures. Furthermore, she rarely comes within shouting distance of the melody, either on the verse or the chorus. Still, by her negative example, Blackstone shows us that there's a lot to be said for singing a melody straight.

Best and *Longest Piano Solo Treatment*

Earl Hines recorded an outstanding ten-minute solo version of "Star Dust" on his *Hines Does Hoagy* in 1974. Taking a contemplative and reflective approach, Hines justifies the extravagant length he indulges in by constantly finding new ways to skewer the melody, continually taking it apart and putting it back together. At times it's rubato, at other points it's in a strong boogie-woogie or stride tempo. Throughout all ten minutes of this performance, Hines's energy and invention never flag, particularly as he builds to a climactic chorus in the windup. This is a marathon triumph.

THE ST. LOUIS BLUES (1914)

words and music by W. C. Handy

"The blues," LIONEL HAMPTON ONCE SAID, "is the mother and father of jazz," and, by extension, much of popular music as well. The blues are such an inescapable part of American music that even though a writer like Richard Sudhalter can demonstrate conclusively (in *Lost Chords*) that it is possible to create great jazz with little or no hint of the blues, no one has troubled to write a book to prove the opposite point of view: from Armstrong to Ellington to Parker to Coleman, the blues remain the lifeblood of most great jazz. It goes without saying that the blues are an infinite source of musical pleasure and artistic fulfillment in themselves, and the pervasive influence that the blues have had on other forms of music is, perhaps, a secondary consideration. However, it's the blues connection with popular song that we're concerned with here, and the piece of music that did the most to establish that connection was W. C. Handy's "St. Louis Blues."

And this was no accident, but exactly what Handy set out to accomplish. Handy's background, as he told it, made him the perfect individual to build a bridge between the blues and Tin Pan Alley, or, in the larger sense, between black music and white music. In his autobiographical writing, Handy does everything he can to portray himself as the crucial link between the two cultures (most notably in *Blues,* a 1926 anthology based largely on information dictated by Handy himself, and in his full-blown autobiography, *Father of the Blues,* from 1941; also of value is his spoken and sung *Father of the Blues—A Musical Autobiography,* recorded in 1952 and '53 for Heritage Records).

In these accounts, Handy was not from the broad class of newly freed poor blacks who produced the blues (bearing in mind that to say the word "poor" before the word "black" at the turn of the twentieth century was pretty much redundant) but from the small black bourgeoisie that flour-ished briefly during Reconstruction. Handy repeatedly insists that black folk music, and the blues that grew out of it, was not second nature to him, that he did not, in fact, have a "mammy" who walked around with a handkerchief on her head singing "Them My Man Done Me Wrong Blues." In the lyrics to "The St. Louis Blues," as sung and acted in the 1929 film of that title, the character played by Bessie Smith is mistreated by her man, who relieves her of her money and abuses and humiliates her before leaving her for another woman. Handy might write about such behavior in the Negro race, but he takes great pains to make clear that no one in his own family ever acted in such a manner.

Handy also never tired of recounting how much his family (particu-larly his father and grandfather, who were both ministers) reviled secular music in general and that they were especially contemptuous of the nascent strain of nineteenth-century black music that eventually became blues and jazz. These first-person accounts (dramatized with Nat King Cole playing the Handy role in the 1958 film *The St. Louis Blues*) invariably depict the Reverend Handy telling his son Will that he'd rather "follow him to the graveyard" than see him playing "the devil's music."

Handy's teacher (and the very fact that Handy had a formal education was notable for the nineteenth century, and for many years to come) preached a similar message. Like Damon Runyon, who once observed that "All hoss players must die broke," this astute pedagogue relentlessly impressed upon young William Christopher Handy that all professional musicians, sooner or later, wind up in the gutter. And, as Handy was quick to acknowledge, he did indeed find himself broke and homeless at least once or twice in the years before he became successful as a song-writer.

Music eventually made Handy rich and famous, one of the most suc-cessful black men of the early twentieth century. Yet far from challenging the validity of his old teacher's assessment, Handy ultimately affirmed it. He seems to have promoted himself less as an artist, a writer of melody, than as a businessman. He rarely even took credit for the act of composi-tion, electing instead to describe himself as a folklorist—but one with a keen business sense and a knowledge of how the copyright office worked. He did not actually write the melodies of his famous songs, he tells us; he cobbled them together from snatches of old Negro folk themes and blues that he'd heard here and there. As a black man, he had far greater access to the Negro subculture than any white man could have had, yet as he came from the middle class, he also had access to the publishing and profit machinery of Tin Pan Alley, which, to be sure, was true of very few Negroes at that time.

The implication is obvious: the larger white world might not respect a black man who could merely write brilliant music, like Scott Joplin, who died, essentially as a result of bad decisions, in his forties, but the culture had to pay attention to this black Rockefeller. Like the oil baron, Handy made his pile by tapping into natural resources, in this case not in the ground but in the air—the melodies that emanated from his own people. In the words of 1920s writer Isaac Goldberg, who opted for a biblical analogy, "Handy is not the inventor of the genre, he is its Moses, not its Jehovah. It was he who, first of musicians, codified the new spirit in American music and set it forth upon the conquest of the North."

"PURISTS USED TO COMPLAIN THAT 'The St. Louis Blues' wasn't really a blues, any more than 'Alexander's Ragtime Band' was really ragtime," says historian Jim Maher. "To them I say, 'Who gives a shit?' " We can reply to these charges on several levels. First, as Maher implies, if it's a great song, a piece of material that inspires brilliant performances, its origin is of secondary importance, and whether it wants to call itself a blues, a waltz, or a schottische is immaterial. (One thinks of Louis Prima introducing a song at a live concert in the early sixties: "Our next number will now be 'Go Back Where You Stayed Last Night, Your Mama Don't Want You Cha-Cha Blues Mambo Waltz Polka.' ") Secondly, one wonders what these purists are griping about, as there's as much genuine blues content in "The St. Louis Blues," in terms of melody, harmony, structure, and anything else you want to discuss, as in virtually any other blues composition you could name.

Each of the song's four strains qualifies as a genuine blues chorus. The only thing that makes "The St. Louis Blues" different from the blues form employed later on is its wealth of material. In small-group jazz and blues performances of the 1930s and forties, a blues consists of a twelve-bar chorus. The end result is less a matter of the composer supplying extra strains that go off in different directions melodically than it is of the performers spontaneously devising their own variations on this basic twelve-bar blues chorus.

When we talk about the blues, above all other musics, the distance between composer and performer is hardly worth mentioning, since those two tend to be one and the same person. Indeed, the model of the blues singer who wrote his own tunes (or picked them out of the air) provided the inspiration for the rock ideal of the singer-songwriter. Even in jazz, your average musicians may play Jerome Kern's "All the Things You Are," but it's almost as easy to come up with a blues of one's own as it is to play a blues of anyone else's authorship. When they do play a blues written by someone else, it's usually because the original composer has done something especially interesting, as in a blues by Handy, Thelonious Monk, Horace Silver, or Duke Ellington. Thus, while the blues as a whole have been enormously influential throughout the history of jazz and pop, there are few individual blues songs that have become widely recorded. One has no hesitation in making the claim for "The St. Louis Blues" that it is by far the most performed and recorded individual blues of all time.

STRUCTURALLY, "THE ST. LOUIS BLUES" is quite extravagant for a pop song: it is fifty-two measures altogether, although in 1914, what would later become the classic Tin Pan Alley mold of the thirty-two-bar *A-A-B-A* was by no means yet standard. Still, "The St. Louis Blues" is unusual for any age. It consists of four distinct strains, and the only time any part of the melody is repeated is in the second strain, which is a complete reiteration of the first. Each of the strains is twelve bars, except for the third, which is sixteen. We can, therefore, describe the overall form as: *A* (12), *A* (12), *B* (16), *C* (12).

Each of the four strains is a single blues chorus. The song was written and published in the key of G (except for the third strain, which shifts into G minor). The key that a piece of printed sheet music appears in commercially often has nothing to do with the composer's intentions but may simply be the key the publisher's house arranger chooses for the ease of the amateur musicians who will be its primary consumers. However, Handy tells us very specifically that when he sat down to write the song, he happened to be thinking about a square-dance caller who barked out instructions in the key of G "and moaned the calls like a presiding elder preaching at a revival meeting." As far as I know, all published versions of the song are in this key.

"The St. Louis Blues" opens with a nine-bar introduction, not always performed, that mainly employs minor chords and offers a hint of a tango section to come later. The opening two strains (the *A* sections) conform to traditional blues harmony: they begin and end on the tonic chord (G). Along the way, they go through only two other chords, the subdominant (IV, or C) and the dominant (V, or D), the chord that traditionally leads back to the tonic. The first *A* section opens with the now-famous line, "I hate to see that evening sun go down" (actually, it's written as ". . . de ev'-nin' sun go down").

The second *A* commences with minstrel show dialect, with "Feelin' tomorrow lak Ah feel to-day. . . ." Cliff Edwards (aka Ukulele Ike), in his 1936 recording of "St. Louis Blues," sings the first line of the second *A* ("Feelin' tomorrow . . ."), then leans into the microphone and says, "Listen close and you're gonna hear me repeat it." The repeated second line is a fundamental characteristic of the blues. Handy prided himself on the way he used the three-line format, which he follows, essentially, in all four strains. Lyrically, the second line is a repeat of the first in all the choruses he supplied, though melodically it's a slightly different story. Rather than repeat the first line exactly, Handy gives us the repeated lyric line set to a slightly different melody—in other words, same words, same chords, slightly different tune. In fact, the second line could be described as a jazz variation on the first line. The words "I hate to see" in the first line are on the notes B-D-B-G, whereas the notes of the second line, "hate to see" (dropping the "I," in the vernacular blues style) are E-G-A.

The leap from the *A* section to the *B* is a most eventful one. The *A* stanza ends on the tonic, G, the *B* stanza begins a fifth higher, on D. The *A* stanza is in major, the *B* stanza is in minor. In the leap from G to D, we also modulate into the parallel minor, G minor. This *B* section, as we've mentioned, is sixteen bars long, though it may also be described as two eight-bar sections. We might also refer to it as a bridge, since it seems to take the place of the bridge in the standard *A-A-B-A* song, although that may not have been what Handy had in mind. All strains of the song use fundamentally the same three chords (I-IV-V), laid out in varying patterns. In the *B* section, the harmonic layout is I-IV-V-I, and it stays on the dominant (V chord) longer than any other.

Most of the melody in this minor section consists of phrases built up of repeated notes—for instance, we open with a string of D's ("St. Louis woman . . .") against the tonic G minor chord, followed by a phrase of mostly repeated C's ("wid her diamond") against the subdominant C minor. Then, in bar 3 ("rings . . ."), we go to the dominant (a D7) and stay there for practically the rest of this eight-bar subsection. These five bars of the dominant start with a long A natural, which is held in the melody for nearly two whole measures. Then, at the end of each of the two minor sections (we could call them B^1 and B^2), we return to the tonic G minor in both the melody and the harmony.

We then shift back into major with style. There are two transitional bars that can either be considered the end of the bridge or the start of the last strain. It contains the last word of the B section ("De man I love would not gone nowhere"), but also it brings us into the major harmony of the C section, matching chords and notes exactly: G minor (the minor tonic), A major, D major (the major subdominant). Handy supplied us only with one "nowhere" in the published music, but many performers, such as Bing Crosby and Louis Armstrong, add a second "nowhere" for emphasis.

As famous as the first three sections of the song are, it's the C section that contains both the melody and the lyric that everybody knows, including the only mention of the title anywhere in the song ("Got de St. Louis Blues . . ."). Again, this is all according to Handy's plan, as he made this final strain the strongest of the three: it's the punchiest and most affirmative, it emphasizes the tonic the most emphatically, and even though the lyric is saying "jes' as blue as Ah can be," the mood is hardly blue at all. Indeed, this is the essential irony of the blues: showing a brave, upbeat face to troubles as a means of confronting them.

As with the A section, the C starts on the major tonic chord (although in the A, that chord had a flatted seventh in it, which it doesn't here). We stay on the tonic for most of this whole section, excepting in bars 5 and 6 (which take us into the IV chord) and in bar 11 (the V). When we hit that dominant in bar 11, it does have a seventh note attached (D7), which serves to direct us even more resolutely to the tonic G for the finish.

Handy also makes full use of blue notes, far more than one would expect to find in the average popular song of the pre-WWI era. The most prominent blue note, the flatted third, first appears in the second bar (written as a B flat on the word "sun"), and is all over the place in the C stanza, this time written as an A sharp. In fact, most of the melody of the C stanza is a three-note pattern that repeats over and over—namely, A sharp, B, and G. The blue notes here are not just thrown in for seasoning, the way that "accidentals" are in most songs. In Handy's music, the flatted third is a fundamental part of the song's tonal character.

If this ain't the blues, I don't know what is.

AS MIGHT BE INFERRED, W. C. Handy was a masterful storyteller, both in his songs and in his autobiographical writings. Over the course of his eighty-five years (1873–1958) he kept two sets of mythologies going—one was the the lifestyle he portrayed in his songs, the other was the ongoing set of no-less-tall tales he told about his own life. Handy describes himself as a member of the black bourgeoisie, the same class of Reconstruction-era Negro families that later produced Duke Ellington in Washington and, still later, Lena Horne in Brooklyn. The years of his youth, the late nineteenth century, were the very years when the elements of jazz and blues were beginning to gel across the South (especially in New Orleans). Yet according to Handy's account, he had no more direct exposure to the music soon to be known as the blues than your average white man with open ears and an inquisitive nature.

The most famous of his stories is the tale of a legendary dance in Cleveland, Mississippi. Against the wishes of his minister-father and his teacher-mentor, the young Handy had become a professional musician, who could sing as well as play piano, guitar, and trumpet. Although he had been through some rough patches early on, as a professional, Handy had sung in a quartet, conducted the pit orchestra in a minstrel show (one of the genuinely black variety), and, by the time he made it to Mississippi, was leading his own dance band. "I hasten to confess," says W.C., "that I took up with low folk forms hesitantly."

As Handy tells the story, he was conducting a dance for the landed gentry of Mississippi, and one gathers by implication that this was a lily-white affair. The request comes from the floor: would the band play some of their "native music." Handy professes to have no idea what they're talking about, and instead obliges with a medley of southern songs, of the sort that any salon orchestra might have played. That wasn't quite what the gentleman had in mind, however. Instead, Handy is kindly asked if another band, a local group, might spell them for a few numbers. Jumping at the chance for a break and a smoke, Handy agrees. Up to the bandstand comes the raggedyest-looking group Handy has ever seen, a trio of guitar, mandolin, and string bass. Handy describes their music as "monotonous," but admits that it has a "haunting quality." He can't quite bring himself to admit that he likes it, rather he expresses the fear that only "the small town rounders and their running mates would go for it."

But when the music stops, Handy changes his tune—literally. The white folks, it turns out, go for this "native music" in a big way, as they demonstrate not only with thunderous applause but with the even louder sound of money. "There before the boys lay more money than my nine men were being paid for the entire engagement." It was only then, Handy continues, "that I saw the beauty of primitive music. They had the stuff the people wanted. It touched the spot. Their music wanted polishing, but it contained the essence. Folks would pay money for it. My idea of what constitutes music was changed by the sight of that silver money cascading around the splay feet of a Mississippi string band."

The image stayed with Handy, but although he would claim that "That night a composer was born, an *American* composer" (Handy's italics), it was several years later, in 1909, that Handy put his new conception of music to work. He was leading a band in Memphis, and his group was hired to play for a series of political rallies, trying to drum up enthusiasm for one Edward Crump, a candidate in the mayoral election. He composed a melody and wrote a set of lyrics to it, and, by Handy's account, the tune caught on so quickly around Memphis that it helped spur Crump into office. And this was, it should be noted, despite how Handy's lyric depicted Crump as a party pooper who would do his best to curtail drinking, gambling, and other forms of merrymaking.

After the election, Handy decided to get the song published commercially, but first he scrapped the political-advertisement lyric and the title, renaming it "The Memphis Blues." (Interestingly, the version of "Mr. Crump" that Handy recorded for posterity forty years later bears very little resemblance to the song that we all know as "Memphis Blues"; actually, it sounds more like the familiar blues variant frequently recorded in the twenties and thirties known as "Mama Don't Allow It" by Cow Cow Davenport, heard in various forms by Count Basie, Cleo Brown, and others.) The song would be politically important, and for more than electing the mayor of Memphis. Handy claimed that this was the first time the blues had been orchestrated and played by a band, by which he means a "proper" dance or marching unit in the Anglo-European tradition, and not a bunch of raggedy-ass black sharecroppers. (To give Handy the benefit of the doubt, perhaps this was his genuine view of the situation as it existed in Memphis, yet we do know that brass bands were playing the blues and even jazz in New Orleans as early as the turn of the century. No wonder the no less self-aggrandizing Jelly Roll Morton went out of his way to pooh-pooh Handy every chance he got.)

However, it's safe to say that "The Memphis Blues" is the first commercially published, genuine blues (as opposed to the conventional pop songs with the word "blues" in the title that would soon proliferate) to really catch on and sell the idea of the blues to the mass public. The way this happened was ironic: Handy was cheated out of his royalties to the song by a couple of white song-publishing sharpies. Yet had he retained ownership, he could never have made the connections it took to get the song as widely played as the unnamed gentlemen he refers to only as "X" and "Z" (actually L. Z. Phillips and Theron C. Bennet). Thanks largely to their efforts, the song became a national hit, and if Handy couldn't reap the profits (the song eventually reverted to him twenty-eight years later, when the initial copyright term expired), there were, nonetheless, significant benefits in store for him.

"The Memphis Blues" awakened the mass music market in general to the commercial possibilities of the blues. Thus when Handy knocked on the doors of other publishing houses, offering them his newer compositions that used both the form of and the word "blues," he didn't have to ask twice. Handy's next song of note, and the next step in the development of "The St. Louis Blues," was an instrumental he called "The Memphis Itch," though he soon changed the title to "The Jogo Blues." He explained that "jogo" derived from a 1913 form of black jive talk, a kind of signifying slang that, although Handy doesn't specify, seems to incorporate pig-Latin. According to the composer, blacks in pre-WWI Memphis were already referring to whites as "ofays," pig-Latin for "foe." Thus, Handy might well have approved of saxist Frank Trumbauer's recording of "The St. Louis Blues." On this 1932 disc, vocalist (and drummer) Leroy Buck, on the same wavelength as Ginger Rogers, who sang a pig-Latin chorus of "The Gold Diggers Song (We're in the Money)" in the movie *Gold Diggers of 1933,* renders Handy's text in pig-Latin. Egged on by Mr. Tram himself, Buck asks the musical question, Why is it, he wants to know, that if we don't like his "eaches-pay" we "ake-shay" on his "ee-tray"?

"Jogo Blues" was a mild success but hardly the hit that "Memphis" had been. Handy decided that his next song would have words, and, equally importantly, it would not be strictly aimed at the black population who knew the meaning of words like "Jogo." Though specific to the Negro, it would be universal in its appeal. It would attempt nothing less than to take the entire black blues experience and make it palatable to white listeners and dancers. It would be faithful to the black sources, but also playable and singable by white folks.

Handy started with the title, remembering an occasion, some twenty years previously, when he and his quartet of the early 1890s were broke and stranded in St. Louis and had to sleep on the streets. "If you ever had to sleep on the cobbles down by the river in St. Louis," he recalled on quite a few occasions, you would hate to see the evening sun go down—hence the opening line. The very nature of the lyric conveyed something quite specific: "Memphis Blues," when stripped of its "Mr. Crump" lyric, had been an instrumental; words were later added by the publisher, and Handy seems to have had no input or approval. The lyric, written by George Norton (who also wrote "My Melancholy Baby"), at least did Handy the service of mentioning him ("a fellow there named Handy has a band you should hear"), and refers to the song itself as "the tune that Handy called 'The Memphis Blues.' "

However flattered he may have been, Handy knew he would have to write his own words for "The St. Louis Blues" to reflect more directly the colloquial speech of black folk music. He is to be forgiven for the distinctly minstrel-show tone of the lyric, the "Ah" for "I," the "de" for "the," as this was the only way he could get the white singers he wanted to even attempt singing with a black feeling. "Memphis Blues" had been a happy song, describing the carefree (presumably colored) folks of that Tennessee town and how much they loved to dance to Mr. Handy's gay old tune. With "St. Louis Blues," Handy tried to document the anguish a woman feels when she's singing the blues. Her man has left her, and now she wants to pack her trunk and make her getaway—that is, either to take a train out of town (just as her estranged beau did), or perhaps, in a more fatalistic interpretation, to make her getaway from this planet and this life.

The blues were as important a contribution to American culture lyrically as they were musically. This is an oversimplification, but the pop songs of the 1890s and the oughts are often described as overtly saccharine and sentimental, while the blues provided a way of expressing grief without resorting to excessive melodrama. It could be said that the popular love ballad, by its own devices, was in itself on the verge of breaking through to a new expressiveness. Within a few years of 1914, the new wave of lyric writers such as Irving Berlin, Cole Porter, Ira Gershwin, and Gus Kahn would be doing, though in quite a different way, what Handy had done with his song about St. Louis.

In addition to summoning up the cobblestone streets when the evening sun went down, St. Louis figures in the song in another key fashion. Handy remembered that during his sojourn there he was once able to forget his own misery by immersing himself in the unhappiness of another. This particular other was a lady who very much fit the profile of the unnamed first-person protagonist of "The St. Louis Blues." Her man had hit the road, Jack, and now she was trying to drown her sorrows in as much Missouri whiskey as she could get her hands on. "But it hadn't worked," Handy recalled. "Stumbling along the poorly lighted street, she muttered as she walked, 'My man's got a heart like a rock cast in the sea.' " Asking a passerby exactly what was meant by this, Handy was informed: "Lawd, man, it's hard and gone so far from her she can't reach it." Thus the B section opens with a curious "Mona Lisa" kind of a line that few people who hear it, or even sing it, quite understand, yet it certainly makes the song more interesting than your average drawing-room drama of 1914. Bessie Smith's 1929 movie version of the song opens slowly, as the Queen of the Blues takes that phrase about the man and the rock and the sea and utters it slowly, a cappella, as if to herself, then starts chanting it over and over like a mantra. From this she gradually eases into song.

Handy threw anything he could think of—every aspect of African-American vernacular music—into "The St. Louis Blues." As we've seen, it is a genuine blues, using blues form, blues harmony, and blue notes, and in addition, he made a point of leaving breaks—open spaces at the ends of lines—where singers and musicians could improvise short personal statements, such breaks being a crucial forerunner of the jazz solo proper. Handy also made a point of incorporating ragtime-like syncopation, although he made sure to tell us in his autobiography that although he considered ragtime to be rhythmically interesting, melodically it left much to be desired. Still, the "SLB" contains clear touches of ragtime as well as the blues.

Handy also presents himself as having been aware, early on, that the blues was closely connected to black church music ("I used plagal chords to give spiritual effects in the harmony"). Of course, had he suggested this to his father and grandpop—that the music of the church had some relationship to that of the gin mill—he would have been excommunicated, or at least gotten his ears boxed. "My aim would be to combine ragtime syncopation with a real melody in the spiritual tradition." The last strain of "The St. Louis Blues" was inspired by a chant that he heard the elder in his native Florence, Alabama (one Lazarus Gardner) use to summon his congregation to come up to the collection plate after the Sunday service. He first utilized this melody as the opening section of "The Memphis Itch," the piece that later became "The Jogo Blues."

Over the years there were any number of church-style versions of "SLB," employing large choirs. There's the 1928 Victor by Warren Mills and His Blue Serenaders, a concert-style treatment built around Duke Ellington's orchestra. This treatment features a ten-voice choir out of the older tradition of spiritual singing, and it's all very proper and "dicty" sounding, as opposed to the funkier and more flexible blues-driven style that would eventually crystallize as gospel music. A virtually identical arrangement would be employed by the Hall Johnson Choir in their twelve-inch version eleven years later. Of Handy's own recordings of the song, the last (from 1952–53) starts with the composer alone, singing and playing guitar, but finishes with a spiritual-style choir, similar to the Warren Mills group, led by his daughter, Katherine Handy.

The Cecil Mack Choir helped Ethel Waters produce one of the all-time terrific versions of "SLB" as part of a *Blackbirds* revue, Broadway's long-running series of "all-colored" productions. (Curiously, the song "St. Louis Blues" is listed as having been heard in the original edition of this famous series of all-black revues, entitled *Blackbirds of 1928,* but Waters and the Mack choir apparently only appeared in the 1930 production. The original cast album, one of the first, was recorded in 1932.) Whatever the source, the Waters-Mack-*Blackbirds* recording is a brilliant transformation of the twenty-year-old blues, building a whole scene around Handy's song.

Using new lyrics (possibly by Dorothy Fields or Andy Razaf, regular librettists for the *Blackbirds* series), the soloists and ensemble comically portray a group of mourners at a southern funeral trying to raise the money to pay the undertaker ("25 bucks is the sum I'm told / He's got to go at Sundown, hot or cold"). The mention of sunset is the cue for Waters to enter, with the only line from the original Handy text, the one about hating to see the evening sun go down. Playing the deceased's widow (and, she implies, possibly his murderer), she laments the passing of this nogoodnik but resolves to move on with her life—literally, by hopping on a train ("15 coaches long") and going back home to Tennessee, her emotional high note seconded by a scream from one of the sopranos.

In addition to blues, ragtime, and church music, Handy had one final trick up his sleeve. He had noticed earlier that when he played Latin-style rhythms, specifically the habanera, black dancers were quick to respond. "The dancers convinced me that there was something racial to this rhythm." Handy may have given voice to this observation from the vantage point of 1941 rather than 1914, but again he's right, on both ends of the Afro-American equation. There are those who believe that in the Old World, the African influence on the Moorish people was one of the inspirations for what we have come to think of as traditional Spanish rhythms. In the New World, Spanish and African rhythmic traditions intersected once again, this time in the Caribbean islands and in Latin America.

Handy also refers to this beat as the "tango," but it's rather unlikely that he would have heard that word in 1914. "Indeed, the very word 'tango,' as I know now, was derived from the African 'tangana' and signified this same tom-tom beat." The tango tempo asserts itself most strikingly in the B section of "St. Louis Blues," as well as in the introduction. There are also entire versions of the song that stress the Latin tinge, such as Paul Whiteman's from 1926. Whiteman commences with castanets, which make Handy's Latinate intro sound even more Spanish (is this "The Madrid Blues"?), and the B section is thoroughly tangofied (again, the accordion solo near the end sounds more like "Lady of Spain"). There are also exclusively Latin treatments in such later Afro-Cuban dance forms as the rhumba (Xavier Cugat) and the mambo (Machito). Even straight-ahead jazz versions used a touch of the tango: it's there in Louis Armstrong's great 1929 recording, and no less so in his 1933 remake, and even vaguely hinted at in the version of the same year by the Washboard

Rhythm Kings, a group as far removed as possible from a Latin society dance orchestra. Even as late as 1942, the drumming (by Ralph Collier) on Benny Goodman's sextet version suggests the "tom-tom beat" described by Handy.

"Altogether," the composer claimed, "I aimed to use all that is characteristic of the Negro from Africa to Alabama."

"WELL, THEY SAY THAT life begins at 40—I wouldn't know—but I was 40 the year 'St. Louis Blues' was composed, and since then my life has revolved around that composition," Handy observed nearly thirty years later. "Memphis" had shown the way, but "St. Louis" truly opened the floodgates; the song was an immediate national hit, even a sensation. It was sung by everyone, from vaudevillians in blackface to high-toned opera divas, it was played by spasm bands in New Orleans with homemade instruments, by the marching bands (Sousa's, for one) that still dominated much of pop music, by salon-style dance orchestras that played in ballrooms in the big cities, and eventually by symphony orchestras. In short, the piece became a staple for everyone engaged in the business of making popular music.

"Handy's Memphis Band," as he billed it, recorded "SLB" in 1922 (Paramount) and 1923 (Okeh), by which time the song had already been committed to shellac dozens of times. We don't know who made the very first recording, but the 1915 Columbia disc by Prince's Band has to be one of the earliest. Charles A. Prince, the director of music for Columbia, had been recording ragtime tunes with the orchestra for over a decade by then, and earlier that year had also cut Handy's "Memphis Blues" and "Hesitating Blues" for Columbia. Prince's Band was considered a dance band then, but heard today on acoustic prewar wax, it sounds as much a military band as anything. Other early discs of "SLB" include Harry Yerkes' Novelty Five (1919) and what must be the first international version, recorded in London in 1917. Billed as the "Ciro's Club Coon Orchestra," this group made sure to offend more than one ethnicity by putting something called "Chinese Blues" on the flipside. The 1919 version by Jim Europe's 369th Infantry Hellfighters Band, then the premier ensemble of the black musical world, was a considerably greater source of race pride.

The first great jazz version came about, indirectly, through Handy himself. In 1918, Pace and Handy, the composer's publishing firm, had moved to New York. Soon, a young pianist, composer, and sometime vocalist named J. Russel Robinson came to work as a "manager" for the company, an early example of a white executive being employed by a black-owned operation. Not long afterward, another young white man visited the office, Al Bernard, a vaudevillian and occasional composer and producer from New Orleans, who was billed as "The Boy From Dixie." With Handy's encouragement, Bernard, a lusty singer in the minstrel tradition, recorded "St. Louis Blues" (with Robinson on piano) for Thomas Edison, one of the earliest blues numbers to be documented by the august inventor of the phonograph.

In addition to the Edison recording, Bernard recorded "St. Louis Blues" for eight other companies, Handy stated, most notably for Victor, in 1921, with the Original Dixieland Jazz Band. The Original Dixielanders were the most celebrated group of the early jazz age—the first to record, the first to headline in New York and London—and it makes perfect sense that they would address the first great jazz standard. It's a driving record, one of the very best the ODJB ever cut, one that supports the consensus that the comparatively later sides by the band are better than the earlier ones that introduced jazz to records and the national audience. Al Bernard sings two brief blues choruses here (not continuous), both of which are variations on the C section, the second being the one about a "black-headed woman" making "a freight train jump a track," the section of the tune that became the most popular in the twenties.

Bernard, who in 1927 recorded "SLB" yet again with another first-rate white jazz unit, the Goofus Five, is just fine as a vaudevillian with a better-than-ordinary understanding of the blues. But it's what happens after the second vocal on the 1921 ODJB record that's truly outstanding. The band's best soloist, clarinetist Larry Shields, takes a solo of two choruses of straight-ahead blues. Any solo on an ODJB record would be notable, since the band was primarily known for its ensemble playing. But this is much more—a beautifully formed and executed statement, with Shields hitting a series of long high notes that get higher and longer as the solo goes on. It's one of the first great jazz solos committed to shellac, predating Louis Armstrong, King Oliver, and Sidney Bechet by at least two years. Clarinetist Harry Shields told anyone who would listen that it was the greatest clarinet solo ever put on record. He was undeniably biased, since Larry Shields was his brother, but his opinion was shared by dozens of New Orleans reedmen, both black and white, who imitated Larry Shields's "SLB" solo note for note for many years to come. Sidney Bechet even hints at it in his 1944 Blue Note disc.

The "SLB" would quickly be taken up by other "Fabulous Five"–type bands of the period, such as Lanin's Southern Serenaders, a variant of the Original Memphis Five, several months after the ODJB in 1921, and by the Original Indiana Five in 1927. The song was also recorded by dozens of New Orleanians, including Sidney Bechet (1944), George Lewis (who cut it both with Bunk Johnson and on his own), Tony Parenti, Kid Howard, and Louis Prima, first with his 1946 big band.

The initial jazz boom coincided with the record industry boom of the 1920s, itself a by-product of margin-buying and stock-market prosperity. As more and more jazz was recorded, "The St. Louis Blues" was heard more and more often. Handy's own Memphis Blues Band version of 1922 sounds more like a brass marching band than a group with any familiarity with jazz or the blues, though it's not without a certain charm. The piece would soon be recorded by the new-style jazz-dance orchestras of the twenties, both white (like Paul Whiteman's) and black. Nineteen twenty-seven saw outstanding recordings by Devine's Wisconsin Roof Orchestra (a slow, deep-blues treatment waxed in Chicago), Fletcher Henderson (under the name the Dixie Stompers, a track that actually sounds earlier than 1927 because Harmony Records was still employing the older acoustic recording techique, but which is nonetheless highlighted by a Buster Bailey clarinet solo), and New York studio baron Sam Lanin. Lanin's is the most surprisingly excellent—one wouldn't expect the prolific leader's contingent of ofay studio musicians to get as blisteringly hot and low-down as Henderson's or Harlemites or a hard-kicking territory band like Devine's, yet that's precisely what they do.

Female singers took to the song immediately—notable interpretations include those by Irene Beasley (with Benny Goodman, 1928), and Bessie Brown (with Clarence Williams, 1926). In the acoustic era (apart from the 1924 Bessie Smith classic), Esther Bigeou (1921) and the 1923 Brunswick disc by Marion Harris stand out. Handy himself described Harris as a "white blues singer," high praise indeed. Indeed, Harris may be the earliest singer on record, black or white, who seems to have anything like a feeling for the blues—her early treatments of Handy songs are considerably more effective than, say, the records of Mamie Smith, the black entertainer credited with sparking the blues trend. Handy also reports that when Harris's record label refused her request to record some of Handy's blues, she took her business elsewhere. Indeed, the discography shows that she left Columbia for Brunswick around this time. An added benefit of the Harris disc is the featured presence of Benny Krueger, one of the most accomplished of early saxophone virtuosi; another is her personalized coda: "another good man gone wrong."

Even though, as George Avakian realized when he used Velma Middleton for the primary vocal on Louis Armstrong's classic 1954 recording, the song is essentially a woman's song, a surprising number of major male singers, in the twenties and early thirties at least, had a go at it. Many of them found interesting ways of dealing with the gender issue, since the lyric simply cannot be converted from first-person-female to first-person-male merely by switching a few pronouns. Bing Crosby tried that, and his version suffers when he gets to the line about a "St. Louis Woman" leading another woman around "by her apron strings." (What is this, a St. Louis lesbian?) Cliff Edwards gets even kinkier, embellishing the familiar line to read: "You got that little ol' mama o' mine all bound 'round with your apron strings."

Gene Austin, foremost among those twenties male singers with high, effeminate voices, sang it, as did studio-band vocalist Scrappy Lambert, on one of his few primarily vocal recordings. Willard Robison, the songwriter-bandleader who doubled (quadrupled?) as pianist-vocalist, did a really intimate, personal treatment (though not as striking as his reading of Handy's "Harlem Blues"). Handy believed that only those "to the manor born"—i.e., colored folks—could sing the blues, yet he admitted that "I was kept busy telling inquiring friends that [Robison] was not colored." He could have said the same thing about Emmett Miller, a sort of early country-blues-minstrel crossover entertainer (much touted—and rightfully so—by recent rock critics like Robert Christgau and Nick Tosches). Miller actually cut two versions, one of the original song itself (1928), the other a rather wry commentary on it titled "The Ghost of the St. Louis Blues" (1929). Jim Jackson, a "songster"—that is, a practitioner of a strain of black folk music that prefigured the blues (think of Leadbelly)—cut it in 1930, as did Cab Calloway, in his very first session. The

young bandleader-vocalist generally avoids the gender problem by skipping most of the lyric, offering instead some generic (gender-ambiguous)
blues stanzas not found in Handy's published music. Calloway also offers
the first recorded sample of his famous scat singing technique, anticipating both "Minnie the Moocher" and the tobacco auctioneer of Lucky
Strike commercials twenty years hence, and concludes with a surrealistic
war whoop.

In 1927, Devine's Wisconsin Roof Orchestra called their version "The
New St. Louis Blues," while Emmett Miller's "Ghost" version came in
1929 and Frank Trumbauer's pig-Latin rendition, from 1932, was titled
"The Newest St. Louis Blues." Abe Lyman's Californians recorded a
horrifically corny, mock-dixieland version called "The New St. Louis
Blues," while a group of young Chicagoans from Ben Pollack's band, led
by nineteen-year-old Benny Goodman and guest-starring Tommy Dorsey, came up with an even cornier treatment called "Shirt Tail Stomp"
that anticipates Spike Jones. In 1934, Guy Lombardo recorded it as his
most convincingly blue treatment of anything, a performance that brother
Carmen Lombardo made memorable with a rather bizarre clarinet solo
in which he held a single note for a whole twelve-bar chorus.

Most of the first virtuoso soloists to address the tune in the thirties
were pianists, none more virtuoso than Earl Hines. Hines is not generally
regarded as a great bluesman, but he made his "Boogie Woogie on the St.
Louis Blues" into something of a showpiece. By decorating the tune with
all manner of boogie-woogie ephemera, in the spirit of Albert Ammons
and Pete Johnson, Hines came up with a spectacular specialty number: if
you went to a Hines concert at any point from the forties to the eighties,
you'd be disappointed if he didn't play "Boogie Woogie on the St. Louis
Blues." Although an aircheck has been issued of the Hines big band playing the standard "SLB" in 1938 (with a vocal by one Katherine Perry), it
was in 1940 that Hines introduced his classic set of boogie-woogie variations. From that point on, he recorded it dozens of times, enough versions
to keep Napster busy for decades. Treatments are especially plentiful during the sixties and seventies, the years of the great pianist's rediscovery
and constant globe-trotting (the first solo versions come from Paris in
1949). Not all versions stress the boogie-woogie aspect, however: his
solo treatment on *Hines Comes in Handy* sounds more like a traditional
blues, and the one on his 1964 *The Real Earl Hines,* far from sounding

like Hines's usual uproarious party piece, is positively solemn. There's an exceptional version on *Blues and Things,* a 1966 album with blues singer Jimmy Rushing and Budd Johnson, Hines's usual tenor sax compadre, and there's a 1977 meeting of Hines and Lionel Hampton, which may be his last recording of the song.

Hines also cut it for—unfortunately not with—Tony Bennett, on *Earl Fatha Hines Live at Buffalo,* released on the great singer's Improv label. This eight-minute magnum opus seems to be typical of the way Hines played it in the later part of his career: he starts with a long, themeless blues improvisation, then gradually gets into the "SLB" melody, boogie-woogie style. The piece climaxes in a long improvisation that seems meticulously worked out and completely free-form at the same time: he plays a long tremolo in his left hand while running in and out of a series of brief quotations in his right: "I Can't Believe That You're in Love with Me," "Jeannie with the Light Brown Hair," "Frankie and Johnny," "Sometimes I'm Happy," "Summertime," "Song of the Volga Boatman." The whole thing seems designed to drive the crowd nuts. Darned if it doesn't.

Hines's boogie-woogie approach to the tune was so pervasive—and persuasive—it seems to have affected even a stylist as distinctive as Art Tatum. In 1933, at the very start of his career, the monster virtuoso recorded a typically thoughtful set of variations on "SLB." Seven years later, around the same time Hines introduced his boogie-woogie version, Tatum rerecorded "SLB," this time with boogie-woogie variations, on which he plays more piano than Ammons and Johnson put together. Harlem pianist Cliff Jackson recorded an outstanding "SLB" in duo with bassist Kansas Fields live at New York's Town Hall in 1944. It's a hard-driving, very affirmative treatment, even in the minor strain. Hines had played the song during his years with Louis Armstrong's All Stars, and after he left that group, "SLB" continued to serve as a feature for his replacement in the All-Stars, Billy Kyle. In recent years, Ralph Sutton has done an excellent job of keeping the prewar traditions of the song alive: he starts with a long intro that sounds as if it wants to go into Meade Lux Lewis's "Honky Tonky Train Blues," and then very subtly makes the transition into the familiar melody. In fact, we're up to the second strain before we even know it.

By the start of the swing era, the song had been recorded so frequently that it made no sense to put it on wax yet again unless one had a truly special treatment up one's sleeve. The Dorsey Brothers (1934) and Benny Goodman brought it into the big band era. This was one of the staples of the jazz repertoire that Benny Goodman loved; as if to atone for "Shirt Tail Stomp," he did "St. Louis Blues" under its real title for a transcription in 1935, then a year later recorded a slightly longer, slightly different chart for Victor, featuring more soloing by the leader, and a year after that performed an even longer version, with sensational solos by all the band's stars, on an aircheck issued only much later, in the LP era. That band's drummer, Gene Krupa, recorded an intriguingly modern treatment with his own band in 1940, one apparently so far ahead of its time that it lay unissued for forty years.

Glenn Miller arranged the Dorsey Brothers' rather scrappy Decca disc from 1934, on which the trombones, led by Tommy Dorsey, dominate. A year later, Miller went to work for Ray Noble, putting together the British bandleader's first American unit, which opened Rockefeller Center's Rainbow Room. Miller also arranged the "SLB" commissioned for Noble, and that record is one of the few swing-era flag-waver-type treatments of "SLB" to use a vocal, in this case, the band's brilliant baritone Al Bowlly, a top-flight romantic crooner from Britain who also knew his way around rhythm songs and the blues. (Miller may also have arranged the instrumental parts of the Boswell Sisters' great 1935 Decca record; its voicings sound suspiciously like Miller's writing.)

With his own band, in 1940, Miller played a really swinging, extended arrangement from Eddie Durham (more closely associated with Count Basie) that's one of the most exciting things the famous Glenn Miller Orchestra ever did. The chart survives on airchecks but was never commercially recorded. Still, Miller made his most vital contribution to the literature of the song with his "St. Louis Blues March." The march form had been used in jazz since Handy's—and Sousa's—day, jazz bands traditionally playing "hot" treatments of such standard marches as the 1861 "Maryland, My Maryland." Generally, the first order of business in such performances had been to separate the melody from its march origins and perform it as a straight 2/4 or, later, a 4/4 foxtrot. In the early forties, Tommy Dorsey had done this with Victor Herbert's "March of the Toys," as did Miller with "American Patrol," a march from 1891 introduced on records by Sousa.

No one had ever quite done it the other way around, however, and this is what "SLB March" pulls off so excitingly: instead of putting a familiar march into jazz-time, the Millerites take the most venerable of all jazz standards and put it into a swinging march-time. In a sense, the march treatment is one of the more faithful swing-era versions, as it goes through all four distinct stanzas. Amazingly, it swings like crazy without ever losing the march tempo; there's even a hint of a march when the soloists play. A cascading brass *tutti* near the end, echoing Harold Arlen's "Blues in the Night," provides one of the most exciting moments in all of big band music, and Ray McKinley's drumming is so powerful, he sounds like a whole percussion section all by himself. Remarkably, the Miller Army Air Force Orchestra played this piece on only a single occasion, a V-Disc recording date, and it has since become the best-known thing the Miller AAF unit ever did.

Like Miller, Duke Ellington enjoyed a special relationship with "The St. Louis Blues." Curiously, almost all of the treatments associated with the Duke turn out to be extended concert versions. In this, Ellington may have been inspired by William Grant Still, an early African-American composer who worked in jazz, pop, and classical forms. In 1926, Still arranged a two-part treatment entitled "Fantasy on the St. Louis Blues" for radio conductor Don Voorhees, and a year later Ellington's first version, for the Warren Mills Blue Serenaders, emerged. This was undoubtedly more the idea of Ellington's ambitious manager, Irving Mills (who named the unit after his five-year-old son), than of the Maestro. Mills augmented the Duke's men with a contingent of studio players led by violinist Matty Malneck and ten gospel–style singers. When the Mills-Ellington disc was reissued on a French LP in the 1970s, the annotator described it as a "monstrosity" and the product of an "emulator" of the sort of symphonic jazz played by Paul Whiteman. Yet, as we've seen, Whiteman's own 1926 "SLB" was nothing if not straight-ahead and swinging (if a little heavy on the Latin and accordion effects).

Ellington's next recording of "SLB" was also a magnum opus, although far from a monstrosity, symphonic or otherwise. This was the twelve-inch Brunswick (1932) that teamed the Ellington group with Bing Crosby, resulting in one of the great combinations of American pop. A four-and-a-half-minute marvel, it has room for two distinct halves, a slow blues and a fast blues, and Crosby is the focal point of both. Both segments open instrumentally, the slow portion commencing with muted trumpeter Cootie Williams growling out the first twelve-bar *A* strain, then we skip the second *A* and cut to the *B,* likewise growled by muted trombonist Lawrence Brown. Again, the famous *C* strain is temporarily withheld, so the second chorus can get underway with Mr. Crosby. He sings the whole enchilada, all fifty-two bars, slowly and sensually, showing an awareness of the blues medium that he's rarely given credit for (the bandsmen respond in kind, particularly in Tricky Sam Nanton and Barney Bigard's obbligati). The second half commences with a peppy alto solo by Otto Hardwicke before Crosby gives out with a fast, blues-based scat improvisation, and we end on a slow coda not found in the original, "And I'll love my baby / Till the day I die." One early Crosby biographer, Dr. Mize, claimed that the session was totally unplanned, that Crosby and Ellington just happened to run into each other in the studio and took it from there. This seems unlikely, given producer Jack Kapp's reputation as musical matchmaker. However it came to be made, it's a highlight in the careers of both of these twentieth-century icons.

So why is it that the next Ellington "SLB," captured live from the band's famous Fargo, North Dakota, dance date of 1940, is also a concert treatment? Five and a half minutes long, it starts with anything but concert finesse. After a piano intro, the bandsmen, starting with trumpeter Ray Nance, tear into the melody almost as if they intend to rip it limb from limb. Three trombones state the minor *B* section, and that, until the end, is virtually the last we hear of Handy's melody, as the piece becomes a set of hard-driving Ducal variations on the twelve-bar major blues. Barney Bigard plays a clarinet solo (three choruses) that seems exciting as we're hearing it but turns out to be tame in comparison with what follows. After a key modulation provided by Ellington, vocalist Ivie Anderson, who never sounded so much like a down-home blues mama, goes at it for five choruses—some actually from Handy's music. Then Ben Webster (tenor) goes to town to the tune of six choruses, pushing the whole shebang well over the edge of euphoria, with Nanton (trombone) wailing in for the finish.

Ellington scholar Andrew Homzy has written: "The combination of concert style correctness and mounting blues hysteria suggests a forerunner of the (1956) 'Diminuendo (Wailing Interval) and Crescendo in Blue.'" The piece ends with a brief quote from Gershwin's "Rhapsody in Blue." Similarly, the "Rhapsody" turns up in Fats Waller's 1939 piano solo treatment of "SLB" (the one done for Associated Transcriptions, which is not to be confused with his pipe organ solo of 1926 or his four-hand duet with Bennie Payne from 1930) as well as at the end of the extended version performed by Bessie Smith in her 1929 film soundtrack performance. In both the Smith and the Waller versions, there's a sense that the quotation is included in the spirit of a tribute. By contrast, in Ellington's gutsy, ballsy, and deliberately over-the-top "St. Louis Blues," the intention seems more satiric than respectful, as if Ellington is lightly ribbing the idea of such a thing as an extended concert work (such as Gershwin's) based on the blues.

Count Basie, on the other hand, recorded a straight-ahead treatment with just his All-American Rhythm Section and the brilliant tenorist Don Byas (who reprised the tune even more effectively on his own for Savoy in 1946). In that same spirit, Ellington finally recorded a simple and swinging standard single-sided 78 version as part of a three-song *homage à Handy* in 1946. Although there are fine solos by Jimmy Hamilton (clarinet) and Al Sears (tenor), the main focus here is an excellent vocal by one Marion Cox, whose stay with the band was unfortunately brief. Of all of Ivie Anderson's replacements (how Duke loved those husky-voiced contraltos), Cox came closest to succeeding her sonically. In this particular treatment, Ellington and Cox keep most of Handy's lyrics but have essentially come up with new blues melodies to go with them.

Interestingly, all four of the major Ellington versions use the lyric—the Maestro was well aware that the words were as much a part of African-American folklore as the tune. He must also have been aware that virtually all the major jazz and pop singers of the era had tackled the song in their own way, performers like the Mills Brothers (1932), Connee Boswell and the Boswell Sisters (1935), Maxine Sullivan (1938 and 1941), Mildred Bailey (1938), Ella Fitzgerald (on a 1939 radio broadcast), Billie Holiday (1940), and Lena Horne (1940).

Oddly, of this highly distinguished body of great American vocalists, the disc with the most authentic blues feeling is that by the white, New Orleans–born Boswells. No surprise, the sisters don't sing Handy's melody straight but, per standard practice for this innovative trio, they rework it into a Boswell creation. Like Ellington in 1946, the Boswells keep the words but set them to largely new melodies which are no less drenched in the blues than Handy's original. The Mills Brothers and Mildred Bailey also know their way around the blues, the light swinging happy kind as opposed to the heavy downer kind. For the Millses, the song is fertile ground for their early-career gimmick of instrumental imitation, and it opens with a convincing faux-trumpet as mimicked by one of the brothers. While their riffs are inspired by Armstrong, much of their lyric seems completely unique to them, and the piece spends a lot of time delineating the extraordinary deeds done by men in love with women of various hair colors. Bailey's treatment, made with husband and longterm collaborator, xylophonist Red Norvo, is one of the toe-tappingest. Bailey almost sounds a little too jubilant when she scats and "hoy-hoys" about how "a baby slaps his pappy down."

The Lena Horne and Billie Holiday versions, both from 1940, are surprisingly of a piece. One thinks of Holiday as being considerably better equipped to sing the blues than Horne, but in this case, both recordings are best described as "theatrical" more than anything else. Holiday cut two Handy songs for which the Columbia producer (Bernie Hanighan?) made the curious choice of Benny Carter as arranger, conductor, and star instrumentalist—curious because though Carter is one of the great jazz heavyweights, the blues was never among his strengths. All the same, Carter and Holiday (who doesn't sound at all the way she does on her own original blues numbers, such as "Fine and Mellow" and "Billie's Blues") turn in a nicely polished treatment.

In a similar vein, Horne cut her version with the Dixieland Group of NBC's "Chamber Music Society of Lower Basin Street," directed by Henry Levine, four months earlier. This group played gimmicky versions of popular jazz classics on a popular radio series (Handy himself made a guest appearance on the show in 1940). In this instance, however, the unit cut out the corn and turned in a surprisingly copasetic eight-song collection of Handy's works, four of which featured Horne.

The same band did equally well on "SLB" that same year with guest artist Sidney Bechet, who played it with the CMSOLBS on the air, a performance later issued by Victor. Full of Jolsonesque bravura, Bechet dominates the disc from start to finish; the most that Levine's men can manage is to stay out of his way. Bechet had officially recorded the song for RCA three years earlier, in a more democratic rendition with solo space for trombonist Vic Dickenson. Though to me the 1940 version is the livelier, either way Bechet is what "The St. Louis Blues" is all about.

So is Roy Eldridge, who recorded the "SLB" with his own orchestra in 1944. Eldridge's treatment is, to use the parlance of musicians of the period, fast as a bastard, with Little Jazz double-timing, triple-tonguing, and quadrupling everything else, almost as if this were "The Flight of the Bumblebee Blues." The piece is less notable for Eldridge's vocal, which uses generic blues lyrics (e.g., "I'd rather drink muddy water . . .") than for the sheer velocity of the piece.

Eldridge also recorded the "SLB" with Billy Eckstine and Ella Fitzgerald, neither of whom is generally thought of as a blues-based performer, yet both of whom turned in superior performances of Handy's venerable blues. Fitzgerald, like Benny Carter, Dizzy Gillespie, and Earl Hines, was a jazz master who certainly knew her way around the blues as a musical form, though rarely did she indulge in what we think of as blues content. Indeed, Fitzgerald's most notable excursion into this music was a 1970s concoction entitled "The Happy Blues," a fast number that included the couplet "Want to leave you happy / Don't want to leave you sad."

In 1963, Fitzgerald recorded *These Are the Blues,* an album that could have been called *Ella Fitzgerald Sings the Blues Songbook.* Assisted by such masters as trumpeter Roy Eldridge and Wild Bill Davis on organ, Ella tackles the whole gamut of traditional blues, from Bessie Smith to Joe Turner to Leadbelly, as well as Handy's "St. Louis Blues." She tries gamely, but the album is not one of her triumphs. It's unfortunate that her best-known studio "SLB" should be so unsatisfying, since she had been doing the number in concert for nearly twenty-five years by then.

Fitzgerald and the "SLB" work beautifully together when she gets frisky and doesn't try to be soulful. There's a big band version orchestrated by Frank DeVol on the 1957 *Get Happy,* which starts half-slow and gets half-fast and goes into a scat sequence. A year later, on *Ella in Rome: The Birthday Concert,* she did an even better live version of this same arrangement, with a scat episode that starts similarly, incorporating a high-speed quote from "It Might as Well Be Spring," and then going off on its own, throwing in the Nat Cole hit "Send For Me." Her 1964 reading from Juan-les-Pins, with Roy Eldridge again, is even better, with Fitzgerald at her most intense and Eldridge's obbligatos turning the piece into a variation of the Count Basie classic "Goin' to Chicago." Fitzgerald's special lyrics at the end, like her more famous text on "How High the Moon," explain precisely why she chose to do the song. "The only reason we sang this song / It was a request from our record [label] / And now we gotta say so long."

The best-ever Ella Fitzgerald "SLB" is a big band radio remote from 1939 (issued sixty years later), in which Fitzgerald is leading the big band of her recently deceased mentor, Chick Webb. Had Fitzgerald and her musical lieutenant, Teddy McRae, realized then that this particular "St. Louis Blues" would eventually be released to the public, they might have titled it "Ella's Blues." They could have easily gotten away with it, too, as there's precious little here that W. C. Handy would recognize as his own. Trumpeter Taft Jordan opens with a smattering of the melody, punctuated with bent notes and smears, while the background behind him retains just the faintest touch of the habanera-tango-rhumba beat. Fitzgerald prefaces her own entrance with a cry of "Tell 'em about the blues, Taft!" and then comes in with about a line and a half of Handy's lyrics. As scant as the reference to the original words might be, the melody has even less to do with "The St. Louis Blues" as we know it. Ella just invents a blues melody of her own that bears a slight similarity to the second strain of Handy's familiar piece. She doesn't even linger on that for very long before launching into one of her most imaginative early scat choruses.

Even side by side with such heavy-duty soloists as Jordan (who solos again at the end of the track), McRae ("Get happy, Teddy! I hear you, Theodocious!"), trombonist Sandy Williams ("Jump! Jump! Jump! Jump! I hear you, Sandy! Talk to me!"), Fitzgerald has little competition as the band's supreme improviser. The track has much in common with Ellington's Fargo version in that it's a marathon jam for a big band. The five-plus-minute track (an eternity in those days of clock-watching commercial-radio sponsors, even though these were sustaining broadcasts) is an epic blues improvisation, both individually and collectively. Even the announcer's interruption at the eleventh hour (just before the band goes into the closing theme) can't detract from the energy and enthusiasm Fitzgerald and her men generate here.

Maxine Sullivan recorded it twice at the beginning of her career, for Victor in 1938 and for Decca three years later. The Victor is a relaxed "theatrical" performance, anticipating Horne and Holiday, opening with a bluesy piano intro that no one would have guessed is by Claude Thornhill (although the "cool"-style reed orchestration is typically Thornhillian). In between, in 1939, Sullivan reprised the song in the Paramount picture titled *St. Louis Blues.* Other than the fact that the song appeared in it, there was no earthly reason to title the film after the song. Still, we have to agree with Handy's own assertion that no matter how lousy the movie was, Sullivan's performance of the song, with Matty Malneck's orchestra and the Hall Johnson Choir, made the whole thing worthwhile. The other participants also recorded the tune at this time, violinist Malneck (who had also figured on the 1928 Warren Mills–Ellington recording) with a salonesque orchestra featuring harp, and the Johnson choir in what is essentially an a cappella treatment of the "Warren Mills" arrangement.

There would be three movies bearing the title *St. Louis Blues,* and the best thing about all of them was the rare opportunity to see African-American talent on the big screen. The 1958 film (also Paramount) is the only feature to star Nat King Cole, and the 1929 two-reeler is the only film whatsoever of the legendary Bessie Smith, probably the greatest blues singer of all time. Both are inspired by Handy mythology: the Cole feature takes as its text the life of Handy himself, although, surprisingly, precious little of it. The whole thing is wrapped around his minister father's opposition to nonchurchly pursuits, in particular the performance of nonchurchly music. There was so much that was dramatic and interesting about Handy's life—his autobiography is one of the great American life stories—so for Paramount to linger so on this one aspect is maddening. As Freudian cineast Krin Gabbard has noted, it's easy to peg the movie as a black variation on the *Jazz Singer* story, a case of (as Francis Davis has observed) boy-loses-Dad, boy-gets-Dad. (Perhaps Cole could empathize to a degree, as his father was also a man of the cloth, albeit a considerably more supportive one.)

The music was the only saving grace, and while there wasn't enough of it in the picture, all three of the principals—star Nat Cole, leading lady Eartha Kitt, and supporting actress Pearl Bailey (as Will Handy's "Aunt Hagar," a character inspired by Handy's 1921 "Aunt Hagar's Blues," aka "Aunt Hagar's Children's Blues")—recorded full-length albums of Handy's songs. (The picture also featured Mahalia Jackson as a gospel singer and Ella Fitzgerald as a nightclub singer—where does Hollywood get these off-the-wall ideas?) All three are sumptuously beautiful albums, three of the very best products of an age that produced hundreds of great vocal LPs.

All three albums put a brilliant new sheen on material that sounds great to begin with: Bailey's is more traditional, whereas Kitt's (arranged by modern jazz flugelhornist Shorty Rogers) and Cole's (orchestrated by Nelson Riddle, who also scored the film) are more contemporary. Bailey treats us to the original Handy composition "Shine Like the Morning Star," while Cole sings a new song by Mack David, inspired by that Handy tune, titled simply "Morning Star." All three treatments of "SLB" are exemplary. Kitt's is the most cabaret-like, Bailey's the most fundamental, and Cole's the most symphonic. The Cole-Riddle skips the *A* section in order to open with the second strain ("St. Louis Woman, with your diamond rings . . ."), which Riddle's masterful orchestration transforms into a haunting, minor-key introduction. It's certainly classically influenced, with Riddle's characteristic allusions to Ravel and Debussy, but far from being overblown "symphonic jazz," it's nothing short of exquisite. (Bailey had already recorded a version of "SLB" for Harmony Records that's far more gimmicky, really just an excuse for Pearlie Mae to do some rather contrived nightclub spieling over blues changes. The Roulette version, however, is superb.)

Bessie Smith's cinematic treatment takes its cue from the story of the song itself, in which a good woman is abused by a no-account man who takes what he can get from her and then gives her the heave-ho. Smith is the most powerful, guttural blues belter of them all, and her potency is not compromised either by the very large choir (Handy claimed it was forty-two voices, though that sounds a little excessive) or the symphonic touches (more *Rhapsody in Blue*) in the orchestration.

As moving as the 1929 soundtrack performance may be, Smith's 1925 Columbia recording, featuring Louis Armstrong on cornet, is the real deal. In several respects, this disc almost seems as if it was produced by a time traveler floating back to us from posterity: here we have the greatest of blues singers, backed by the greatest soloist in all of modern music, performing the song that had already become the national anthem of the blues. Just the same, there are a couple of wrinkles that history hadn't counted on: this is 1924, and one wishes that the woman, the man, and the song had waited a year or so until this masterpiece could have been documented by the far more sophisticated electrical recording technology. And one has to question the decision (presumably by producer Frank Walker) to back this duo with a Martian-sounding, organ-like keyboard known as the harmonium. Still, like the choir on Smith's soundtrack, these liabilities do not significantly undercut the strength of the record. It's often said that Armstrong was too much the star himself to play second fiddle to anyone, even the great Bessie Smith, and that Smith, for her part, wanted her accompanists to stay more in the background, but you'd never know it by listening: it's almost a voice-cornet duo rather than a cornetist merely playing obligatos behind a singer. Armstrong's fill-in figures are tasteful and tactful, and Smith has more than enough confidence and charisma—not to mention pure chops—to outshine any brassman who would even think of trying to steal her spotlight.

This 1925 disc also served the no-less-crucial function of bringing Armstrong and the "SLB" together in the studio for the first time, and it would be far from the last. He recorded the Handy classic three times, with different editions of his orchestra—1929 for Okeh, 1933 for Victor, and 1934 (in two takes) for an obscure label in Paris—and dominates all three from the git-go. The 1929 opens with a bit of the minor section as intro (as usual, retaining the habanera), Armstrong then tearing into the opening strain, following the published A-A-B-C pattern, allowing trombonist J. C. Higginbotham to take the minor "bridge." Comes time for the C strain, Armstrong reenters singing, giving us a taste of Handy's lyrics before switching to standard blues phrases and wild scat. The climax is wilder still, with Armstrong punching out a series of high G's. The 1933 is an even faster and more aggressive treatment of the same arrangement, again with a trombonist (Keg Johnson) taking the minor B, which this time launches a string of twelve-bar blues solos by Scoville Brown (alto), Charlie Beal (piano), Mike McKendrick (banjo), and Budd Johnson (tenor). This time there's no Armstrong vocal per se, but the leader's voice is heard egging the soloists on, and Armstrong climaxes by soaring above the band and knocking out a string of high D's. (There's also a short radio transcription of Armstrong's big band racing through Handy's tune in 1937.)

Producer George Avakian was intimately acquainted with all four Armstrong recordings of "SLB" when, in 1954, he convinced the powers that be at Columbia Records to let him record Armstrong doing a fifth. This was to be the opening track of an entire album of Handy's music by Satchmo the Great. Made with Armstrong's regular working group, the All-Stars, *Louis Armstrong Plays W. C. Handy* is one of the greatest of all jazz albums from start to finish, and the disc gets going in a big way with a marathon reading of "SLB." Wisely, Avakian assigned the plum spot on it to the band's resident vocalist, blues and comedy specialist Velma Middleton. The producer was well aware that, as we've seen, it's hard to make the song's basic lyrics work for a male singer, and though Middleton may not be Bessie Smith, she more than conveys the combination of vaudeville spirit and down-home blues feeling Handy was trying to inject into his song. Even better, Armstrong gets to sing as well, joining Middleton for some choruses later on in this nine-minute track (including one rather violent episode in which Satchmo expresses the ambition to go upside Velma's head with a wooden picket from a fence), a prime example of how to make a good thing even better.

This wasn't the end of Armstrong's relationship with Handy's classic, although we might well wish that it had been. He had played the tune fairly frequently in the early years of the All Stars, particularly when pianist Earl Hines costarred in the group and did his famous set of variations ("Boogie Woogie on the St. Louis Blues") almost nightly. In 1956 Armstrong made a sixth commercial recording, also for Columbia, this one done live at Lewisohn Stadium, New York, the All-Stars supplemented by all eighty-eight pieces of the New York Philharmonic under the baton of no less keen a fan of jazz than Leonard Bernstein. This ten-minute extravaganza is not a total waste of time, as the unencumbered All Star sextet gets a generous piece of the proceedings all to itself, and Satch's solo trumpet sounds spectacular indeed when soaring over Lenny's players. Handy himself was in the audience that night ("eighty-three and blind," as Edward R. Murrow tells us), and both the performance and Handy's reaction were filmed by CBS TV. Although he might have been flattered by the tribute, the composer undoubtedly was remembering an observation he made in his 1941 autobiography—that symphonic jazz was the cultural equivalent of a farmer plowing his field in a tuxedo. When Bernstein self-deprecatingly describes the Philharmonic treatment of the tune as "a blown-up imitation of what [Armstrong] does," we can't help but agree.

The Philharmonic treatment of "SLB" must have been the last great public moment of Handy's lifetime. He died in 1958, shortly before the release of Paramount's feature film *St. Louis Blues*. Surely, he couldn't have been surprised that the classical world, too, wanted a piece of that St. Louis magic. Nearly every other genre of music had already had a go at it—in addition to jazz, blues, and pop, there were also a number of country versions. The "Father of Western Swing," Milton Brown and His Musical Brownies, recorded "SLB" in 1935 and played it frequently at dances of the time. According to Brown's biographer, Cary Ginell, the Brownies stretched it out in such a fashion that the crowds would literally go wild while waiting for the band to resolve the chords and the tension. In 1946, Bob Wills, best known of all cowboy swingsters, cut an extralong, two-part treatment for Tiffany transcriptions. This mainly consists of overlong minstrelsy-style banter back and forth between Wills (sort of a goyish Ted Lewis) and cowboy crooner Tommy Duncan—had there been an Anti-Defamation League for rednecks, they would surely have objected.

The song was performed almost as frequently in Europe as in the States, starting with that unfortunately named Ciro's Club Coon Orchestra in 1917. Friends of Handy's reported that when they were recognized as Americans overseas, the local bands would frequently strike up "SLB" as if it were "The Star Spangled Banner." Django Reinhardt played it under Stephane Grappelli's leadership in 1935, with expatriate New Orleans reed colossus (physically) Big Boy Goudie, and as a solo feature two years later. Lew Stone, whose ace British swing band took a backseat to none on his own continent and to precious few elsewhere, swung the heck out of it in 1935. The soloist who enjoyed the most "SLB" activity in the shortest time would have to be the London reed virtuoso Freddy Gardner, who cut it five times between '34 and '36.

Like hillbillies and Euro-swingers, modern jazzmen who wanted to demonstrate their connection to the older jazz tradition also took on Handy's venerable blues. Dizzy Gillespie cut it three times, starting with his original Victor big band in 1949, in an orchestration that opens with a phrase that Charlie Parker also used at the start of his famous solo "Parker's Mood" (the line that Eddie Jefferson lyricized as "Come with me / If you wanna go to Kansas City"). He returned to the "SLB" ten years later on his Verve album *Have Trumpet, Will Excite,* and again in 1976 on *Dizzy's Party,* under the title "Shim-Sham Shimmy on the St. Louis Blues," an obvious allusion to Earl Hines's perennial "Boogie Woogie on the St. Louis Blues." Like Ella Fitzgerald and Earl Hines, yet unlike Parker, Gillespie was hardly a blues specialist, but he, too, managed to say something unique and worthwhile with the "SLB."

It would be pianists wanting to pay their respects to the jazz tradition who would have the most to say regarding "The St. Louis Blues" in the modern era. For instance, Tommy Flanagan, in his 1989 trio version with George Mraz and Kenny Washington, pays homage to Gillespie by opening with the "Come with me if you wanna go to Kansas City" line. Likewise, Sun Ra concocted an elaborate piano fantasy on the "SLB" in 1978, one not based on his usual science-fiction jazz; it's a very believable performance done in the stride tradition of Fats Waller and James P. Johnson. The most elegant "SLB"s on record have to be those of Ellis Larkins, which opens with George Duvivier before the pianist enters with the second strain, and the duo of John Lewis and Hank Jones, who, by quoting "Mountain King," make reference to both Waller and Nat Cole.

Dave Brubeck's live 1963 recording from Carnegie Hall has the pianist playing the first two strains; then, when Paul Desmond enters, it becomes an exuberant, extended (eleven-minute) jam session on the blues, no longer based on Handy. Herbie Hancock's version, on his *Gershwin's World* album, is somewhat disappointing in that the focus isn't on Hancock playing Handy but on guest star Stevie Wonder, on harmonica and singing—within a short while the track becomes just another Little Stevie rave-up.

It's also gone on being sung, although principally by older singers, including three of the classiest ladies in jazz: Helen Humes did a loud and brassy yet tasteful treatment on *Songs I Like to Sing,* and when Humes is singing the blues, she really gets into it. Adelaide Hall and altoist Benny Waters sang it in London in 1989 (recorded and broadcast on the BBC) at a time when they were about three hundred years old between the two of them. The performance, which incorporates a lot of Latin rhythm, scat, and other interplay between the two principals, more than makes the point that Hall is still a game gal. Maxine Sullivan, who'd cut it twice in her youth, returned to "SLB" in 1978, turning in a hard-swinging rendition in a blues-and-boogie groove with pianist Art Hodes.

The two major white pop stars who were most conversant with the blues were Kay Starr and Peggy Lee. They had very different approaches to the tradition, yet both came out of Louis Armstrong, Lee with a little more indebtedness to Billie Holiday. Kay Starr's early recording is exciting and inspired, with a clarinet solo by Barney Bigard, who gets more to do on the song here than on any of the occasions when he recorded it with Ellington or Armstrong. Peggy Lee sings it very well on *Blues Cross*

Country, although the slightly dated arrangement credited to Quincy Jones indulges in a few sixties schlockisms. Both Starr and Lee are truly in touch with the spirit of the blues.

The song was performed by singers who had an even stronger connection to the tradition, among them Jimmy Witherspoon and Etta James, and those who had considerably less, such as Perry Como and Jo Stafford. Witherspoon's is a live, straight-ahead jam session, with sax soloists Ben Webster and Gerry Mulligan showing that they more than have the right stuff for the blues; there's a lot of handclapping by the crowd. Etta James not only has all the right feeling, she shows a keen appreciation of Bessie Smith, using an a cappella opening and a choir in the same fashion as the Empress's 1929 soundtrack. The Como and Stafford treatments were simply a mistake. One feels ungentlemanly even in bringing them up. Both are overdone, but Como's, on *Como Swings,* is particularly over the top, and the use of Latin rhythm only underscores how the normally smooth singer is out of his depths here.

It would be hard to think of a fashion in which "The St. Louis Blues" has *not* been recorded—in 1933, for instance, Bluebird released a disc by an ensemble billed as the Whiskey Bottle Boys titled "Blue Songs," a medley that opens with the familiar blues. The WB Boys get all the notes right and, surprisingly, do not sound as if they've just consumed the contents of their chosen instruments. In 1991 it was recorded by String Trio of New York (on *Time Never Lies*), a band that's easy to classify as a "chamber group" but impossible to categorize as either jazz or classical; it embraces elements of both, as well as folk, bluegrass, and a heavy dose of rural blues. To hear them run faithfully through all of Handy's stanzas, one might imagine this threesome has much of the feeling of the original string trio that inspired Handy to play the blues back in Mississippi at the turn of the last century.

The ultimate tribute may well have come from Dorothy Fields, in her lyric to "Never Gonna Dance" (to music by Jerome Kern), from the Fred-Ginger masterpiece *Swingtime.* Here, Fred Astaire sings of a drum beating the "weird tattoos / Of the St. Louis blues."

It's tempting to conclude with some remark like "Fashions come and fashions go, but 'The St. Louis Blues' lives on." For the past fifty years the song has chiefly been the province of traditional jazz and dixieland bands. Gillespie notwithstanding, bop bands rarely address it, and neither do blues acts from the 1940s or later. Does it matter? Well within Handy's lifetime, the song had proven itself the single most familiar set of words and music in all of jazz, and it's unlikely that any other number will come along to displace it from its perch. There are also fashions within the song itself: in the twenties most every singer included the line about how a black-haired mama made a freight train jump its track, whereas in the thirties, the line about not liking one's peaches and therefore not shaking one's tree became fashionable. By the forties, singers wanting to extend the finale C section added the stanza about "I love that man like a school-boy loves his pie" (when did pies become synonymous with schoolkids, I'd like to know?).

Yet there's one passage in the published sheet music I have yet to hear any singer utter. It goes:

> *Ashes to ashes, dust to dust.*
> *Ashes to ashes, dust to dust.*
> *If my blues don't get you, my jazzing must.*

BONUS TRACKS

Bet You Never Knew "The St. Louis Blues" Was a Love Song

The award for the sweetest, tenderest "St. Louis Blues" goes to Billy Eckstine. His 1953 version was released as by the Metronome All Stars, and while side B is a jam session on the tune with spectacular solos by Lester Young and Roy Eldridge (plus an unexpected scat vocal by Eckstine), side A is Mr. B. all the way. Eckstine's singing is not essentially blues-based; he comes more out of Crosby and Russ Columbo (though, as we've seen, Crosby knew a thing or two about "The St. Louis Blues" himself) than out of Robert Johnson. Yet Eckstine had enough of a combination of blues chops and pure class to pull off one of the great pop vocal versions of the "SLB"—having Lester Young to play obbligatos sure doesn't hurt—by crooning it as if it were "I Apologize." It may not be the "St. Louis Blues" that Handy had in mind back in 1914, but it more than works for me.

Most Unusual and Outrageous "SLB"s

A year after the Bessie Smith *St. Louis Blues* featurette, who would have guessed that the individual responsible for the song's next milestone appearance in a motion picture would be . . . Mickey Mouse? Believe it or not, in the 1930 Disney cartoon *Blue Rhythm,* the Mouse plays a maestro (a mousetro?) at a band concert in which he and his cartoon cronies savage the hell out of "The St. Louis Blues."

Coincidentally, there's an equally audacious treatment from that same year, unearthed by Sherwin Dunner and Ron Hutchinson of the Vitaphone Project, that also comes from an early talkie short. Bandleader Vincent Lopez was, for a time, regarded as the chief rival to Paul Whiteman. But though Lopez, like Pops Whiteman, led an excellent straight-down-the-middle jazz-and-show band, he rarely went to Whiteman's extremes, and never made a point of playing as much symphonic jazz (or even non-symphonic jazz) as the more ambitious Whiteman. In 1930, Lopez recorded a super-duper eight-minute version of "The St. Louis Blues" that was pressed only on a ten-inch microgroove transcription distributed for playback in movie theaters by Paramount. It's nine choruses long and features just about everything that they thought could be done with the "SLB" in 1930: the second strain is done in minor, but not as a tango; a gospel choir comes in and sings the lyrics while a pennywhistle soloist noodles about them; a trombone improvises twelve bars of blues over the choral background; a solo vocalist sings two nonconsecutive choruses over the gospel choir; a very tightly muted growling trumpeter goes into a call-and-response chorus with the band that seems much inspired by Bubber Miley's solo on Ellington's "Black and Tan Fantasy"; and a hot violin solos with rhythm section only. Other than in the use of the choir, which relates it to Warren Mills–Ellington, this is not in the least a concert or symphonic version, just an extra-long treatment in which the band seems to have done everything it could think of.

If the Lopez performance is more astonishing than outrageous, the same can't be said of an extra-long performance by the Casa Loma Orchestra. This is a two-sided private-issue disc, apparently produced by the band for its own amusement and unearthed seventy years later by engineer Mike Keiffer. Side one starts out like a parody of a sweet dance orchestra like Lombardo's trying to play the blues and overdoing it, leaning too hard on the brass smears and making the ensemble playing sound rougher and rattier than is necessary. Trombonist Pee Wee Hunt growls too much and then clarinetist Clarence Hutchenrider strains exaggerat-edly, to the verbal encouragement of the band, for a high note. There follows the first set of vocals, which begin with new blues lyrics ("A billy goat stepped in a bumblebee's nest / And from that minute on he didn't get no rest"). Side one ends and side two begins with the work in progress, as if the band wasn't willing to pause while the engineer switched acetates. We get two of the bandsmen indulging in some in-creasingly inane scatting. There's also a conversation/battle between two trombones, and more weird scatting. On the whole, I wouldn't be sur-prised to learn that the Casa Lomans had been partaking from the instru-ments of the Whiskey Bottle Boys.

Most Authentic "Modern-Era" Version of "SLB"

If Bessie Smith, whether with Louis Armstrong on her acoustic Columbia disc or with that big choir on her soundtrack recording, can be credited with making the most authentic 78-era treatment of the "SLB," the prize for the most authentic LP-era recording goes to Smith's con-temporary Ida Cox. Like Bessie Smith (and unlike, say, Mamie Smith) Cox was less of a vaudevillian than most of the so-called classic blues singers of the twenties and more of an authentic blueswoman. According to varying sources, Cox was born somewhere between 1889 and 1896; in any event, like Bessie Smith (born 1894), she would have been an adult in 1914, when the "SLB" was first heard. Although supported by obbligatos from such stars as our old friend Little Jazz Eldridge and Coleman Hawkins (who, unlike disciples such as Ben Webster, almost never accompanied a singer after his own apprenticeship with the wrong Smith girl— Mamie), the main attraction here is Cox herself. She's at least in her mid-sixties, but her voice still sounds powerful and her articulation could cut steel. This is a thoroughly believable rendition, a performance one can have complete faith in, sure as a Kentucky colonel loves his rock and rye.

Mack The Knife

A THEME FROM "THE THREEPENNY OPERA"

Music by
KURT WEILL

English words by
MARC BLITZSTEIN

Original German words by
BERT BRECHT

Featured by LOUIS ARMSTRONG

Price
50¢
in U.S.A.

WHEN PERFORMING THIS COMPOSITION KINDLY GIVE ALL PROGRAM CREDITS TO
HARMS, INC.
NEW YORK, N. Y.

Printed in U. S. A.

MACK THE KNIFE (1928)

(aka "Moritat," or "A Theme from *The Threepenny Opera*")

music by Kurt Weill

original German lyric by Bertolt Brecht

English lyric by Marc Blitzstein

WITH THE SUCCESS OF "Mack the Knife" in America, the music of Kurt Weill came full circle. (I stress the career, rather than the composer himself, Weill having died in 1950, a good half-decade before "Mack" would appear on the charts.) Weill, as portrayed by his biographer Ronald Sanders in the definitive *The Days Grow Short,* reminds me of the Robin Williams character, a robot named "One," in the movie *Bicentennial Man,* a very touching piece of science fiction based on an Isaac Asimov short story. Much the same way that One strove to become human—a *mensch* would be another way to put it—Weill spent the better part of his creative years trying to become American. He had prospered for the first decade or so of his mature professional life in his native Germany before being chased out by the Nazis in 1933. When the country of his birth rejected him, you might say that Weill returned the favor by rejecting German culture, and with every one of his American works he sought to prove himself capable of creating the same kind of glorious melody as such fellow Broadway Jews as Irving Berlin, Richard Rodgers, and, most of all, George Gershwin.

Yet, ironically, the single most successful song in the Weill catalogue would be an English translation of one of his earlier, Weimar-era works. "Mack the Knife" wasn't just a chart-topping hit, one of the biggest sellers of all time, but a song that virtually all the most important vocalists in the American idiom felt impelled to perform, including Ella Fitzgerald and the three central male singers of the century: Louis Armstrong, Bing

Crosby, and Frank Sinatra. The song also made the career of Bobby Darin, a major talent very nearly on their level.

It's fitting that Weill's centenary (he was born in 1900 and died in 1950) arrived a year after Noel Coward's (1899–1973). The obvious similarity is that Weill and Coward were the two major songwriters of their era who established their reputations in Europe and then proceeded to have a major impact on America and Tin Pan Alley, the home base of the modern popular song. But beyond that, devotees of their work have claimed that Weill and Coward were somehow more than "mere" songwriters. In Coward's case, the fact is plain, since his career as composer, lyricist, playwright, actor, singer, novelist, raconteur, and legendary, quotable wit was . . . legendary. Weill, by contrast, achieved the status of a great intellectual without writing a single word of text.

Ordinarily, a composer of melodies—a Harry Warren, a Jerome Kern—isn't held responsible for the literary content of the words that accompany his tunes. Yet the libretti that go along with Weill's music are so consistent in their point of view that one is tempted to credit the composer. He is, indeed, generally perceived as a political ideologue who spent his life fighting fascism and injustice.

Weill himself may have been flattered by such a notion, but probably he wanted to be thought of for what he was: a maker of melody. Although it's clear where he has influenced later American theater composers, particularly Stephen Sondheim (*Sweeney Todd* has more than a touch of Brecht and Weill about it), in a sense he lived their careers in reverse, since most Americans start by writing traditional musical shows and drift into experimentation later on. Weill, however, spent his career in search of melody: he began as a young avant-garde composer in Germany, where he was encouraged to follow in the footsteps of Schoenberg, and from there became involved in modern opera, then in experimental music for the theater, and only later in Broadway-style musical comedy and the American popular song idiom. Both as a refugee from Hitler and as an artist, Weill was the archetypal modernist who came in from the cold.

IN JAZZ, THE STORY one encounters again and again is that of the supremely talented yet self-destructive "young man with a horn" who burns himself out in his twenties or thirties with alcohol or drugs. In the world of musical comedy, the story you hear again and again is of the show that needs an additional song at the last minute. With only hours to go before the opening, the composer and lyricist sit up all night and bang something out. Then, often as not, it's that very eleventh-hour addition that becomes the show's big hit. Thus did "Comedy Tonight" become the most memorable song in *A Funny Thing Happened on the Way to the Forum,* and "Soliloquy" was written while *Carousel* was already in rehearsal. Even more than most writers of musical scores, Weill had made something of a career-long practice of these last-minute hits: "September Song" in *Knickerbocker Holiday,* and the entire "circus dream" sequence featuring "The Saga of Jenny" in *Lady in the Dark.*

"Mack the Knife" himself began life as "Captain MacHeath," the dashing bandit antihero of John Gay's *The Beggar's Opera,* which was first performed in 1728. (As one Broadway wag put it, "That's even before Al Jolson!") In the most famous modern document of Gay's work, the 1953 British film of *The Beggar's Opera,* Mack is portrayed as a rather dashing figure by Laurence Olivier. Brecht and Weill had first conceived of *Die Dreigroschenoper* as a comparatively simple update of *The Beggar's Opera,* but the more they worked over the material, the more it became their own. Still, the central characters—MacHeath, Lucy Brown (Lucy Lockit, Gay's original), Polly Peachum—and the London setting (updated from the early eighteenth to sometime in the late nineteenth century) come from Gay.

Just a few days before the August 31, 1928, premiere of *Die Dreigroschenoper,* it occured to Brecht and Weill that their MacHeath (no longer called "Captain," although it's still understood that he's had military experience) was becoming too much of a conventional hero and not enough of the antihero they'd sought to make him. Harold Paulsen, the actor portraying MacHeath, was quite the matinee idol, and he played Mack as a gentlemanly gangster—a relatively new concept in the age of American prohibition. MacHeath would be handsome, virile, impeccably dressed, and catnip to women, in spite of the fact that he'd murdered several, robbed many, and seduced and abandoned far more. How, then, to properly convey the menace and the evil that was MacHeath?

It was Brecht's idea that they should add a number at the very opening of the play, immediately after the overture, that would show the audience what a rat-bastard this MacHeath was. Brecht started by comparing Mack to a shark: the latter may be a murderous, man-eating fish, Brecht reasons, but at least he's honest about what he does. When you see a shark coming, you can hardly fail to miss his terrible dagger-like choppers and at least try to get the hell out of his way. Mack's razor, on the other hand, is more deadly than a shark's teeth because you never see it coming. This charming gentleman will smile at you warmly as he picks your pocket, and feels no compunction in patting you on the back with one hand while slitting your throat with the other. When a shark attacks, there's no doubt about it—mainly because there's blood all over the place. When Mack strikes, he's careful to cover it up, and doesn't get so much as a spot of blood on his elegant white kid gloves.

The song is divided into seven sixteen-bar sections. The first two establish, through elegant use of simile and metaphor, the unsharklike nature of MacHeath. The balance of the lyric is a rather straightforward cataloguing of MacHeath's grisly misdeeds: a bloody corpse is found on the street one Sunday morning and someone gets a glimpse of a vaguely Mackish suspect slipping 'round the corner. A rich man has disappeared—along with his money—and all of a sudden MacHeath seems to have a lot of cash on hand. A coincidence? Unlikely. You can't directly link Mack to any of these crimes, not when the body of a woman is found with a dagger in her breast and Mack is spotted nearby, nor when a fire in Soho kills seven children and one old man, nor when a young widow ("still a minor") is raped in the middle of the night.

Various productions of the show pick and choose which of MacHeath's numerous atrocities they will include. This holds true for both German and English treatments and is not merely a matter of a given translator trying to cover something up, although it's true that the American "pop version" does omit some of Mack's more abominable acts. One of the most famous sections of the song, the ending, in which the lyric recites the names of MacHeath's romantic victims (Suky Tawdry, Polly Peachum, Jenny Diver, not to mention good old Lucy Brown) seems to be entirely the invention of translator Marc Blitzstein; nothing like it appears in any other English version. Blitzstein also came up with the idea of reprising the opening stanza (the one about the shark) at the end, although this seems to have been done only in the 1954 Theatre De Lys revival (and the cast album), not in any of the pop versions.

After coming up with the idea for the song, Brecht went home for the night and returned the next day with the words, which Weill, in turn, also took all of one night to set to music. Brecht supposedly told a few friends that the melody, too, was basically his idea (as he would also boast of "Alabama Song," from the two collaborators' *Mahagonny*). Weill, for his part, is said to have been inspired by noises he heard in Berlin traffic while taking a streetcar home that night. He wrote the tune in C, which is how it appears on the recordings of the 1928 original production and the 1954–55 off-Broadway version. Just as the structure is simple—it's essentially a four-line *A* section heard over and over (well, seven times)—the melody is quite simple, as well, being based primarily on three notes, the third, fifth, and sixth tones of the scale. In the key of C, that's E, G, and A; and this basic pattern is repeated twice in the first line, then again starting a step lower, on D (the scale's second tone) in the second. The third line makes the only significant departure from the basic E, G, A line, but the fourth line returns to that original melody. Although Weill chose not to end on the tonic note C (preferring instead the mediant, A), he does use the conventional harmonic progression of I-II-V-I, which perhaps explains why the song seems so at home with American pop and jazz performers.

Brecht titled the tune "Moritat," a German term meaning "murder song" or "murder ballad." In German, "*mord*" means "murder," and "*tat*" means "deed," a possible origin of the English expression "tit for tat." Guy Sterns's English translation (included as the libretto in Columbia Records double-LP German-language recording from 1958) describes it as a "penny-dreadful ballad." Whatever you call it, such songs are part of a shared English-German tradition, ballads for performance on music hall stages (or, in the case of this one, by a street-singer) that cry out the news, offering grisly details of the latest crime. (The most famous "murder ballad" in the traditional English repertory is "Sweeney Todd the Barber," the source for that most Brechtian of Sondheim musicals.) Eventually, the song title was changed from the more general "Moritat" to a more specific title containing the name of the character it describes.

On opening night in 1928, it wasn't until they reached the "Cannon Song" that the company knew they had a hit. In fact, "Mack" originally didn't make much of an impression: it was supposed to be sung by a street performer, played by Kurt Gerron (who doubled as the crime overlord's pal, the corrupt Police Chief Tiger Brown), as he operates a hurdy-gurdy. Unfortunately, no one had remembered to wind the organ, so the Streetsinger found himself singing a cappella. By the second stanza the pit

orchestra jumped in and ad-libbed an impromptu accompaniment, but by
then the song had lost some of its impact.

Despite this inauspicious beginning, the show was a hit—by far the
biggest of Weill's pre-Broadway career—and "Moritat" was the song that
Berliners were humming in the streets the next day. Cast recordings were
made two years later, featuring Weill's wife, Lotte Lenya, not only singing
the songs she introduced in her original role as Jenny Diver but most
of the other women's songs as well, while Gerron performed both the
"Moritat" (as the Streetsinger) and the thunderous "Cannon Song" (as
Tiger Brown). Original cast albums were more common in Europe than
in the States at that time, but even overseas such projects were by no
means as common as they would be in the world after *Oklahoma!*

The *Dreigroschenoper* discs were not best-sellers in Europe or America,
but many people with a keen interest in theater music owned a copy of
the 78 album, among them the Gershwin brothers. On the other hand, no
one seems to have gone to see *Die Dreigroschenoper* when it played briefly
at Broadway's Empire Theater, a mere twelve performances, in 1933.
The translation, the first of four that would eventually reach Broadway or
off-Broadway, was by the coproducer, Gifford Cochran. No, I never heard
of him, either, but Burgess Meredith, who played one of the supporting
roles (and later became a friend of Weill's in his early Broadway years), is
still well known. This was the first time that the work was known, in English, as *The Threepenny Opera*.

The 1930 German film of *Die Dreigroschenoper* (directed by G. W.
Pabst) was better received internationally than in America. The "Mack"
song is woefully underplayed there, almost thrown away. The overture is
hardly present at all (replaced by "What Keeps a Man Alive" under the
main titles), and the story commences, as usual, with *Die Moritatensanger*
performing this opening song, this time with the aid of an easel bearing
cartoon-like illustrations of corpses and sharks. The idea of starting the
story with Mackie's spotting Polly and following her down the street
even as we hear the "Moritat" is a good one, but most of the other departures from the show (approved of, and many even suggested by, Brecht)
are not nearly so successful. (Even less wise was the decision not to use
most of Weill's score, which unfortunately also occurred all three times
that Hollywood filmed one of Weill's Broadway hits). This film's major
asset is the visual presence of Lenya in her role as Jenny at roughly the
time of the original Berlin run. (The film was also apparently shot in

French, and excerpts from the French soundtrack are included on the same Telefunken LP that contains the original cast recordings, but, alas, a French "Mac le Dagger" is not among them.)

By 1930, "Mack" was already a hit song around Berlin, and was being heard in cabarets and various kinds of theaters. Around this time, a band known as the Haller Jazz Revue Orchestra recorded a double-sided instrumental medley of tunes from *Dreigroschenoper*. Judging by the name of the band as well as by the style of their playing, they were more likely a theater pit orchestra than a band that played for dancing (undoubtedly in those days there was more jazzlike music in Berlin's cabarets than in its ballrooms). One side of the Haller disc is given over to what record collectors would call a "hot dance" treatment of "Barbara Song," highlighted by a dark, plunging trombone solo. The flip side is even juicier: it starts with a thirty-second chorus of "Das Lied von der Unzulänglichkeit" (Peachum's second-act aria, known in Blitzstein's version as "Useless Song"), and from there we segue into the famous "Moritat." The Hallerites start by phrasing the melody pretty much as heard in the show, on a calliope (with low-pitched guitar accompaniment), and from there launch into an attempt to put the piece into a jazzy fox-trot tempo, as if they were a New York or London dance orchestra. There's even a stanza played on three soprano saxophones, in the manner of Fletcher Henderson, followed by more hot, pumping trombone. It still has a heavy Weimar feeling, and as on the 1930 original cast recording, "Moritat" is played in C, but this was the first indication that the song might make it on its own, removed from the *Dreigroschen* context.

The Haller recording, as far as is known, has never been distributed outside Germany or reissued on any kind of long-playing release, yet it makes several important points for Weill. It's been noted that he was part of the first generation of European composers writing for either the theater or the concert hall who were deeply influenced by American jazz: Lenya later reported that as early as the *Threepenny* period Weill had already amassed a collection of Louis Armstrong records, which would place him in the vanguard of Eurojazzophiles. (Dan Morgenstern advises taking this story with a grain of salt, as Armstrong was barely known to white people in America, let alone Europe, at this time, but it is certainly possible.) More than his earlier symphonies, operas, or theater works, *Dreigroschenoper* was the work in which Weill most fully indulged his love of jazz—perhaps not in rhythm or the concept of the solo improvisation, but certainly in the loose, dissonant nature of the harmonies. The Haller side may well be the first example of the world of pop and jazz claiming Weill's music for its own purposes, and early proof that "Moritat" had what it took to succeed not only outside *Dreigroschenoper* but far outside Weimar Germany itself.

THE SONG DID NOT, however, attain that status for a good twenty years. After leaving Berlin, Weill himself showed little interest in keeping *Dreigroschenoper* alive, or even in maintaining his partnership with Brecht. In 1946, Duke Ellington presented his own update of John Gay's *Beggar's Opera,* titled *Beggar's Holiday,* on Broadway. Boasting a libretto by John LaTouche and a mixed-race cast, the production ran for 111 performances—about a hundred more than the 1933 Broadway *Threepenny Opera,* but still short of a hit. After these German and American adaptions, in 1953 the British reclaimed John Gay in a big-budget movie musical of *The Beggar's Opera* (one of the best of all British musical films, in fact), with Laurence Olivier not only acting but singing the heck out of the role of Captain MacHeath.

With the Nazis out of power in Germany, the time seemed ripe for *Dreigroschenoper* again. According to Ronald Sanders, "Almost as soon as the war had ended, *Dreigroschenoper* was back in the repertory of German theatres, and other Weill works followed suit." So the seeds of the postwar revival of interest in Weill's early German work were sown, fittingly, in Germany itself, as the country began to look to its pre-Nazi past.

The Philadelphia-born composer Marc Blitzstein (1905–1964) had been studying with Arnold Schoenberg in Berlin in 1928, which is when he saw *Dreigroschenoper* and became infatuated with Weill's music in general and that work in particular. Blitzstein's own music is often described as being written in the Weill style, partly because Blitzstein's career paralleled Weill's own: he started by writing modernist instrumental music, then switched to politically motivated theater works, and finally succumbed to the lush Broadway sound. Blitzstein's best-known earlier work, *The Cradle Will Rock,* is leftist in content and at least vaguely Brechtian in form, although the dramatic style also recalls Clifford Odets's *Waiting for Lefty.* Blitzstein's final show, *Juno* (which lasted a mere sixteen performances), boasted rich melodies that could be said to be influenced by *Lady in the Dark* and *One Touch of Venus,* but just as much by the work of

Jerome Kern and Richard Rodgers. In real life, however, Blitzstein ended up like a "Surabaja" Brecht character, dying in a bar brawl with three drunken merchant marines in Martinique.

In January 1950, not long after the short run of his opera *Regina* (based on Lillian Hellman's *The Little Foxes*), Blitzstein, on his own initiative, made an English translation of "Pirate Jenny" and showed the results to Weill and Lenya, who were much pleased. It was four months later, at Weill's funeral, that Blitzstein decided to continue the process, with "Solomon Song." In an interview, several years later, he recalled, "Soon I was translating other songs and snatches. By that time I had reached the point of no return, I had to do it all." Undoubtedly he was encouraged by the success of a memorial concert at Town Hall in February 1951, at which Lenya and others performed Weill's German works; he was also egged on by conductor Maurice Abravanel, a former student of Weill's who performed many of the composer's works in the New World (and who had also worked the podium on Blitzstein's *Regina*). Blitzstein's *Threepenny* translation was performed for the first time in Massachusetts, at Brandeis University, in 1952, under the baton of Leonard Bernstein.

This "workshop" production was so well received that Blitzstein and Lenya immediately received offers to take the translation to Broadway. However, all the producers who extended these invitations wanted to monkey with the material in some fashion, to change the setting or update the story. Blitzstein and Lenya finally went with Carmen Capalbo and Stanley Chase, the first producers who agreed to accept the work as Brecht, Weill, and now Blitzstein had written it. The catch was that they were working in the new theater universe known as "off-Broadway."

In theater histories, 1953 is given as the year that the modern concept of "off-Broadway" was introduced, and at first the term usually referred to productions staged in Greenwich Village. Brooks Atkinson wrote in the *New York Times,* "The brains, taste and inventiveness of the musical theatre have moved off-Broadway this season. Broadway is left with a gaudy wardrobe of old hats."

Brecht was still alive to hear of the success of *The Threepenny Opera*—and to bristle at Blitzstein's name appearing above both his and Weill's—when it opened off-Broadway at the Theatre De Lys, near Waverly Place (in Greenwich Village), on March 10, 1954. It initially ran for a limited engagement of ninety-four performances, then reopened on September 30, 1955, for 2,611 more. In addition to Lenya, then on the safe side of sixty, portraying the hooker Jenny Diver, the American cast included such rising stars as Bea Arthur, Charlotte Rae, Jo Sullivan, John Astin, and Gerald Price, the latter in the role of the Streetsinger, who sings "The Ballad of Mack the Knife" immediately after the overture. A month later, producer Ed Cole of MGM Records recorded the original cast album of the American *Threepenny Opera*—the first-ever cast recording of an off-Broadway production—on which "Moritat" is once again played in C major. According to David Farneth of the Weill-Lenya Research Center, some of Blitzstein's translation (and indeed, Brecht's original libretto) was deemed too violent and erotically explicit for a family-oriented label like MGM Records. Thus, at least two of the more questionable stanzas of "Mack"—the woman stabbed, the child-bride violated in her slumbers—were deleted in the recording session, although they were, in fact, performed nightly at the De Lys. Like the show, the album was a major commercial success. To Brecht, Blitzstein, and Lenya it must have seemed that *Threepenny Opera* and "Moritat" had reached their final destination. They couldn't have known that "Mack"'s status as a legendary pop song was only beginning.

THE MEN BEHIND THE SCENES most responsible for transforming "Moritat" from the avant-garde Berlin theater song into the American pop hit "Mack the Knife" were producer George Avakian and trombonist, arranger, and bandleader Turk Murphy. Immediately after the war, Avakian was writing a column on music for *Mademoiselle,* where he became friendly with the magazine's editor, George Davis. In the early 1950s, Davis married Lotte Lenya, and Avakian, who remained friendly with the couple, and who was by then in charge of pop and jazz albums at Columbia Records, thus got in on the ground floor of the Weimar-Weill revival. Avakian was there in March '54 for opening night of the De Lys production, and returned many times.

"All of a sudden, it hit me like a ton of bricks, that the opening song would make a great jazz instrumental," Avakian recently recalled. "It was only a few bars, but those changes and countermelodies—I kept thinking what a great jazz musician could do with it!" When the original cast album was released on MGM Records, Avakian dubbed off acetates from "The Ballad of Mack the Knife" and began circulating them, along with the sheet music, among jazz musicians he knew. He started with Erroll

Garner and Dave Brubeck, the two star pianists on his home label, Columbia Records, but both of them turned it down. In fact, every musician he submitted it to refused it, even when he began trying players who were not under contract to Columbia, such as the Modern Jazz Quartet and Gerry Mulligan.

Finally, Avakian got the idea of bringing it to Turk Murphy, who led one of the major traditional jazz groups on Columbia Records and was one of the key figures in the dixieland revival on the West Coast. When Murphy was next in New York, Avakian brought him down to the De Lys and Murphy agreed that the song was a natural for jazz purposes, although Avakian was still thinking of it as an instrumental. "No one's going to want to hear this bloodthirsty lyric," Avakian thought, but Murphy's band would be perfect, particularly as his six-piece dixieland group was so close in makeup to Weill's original pit orchestra. But Murphy, it turned out, had a better idea. "I know the perfect guy to do this song," he told Avakian, "but I'm not going to tell you who. Come out to Los Angeles and I'll show you." Murphy's band was appearing at an L.A. club called the Tin Roof, and when Avakian arrived, the trombonist offered to drive him to another club where the as-yet-unnamed artist he had in mind was appearing. They drove off to the Mocambo, and as Avakian saw the big sign in front reading "Appearing Tonight: Louis Armstrong and His All-Stars," it immediately hit him—"Well, of course! I don't know why I hadn't thought of that myself."

In a way, "Mack the Knife" was almost predestined to make it as an American pop song, especially in the 1950s, and especially for Louis Armstrong. This was the most diverse era of American pop, when anyone from Nat Cole to Elvis to Liberace to Spike Jones had a shot at landing a hit. As contemporary jazzman Don Byron has observed, "In the transition between swing and rock—a period too wacky to have a name—it seemed as if any song from anywhere in the world could score on the charts. Music from all over Europe hit the pop charts alongside country tunes. Such a diversity of material . . . might lead one to think that this period was a time of cheerful pluralism." The repertoire of Louis Armstrong was especially pluralistic: a typical evening with Armstrong and his All-Stars might include "The Gypsy" (English), "The Faithful Hussar" (a German song that Armstrong first recorded at a live concert in Milan), a pairing of "La Vie en Rose" and "C'est si Bon" (French), "High Society Calypso" (Cole Porter's approximation of Jamaican jive), "Skokiaan" (Zimbabwean), and "Cold Cold Heart" (from a country even farther afield—Nashville).

Murphy later recalled that when Armstrong heard the lyric for the first time, the trumpeter rejected it as being too bloodthirsty for his taste. Avakian, however, remembers that the mighty man took to it at once when he and Murphy played him the Gerald Price recording in his dressing room at the Mocambo. "Pop's face just lit up as he heard the lyrics. It took him about forty seconds before he said, 'Well, I'll be! I used to know some cats just like that in New Orleans!' " Armstrong agreed to sing it and Murphy presented the trumpeter with his six-piece orchestration, which Armstrong entrusted to his valet, one Doc Pugh, for safekeeping. They made plans to record the song a few weeks later, when Murphy's band would be playing at a Child's restaurant in New York. Armstrong had no New York engagement in the immediate future, but he was due to start on a tour of Europe in the fall of 1955 (this is the trip that Edward R. Murrow of CBS-TV and Columbia Records would extensively document), and would be able to spend a day in New York to do a short session.

Now, it happened that Avakian's wife, classical violinist Anahid Ajemian, was working as half of a duo with her sister, pianist Maro Ajemian. The sisters at that time had a recording contract with MGM Records, which had an extensive classical catalogue, and by coincidence their producer was Ed Cole, the man who had done the original cast album of the De Lys production of *Threepenny*. When word got to Cole that Louis Armstrong was just about to record "Moritat," he went to Harry Meyerson, who ran MGM's pop division, and suggested that they do a single of their own.

Meyerson got together with the versatile Dick Hyman, who doubled as a studio keyboardist and as MGM's star jazz pianist. Coincidentally, in 1953, Hyman had recorded an entire album of Kurt Weill songs, although this consisted entirely of American works and nothing from *Threepenny*. At the suggestion of Cole, Hyman came up with a unique treatment for the "Moritat" theme: it would utilize a piano trio, with bass and drums, but instead of a conventional piano it would feature what Hyman describes as a "harpsichord piano." This was an instrument that had been altered, by means of a special kind of staple affixed to the hammers, to sound like a harpsichord. "The main difference," Hyman told me, "is that a harpsichord has no dynamic controls, you can't alter how loud or how soft it plays"; by contrast Hyman's harpsichord piano possessed piano-forte capabilities. It was an intriguing way to treat a melody that was already intriguing on its own.

Hyman recorded his version, released as "Moritat (A Theme from *The Threepenny Opera*)," a few days before Armstrong, Murphy, and Avakian laid down theirs on September 28, 1955, which was two days before the reopening of the show at the Theatre De Lys. On September 22, Avakian had Murphy record his arrangement in an instrumental version, the leader's trombone standing in for Armstrong's vocal, a track that Avakian intended to use as a backup in case the Armstrong record didn't come off for any reason. He also recorded a new treatment of "Moritat" featuring Lotte Lenya, singing in German, backed by Murphy's band, for European release.

Avakian might well have needed to use his plan B—the Murphy version—because shortly after Armstrong arrived at the studio, he informed Avakian that Doc Pugh had lost Murphy's manuscript and that he and the band hadn't had a chance to rehearse the arrangement. But none of this fazed Avakian, who knew that Murphy, who was present, had kept a duplicate copy of the chart. The arrangement was comparatively simple and Armstrong was a fine sight reader, so he and the All-Stars cut it cold. Armstrong certainly sings it as if he knows it, and it's hard to believe that he's actually performing "Mack" for the first time.

The producer made three suggestions, and Armstrong took him up on two of them: the substitution of "the cement bag *drooping* down" instead of "dropping," because it sounded funnier; and the insertion of the name Lotte Lenya (Bobby Darin later made her "Miss Lotte Lenya") in place of Suky Tawdry in the list of MacHeath's paramours, which is generally how the song has been performed ever since. Armstrong rejected the producer's suggestion that he refer to Lucy Brown as "Juicy Lucy" because he thought it was too salacious—"Pops could be a little straitlaced," says Avakian, even though his inspiration for the phrase came from Armstrong's own line in "Baby, It's Cold Outside": "Take your shoes off, Lucy / And let's get juicy!"

The band laid down several takes, and the finished single incorporates more than one performance, plus overdubs, which explains why during the stanza that begins "On a sidewalk, Sunday morning . . ." we can plainly hear Armstrong's trumpet playing obbligato to his own vocal in a theme reminiscent of his original composition "Coal Cart Blues." The Armstrong-Murphy treatment is, obviously, the first flat-out jazz take on "Mack," but it retains strong connections to earlier interpretations: in order to provide some relief from the potential monotony of a single sixteen-bar strain repeated seven times, Weill wrote all sorts of counter-melodies. Murphy, too, supplies little bits of business behind the vocal, and some of these are Weill-like background figures, while others—like Trummy Young's statement behind Armstrong—are improvised obbli-gatos in the best jazz tradition. Most of the record, including the entire vocal, is in C, but as soon as Armstrong is finished, the piece modulates to E flat. This is a much more common jazz key, and by going there, Mack is spreading the news that he's leaving Old Berlin behind for New Orleans. Armstrong tended to play the E flat section less and less over the years—it's still there in a 1959 Swedish concert but gone in a 1962 Chicago appearance, which ends immediately after the vocal.

For the flipside, Avakian had the All-Stars do "Back o' Town Blues," an Armstrong original and perennial, which he knew they could lay down without a hitch and which featured several members of the group (among them Doc Pugh) voicing their responses to Armstrong. Apart from the two issued sides, the group laid down another version of "Mack," this time with Armstrong and Lenya singing a duet that Avakian had worked out beforehand. The duet itself wasn't released until thirty years later, as part of a Book-of-the-Month Club package, but even more entertaining is a sampling of the original recording session edited for release in anticipa-tion of the Weill Centennial in the year 2000, in which we can hear Lenya trying hard but in vain to sing with something approaching a swing or jazz feeling, and Armstrong patiently trying to coach her through it.

It wasn't exactly an arms race between Louis Armstrong and Dick Hyman, as frequently could be observed at that moment in the music business, when different labels promoted rival versions of the same song. MGM had a distinct advantage, in that at Columbia only two singles could come out each week and it was difficult to move something up the schedule. As it happened, both the Hyman record and the Armstrong records were hits. Les Paul and Mary Ford also got a piece of the action, and their own version of "Mack" became a big seller on Capitol. The Hyman record came out first and seems to have sold the most copies in 1955 and '56, but the original Armstrong version became the definitive jazz version, the one that established "Mack" as a pop song and made other jazz and pop artists want to perform it. For the first few months that the two singles were out, the song was still titled "Moritat (A Theme from *The Threepenny Opera*)" on the labels; only a few months later did the publisher, Chappell Music, relent and give permission to officially change the name of the song to "Mack the Knife."

(Murphy later recalled that Columbia Records had offered him the choice of either a royalty or a flat fee for his arrangement, and that he was sorry he chose not to take the royalty, in light of the hit the song became. This seems unlikely, however, as royalties for orchestrators were quite unusual at the time. Avakian remembers that Armstrong offered to give Murphy a share of his own royalties from Columbia but that the arranger graciously declined.)

By the time Armstrong had returned from Europe (they were back in New York on December 31, 1955) and was headed for Miami, the single of "Mack" had been released to great acclaim. His opening night audiences in Florida were clamoring for it, but the normally obliging Armstrong was unable to satisfy the request. He had completely forgotten about the song since recording it in September, and, as it happened, once again the band's valet had lost the orchestration. As a result, Armstrong and company were forced to take a roll of nickels and some manuscript paper and transcribe their own chart off the jukebox in the hotel coffee shop. From that point on, it was an Armstrong perennial. All subsequent interpretations would refer back to his in some way, and he would keep performing it until the day he gave his last show.

Armstrong instantly made "Mack" part of the traditional jazz repertory, and countless performers have done it since, in tribute to its satchel-mouthed originator. Among the first of these was Bing Crosby, on his 1957 album *Bing with a Beat.* In *Threepenny,* the opening song concludes with Lenya speaking the words "That was Mack the Knife," and on his record, Armstrong opens with "Dig, there goes Mack the Knife." Crosby commences with the wildest spoken intro of all: "Lay way back, you cats! Dig in! Bivouac!"—by which he apparently means entrench yourself and prepare for attack—"Mr. Mack is movin' in."

Although the force of Crosby's own trenchant personality is unmistakable, this 1957 recording is an effective salute to Armstrong. Whereas the trumpeter had collaborated with Turk Murphy, Crosby is in cahoots with the other great brass-playing leader of New Orleans–cum-California jazz, trumpeter Bob Scobey. Like Ruby Braff, the short-lived Scobey was one of the few trumpeters of his generation to successfully evoke Armstrong's open-horn fire and sparkle. The Crosby-Scobey treatment closely follows the pattern of the Armstrong-Murphy. For one thing, it uses countermelodies in the same way, although they're arranger Matty Matlock's own original countermelodies—with Scobey even throwing in a characteristic Satchmo lick to announce Crosby's entrance. In terms of key, this is the first "Mack" to get completely away from C major—it's a third lower, in A flat—but unlike later "Mack"s, this one has no modulations whatsoever. Crosby's approach is a trifle subtler than Armstrong's (certainly far more so than Bobby Darin's); at least he's a bit more guarded in his admiration for the murderous MacHeath. As he nears the closer, the band plays an orchestration of the "Coal Cart Blues"–like trumpet figure Armstrong had overdubbed behind his own vocal.

IT SEEMS ALMOST PERVERSE to describe Bobby Darin's 1959 version of "Mack the Knife" as anything but definitive. It's one of the great pop records of all time, as well as one of the biggest hits in the history of the recording industry, and surely the song is more identified with Darin than with any other performer. Still, Darin was highly inspired by Armstrong, from the grand, swooping strokes, such as the basic idea of doing "Mack" in swingtime with touches of ironic irreverence, to such nuts-and-bolts details as his use of "drooping" instead of "dropping," not to mention the insertion of the name Lotte Lenya in the list of Mack's floozies in the last stanza. Darin was one of the most exciting performers American showbiz has ever known, but it would be inappropriate to describe him as a great original. Armstrong is hardly the only icon Darin evokes. In fact, he's not even the only singer-instrumentalist named Louis who appears in Darin's arsenal: "Mack" is set to an irresistible shuffle-rhythm pattern that both Louis Prima and Louis Jordan had been using for about twenty years by 1959. And Darin's whole swaggering approach, his swinging machismo, was handed to him directly by Frank Sinatra via such classic albums as *Songs for Swingin' Lovers* and *A Swingin' Affair. That's All,* the Darin album that introduced "Mack," bore a congratulatory telegram from Sammy Davis, Jr., on the back cover, as if to signify the approval of the Sinatra camp.

Darin's recording of "Mack" signified the first of his many stylistic evolutions, from tight-jeaned teeny-bopper idol ("Queen of the Hop") to Vegas lounge lizard, and, eventually, to hippie, folky, and cowboy. Originally, Darin conceived his treatment of "Mack" not as a single but merely as one track among eleven others for *That's All*. This was Darin's first major statement as a singer of adult popular standards, arranged by Richard Wess (who also did charts for Chris Connor and Betty Carter, among others). Around the time *That's All* was coming together, Ahmet Ertegun, the president of Darin's label, Atlantic Records, had a power lunch with Lotte Lenya, who encouraged him to record more Weill songs on Atlantic. "I told her that we were not a general record label, that we just did rhythm and blues and rock and roll," Ertegun told Darin biographer Jeff Bleiel, "but I said I'd think about it. I didn't have the opportunity to mention it to Bobby. So when he came up with 'Mack the Knife,' I said, 'I can't believe it—three days ago I had lunch with Lotte Lenya and I was going to suggest it to you.' "

Ertegun said of Darin's "Mack," "I knew it couldn't miss. Once in a while, you hear something and say, 'The magic is there.' Bobby worked out the arrangement with Dick Wess and it was fabulous. We put together a great band. It was just one of those forever records." Darin and Atlantic made sure that "Mack" was the lead-off track on the *That's All* album, and after it appeared, the immediate reaction of disc jockeys necessitated its release as a single. The 45 was released in August of '59, and by the fall it was the biggest record in the country, and of Darin's whole career. Darin said in 1960: "My record, which is completely away from rock and roll, came at a time when tastes were shifting. It was perfectly timed and turned out to be the luckiest thing I ever did. It's the sort of thing I intend to concentrate on because adults like it as well as kids." On another occasion he added, "I had to go beyond rock and roll. 'Mack' introduced me to the adult world."

What makes Darin a great pop singer, finally, is that he's more than just the sum of his influences (Armstrong and Sinatra especially); he brings to the table something that's uniquely his. We've noted his musical roots in Sinatra and all three of the Louises—Armstrong, Jordan, and Prima. Instrumentally, the Wess-Darin chart is very much inspired by the Armstrong-Murphy session in the way it uses countermelodies and obbligatos. Yet it's even more indebted to the Frank Sinatra–Nelson Riddle tradition, starting small and building to a boffo climax, like their "I've Got You Under My Skin," and starting with the rhythm section and gradually adding instruments, like their "The Lady Is a Tramp." Darin and Wess take two other ideas found in the Armstrong record and expand on them: the first is the remnant of Weill's countermelodies heard in the Armstrong, which Wess modifies so that the instrumental background changes constantly. Second, where Armstrong's arrangement includes one major key modulation, the Darin-Wess disc changes keys, rising chromatically, with almost every new section.

Darin's "Mack" chart is laid out in seven sixteen-bar stanzas, and the instrumental background keys change thus:

Intro	Starting out in B flat, instrumental, we hear the rhythm section phrase the shuffle pattern.
I.	The saxes start playing long and sustained just before Darin's entrance.
II.	Muted trombones come in behind the vocal, complementing the saxes. The reeds are legato and the bones are deliciously staccato. (Now we climb a half-step to B natural.)
III.	The reeds drop the long sustained notes and play a more agitated figure in response to Darin; the trombones drop into the background. (To C natural.)
IV.	The saxes get even more aggressive, with trombone fills lunging in and out. (To D flat.)
V.	The bongo drums become especially pronounced, although the whole show is still essentially reeds and bones. (To D natural.)
VI.	Finally! The trumpets come in and we now have a unified brass section, as we start building to a climax. (To E flat.)
VII.	This might be called VI-redux, as, lyric-wise, it's a repeat of the sixth stanza. All the sections are going great guns now, playing louder and louder countermelodies, and the difference between the two types of musical statement now becomes moot. The whole thing comes together in a delirious climax.
Coda	Darin's spoken exclamation, in reference to the spoken intros and outros from the cast albums, Armstrong, and Crosby: "Look out, ol' Mackie is back!"

Even on paper it seems exciting, thanks also to Mel Lewis's propulsive drumming. The ending all but explodes on a sharp eleventh chord (a raised fourth)—a very strong jazz chord. Still, Darin's contribution to the "Mack" legacy isn't apparent in the music so much as in the attitude. Kurt Gerron and Gerald Price, the Street singers of the Berlin and off-Broadway productions, sang "Mack the Knife" with a reporter's detachment. They provided a very straight inventory of the master criminal's evil deeds—a very Brechtian approach.

Armstrong gave Mack a lot more immediacy, making him, in a sense, an update of the second-person protagonist in his "(I'll Be Glad When You're Dead) You Rascal You," an uproarious "ranking" (as we used to say back home in Brooklyn) of an incorrigible character. The "rascal" in that 1931 song goes into Armstrong's home, eats all his fried chicken, and flirts with his wife. (Best line: "You gave my wife a bottle of Coca-Cola / So you could play on her Victrola!") MacHeath's crimes—serial homicide, grand larceny, polygamy, child rape—are no doubt more serious than grand theft poultry, but Armstrong retains that same attitude, singing of MacHeath laughingly, and perhaps ever so faintly admiringly.

Darin goes considerably further in that direction. His "Mack the Knife" is a swingin' cat, to be sure, not only because all the chicks dig him, like the most, but because he breaks the rules—makes his own, in fact—and doesn't get caught. Jeff Bleiel writes, "Many Brecht-Weill purists ridicule Darin's 'Mack the Knife' because it is a complete bastardization of the song's original *mise-en-scène*." Well, not so fast there, Kemosabe. Darin's may be an extreme interpretation, but one can't help feeling that Kurt and Bert would have approved. (Brecht died in 1956, six years after his former partner, but Blitzstein and Lenya were still around; one wonders how they felt about the Darin recording, other than considerably richer.)

Remember that Brecht was, politically, a radical at the very least. (And Weill, if he was less radical, was certainly a committed leftist; witness the fact that he succeeded in mounting *Lost in the Stars,* a full-scale Broadway musical on the unlikely subject of apartheid.) For Brecht, Mack was the embodiment of the perfect capitalist who would slit your throat for a nickel, rape your sister if it pleased him, and just as quickly throw your poor old mother out on the street if he could somehow profit from it. Robbing a bank may be a crime, but founding a bank is a far more profitable one: Brecht elaborates on this point in his two revisions of the *Three-*

penny plot, the 1931 film and his 1933 *Threepenny Novel*. Still, he would have been denounced by the Soviet Politburo as resoundingly as he was by the HUAC. In true Marxist art, attacking and ridiculing the bourgeoisie is only about half the job. The rest is about glorifying the proletariat, the working class, and the Soviet mass-hero. Then, too, the *Überkapitalist* Mackie Messer isn't only "anti-," he's also a hero, who not only gets a happy ending in the windup but the audience's sympathy throughout the story. The reason that Armstrong and Darin can revel in and glorify the gangster MacHeath is because Brecht and Weill have already done so.

None of which quite prepares us for the near-hysterical level of irreverence displayed by Darin in his many performances (on the later live versions he's even more frantic, but we'll stick to the original 1959 studio version here). In translating "Mack" from Brecht's original German, Blitzstein indulged in some poetic license—some might say that he cheated. Whenever he translated a line and came up a beat short, he threw in the word "dear," mostly just to take up the space. It serves for emphasis, and it serves to mark time. (No other English translation of "Moritat" uses the word "dear.") Darin's first move, then, is to retranslate many a Blitzstein "dear" into a "babe," as in, "Oh the shark—babe! / Has such teeth, dear." And that's only the beginning. Throughout, he plays with sonics, the very sounds of vowels, consonants, and contractions, and even his own breathing apparatus; he gasps in time, and throws in all manner of "hup-hup"s and "ho-ho"s, "uh-huh"s; instead of "Could it be that our boy is back in town?" he wagers "Five'll get you ten that our boy . . ."; the line about spending like a sailor is sung with a slightly drunken inflection; and when he gets to the part about the corpse on the corner, he throws in an "eek" to obliterate even the slightest possibility that anyone might take the story literally or seriously.

Why should a dead body bother anyone, you almost begin to wonder. Darin does everything he can think of to informalize, almost trivialize, the lyrics, taking his irreverent attitude to a completely manic level, and, as the singer intended, it has precisely the opposite effect. The more you sing about death and destruction in a happy, carefree tone, the more sinister it seems—rather like historical recordings of a happy Nazi soldiers' chorus (yes, such things exist), or Sweeney Todd and Mrs. Lovett happily crooning about all the people they're going to slaughter and devour at the end of act I of Sondheim's show.

Who better to croon about death than Darin? Robert Johnson's own hellhound was forever on his trail. As writer Darcy Sullivan has noted, Darin suffered from a heart condition his entire life and was always acutely conscious that "the man in the bright nightgown" (as W. C. Fields referred to death) was only a step behind him. Weill, Brecht, and Blitzstein all died in their fifties, yet compared to Darin, who kicked the buck-buck-bucket at age thirty-seven, they seemed like old men.

Darin had recorded various items that could be considered sequels or follow-ups to "Mack." The second track on *That's All* was "Beyond the Sea," another attempt at giving the *le swing américain* treatment to an older European song, while Darin's own "Gyp the Cat" was as bald-faced a rip-off of "Mack" as ever I hope to hear. His most successful attempt to duplicate that song's success was another tune from a musical depicting the Victorian era, in this case "Artificial Flowers" from *Tenderloin*. If anything, "Artificial Flowers" is even more morbid than "Mack," detailing as it does the painful death of a little girl. It was somewhat camped up in the original 1960 Broadway production, done almost straight in the 2000 City Center Encores revival, but done to a maniacal fare-thee-well that could only be described as bloodlust by Darin, who, even more than on "Mack," sings it as if he's jubilantly defying the hellhound.

Darcy Sullivan also points out that Bobby Darin was one of the reigning gods at Las Vegas at a time when nuclear devices were being tested just a few miles away in the deserts of Nevada. What better spot to party away the flop sweats caused by the Cold War and the threat of the coming Armageddon than at ground zero for the very weapons that were responsible for the age of anxiety? And who better to help one confront that long, hard, postatomic big sleep than a crooner with a time bomb for a ticker singing about dead little girls and a serial killer who would just as soon cut your throat as look at you?

I'M TEMPTED TO REGARD the Darin "Mack" as the number-one version, but Armstrong's is so strong and Darin's owes so much to it that we have to rate the two neck and neck. Both of the two most important subsequent recordings—those by Ella Fitzgerald (a live recording from 1960) and Frank Sinatra (a studio recording originally made in 1984 and remade a year later)—make heavy reference to both Armstrong and

Darin. In fact, Fitzgerald launched the tradition of referring to previous versions of "Mack" in her own special-material lyrics, and Sinatra not only picks up on that idea, but he includes "Lady Ella" in his sung list of previous interpreters of "Mack" who "sung this song nice."

In Fitzgerald's case, she wanted us to believe that these special lyrics were improvised spontaneously by her. As the introductory vamp starts, she informs the audience, speaking in the "royal" first person plural, that "We'd like to do something for you now . . . we haven't heard a girl sing it . . . and since it's so popular we'd like to try and do it for you . . . we hope we remember all the words." Fitzgerald's treatment is the most musically playful of them all. As early as the second stanza she repeats the phrase "could it be" over and over for emphasis. As she predicted, by the third stanza she shows every sign of having forgotten the lyrics (singing "What's the next chorus / to this song now? / This is the one now / I don't know . . ."). The fourth stanza finds her getting some of the lines right and mangling others, while on the fifth she explains that she's singing "Mack" mainly because of "Bobby Darin and Louis Armstrong" who made a record of it, whereas "Ella bella" is merely making a "wreck" of it. Over the next few stanzas she elaborates on the process of singing the song, but, more memorably, to digress into her crowd-pleasing imitation of Armstrong's gravel-voiced scatting.

It's interesting that Fitzgerald follows "Mack" with "How High the Moon." She sets up this most famous of all her improvisations with a sung introduction in which she forewarns the crowd that she's about to scat. What was observed at the time is no less true today—that the show Fitzgerald makes of forgetting the lyrics is even more entertaining than the song itself.

If blowing the lyrics was a deliberate maneuver, Fitzgerald was careful to cover her tracks: she kept "Mack" in her concert repertoire, and on the post-1960 performances that I have been able to hear she does not repeat the shtick about forgetting the words. Her two best later "Mack"s come from the Côte d'Azur in 1966 and Budapest in 1970. In the first, she swings perhaps even more excitedly than in '60 (having Duke Ellington's orchestra to back her up certainly doesn't hurt), and she scats like crazy and spends even more time growling like Satchmo. In France, she pays homage to Maestro Ellington with a quote from "I'm Beginning to See the Light." In her Hungarian "Mack," during an eight-minute masterpiece at an even faster, more frenetic tempo, she takes a left turn through "On the Trail," "Take Me Out to the Ballgame" and, on a related note, "Say Hey (The Willie Mays Song)," the "Call for Philip Morris" jingle, "Twelfth Street Rag," "Rockin' in Rhythm" (more Ellingtonia), and "Jumpin' with Symphony Sid." Then, she makes like Pops crooning "That's My Desire," introduces the trio in his voice, and finally returns to her own for "Work Song." She ignores most of the familiar lyrics, concentrating again on special material about making a "wreck" as opposed to a record of the song. But she does not claim to have forgotten the words. Fitzgerald finally brought "Mack" into the studio on her 1978 *Lady Time* with organist Jackie Davis and drummer Louis Bellson; this time she sings all the Blitzstein lyrics and omits all extra business. Even without the sound of the roaring crowds, the scatting, the special material, and the Armstrong impression, it's pretty darn exciting.

Like Darin, both Fitzgerald and Frank Sinatra modulate a half-step upwards with just about every stanza. Sinatra and his arranger, Frank Foster, seem to have gleaned the inspiration for their chart from Fitzgerald more than from any other previous interpreter. Both Fitzgerald and Sinatra start in G natural and proceed upward, chromatically, until they reach D flat. Sinatra also picked up on Fitzgerald's supposedly spontaneous notion of singing *about* the song: after listing Armstrong, Darin, and Fitzgerald, he expresses the doubt that he's capable of adding anything new. And he's more or less right. Sinatra's "Mack the Knife" is not classic Sinatra. The special-material lyrics (and there's almost more of that than there is of Blitzstein) allow him to step out of the story a little too far, and he never really sounds fully invested in it. As Ol' Blue Eyes (as he refers to himself) says, it's pretty much a feature for the band, a welcome chance for the ensemble to get to shine out in front more than they generally do at a Sinatra concert. Sinatra originally recorded "Mack" for his 1984 album *L.A. Is My Lady,* then a year or so later rerecorded his vocal on top of the original orchestral track. He had been singing "Mack" nearly every night in concert and apparently felt that his later approach to the song was more authoritative. He does indeed sound more in command on the remake, but the original has a friskiness, a jazzy playfulness that the remake can't match. Foster's orchestration is awfully busy in its attempt to override the possibility of seven stanzas getting repetitious, and some of the more audacious elements of the orchestration, the very up-front trombone solo, for instance, have been minimized in the remix.

After treatments by Armstrong and Fitzgerald, the song was pretty much divorced from its *Threepenny* origins and was picked up by jazz musicians as another pop melody to be played with. When Sonny Rollins cut it in June 1956, on his seminal album *Saxophone Colossus*, it still had something of the pre-Armstrong *Threepenny* time feel, and still bore the title "Moritat," but Rollins's was perhaps the last jazz version to convey that feel. (Anita O'Day and Jimmy Giuffre did attempt to incorporate something of that ambling, stop-and-start tempo in their treatment on their 1959 *Cool Heat*, but this is the least successful track on that otherwise fine disc.)

Earl Hines did a solo piano treatment in 1972, while in that same year Mary Lou Williams played it with her trio on an exceptional live recording in Chicago, at Rick's Cafe Americain (no, she didn't play "As Time Goes By"), a straight-ahead, swinging treatment that she spices up even further by throwing in bizarre clusters of note at points that seem almost random. There are also jazz organ versions (Jimmy Smith on *Crazy, Baby!*; Jackie Davis with Ella Fitzgerald on *Lady Time*) and even a jazz violin-organ-guitar-drums version led by Stephane Grappelli in 1972, with Eddy Louiss, Jimmy Gourley, and Kenny Clarke. André Previn and J. J. Johnson included it on a 1961 album of jazz treatments of Weill's German works (a set that should have been reissued for the composer's centennial). The fine modern jazz trumpeter Kenny Dorham cut a trumpet-and-rhythm reading in obvious and euphoric tribute to Louis Armstrong.

"Mack" and *Threepenny* live on in other guises: the song has been heard in various incarnations, such as a 1962 German film (which was relatively faithful to the original show, although the American-released version interspliced Sammy Davis, Jr., as the Streetsinger). There were other New York productions, like a 1976 production by the Public Theater at the Vivien Beaumont, and a new Broadway production starring Sting, in 1989, which launched a brief vogue for the Brecht-Weill material among British rockers. The Who's Roger Daltrey played the Streetsinger in an American film from that year, titled variously *Threepenny Opera* and *Mack the Knife*, which starred Raul Julia repeating his role as Mack from the Public Theater production. Marianne Faithfull, with a voice like a cockney Tallulah Bankhead, played Pirate Jenny in a 1992 Dublin production and recorded "Mack" on her album *20th Century Blues.* These later *Three-penny Operas* had several things in common: all of them (except the 1989 film) eschewed the Blitzstein version, instead scouring the Brecht libretto to find as many dirty words and ghastly deeds as they could possibly attribute to Mack. In addition, instead of displaying the characteristic detachment of Kurt Gerron and Gerald Price, or even the swinging style of Armstrong and Darin, they seemed to be snarling out the "Moritat" as nastily as they possibly could—Faithfull was practically croaking.

It's the Ella Fitzgerald disc that provides us with the perfect note to end on: I mentioned above that her 1960 recording was from a live per-formance (obviously, the bit about forgetting the lyrics would have made no sense in a studio session), but what I deliberately omitted above is the salient fact that this happened at a concert in West Berlin—at no less a nexus of *deutsche Kultur* than at the the *Deutschlandhalle* itself, an even more crucial epicenter of Cold War politics than Las Vegas. I've also noted Fitzgerald's spoken introduction, but again what's most noteworthy isn't what she says but what she leaves out. Fitzgerald doesn't acknowledge—doesn't even seem aware—that it was in this very city, some thirty-two years earlier, that Mack the Knife first began his one-man, one-song crime wave. She doesn't care that she's bringing the Berliners a little bit of their own back to them. She's presenting "Mack the Knife" for what it was then—an American pop hit, even a piece of genuine Americana.

Weill, who died in the middle of writing a musical version of that quin-tessential American novel *Huckleberry Finn,* would no doubt have been delighted. In 1956, Lenya wrote to a friend: "The 'Moritat' has been recorded by 17 different companies. You hear it coming out of bars, juke-boxes, taxies, wherever you go. Kurt would have loved that. A taxi driver whistling his tunes would have pleased him more than winning the Pulitzer Prize."

"Mack the Knife" has not been heard in jazz or cabaret circles as much in the past thirty years as, say, "I'll Remember April" or "There Will Never Be Another You." Indeed, Dave Frishberg refers to "Mack" in his song "I'm Hip," as if it were a cliché of pseudo-hipness. But, despite its remote origins in prewar German experimental theater, it remains one of the pivotal works of postwar American pop. Will great interpreters con-tinue to reimagine "Mack" in the future? The line forms to the right, babe.

BONUS TRACKS

Two Sublimely Surreal Female Vocal Versions

Virtually everything Eartha Kitt ever sings is at least slightly surreal, and her "Mack," on *The Fabulous Eartha Kitt,* is no exception. It's a pop treatment, with a background choir (first singing wordlessly, then intoning the riff line "Mackie's back, back in town") that adds considerably to the camp quotient. Yet Kitt's vocal has far more menace in it than any of those treatments that are generally regarded as faithfully Brechtian. The way this Kitt-cat sings, you can practically see her displaying her milky-white teeth.

Peggy Lee's version, on the 1963 *I'm a Woman,* is downright bizarre, and can only be regarded as both a self-parody and a send-up of the pop conventions of "Mack" that had already been established. She gives the melody line a singspiel treatment, more or less just speaking it approximately in tempo, while in the background there's a prominent counter-melody that sounds like circus clowns lampooning classical ballet. What really makes it weird are the sound effects—for example, jangling coins on the line "all his cash." The whole thing is vaguely Spike Jones–ish, but way more subtle than that—perhaps more like Ernie Kovacs. (Kovacs, easily the most intellectual satirist of the early years of televison, himself had used Lotte Lenya's German-language record of "Moritat" as background for visual comedy sketches on his TV show.)

The Two Most Egregiously Awful Instrumental Versions

They're both by Morton Gould, on a dreadful RCA album entitled *The Two Worlds of Kurt Weill* (1966) that took advantage of the two-sided LP format by devoting one side to Weill's Berlin compositions and the other to the composer's Broadway phase. "Mack," astutely, appears on both sides. But it's hard to tell which overorchestrated, overbaked treatment is more abominable. The "German" arrangement makes much of the tuba and banjo and plays little tricks, like going into waltz time for no reason. The "American" treatment sounds like a badly mangled parody of space-age bachelor-pad music. Both versions represent the kind of orchestration that gives stereo a bad name, and can safely be described as strange and yet hideous.

The Hidden History of the Latin Tradition of Macko el Knifo

There are American jazz-pop singers who have sung "Mack" with a Latin tinge, like Della Reese on her 1978 *Live at Chumley's,* on which this future angel touches us with the aid of Lou Levy on piano and a heavy dose of bongos. The Latin presence on *A Touch of Tabasco,* Rosemary Clooney's brilliant meeting with Perez Prado, is considerably more than a tinge. In fact, this is an inspired album on the whole, and along with *Latin à la Lee* and *Lawrence Goes Latin* (Peggy and Steve, that is), it shows that Latin rhythms were inspiring superior gringo pop singers long before the coming of the bossa nova.

There is, however, a more direct connection between Latin music and "Mack." The actor and salsa singer Ruben Blades had a hit with an original song entitled "Pedro Navaja." As translated by Ivan Santiago, this number details the activities of a charismatic barrio crime kingpin whose name could be given in English as "Peter Knife." Blades spends much time talking about Pedro's razor, which is compared to his flashy golden teeth. One line explains that Pedro keeps both of his hands in his pockets at all times, so that his victims will never know which hand is holding the weapon. Eventually, Pedro gets into a knife fight with a streetwalker, and both of them are killed. "Oh yeah! . . ."

Best Danish Tenor Versions

Helge Roswaenge, one of the finest operatic tenors of his time, sang the role of the Streetsinger in a late 1950s recording of the *Threepenny* score, with the chorus and chamber orchestra of the Vienna State Orchestra, conducted by Charles Adler. Roswaenge uses the familiar Weill orchestration and really projects it as if it were genuine opera, not necessarily the threepenny variety.

It might be a stretch to put Ben Webster in this category, but he did spend enough time in Denmark to be considered an honorary Danish tenor. His is a straight-ahead jam version taped live in Copenhagen in 1965, completely outside of the *Threepenny* context, but there's no one who embodies the dangerous romanticism that is Mack the Knife as completely as Ben Webster.

OL' MAN RIVER (1927)

music by Jerome Kern

words by Oscar Hammerstein II

Better ask ol' man river what he thinks. He knows all 'bout dem boys. He knows all 'bout ever'thin'.

—JOE, from *Show Boat,* act 1, scene 1

THERE IS A MOMENT in P. G. Wodehouse's story "Quick Service" where a certain Lord Holbeton breaks into song—

He sang as he floated along, naturally selecting his favourite melody ("Trees"), and he had just gotten as far as the line about nests of robins in the hair and was rendering it with even more than his customary brio when there impinged upon his ears one of the gloomier passages of "Ol' Man River," and he perceived coming towards him the bowed figure of the chap Weatherby.

When a man singing "Trees" meets a man singing "Ol' Man River" something has to give. They cannot both continue to function. Lord Holbeton generously decided to be the one to yield.

What Wodehouse would never mention—although Oscar Hammerstein frequently did—was that Wodehouse himself had been a kind of cousin to the creation of *Show Boat,* the Broadway musical that introduced "Ol' Man River." In 1918, during PGW's Broadway phase, he and Jerome Kern had cowritten the songs for a show called *Oh Lady, Lady,* which included something called "Bill." The tune was cut but was exhumed from the trunk nine years later when Hammerstein and Kern were writing *Show Boat* and needed a heart-stopping torch song for Helen Morgan in act two. Hammerstein rewrote the lyrics for the first half of each of the song's two sixteen-bar choruses, but was quick to point out to anyone who would listen that "Bill" was essentially Wodehouse's work. Perhaps out of gratitude, Wodehouse managed to work "Ol' Man River," *Show Boat*'s biggest hit, into several stories. "Ol' Man River" figures also in Wodehouse's "Big Business," in which story two men argue as to the correct spelling of the title, whether it's "Ol'" or "Old." Eventually, Reginald Mullins takes to the stage at the village concert and renders the song with such passion that his estranged fiancée returns to him.

AT FIRST GLANCE, "Ol' Man River" is a comparatively simple, thirty-two-bar popular song. But apart from the length of the chorus itself, everything else about it is big, big, big. That description encompasses the scope of its philosophical content, the list of artists who have recorded it, the length of its verse (and the way it has two separate verses, one of which is nearly as long as the refrain itself), and, of course, the stories that are told about it.

Maybe you've heard this one: Florenz Ziegfeld, producer of *Show Boat,* was infamous for devoting all of his professional (and often personal) energies to the women in his shows. The line in the Warren and Dubin song "Dames" that goes "Who cares if there's a plot or not / If you've got a lot of dames" could have been written with Ziegfeld in mind. The leitmotif of Ziggy's career was summed up perfectly in "A Pretty Girl Is Like a Melody," which Irving Berlin wrote for the *Ziegfeld Follies of 1919* and which later climaxed the producer's posthumous screen biopic, *The Great Ziegfeld.* Berlin was being deliberately arch when he opened his verse with the words "I have an ear for music / And I have an eye for a maid!" Everyone in showbiz knew that while the latter was eminently true of Ziegfeld, the former was anything but. Then again, Ziegfeld's alleged indifference to music may have been overstated. One has only to consider the caliber of the songwriters whom the producer hired over the years, from Berlin to Kern to Gershwin to Walter Donaldson, to realize that he must have had some kind of "ear for music."

Anyhow, the story goes that when *Show Boat* played its first preview, at the National Theater in Washington on November 15, 1927, it ran way overlong, as most musicals generally do during their tryout performances. Entire ballets, not to mention musical numbers, had to be chopped willy-nilly, and supposedly Ziegfeld suggested that "Ol' Man River" be deleted. As it happens, *Show Boat*'s investors included Evelyn Walsh McLean, who at that time was the owner of the legendary Hope Diamond. When Mr. Ziegfeld informed Mrs. McLean that he was considering dropping "Ol' Man River," she was aghast. She felt so strongly that the song should be left in, she made the producer, ever the gambling man, a sporting proposition: the song remained, and, if it failed to become the instant hit of the show, she would make Ziegfeld a present of the Hope Diamond. When *Show Boat* opened on Broadway six weeks later, on December 27, 1927, Mrs. McLean did not have to part with her jewel.

THERE'S ANOTHER STORY ABOUT "Ol' Man River" that bears repeating here. Oscar Hammerstein's wife, Dorothy, frequently complained that she was tired of hearing the song referred to as "Jerome Kern's 'Ol' Man River.' " She voiced her objection as follows: "My husband wrote 'Ol' Man River.' Mr. Kern wrote 'da-da-de-da. . . .' " Mrs. Hammerstein, it would seem, was a great believer in the primacy of the lyric.

So, too, was Robert Russell Bennett, who orchestrated *Show Boat* and dozens of other classic Broadway musicals. As he told Max Wilk (in *They're Playing Our Song*):

> Kern would play pieces for me, and I'd always say, "Is that the verse or the chorus?" And Jerry used to die because I couldn't tell which was which. One day he showed me this thing and I put a piano part to it. This one didn't fall into the same category—the kind of piece Kern wrote that confused me—but it was a meandering sort of thing. It didn't go much of anywhere when you just took the tune by itself. But the minute you got Oscar's words to it—"Tote dat barge, lift dat bale / Get a little drunk an' you land in jail"—you had a real poet.

However, as important as the lyric always is to a good song, in the case of "Ol' Man River," Mr. Hammerstein's role was even more crucial than usual. If "OMR" was one of the first songs Ziegfeld considered for cutting, it may have been because it was just about the last song to be added. The score and book were almost finished when Hammerstein happened to be pondering the way in which Edna Ferber had used the Mississippi River in the book from which the musical was taken. "Edna Ferber had written a sprawling kind of novel in *Show Boat,* it didn't have the tightness that a play requires," Hammerstein later said in an interview. "I wanted to keep the spirit of Edna's book and the one focal influence I could find was the Mississippi River, because she had quite consciously brought the river into every important turn of the story. So I decided to write a theme, a river theme."

In the novel, the river was practically a character in and of itself: it's a unifying force that binds all the characters together, dictates their relationships, and determines the course of all their lives. It allows the Hawks family and all who work with them to earn their livings, even as it makes possible the entire economic system of the nineteenth-century South, with its dependency on water-based cargo transport. In a sense, the show boat itself, the *Cotton Blossom,* is also a cargo ship, transporting culture from port to port as if it were cotton or yams. When Julie and Steve are judged and found guilty of violating the racial (antimiscegenation) laws of the day, they're punished by being banished from the show boat and the river, and soon come to a bad end. When the younger couple, Magnolia and Gaylord (are those names southern enough for you-all?), voluntarily leave the river, they, too, fall upon bad times and split up. Decades later, they are reunited at the conclusion of the story, when they both come home to the Mississippi and to each other.

Years later, in a letter to his daughter, Hammerstein called her attention to a poem by Tennyson, "The Brook," which includes the line "Men may come, men may go / But I go on forever." "I became a little self-conscious as I wrote it down just now," his letter continues, "because the philosophy is strangely like 'Ol' Man River, he just keeps rollin' along.' The young man who wrote this song was not consciously imitating Tennyson, but there you are—the ideas are similar, aren't they?" Gary Giddins has further identified another source for Hammerstein; in St. Augustines famous *Confessions,* the author confesses to be "thoroughly tired of living and extremely frightened of dying." Yet in Hammerstein even more than in Tennyson or Augustine, the river is the provider of all things: business and money, culture and entertainment, family and faith, even love and romance. The way most productions of *Show Boat* use a gospel-style choir as background for "Ol' Man River" reflects the idea that there's a kind of spirituality to the river. Maybe it has to do with the cleansing power of the waters, in the sense of a baptism: to achieve an affinity for the river is to grow closer to God.

Hammerstein wanted to capture that spirit of the river in song, and he realized that this piece of music would be the lifeblood of the musical the same way that the Mississippi is the heart and soul of the characters in the book. According to Hugh Fordin in his biography of Hammerstein, *Getting to Know Him,* Hammerstein then brought the idea for the river song to Jerome Kern, but discovered that Jerry was too busy at that moment to write a new song. Hammerstein then came up with the idea of reworking a few of the melodies Kern had already written.

"There is that fast-paced banjo that introduces the show boat *Cotton Blossom* in the first act," said Teddy Holmes, who published the score in England as general manager of Chapell, Ltd. As he told Max Wilk, "Listen to that banjo music and you'll hear the River strain imbedded in it. It was simply that Hammerstein heard it before Kern did." According to Holmes, Hammerstein went to Kern and said, "Why don't you take that banjo music and merely slow down the tempo?"

But there was considerably more to it than that. Essentially, Hammerstein (first by himself and then with Kern) reworked the opening choral segment of act one, scene one, into "Ol' Man River," and to understand how that "banjo music" evolved into "River," we first have to look at the "Cotton Blossom" sequence. This entire scene is in fact a montage of different melodies, most of which are developed enough to be considered songs in themselves. The first few of these songs-within-the-big-number are the ones that turn up again in "Ol' Man River."

Curiously, Kern opens with a few bars of an instrumental, not with a banjo but with staccato plinks on a xylophone in a manner that suggests *Flower Drum Song* more than the Old South. This melody comes back at the end of the opening, this time with the choir singing "See the show boat . . ."

The first of these themes (for our purposes, let's call it "Cotton Blossom A") is a twenty-five-bar theme sung by the black chorus that describes a laborer's life on the Mississippi, although the show boat itself is not yet mentioned. The show boat (the *Cotton Blossom*) itself is then introduced by the next theme ("Cotton Blossom B"), which is heard only for eight bars at this point but reappears a few minutes later in the opening sequence. The division of the piece into A and B may appear at first to be somewhat arbitrary, as they're both sung by the "colored chorus." However, the distinction is necessary, because the A section, as we shall see, has an especially direct connection to "Ol' Man River."

In fact, "Cotton Blossom A" provides about two-thirds of the "Ol' Man River" melody—all of that famous song except its best-known strain, the central "Ol' Man River" melodic line itself. "Cotton Blossom A," to all intents and purposes, *is* the verse, although it's heard at a much faster tempo and in a more jubilant mood than the way "OMR" is performed (in the show, at least). The first eight bars are melodically and lyrically identical, although when those eight bars are first heard as the opening section of "Cotton Blossom," they're considerably lighter and less foreboding than they will be at the end of scene one, when "Ol' Man River" itself is first heard. Indeed, at the opening, this same piece of music is incredibly light and cheery. The black laborers—this may be after the Civil War but they seem hardly better off than slaves—come out singing joyfully as if this is going to be some kind of happy frolic about carefree colored folk in the old antebellum South—or even a minstrel show. If, however, one listens closely to the lyrics (which begin with the N-word), one gets quite the opposite message. Lurking beneath all this gay and colorful clothing is, as Hammerstein hinted, a protest song.

That's the first eight bars of the "Cotton Blossom" opening. In the second eight bars, a chorus of young, gifted, and black chorus girls strut out and sing a new melody, with lyrics along the lines of "There's a lot of lovin' on the levee for you." Next, the male and the female choruses come together for the third and final section of this segment, which totals twenty-five bars, as the final stanza gets an extra bar at the end; the form is *A-B-A¹* (*A¹* being a variant of section *A*). Although the opening eight bars use the exact same lyrics as the first verse to "OMR," the other two sections of "Cotton Blossom A" are heard with different lyrics from what will be heard later when "OMR" itself is sung.

The second eight-bar segment, the one sung by the women, will not only be heard again as the middle section of the verse to "Ol' Man River" but is also reused as the bridge to the central refrain itself. The first time, as sung by the female chorus, the words are "Git yourself a bran' new gal" in the original 1927 ("Drop that bale and have some fun" in the 1962 Columbia album); later, as part of the verse, it's "Don' look up / An' don' look down"; and finally, as the bridge to the refrain, it's "You an' me, we sweat an' strain."

Hammerstein may have been able to cannibalize roughly two-thirds of "Ol' Man River" from "Cotton Blossom," but he had to recruit Kern to help him with the rest, especially as the melody that gets the title words is the most important part of the song. For this, they seem to have gone to "Cotton Blossm B," which is the part of the opening number where the words "Cotton Blossom" itself are first heard. Kern and Hammerstein essentially adapted one title phrase into another: the four notes that form the words "Cotton Blossom" in the key of C would be C-C-A-G; if these are inverted, or played as a mirror image, they become G-G-A-C, which are the four notes that go with the phrase "Ol' Man River." The crucial difference between "Cotton Blossom" and "Ol' Man River" is not one of melodic content but of tempo and attitude: on the whole, the piece is slowed down and the mood darkened. As Wodehouse put it: ". . . one of the gloomier passages of 'Ol' Man River.' "

It shouldn't be implied that Hammerstein and Kern were merely rummaging around for snippets of melody; in fact, they were introducing into musical comedy the notion of the leitmotif, with "OMR" serving as a theme that runs through the whole story. It's anticipated at the start, as the very first notes sung in the work, then heard in full at the end of the first scene, and is referred to throughout the work, and reprised at the conclusion. By the time the two men were finished, the song indeed ran through the entire production much the way that Ol' Man Mississippi chugs its way through the South. This had been done in opera, particularly in the *Gesamtkunstwerke* of Richard Wagner, but was fairly untried in a Broadway show.

Up to now we have been referring to the "verse" as it appears in the sheet music, which is not exactly the same as the way it was heard in the theater in 1927. In the show's score, the number is laid out as follows:

Joe: "show" verse ("'Dere's an ol' man called de Mississippi . . .")—8 bars.

Joe: full refrain ("Ol' Man River, / dat Ol' Man River . . .")—32 bars.

Joe: "sheet music" verse, *A* section ("Niggers all work on de Mississippi . . .")—8 bars.

Black Male Chorus: "sheet music" verse, B section ("Don' look up / An' don' look down . . .")—8 bars.

Joe: "sheet music" verse, A^1 section ("Let me go 'way from de Mississippi . . .")—9 bars.

Black Male Chorus with Joe: A and A of refrain ("Ol' Man River, / Dat Ol' Man River . . .")—16 bars. (The relationship of Joe to the chorus here might be described as "outlining"—about which more later.)

Joe, with Male Chorus humming (or singing wordlessly) in the background: B section of refrain ("You an' me, we sweat an' strain . . .")—8 bars.

Joe, with Male Chorus in harmony (singing with him): A^1 section of refrain ("Ah gits weary . . .")—8 bars.

As with "Summertime," it is perhaps inappropriate to think of "Ol' Man River" in terms of verses and choruses; it is, after all, not an individual song but a part of a fully integrated score. It's also one of the few songs in which verse and chorus share melodic material. What's also unusual is that the verse has a definite tempo, and that the verse is generally performed at least slightly faster than the chorus. (In the sheet music, the tempo indication for the verse is "*moderato*" while the refrain is "very slowly *con sentimento.*") The verse and the chorus are both in the same key (not true of all songs) and are built primarily on the same chords. The verse almost sounds like a variation on the chorus, a riff on the same chord changes.

As mentioned, it's the longer of the two verses that actually appears after the first hearing of the refrain in the show. Outside the show—that is, in the published sheet music, and as performed by most popular singers, who follow the example of Frank Sinatra—it has been codified as coming before the chorus. Musical-comedy performers associated with the show tend to mix the two verses: the recordings by Jules Bledsoe (1931) and Paul Robeson (in 1932, anyhow), the two actors identified with originating the role of Joe, both start with the complete "show" verse ("Dere's an ol' man . . ."), but after the eight bars of that are over, they go right into the last seventeen bars of the "sheet music" verse (from "Don' look up . . ." to ". . . I long to cross"), thus melding the verses. It's hard to understand why, since both the '32 Robeson and the '31 Bledsoe are pressed on twelve-inch records (4:06 and 4:19 respectively) that would easily allow for both sets of verses, the before and the after, as heard on the stage.

In the original score (as recorded by John McGlinn) and in the published music of the individual song, the key is C (although Paul Robeson was shortly to take it a half-step lower, to B). In some ways, it's a simple song, but it's a very rangy one; even in the sheet music, which was rearranged for avocational players and singers, it starts down at a low G ("*Ol' Man* River . . .") and builds all the way up to a high E (particularly in the final three bars: "*Ol' Man* River, / He *jes' keeps* rollin' . . ."). This makes it awkward in the published sheet music—since low G is well below the ledger lines; the key would have to be E flat. This range of nearly two octaves is quite atypical for a popular song.

As we have seen, the sheet music verse is set in a form of A-B-A^1. The third strain opens the same way as the first but is different enough to be considered an *A prime* rather than a complete melodic reiteration of the initial *A* (on the third line of this section—"Show me dat stream"—Kern goes to a diminished chord, and from there to an augmented chord). This third line also starts a half-step higher, on F, whereas in the first segment it began on E. As mentioned above, the third part of this verse also has an extra bar at the end, which allows the concluding word "cross" to be held for an extra beat before a three-beat rest, allowing for a dramatic break before the chorus proper begins.

The refrain is essentially A-A^1-B-A^2 in that the main melody—the "Ol' Man River" melody itself—is heard three times, but with variations each time. The harmonies of both the verse and the chorus (excepting the bridge) are very major and strong, primarily the I and the IV chords. These are the two chords most often employed when the intention is to evoke the feeling of folk music, and as such they're heard in "Summertime," "The St. Louis Blues," and much of Aaron Copland's rustic Americana.

The main melody principally goes back and forth between the progression of I (C) and the minor vi (A), and I (C) and IV (F) major. The song uses a lot of minor in the bridge, or, to be more technical, it goes to the mediant chord (E).

Over the course of the chorus, the melodic trajectory gradually gets higher and higher: from low G to high A in the first eight-bar section (*A*), and then from that same G up higher to C in the second (*A'*). In the bridge, it stays within a more closely confined space of high C to low F sharp (the only accidental in the whole song, which occurs on "barge," "bale" and "drunk"). The bridge reaches its lowest note on the last word, "jail," which occurs on a low D. However, certain interpreters, most notably Robeson and Sinatra, take this note considerably lower for an even more powerful, dramatic effect.

The bridge (in both the verse and the refrain) ends on the II and the V chords, which is not a folkish progression but more of a convention of Tin Pan Alley and Western music in general. As we get closer to the conclusion, Kern uses a IIm7 chord (Dm7) to point us in the direction of the eventual resolution. In the final eight bars, the melody gets higher and higher until it reaches the high E, and the last two notes, high D and then high C, are generally held for a big ending.

"Ol' Man River" is a song about man's inhumanity to man, and thus one might expect it to be built on a harmonic structure that conveys a lack of resolution or perhaps employs a lot of dissonance. On the contrary, "Ol' Man River" doesn't use fancy chords but very fundamental harmony. It emphasizes its tonic C chord, the most basic of all chords (one without sharps or flats), very firmly and consistently. Both the melody and the harmony are rock solid, and when an equally well-grounded basso like Paul Robeson belts it out, the attitude conveyed is not one of complaint but of overwhelming strength, which could be interpreted as representing the solidarity of the black race. Perhaps because its harmonies are so basic and the main melody affirmatively ascending (not all that different from "I Got Rhythm"), the song spent most of its first twenty years as a vehicle for hot jazz units—usually black bands.

"Ol' Man River" belongs to two different kinds of show tune: the first is the genre that Hammerstein all but created, the impassioned plea for racial and social equality, as heard in "The Eagle and Me" from *Bloomer Girl* and Hammerstein's own "You've Got to Be Taught" from *South Pacific*. But we also have to consider "Ol' Man River" in the context of the Broadway anthem, those gut-busting baritone ballads in which manly men assert their manliness—"They Call the Wind Maria" from *Paint Your Wagon* is one, as is Hammerstein's own "The Riff Song" from *The Desert Song*.

Still, no matter which angle you view it from, "Ol' Man River" is, more than anything else, a heroic song.

THE CONCEPT OF TURNING THE Edna Ferber novel into a stage show originated, surprisingly, not with Hammerstein but with Kern. The composer seems to have read her *Show Boat* in October 1926 and was so excited about making a musical out of it that within a month he had arranged a series of meetings—first with Ferber herself, then with Hammerstein (his collaborator on the 1925 hit *Sunny*), and, finally, with producer Ziegfeld. That November, the four parties finalized the idea in a legal contract. The show, however, didn't open on Broadway until thirteen months later—in those days a ridiculously long time for the writing and staging of a musical. Old movies are always showing us how Rommy or Georgie and Ira came up with a whole show in a single weekend, and that's only a slight exaggeration. In fact, the original agreement provided that the finished book, music, and lyrics be delivered by January 1, 1927.

Obviously, this didn't happen. In his biography of Hammerstein, Hugh Fordin explains that the delay was due largely to Ziegfeld; he wasn't particularly eager to produce an entertainment bereft of his customary display of showgals parading about in flowering hat and towering heel. He kept postponing the production, which turned out to be to the benefit of the authors, as the delays gave them time to further polish the work. Miles Kreuger, in his indispensible *Show Boat: The Story of a Classic American Musical,* comes to the opposite conclusion: that Ziegfeld was quite keen on mounting *Show Boat* and that it was Kern and Hammerstein who kept the producer waiting.

Either way, the extra time that it took to write the book and score to *Show Boat* relates directly to "Ol' Man River" in two key ways. If the writers had rushed out the score in two months, as originally planned, they probably wouldn't have even thought of "Ol' Man River," considering how late in the process that song was added. Unfortunately, those same delays that allowed for the song's creation would cause Paul Robeson to be no longer available. He had been the natural first choice to play Joe, and thereby introduce "Ol' Man River," but by the time the work was finished, the great basso was committed to doing concerts in Europe.

The second choice was Jules Bledsoe (1899–1943). The situation would seem perfectly consistent with Bledsoe's career, in that, as a black bass-baritone who gave concerts, largely of African-American folk songs, and occasionally acted in musical shows, he was always coming in second to Robeson. Generations later, Bledsoe is remembered only for two things: playing Joe when Paul Robeson was unavailable and inspiring a line in Billie Holiday's first record. (In "Your Mother's Son-in-Law," words by Mann Holiner, a young Lady Day sings, "You don't have to sing like Bledsoe / You can tell the world I said so.")

Typically, Robeson had already recorded "River" three separate times before Bledsoe made his first and only record of it, in London in 1931 (one of only twenty sides that Bledsoe ever cut). Throughout the show, other characters keep describing Joe as lazy—Stepin Fetchit played him in the 1929 film—but Bledsoe on this recording, which we can only assume reflects the way he sang it on stage in the show, is anything but. There's no doubt that he can sing, and he's especially convincingly when holding the "Aaaa- . . ." on "along" at the song's end (the key is C, he holds it on a high G). Quite the opposite, he tries much too hard to make the song as dramatic as possible (like Lawrence Tibbett snarling out "Song of the Whip" or some other operetta piece). He rushes out the second "let me go 'way" in the verse, clips "sick" in the out-chorus, and in general sounds even hammier than Al Jolson (who recorded a comparatively subdued "OMR" in 1928). Bledsoe is accompanied by the Decca London house band, which supplies an instrumental entr'acte between his first full vocal and his out-chorus. It's ultimately a dance-band performance, with the emphasis on mellow trombones, which achieves the unfortunate side effect of making Bledsoe seem all the more agitated by comparison. He's just too far over the top; he nearly stomps the song to death.

Although Robeson missed the Ziegfeld production, he played the role in all the other important early incarnations of the show: the 1928 London production, the 1932 Ziegfeld revival, the classic 1936 Universal film, and in between and in conjunction with these productions he recorded the song at least six times between 1928 and 1936 alone, and kept it in his concert repertoire for the rest of his career. (Surprisingly, *Paul Robeson,* Martin Bauml Duberman's exhaustive biography of the singer-actor-lawyer-athlete–political martyr, makes no mention of how Robeson served as the inspiration for Joe or that Kern and Hammerstein were eager for him to introduce the character in the original 1927 Broadway production.)

Just as Robeson was an improvement over Bledsoe in the role of Joe, so too was the London Queenie, Joe's wife. On Broadway, she had been played by vaudeville headliner Tess "Aunt Jemima" Gardella, an Italian-

American woman who was perhaps the only female star of this century who specialized in blackface performances (indeed, she never appeared in any other guise). Although films and recordings reveal Gardella to be a fine entertainer, in England Queenie was played by one of the great American blues and cabaret singers, the soon-to-be-legendary Alberta Hunter. Hunter later told biographer Frank Taylor that the London producer originally had a white English actress in mind, but that Hammerstein himself insisted on authenticity. (Why the author didn't insist on this on Broadway is not known.)

Hunter also recalled that Robeson refused to play Joe unless the offending word "niggers" was replaced by the somewhat softer term "darkies." However, Hunter's memory is at odds with reports from the black press at the time, which are extensively documented in Duberman's Robeson biography. The *Amsterdam News* and the *Pittsburgh Courier* both reported (in the same editorial) that some black people resented Robeson "for loaning his talent and his popularity towards making the production a success" and added that "if anyone were to call [Robeson] a nigger, he'd be offended, yet here he is singing 'nigger, nigger, nigger' before all those white people." It should be noted that Robeson does not, in fact, sing "nigger" in any of his many recordings of "River," which cannot be said of several white entertainers who recorded the song in 1928, including Al Jolson and the Revelers.

The reaction of the black press was altogether appropriate, although it misses Hammerstein's point. The very first word of the show is the N-word, but it can be argued that Hammerstein is using the offensive term not because he endorses the hatred that the word conveys but for its shock value, much as Mel Brooks and Spike Lee have in more recent times. As is obvious to anyone who's ever heard the song, the N-word was almost immediately replaced by "darkies" and "colored folk" and, by the time of Frank Sinatra's 1944 recording, it had morphed to "Here we all work on the Mississippi." Sinatra is nonetheless still identifying himself as a member of the black race as he clearly targets "the white man boss" as the symptom of his unhappiness. Still later versions, such as the otherwise excellent 1959 recording by baritone Gordon MacRae, sanitize it too much when they refer to the heavy as "the big man boss." (He could be talking about Edward G. Robinson.)

In 1927 it was considered daring to show the humanity of Negro characters on stage, and this *Show Boat* surely does. Still, were Ferber alive today she might be surprised to find herself in the same show boat as Harriet Beecher Stowe. When Mrs. Stowe wrote *Uncle Tom's Cabin,* she intended it as a passionate polemic against the evils of slavery, and would have been aghast to learn that generations later, black people held up her leading character as anything but a symbol of racial pride. Likewise, Hammerstein, and to an extent, Ferber, were also trying to illustrate the madness of a society where "the land ain't free" and people of one skin color are considered better or worse than people whose skins are a different shade. Perhaps Ferber's dramatic invention hasn't held up so well. The famous miscegenation scene, in which Julie's husband, Steve, makes the ultimate sacrifice for his wife by persuading a lawman to believe that he's black, may have moved audiences in 1927 but seems hardly any more convincing today than Eliza on the ice.

Hammerstein, by being less specific, came up with a song that over the long run has been enthusiastically embraced by performers of all skin colors and all musical genres. It's no longer just about black folks and racial hatred; it's about man's inhumanity to man on a much broader level. The content is intriguing enough, but the form in which Hammerstein puts it across is itself remarkable. For much of the time since his death, Hammerstein's stock as a lyricist has steadily fallen, and many a cabaret cutup worships Richard Rodgers's first partner, Lorenz Hart, at the expense of his second, Hammerstein. Unlike Cole Porter or Hart, Hammerstein did not write lyrics that called attention to themselves with a lot of tricky rhymes—he was more interested in putting over the story, the character, and the message than showing off the fact that he owned a rhyming dictionary. His entire output is a testament to the idea of how difficult it is and how ultimately satisfying it can be to say something in the most direct, possible manner.

The main difference between the verse (and even the part of the verse that reappears as the bridge to the chorus) and the refrain is that the verse rhymes and the chorus doesn't. "There are no rhymes at all for a long part of the song's refrain," said the lyricist, "and when you imagine the refrain with rhymes you realize how much weaker it might be." Actually, a completely rhymeless song ("Moonlight in Vermont" is the most famous example) would also have called attention to itself, which is to say, it would have attracted attention to the form and away from the content. However, each of the three *A* (or *A* variant) sections in "OMR" does have what we could call a "soft" rhyme. In the first, it's the especially subtle, implied rhyme of "nothin'" and "somethin'"; in the second, it's "cotton" and "forgotten"; in the third, it's "tryin'" and "dyin'." Fancier, more pretentious rhymes, Hammerstein is telling us, would distract from the message, and he wants nothing to stand in the way of what he's trying to tell us, least of all language itself.

Simple forms empower the poet to express profound thoughts. According to Hugh Fordin, Hammerstein did not get up in the morning determined to write a "protest song," but in depicting the confusion of a simple black laborer on the river he came up with something universal, something that symbolized the plight of mankind throughout history. On one occasion, Hammerstein did agree that the song could be interpreted as an anthem for civil rights, but he averred that he "wasn't conscious of writing that at the time." Yet on another occasion he said, "I put the song into the throat of a character who is a rugged and untutored philosopher. It's a song of resignation with an implied protest."

Nonetheless, Hammerstein's later track record—his involvement in the Hollywood Anti-Nazi League (years before World War II), for example—speaks louder than his denials. Later, his "You'll Never Walk Alone" (from *Carousel*) also gained new life as a civil-rights anthem. Hammerstein might have argued that he wasn't trying to write anything political with that one, either, but there's no denying that "You've Got to Be Taught" (from *South Pacific*) is an out-and-out attack on prejudice and bigotry. Still, none of these later songs was more effective than "Ol' Man River." And as it happens, "OMR" is from *Show Boat,* acknowledged as the first musical in which song and story organically flowed from each other, each supporting the other (although this would not become standard procedure on Broadway for another sixteen years, until Hammerstein perfected the approach in *Oklahoma!*). In that sense, the first integrated musical is also the first integrated musical.

SOME SONGS ARE PERFORMED in many different ways, as we have seen and will continue to see, but "Ol' Man River" is not one of these. You will never hear it played as a waltz (like "Take the A Train"), as a march or a boogie woogie (like "The St. Louis Blues"), or as a bossa nova (like "Star Dust"). Essentially, "Ol' Man River" has only surfaced in two distinct identities: as an anthem, as Kern and Hammerstein intended, and as an up-tempo killer-diller, which undoubtedly sent those two gentlemen into conniption fits.

By some kind of bizarre coincidence, both identities of "Ol' Man River" were established on records by Paul Whiteman, the bandleader and showman who was unquestionably the single most central figure in the popular music scene of the 1920s. On Janury 11, 1928, White-man recorded "Ol' Man River" as an up-tempo fox-trot for a standard ten-inch Victor dance disc, complete with a peppy vocal by twenty-four-year-old Bing Crosby in one of his first recorded solos. On March 1, Whiteman returned to the song, this time presenting it under the band-leader's other identity as a maestro of semiserious "concert" music, which generally consisted of some popular song dressed up in symphonic trappings.

The Whiteman concert treatment of "OMR" features Paul Robeson as its primary voice, and as such it has the distinction of being the first pop-ular song ever recorded by him. This is sometimes regarded as an original cast recording, but technically it wasn't: Robeson, as noted, was not a member of the original cast on Broadway and would not open in the show until two months later, in London. In fact, he was only home in America for a short while in early '28, between concert dates in Paris and the *Show Boat* opening at the Drury Lane, in May of the same year. This Whiteman treatment qualifies as one of the bandleader's more successful concert elaborations on a pop song (it's certainly better than the ghastly sym-phonic version of "Chloe," recorded three days earlier), since "OMR" is something of a concert piece to begin with. As with Whiteman's other such ventures, much of the symphonic elaboration takes the form of tempo changes—playing the piece fast and slow, slowing down and speeding up. The secondary voice is Mike Pingatore, Whiteman's long-time banjo virtuoso, who adds to the Old Southern atmosphere, and there's another singer, the band's own tenor, Austin "Skin" Young, who sings the middle section of the verse ("Don' look up . . .") after Robe-son's first chorus.

Robeson sings two choruses on the Whiteman disc, one at the begin-ning in solo, the other at the end with a full mixed choir, and while he's hardly the whole show, it's clear that for the man and the music, this was the beginning of a beautiful friendship. Two months later, and two weeks after the West End opening of *Show Boat,* Robeson was in a London studio recording "River" again, this time with the Drury Lane Theatre Orchestra and Chorus. Interestingly, of the six occasions when he recorded the song from 1928 to 1936, no two use the same arrangement. The 1928 Drury Lane version starts with the "show" verse ("Dere's an ol' man . . ."), but then Robeson goes into the last eight bars of the published verse ("Let me go 'way from the Mississippi") before singing another full chorus, this time with the male choir from the show. The 1936 recording, made at the time of the Universal film, is the only one that features Robeson using the sheet music verse, still avoiding the N-word but singing "Darkies all work on de Mississippi." Both the May '28 and the '36 feature the "outlining" chorus, which, in a tradition that originated in black spritual singing, has the choir singing the body of the melody while the lead singer kind of circles around them melodically— when they get to "rollin' along," he sings " 'Long, old river keeps rollin' along. . . ."

Apart from the N-word and the D-word, the lyric is throughout peppered with what Duke Ellington would call "lampblack Negroisms." As with "St. Louis Blues" before him and "Summertime" after, in writing for black characters, Hammerstein didn't hesitate to use a kind of black dialect ("Dere's an ol' man . . .") that future generations have come to condemn as a condescending caricature of black speech.

Most of the early Robeson recordings were made in England; the exceptions are the two "concert" versions, the 1928 Whiteman and one in 1932 with Victor Young and the Brunswick studio orchestra. This latter was recorded at the same time as Ziegfeld's 1932 Broadway revival of the show as part of an original cast album released by Brunswick Records, which Miles Kreuger has identified as "the very first American record album ever made from the score of a Broadway musical." Even so, musical director Victor Young and producer Jack Kapp (who would reunite with Hammerstein for the albums of *Oklahoma!* and *Carousel* a decade later) didn't get it quite right. This wasn't a true original cast album, since only Helen Morgan and Robeson were selected from the company then playing on Broadway, and they weren't presenting the music as it was heard in the show. Instead of letting the principals sing the show's Robert Russell Bennett orchestrations, Young and Kapp treated the eight twelve-inch sides (currently available on a two-CD set from Pearl Records) as a kind of a symphonic suite.

Generally speaking, the result is a little sleepy (although not as dreadfully dull as the *Show Boat Scenario* suite recorded in 1941 by the Cleveland Orchestra). But although Morgan especially suffers, Robeson's "Ol' Man River" comes off rather well, and the concert-style arrangement can't sabotage a song that had long since evolved into a concert showpiece. While the minute or so of symphonic-style intro that proceeds Robeson's vocal is far from bad, one still wishes that the extra space on this four-minute side had been given over to a more complete representation of the full "Ol' Man River" as they were performing it every night on Broadway, with both the verses documented intact. (This was not achieved until several decades later on an English studio album of the *Show Boat* music, and the entire score was not recorded in full until John McGlinn's definitive, three-CD treatment of the show from 1988.)

Norma Terris, the original Magnolia on Broadway, told Kreuger that "Robeson was a brooding 'Ol' Man River' and Bledsoe was a happy 'Ol' Man River.' " This observation is not borne out by their recordings, since Bledsoe is more accurately described as an over-the-top "Ol' Man River." Robert Russell Bennett also compared the two Joes, pointing out that Robeson's voice was deeper and that he sang "Ol' Man River" a step lower. In the recordings, Bledsoe, a baritone closer to tenor range, sings in C (the key of the show and the sheet music edition of the song), while Robeson, a deep bass-baritone, sings it in B flat. The discs support all testimony that Robeson was a deeper and more powerful Joe, and it's easy to imagine the power his voice and presence must have had in the theater. Where Bledsoe spits the song out overtheatrically, Robeson is considerably more subtle: he doesn't have to turn on the histrionics because he realizes that the words are powerful enough to speak for themselves. In what might be called the climactic moment of the song, at the end of the bridge, on the words "land in jail," Robeson goes from C all the way down to low F, and the sheer power he conveys is nothing less than electric. So, too, is the ending, where he holds the concluding note (a-*long*) for four bars.

The song remained Robeson's signature for the rest of his career. A concert recording from 1952 finds the great baritone making the song more political than ever, thanks to several lyric changes. By changing "Git a little drunk . . ." to "Show a little grit / An' you land in jail," and then altering the last *A* section from "Ah gits weary . . ." to "I must keep fightin' until I'm dyin'," Robeson takes the lyric closer to Woody Guthrie than to Hammerstein. The voice sounds older, with lots of vibrato, but it's still beautifully resonant. By now, Robeson is no longer singing as Joe, riverboat laborer and rugged philosopher; he's singing as Paul Robeson, freedom fighter.

Robeson's hold on "Ol' Man River" was so authoritative that for years no one attempted to challenge him. Al Jolson seems to have been the only other major singer to perform "OMR" as anthem after Robeson and Bledsoe, and his 1928 Brunswick (in D flat) is actually quite convincing. A radio version, from his *Kraft Music Hall* program of twenty years later, is even better; the combination of his vocal quality, his total conviction, and the superior sonics make this one of the great readings of the song and indisputably the greatest Jewish performance of the song. And I don't mean that flippantly: his intonation and his attitude are unmistakably Hebraic. Jolson underscores the universality of the text by showing how it applies as much to the plight of the Jews as it does to blacks in the American South. The 1928 Jolson disc opens with Hammerstein's original word, "Niggers," which is especially shocking today, and the later radio treatment offers a wimpy substitute in "Lots of folks work on the Mississippi. . . ." Even on the 1928 disc, Jolson isn't using the word lightly; like Hammerstein, he knows the term is a lightning rod for racial discord, and he makes full use of its disturbing power.

The same can't be said for the Revelers, who cut "OMR" for Victor on the same day as the first of the two Whiteman recordings (January 11, 1928). This vocal quartet was harmonically quite innovative and was an important influence on such later groups as Whiteman's own Rhythm Boys and the German Comedian Harmonists. Rhythmically, however, the Revelers were stiff beyond words and even the most rudimentary syncopation seems quite beyond them. For that reason, although they were enormously popular in the mid-twenties, the group is rarely reissued or listened to today. Their "Ol' Man River" uses an overdone specialty arrangement rendered in a staccato, almost arhythmic style. Basso Wilfred Glenn sounds unsettlingly naïve when he croons "*Us* niggers all work on the Mississippi. . . ." Later, he makes like an overseer and chants "Tote that barge!" and "Lift that bale," while the other three Revelers answer back "Yassuh!" Throughout, the Revelers don't seem to realize that there's meant to be a suggestion of unrest and protest in the material; they sing it as if it's a minstrel-show celebration of the Old South. Wilfred

Glenn did better when he supplied the vocal refrain for the Columbia recording by Donald Voorhees and His Orchestra, one of the very rare instances of such a deep basso singing on a standard dance disc.

As noted, the tradition of swinging "Ol' Man River" also begins with Paul Whiteman, whose January 11, 1928, Victor version set the standard for "River" fox-trots. It starts with a tantalizingly slow violin intro, although the balance of the recording is noteworthy as an early example of using strings in an up-tempo jazz setting. The trombones get a lovely section *soli* on the first and last eight bars of the verse, and C-melody virtuoso Frank Trumbauer rates a worthy eight-bar statement of his own. But the star of the disc is undoubtedly Bing Crosby, whose one chorus makes it clear why he's about to shake up the world of popular singing, much as this particular record shook up whatever notions about "Ol' Man River" had emerged in the few weeks since the song was introduced on Broadway. Crosby is brimming with *brio,* and far from sounding forlorn when he gets to the part about getting drunk and landing in jail, he sounds as if he might enjoy it. (On a biographical note, thanks to Gary Giddins's life of Crosby, we now know that getting smashed and winding up in the calaboose were part of the singer's history.) In a word, Crosby swings "Ol' Man River," which in this case means approaching the song from an ironic perspective closely related to the blues. His way of dealing with the troubles that the song describes is to laugh right in their faces and tell them to just keep rolling along.

The first great soloist to go to work on "Ol' Man River" was Bix Beiderbecke, then the star of Whiteman's brass section, who recorded it under his own name as "Bix and His Gang." This hymn to African-American solidarity may seem an odd choice of material for the greatest of all Caucasian jazzers, yet the opening melody solo is pure Bix, with his unique approach to reshaping a melody—it's his swinging way of cutting off certain notes that really impresses one here. He doesn't improvise per se on this particular track, but rather lingers around the melody and recasts it in his own image. At one time, Beiderbecke was thought to be present on another 1928 version of the song, by dance-band leader Lou Raderman, who, because he was under contract to the technologically challenged Harmony Records, had the dubious honor of making what is probably the only acoustically recorded version of "Ol' Man River." It's no longer believed that the cornet soloist on the Raderman disc is Beiderbecke, but whoever he was, he was certainly taking his Bix pills. Like the Voorhees disc, the Raderman has a basso vocalist who's a few octaves lower than the lightweight tenors heard on most dance discs of the period.

If recording frequency is an indication of popularity, "Ol' Man River" was a successful tune indeed, having been waxed at least ten times in its first year. Sammy Stewart and His Knights of Syncopation were a black band based in Chicago, yet their "OMR" has some echoes of the Bix–Red Nichols New York school—particularly in its harmonically open sound. Willard Robison also cut it with his Deep River Orchestra for Pathé and Perfect. Robison was a brilliant composer, singer, and pianist, but his big band was comparatively undistinguished, though extensively recorded. For whatever reason, Robison did not handle the vocal refrains with his own dance band, which is a pity, as his singing would have greatly improved most of its recordings. The vocal chorus of Robison's "OMR" is handled by a typical Coolidge-era drone who sounds as if he hasn't the foggiest notion of what he's supposed to be singing about.

It would be nice to report that after the show became a hit and the song was widely heard, "Ol' Man River" became an instant standard (even though the concept of the pop standard was only in its infancy then). However, like most pop songs of the period, it seemed to have stopped being played a few months later. "OMR" didn't really catch on for keeps until after the 1932 revival. Then, in the years immediately before and after the dawn of the swing era, it became one of the most frequently and energetically swung of all melodies. The disc that relaunched it as a swing anthem was made by Horace Henderson in 1933. Although he uses musicians associated with his more famous brother, Fletcher (among them Red Allen and Coleman Hawkins), make no mistake, this is Horace's date. Horace did all the arrangements and preparation, and as a result this is a much more together performance than most of those done under the imprimatur of the more lackadaisical Fletcher. Red Allen's vocal is exuberant, as is his trumpet solo, while Coleman Hawkins is as ferocious and hawklike as his nickname suggests—and the ensemble as a whole takes a surprising detour through the blues "St. James Infirmary." The piece is suitably propelled along by the bass playing of John Kirby, whose pizzicato plucking is so strong you could almost believe there's a washboard somewhere in the rhythm section.

Obviously, the piece's diatonic, scalelike melody appealed to jazzmen, who for a few years made it virtually their favorite jam number after "I Got Rhythm." Other early swing bands recorded it in 1934: Luis Russell, Tiny Bradshaw, and the Casa Loma Orchestra. Although they all sound different, they all follow the Henderson format in their mixture of swinging ensemble riffs, spectacular solos, and increasingly hysterical vocals. Sonny Woods with Russell, and Bradshaw with his own band, sound as if they're trying to out-manic each other. On the Russell, cornetist Rex Stewart (soon to join Ellington) plays a virtuoso solo over an impossibly fast beat led by New Orleanians Pops Foster on bass and Paul Barbarin on drums. Bradshaw opens with a Gershwinesque fanfare (both place the vocals way up at the front) and features another future Ellingtonian, altoist Russell Procope. The '34 instrumental by the Casa Loma, first of the white swing bands ("the band that made swing commercial," was how leader Glen Gray later put it), is less frantic than Russell or Bradshaw, but no less swinging. It uses more of a staccato approach to the rhythm and features two pianos, several standout episodes by clarinet champ Clarence Hutchenrider, and a baritone sax statement by Hutch as well. All three versions build to an exciting call-and-response climax in which the individual sections play off each other, the essence of swing-era style.

Putney Dandridge, as Dan Morgenstern points out, served as Bill Robinson's pianist for his day job but rarely played on his own sessions, preferring to concentrate on singing vocals somewhat in the spirit of Fats Waller, though considerably more agitated. His "River" uses all-star accompaniment featuring trumpeter Bobby Stark and tenorist Teddy McRae, not to mention pianist Teddy Wilson. Dandridge is higher up the manic scale than other swingers of "Ol' Man River," and his ad lib "You drink a little corn and I'll throw you in jail" is even more priceless than Tiny Bradshaw's "Why, you'll land straight in jail!"

Red Allen, who had helped launched the vogue for swinging "OMR" in 1933, returned to it eight years later in a solid, small group treatment, featuring his trumpet and vocal again as well as profoundly blue clarinetist (and fellow Crescent City wanderer) Edmond Hall, all set to an irresistible vamp that comes dangerously close to a boogie-woogie. Nat Gonella, who was a New Orleans trumpeter-singer-funster cut from the same cloth as Red Allen, Wingy Manone, and Louis Prima, but who happened to have been born and raised in London, recorded it in 1936, starting in medium tempo, double-timing on the bridge, and then getting hot and frantic on the second chorus.

Willie Lewis, the Harlem bandleader who earned his reputation in Europe, recorded it twice over there in increasingly smooth instrumentals, from Paris in 1938 and Zurich in 1941 (the latter builds to a bass solo, itself a rarity in the premodern era). The song had hopped the pond with the London production, and was recorded there in a dance treatment by Jack Hylton and His Orchestra. Hylton was regarded as an approximate English equivalent of Whiteman—he was the single most popular bandleader in Europe and also regularly went in for concert orchestrations of pop songs. Hylton's instrumental is very much in the fast-moving spirit of the Whiteman-Crosby, featuring solo spots by jazz violin and vibraphone (Rudy Starita). In 1928, bandleader-composer Noble Sissle cut "River" as a vocal record while in Paris, and Jack Hamilton and His Entertainers recorded "OMR" for Azurephone. In 1947, Django Reinhardt and Stephane Grappelli swung "River" six ways till Sunday.

Some of the swinging versions of "River" came from surprising sources. Just like the "dem" who plant taters and cotton, it's too often forgotten what a great jazz singer Martha Raye was. Her 1939 "OMR" comes in two tempos, and the first is one of the most extraordinary treatments of the tune ever. We've heard "River" fast and slow, but whenever it's slow, it's been like a stately anthem. Raye's first chorus is slow (reworking the melody as she goes along and popping a high note on "I gets weary . . ."), but slow like a romantic ballad; she sings it tenderly and caressingly, as if it were a declaration of boy-girl love. Then all hell breaks loose in the second chorus as Raye the scat singer emerges, parading Kern's melody up and down and all over the place, climaxing in a lick that predates Billy Eckstine's "Rhythm in a Riff."

Likewise, one associates trumpeter Harry James and crooner Dick Haymes with softer, more romantic sounds, yet here they are in 1941 with, of all things, a swinging, up-tempo "River" (in D flat—could they have picked it up from Jolson?). James is in fine fettle—after all, he was a superior jazzman, even if it was his more sentimental numbers that put him on the charts. Haymes, for his part, sounds less uncomfortable than one might have anticipated, since he almost never sang anything but slow ballads. Still, he isn't quite right for this treatment, which probably should have been strictly instrumental—the vocal, on the whole, seems unnecessary.

Trumpeter Cootie Williams recorded one of the more extraordinary "River"s, putting the focus on his own tightly muted instrument with its instantly recognizable wah-wah growl, phrased on top of an early example of what eventually became known as a shuffle pattern. No less remarkable is the contribution of vocalist Jerry Kruger (whom the reader will encounter again in our discussion of "Summertime"). This vocal is a little less overwhelming than her treatment of "Summertime," but Kruger still has originality and invention to spare in translating "River" into jive doubletalk. She also gets in some uproarious interjections, such as, apropos of nothing, "I want some lyonnaise potatoes and some pork chops," as well as "He's been there for years / Sheddin' his tears / The old oaken bucket is a-dunkin' again!" Then, most audaciously, at the end of the bridge, after giving us the barges and bales, instead of going on about getting intoxicated in the traditional alcoholic fashion, she substitutes "Smoke a little tea-o and sing 'O Sole Mio' "!

Also featured with Williams are Johnny Hodges and Lawrence Brown, and Duke Ellington himself is at the piano. This was part of a remarkable series of sessions that Ellington participated in beginning in the late thirties, featuring small groups out of his Famous Orchestra, working under the names and leadership of his best-known sidemen.

In the thirties, both Ellington and Glenn Miller included the tune as part of an extended *Show Boat* medley. Miller's medley survives as an aircheck, Ellington's only as an incomplete orchestration in the Library of Congress.

Thirteen years after Cootie William's 1938 swinger, Ellington returned to the "River" with a small group, this time in a slow treatment. It's one of the more obscure slices of Ellingtonia: like "Summertime," "OMR" here serves as a vehicle for band vocalist Al Hibbler in 1951, and, as with the Gershwin song, this treatment was never commercially recorded, surviving only on a radio transcription. It's one of the better examples of the often-perverse Hibbler singing almost completely straight, accompanied principally by Ellington's piano and violinist Ray Nance. This time it's Ellington's turn to go bizarro; his keyboard work here seems deliberately arch, and he hits all kinds of discordant notes that seem to suggest that you'll never know what you'll come up with when you start dredging this river.

Which makes Ellington one of three major artists who addressed "River" both as a swinger and as an anthem; the others are Paul White- man, as we've noted, and Bing Crosby. Crosby's 1928 vocal (with White- man) is one of the most famous sides of his early career, but his 1941 solo version is one of his most obscure. It's one of a series of standards Crosby cut circa 1939–41 that were not directed by John Scott Trotter, his customary conductor, but by Victor Young, who, thankfully, is consider- ably more low-key here than he was on the 1932 *Show Boat* album. The Crosby-Young "Ol' Man River" is an oddity in that it's one of the only versions of the song between Robeson and Sinatra that doesn't break into swingtime at any point. Like the Martha Raye, this is a unique version, a relaxed, even casual "Ol' Man River," which Crosby achieves without being flippant or trivializing the text. In keeping with the intimate mood, Crosby seems to be minimalizing the range of the piece and reining some of the intervals in, making the lows higher and the highs lower.

Thus for its first fifteen years, "River" was heard almost exclusively as an up-tempo swinging number. The song was reclaimed as a "serious" piece of music thanks almost entirely to Frank Sinatra. Crosby's had been the major slow version previously (since Robeson's, that is), but his, with no disrespect intended, still seems like the work of a crooner. Sinatra's interpretation, first documented in 1943, marks a concerted attempt to build a bridge from the Paramount Theater to Carnegie Hall, and to create a kind of concert repertoire for a popular singer. Therefore, it's appropriate that our earliest hearing of the Sinatra "River" should originate from what could be considered the first series of concerts (as opposed to nightclub or theater appearances) by a modern popular singer, Sinatra's summer of 1943 symphonic tour that culminated in an appear- ance at the Hollywood Bowl.

Sinatra's musical and cultural aspirations also had political ramifica- tions: in both of the eras when Sinatra sang "Ol' Man River," the mid- forties and the mid-sixties, civil rights was a prominent social issue. In 1943, America was fighting the war against Nazism, although "tolerance" at home (as they used to call it back then, somewhat patronizingly) was more of Sinatra's own private battle than a national cause célèbre. Sinatra did not publicly ally himself with the civil rights movement in the 1960s, but as Tony Bennett and historian Patricia Willard and many other partic- ipants in that cause have acknowledged, they were there, at least in part, because of Sinatra, who twenty years earlier had inspired them to be there.

Like the 1941 Crosby record, both sets of Sinatra readings, from the forties and the sixties, are very personal, although Sinatra, more than his predecessor, succeeds in making "River" sound anthemic as well as intimate. "OMR" is a highlight of the Hollywood Bowl concert; on other numbers here, he seems to be saving himself, as if perhaps in awe of his surroundings, but he gives "OMR" everything he's got. He sticks to the melody closely on this first documented reading, and it's also the only time when he uses a term that specifically connotes African-Americans— in this case, as with Robeson in 1936, it's "darkies." On an October 1943 radio show, he eliminates the verse entirely.

By the time of his first commercial recording of "River," made for Columbia in 1944, he has his approach perfected: the sheet-music verse, followed by the chorus, done slowly so that, like all FS recordings of the tune, this one requires four minutes, although it includes only one run-through of the verse and chorus. He also eliminates any reference to the specific racial identity of the collective protagonist. Hammerstein and Robeson had used the harsh language for shock value, but Sinatra's approach is more subtle and more universal. As noted earlier, there's no doubt as to who's oppressing whom, especially as Sinatra still describes the heavy as "the white man boss."

After the Bowl, all versions find Sinatra taking more liberties with the melody. Again, following Crosby's example, and even improving upon it, he personalizes the melody without sounding jivey, which would risk undermining the song's message; in fact, he makes the point of the song clearer than it's ever been, except perhaps with Robeson. Both the forties and the sixties versions are in C, and Sinatra, more than Robeson or Crosby, puts most of the dramatic emphasis on the second half of the chorus. At the end of the bridge, there's a feat that ranks as one of the more astonishing acts of vocal virtuosity in his canon, when he goes from the last note of the bridge ("jail") down to the first note of the final *A* section of the chorus ("Ah"). In the music, "jail" is on D and "Ah" is on G, but Sinatra connects them and sings them on a single breath. Essentially, he begins his descent while still on the word "jail," and glides down from D to G while still sustaining the note. He wasn't yet doing this at the Hollywood Bowl, where there is a clear break between the two notes, but he does it on the 1944 Columbia and all subsequent versions. On the forties versions, Sinatra's boffo, opera-like ending attracts the most attention: he sounds as if he's going to bust a gut shooting for a high D (on "*a*-long") and holds it for measure after measure before landing on the tonic C.

In the sixties, Sinatra elaborated on the "jail"/"Ah" device (doing something similar in "Fools Rush In" and, more notably, in "Moonlight in Vermont"). He began performing the song again on his 1962 world tour for children's charities; although he traveled with a sextet, the live versions from this decade are generally sung just with Bill Miller's piano. Emil Richards, who played vibes in Sinatra's sextet, remembers studying "The Old Man" as he did this number and trying to breathe along with him, which always turned out to be impossible. He would sing it all with one breath, including the phrase "Ah gits weary," and, said Richards, "By the time he got there, let me tell you, he was friggin' weary!"

In the verse, roughly the same slice of melody ("until yo' dead") goes up from E to F, whereas here it goes down, and on his 1963 album *The Concert Sinatra,* Sinatra goes down further still, not just down from D to G but to F and possibly, very briefly, to low E—just about the lowest note he hits in his whole career. But, metaphorically speaking, it's quite a high note, and it continued to be so when he sang it on his 1967 *A Man and His Music* TV special (where the presence of Ella Fitzgerald inspires him to even greater heights) and at a 1968 concert in Oakland, California (at which he introduces it as "probably one of the greatest pieces of music in our American library"), which is also primarily a duet with Bill Miller, the rest of the orchestra joining in only for a dramatic conclusion on the final note.

All of these Sinatra versions have a big ending, which is atypical for the singer. At virtually every stage in his career, Sinatra preferred to place his climax at least eight bars or so before concluding, and then wind down to an intimate, quiet coda. Big endings were more Judy Garland's style. Perhaps influenced by Sinatra, or possibly even at his suggestion, she added "River" to her repertoire in 1963, when she was doing her weekly TV show. A later performance recorded *Live at the Palace* was commercially issued within Garland's lifetime, but the 1963 TV reading is far superior.

Sinatra may be intimate, but Garland is downright vulnerable. She makes it sound as if the first step toward conquering the world's evils is to best one's personal demons. This, unfortunately, she would never achieve in real life, but you'd never know it from the way she builds from terrified to triumphant here. Taped in June 1963, it anticipates the patriotic, world-beating mood Garland would soon express in more literal anthems like "Battle Hymn of the Republic," an attitude largely inspired by the assassination of the chief executive in November of that year.

Jerome Kern supposedly once told Sinatra that "My idea with that song was to have a rabbity little fellow do it, somebody who made you believe he was tired of living and scared of dying. That's the way you do it, Frankie." The composer's description much more accurately fits Garland's performance.

Garland may be virtually the only performer in Sinatra's field who had the heart, the brains, and the nerve to challenge him in the "Ol' Man River"–as-anthem stakes. One surprising contender was the alto sax giant Art Pepper: two years before his death in 1982, Pepper recorded an album with strings that included "OMR." For the first chorus, he phrases in slow ballad time, and it's clear from the first note that he's been listening to *The Concert Sinatra,* as this marks one of the only occasions when a jazz instrumentalist plays the whole thing in ballad tempo, starting with the verse (although in this case it's the shorter, eight-bar version of the verse). After the first chorus, Pepper opens up, both time-wise and harmonically, as the tempo increases and pianist Stanley Cowell starts laying down a modal vamp similar to what McCoy Tyner played behind John Coltrane on "My Favorite Things." Pepper's arranger, Bill Holman, had done his own treatment in 1960 with a hard-swinging studio band consisting largely of one-time Kentonites like himself. The chart, which features Holman's own tenor (as well as trumpeter Conte Candoli and pianist Jimmy Rowles), is especially notable for the subtle, almost "stealth" manner in which Holman phrases the final chorus.

The song continued to be occasionally sung as an up-tempo in the postwar era, generally by singers who grew up with the swing treatments of the thirties. Joe Williams has one of the best swinging "River"s; even though it's fast and dynamic, somehow it doesn't seem disrespectful. Gloria Lynne just revs through the thing, sounding as if she just happened to need an up-tempo at this point and "OMR" would do as well as anything else. She sings it well, but it sure don't sound as if she's been doing a lot of liftin' and totin'. The treatments by Hadda Brooks and Della Reese are a bit sillier. Brooks, a female pianist-singer in roughly the same tradition as Nellie Lutcher, Julia Lee, and Rose Murphy, uses an engaging clip-clop vamp and an irreverent cry of "Ha ha!" Reese, who recorded it live, makes some wacky lyric changes, such as "All them folks that plant that stuff are pretty soon forgotten" and "Let's get drunk and spend the night in jail." It's certainly a lot of fun, and the only time "Ol' Man River" went "ro-ro-rollin' a-long."

Tony Bennett and, more recently, Rosemary Clooney (the latter on *Still on the Road*) have swung it. Bennett did "River" as the climax of his 1958 meeting with Count Basie, a package that was passed off at the time as having been recorded live in a nightclub but was actually made in the studio, the applause added on a separate track. The producers of the most recent Columbia CD elected to leave off the applause, which leaves the album sounding kind of hollow, as if it's missing something. This is especially true of Bennett's unique take on "River," arranged by pianist Ralph Sharon, which was done largely as a feature for Latin percussionist Candido. Bennett exuberantly swings through his chorus in about fifty-five seconds, and then the master *conguero* takes over. The bulk of the track is by Candido, but because this is the kind of crowd-pleasing turn that we expect to be followed by tumultuous applause, it seems especially puzzling when there's no ovation at the end.

Satisfying as Bennett's treatment is, it's hard to think of any of Sinatra's mainstream pop offspring or colleagues, apart from Garland, who did a "serious" "Ol' Man River." Sammy Davis, Jr., bit one off, on his live album taped at Town Hall. He can't make up his mind if he's trying to work in the tradition of Sinatra and Garland, by doing it intimate and with minimal accompaniment, or big and gut-busting as in the black basso tradition of Bledsoe and Robeson. The end result is unsatisfying, with Davis overacting terribly, as if he were lobbying for an Academy Award.

THERE WAS, HOWEVER, a genre of singers who picked up on Sinatra's cue and continued to perform "River" as an anthem, and they came not from big bands but from rhythm and blues, an area that would have surprised Sinatra as much as Jerome Kern. *Show Boat* was ubiquitous in the early postwar years. In 1946, there was a very successful revival on Broadway, which led to an equally successful cast album on Columbia. That same year, MGM released *Till the Clouds Roll By,* a film biography of Kern that began with a lengthy excerpt from *Show Boat* and concluded with Sinatra doing "River" in a white tuxedo atop a white column in front of a great white set. It's an image that every cultural historian in America, whether writing about film or music or even white tuxedos, has taken a potshot at. Yet the white man bosses at MGM did not frown; instead, they proceeded to film a third cinematic version of *Show Boat,* in 1951.

The 1951 film is often compared unfavorably to the classic 1936 Universal version, but that isn't totally fair as the MGM version is a more than serviceable color remake, and it does especially well by "Ol' Man River." The song was beautifully staged by Roger Edens (who filled in for director George Sidney on this one number) and sung by William Warfield (the next great singer of African-American folk and concert music after Robeson, Bledsoe, and Todd Duncan). There's one other crucial difference: *Show Boat* purists undoubtedly object, but this time around, "OMR" is not sung at the conclusion of act one, scene one, apropos of nothing, as it was on Broadway. Here, Joe sings it right after the famous "miscegenation" scene, which makes it doubly clear that "Ol' Man River" is intended as a song of social protest. Compared to the more lavish spectacle mounted by director James Whale in the '36 film, and also compared to the big production number outlined in the Broadway score, the 1951 Edens-Sidney arrangement stays simple and direct: Warfield sings the eight-bar verse, then just one chorus of the song, and there is no choir behind him. It's a comparatively short and intimate "Ol' Man River," but an undeniably powerful one.

MGM's *Show Boat* was an unforeseen blockbuster, grossing eight million dollars as the second most popular film of the year. Already established as the definitive postwar Porgy, Warfield also became the most sought-after Joe of the fifties and sixties: he essayed the role in Columbia's third album of *Show Boat,* a studio cast taped in stereo in 1962 with John Raitt as Ravenal, and again at the Lincoln Center revival of 1966, produced by Richard Rodgers and recorded by RCA. (The 1962 and '66 recordings also shared the same Magnolia, Barbara Cook, and the same musical director, Fritz Allers.)

Other notable *Show Boat* cast albums with notable "OMR"s include an all-operatic version released by RCA in 1956, with Risë Stevens and Patrice Munsel, and with Robert Merrill, sounding like Victor's answer to Gordon MacRae, singing all the male numbers, including "River." Two English albums, a studio cast from 1959 and the Adelphi Theatre production of 1971, use the most famous black female singers in England as Julie: Shirley Bassey on the '59, Cleo Laine on the '71. Both of these albums include the full treatment of "Ol' Man River" as outlined in the complete score (as does the 1988 John McGlinn recording, which, unlike the English LPs, uses the N-word). The fine Maori baritone Imia Te Watia sings "River" on the '59 and Thomas Carey sings it on the '71. On the '59, the choir behind Joe sounds as if the river they're singing about is the Thames rather than the Mississippi, but Te Watia's performance is strong and moving; he's as good a Joe as any.

Thus, given MGM, Sinatra, and William Warfield, there can't have been many English-speaking individuals at the start of the rock era who couldn't hum "Ol' Man River." Significantly, most of the mainstream black pop stars of the 1940s and fifties—Cole, Eckstine, Vaughan, Fitzgerald (who left it off her *Jerome Kern Songbook* even though it's proba- bly Kern's single best-known song)—all stayed aweyed from it. Yet the first generation of black R&B and soul singers had grown up with "OMR," so it shouldn't have been surprising that they'd want to put their own stamp on it, and several recognized it as a potential concert vehicle tailored specifically for the black experience.

By far the best of these is by the uncategorizable Ray Charles, who included it as one of his *Ingredients in a Recipe for Soul*. Marty Paich, best remembered as a modern jazz arranger, put together a background for Charles that's so plain vanilla, I can't imagine any self-respecting Cau- casian ever wanting to sing in front of it. It starts with a choir—singing the full twenty-five-bar verse—that's got to be the pastiest I've ever heard. Charles's vocal is something else again, however. He changes more lyrics, throwing in more than Sinatra at his most extreme (such as "And if you drink a little scotch / I want you to know you're gonna land in jail") and does it all in that beautiful wheeze of a voice. The chalky white background makes Brother Ray sound even bluesier by comparison. Con- trast is the primary weapon here: the background singers are so *not* what the song is about, while Charles *is*. Kern and Hammerstein probably wouldn't have approved of what he does to the music and lyrics (the tempo, too, is much slower than they ever sanctioned), but Ray Charles's passion and soul must be precisely what they had in mind.

It's hard to ascertain whether or not the disc of "River" by Screamin' Jay Hawkins should be described as a "serious" performance or not, even

by the artist's own standards. It's a dramatic, anthemic performance that
starts off with a slightly overtheatrical eight-bar instrumental verse.
Hawkins sings the chorus straight until the end of the first *A* section,
which he suddenly emphasizes by screaming "a-*long*" at the top of his
lungs, underscored by a cacophonous clatter from the rhythm section.
Second eight bars, same deal, and the bridge is completely straight, after
which the final *A* gets a bit of sensual R&B backbeat. Following a scat
break that sounds like Louis Armstrong gargling, he goes into a second
chorus sung in swingtime but punctuated with sustained notes and a
killer vibrato that could be Billy Eckstine impersonating Bert Lahr.
Among the hundreds, nay, thousands, of recordings of "River," this one
surely is unique.

The definitive doo-wop "Ol' Man River" is by the Ravens and features
the legendary basso Jimmy Ricks, who might well be described as the
Paul Robeson of R&B. A major hit for the National label in 1947, the
Ravens' treatment is light and airy, bereft of any trace of social protest.

Two decades or so later, the Motown-based Temptations tackled the
tune, their own superstar basso Melvin Franklin the featured vocalist.
Unlike the Ravens, the Temps treat it as a concert piece enlivened with
broad comic accents. This stately, nearly five-minute track (an eternity by
Motown singles standards, but then Ray Charles went five a half and
Screamin' Jay went over six) also contains sequences in which the voices
act the story out as if it were a radio drama, with spoken dialogue and
sound effects. The fivesome goes back and forth between rubato, conventional ballad time, and the sixteenth-note-based backbeat of sixties
pop. Lead voice Franklin alternates between crooning, bellowing, and
recitative.

Someone once wrote that camp and soul are not compatible, yet here
the Temptations mix the two approaches very effectively. The group also
included the song on *The Temptations Live!*, taped at the Rooster Tail in
Detroit in 1967, and it's a howl to hear the crowd laughing along at every
gag and every camped-up bit of business. The end of the verse is done relatively straight, and this portion of the performance is the most gospel-
like of all recordings of "OMR."

Following the example of the Ravens, not all the R&B and soul versions take the anthem approach; there are also up-tempo doo-wop versions of "Ol' Man River." Both Ruth Brown and Sam Cooke recorded

hand-clapping, foot-tapping treatments. Brown opens rubato with the last line of the verse ("That's the old stream . . .") before a back-up group of doo-woppers, including a Jimmy Ricks–like basso, falls into line behind her and goes into long sustained notes on the bridge. Where Brown is backed by a male chorus, Cooke has a female choir and a rhythm section with prominent vibraphone for accompaniment. This short, two-minute treat is graced with a countermelody based on the brief phrase that goes "rollin' along, rollin' along." When he reaches the line about his body being all aching and racked with pain, Cooke gives the merest nod to the anything-but-cheerful content of the lyric as he goes happily doo-wopping along. As always, Cooke combines irresistible rhythm with one of the sweetest voices in all of pop.

These are far from the only performances of the song outside its home turf of Broadway, jazz, and mainstream pop. Country guitarist and pro-ducer Chet Atkins recorded an instrumental treatment that's half-jazz and half-country; it's a melodic and harmonic improvisation, but done with a distinctly Nashville sensibility. Jim Croce, who encroached upon the genres of country, folk, and rock, recorded a lovely Willie Nelson–style hillbilly treatment not long before his tragically early death (in a plane crash) at the age of thirty; it doesn't sound anything like "Bad, Bad Leroy Brown."

And there continued to be jazz performances: among pianists, Oscar Peterson set the standard with his live trio recording of 1959. This is a two-minute marvel of melodic invention: one of the only up-tempo ver-sions to contain the verse, it opens with Peterson playing each line of the twenty-five-bar verse in very rapid time, after which there's a long break in which drummer Ed Thigpen or bassist Ray Brown throws the line back at him. His blazingly fast treatment of the chorus isn't anything to sneeze at, either. One is especially greatful that Peterson bit off "OMR" with this particular trio; the Brown-Thigpen combination clearly brought out the best in the pianist. He always swings like mad, but there's a relaxed, inti-mate quality in his work at this time that's unique in Peterson's prodigious career.

Following Peterson's example, other pianists have recorded it as a kind of show-off piece to test for the ultimate speed that human fingers can fly across an ivory keyboard. Derek Smith's reading is finger-bustingly fast, as is that of Adam Makowicz, who suggests what Art Tatum might have done with the tune (he plays the melody very fast, and his improvisation moves about twelve times faster still). Dick Hyman and Ralph Sutton recorded a duo-piano version (no bass or drums, just the two pianos) that starts anthemic in the verse and gradually works its way up to swingtime. Two keyboard superstars who could have competed in the "OMR" speed derby but elected not to were Dave Brubeck and Erroll Garner. Brubeck turns the song into a feature for bassist Eugene Wright in which the rest of his famous quartet concentrates on supporting him. (Perhaps because the bassist was the only black member of this, the greatest of all Brubeck groups, he regarded the song as his birth-Wright.) Erroll Garner doesn't go for raw speed, just that familiar rollicking, bouncing happy piano sound that was especially his. Garner's statement on the tune is forceful, intense, and exciting, and it just keeps rollin' along.

There's also a bunch of tenor treatments by players with a foot in the worlds of swing and bop. Don Byas, recording in Paris in 1950, plays it most like a song, without the anthemic baggage "OMR" traditionally carries; even swinging, it's still an awfully pretty tune. Both Charlie Ventura (1951) and Gene Ammons (1961) open with the verse in ballad time, and both use the eight-bar version, although what happens after the verse is completely different. Ventura, with a group called the Big Four, goes into a jam session; bassist Chubby Jackson plays the chorus melody first, interrupted by breaks from drummer Buddy Rich and Ventura joining in on the bridge. Ventura takes over completely at the second chorus, and his entrance (diving down to some especially resonant B flats) is most attractive. There's also an exciting drum solo by Rich before Ventura builds to bluesy climax. Pianist Marty Napoleon is about the only one who doesn't get to solo. In the Ammons version, on the other hand, when he reaches the chorus, he settles into a semi-slow, extremely sensual ballad groove, supported by congas (not to mention pianist Richard Wyands and bassist Doug Watkins). This is an "Ol' Man River" for lovers.

Although the *Show Boat* score as a whole never attained the mass popularity among jazzmen enjoyed by *Porgy and Bess* (*My Fair Lady* and *West Side Story* tie for second place), there are at least two full-length jazz albums of *Show Boat* music—one sublime, one ridiculous. Columbia's *The New Jazz Sound of Show Boat* has got to be one of the strangest albums ever released. Apparently, studio guitarist Barry Galbraith and composer-arranger John Carisi (best known for "Israel" and "Springsville," two tunes he wrote for

Miles Davis) came up with the idea of a new ensemble called the Guitar Choir, which consisted primarily of five of those instruments. The Guitar Choir made only this one recording, which features the guitars, bass, and drums, plus three horn soloists in altoist Phil Woods, trombonist Bob Brookmeyer, and Carisi himself on trumpet. It was a strange idea and an even stranger sound, and the LP included songs from the 1936 film and the 1946 revival. However, "Ol' Man River," one of the most straight-ahead charts on the disc, probably fares the best here, since it's primarily a vehicle for Brookmeyer.

Trumpeter Kenny Dorham was also one of the great jazz composers, but luckily he wasn't tempted to tamper with "Ol' Man River" or play it in any fashion other than satisfyingly straightforward. Done with the tra-ditional hard-bop lineup (which Dorham had helped invent) of trumpet, tenor (Jimmy Heath), and rhythm (three pieces), the cut opens with the twenty-five-bar verse played by the two horns rubato and without the rhythm section, intriguingly shifting to march time in the middle eight, then picking up a standard fast bop tempo for the chorus. All three soloists, Dorham, Heath, and Kenny Drew, are at the top of their form. Unfortunately, Dorham's album, *Jerome Kern's Show Boat,* made for the obscure Time label, is one of that great trumpeter's hardest to find.

Dorham's "OMR" is boppish and swinging with just a hint of defi-ance—a perfect "River" for the start of the sixties. It marked the start of "River" reclaiming its status as anthem, which, once again, happened thanks largely to Sinatra. Over the years, the song had become so overly familiar that anyone performing it had to work twice as hard to defeat the expected clichés. In Eddie Cantor's 1930 film of his Broadway show *Whoopee* (originally produced by Ziegfeld), the comedian sings a brief parody of the song. In the Our Gang short *Mush and Milk,* the little black kid known as "Stymie" (George Beard) includes it in a list of three famous rivers. Other songs like "Roll On, Mississippi, Roll On" (1931) refer to it in the lyrics ("Come on, you old man river, come on!"); jazzmen hint at it in the titles and sometimes the melodies of Duke Ellington's "Old Man Blues" (which has an ascending line that may be considered a relative of "OMR" and a bridge that's practically identical), and Dizzy Gillespie's "Old Man Rebop." Many jazzmen have quoted it in their solos—for instance, Lester Young at the start of his famous opening gambit on Count Basie's "Taxi War Dance."

That the song could still touch a nerve thirty years after it was written was aptly demonstrated by comic Stan Freberg in one of his all-time classic routines, "Elderly Man River," a bit he first performed on his radio series of the mid-fifties and shortly thereafter refined and recorded for Capitol Records. In this routine, radio star Freberg announces his intention to sing "Ol' Man River" to help celebrate the rather spurious-sounding holiday "National Mississippi Riverboat Paddlewheel Week." But before he can get under way, he's interrupted by a Mr. Tweedley (Daws Butler), a censor appointed by the "Citizens Radio Committee." As the routine proceeds, whenever Freberg comes to something that the network censor considers offensive, Mr. Tweedley sounds an irritating buzzer and the music stops.

It doesn't take long, as Mr. Tweedley finds the very first word ("Old") objectionable. "The word has a connotation that the more elderly people find distasteful," so Freberg is stuck singing it as "Elderly Man River." The more Freberg sings, the more the censor chimes in with his buzzer, and the more absurd euphemisms Freberg has to substitute for original lyrics. Of course, by taking out everything that's objectionable—which includes cleaning up Hammerstein's use of dialect slang ("Somethin'" and the double negative "he don't say nothin'"—and even mock-correcting "cotton" to "cotting")—Mr. Tweedley succeeds in draining all the meaning out of the song, neutralizing its power. After "You and I, we perspire and strain," Freberg and his chorus are about to get to the line about getting you-know-what and landing you-know-where, Freberg realizes that he's licked and ends the song right then and there. The irony is that the censor corrects everything about the song except the racial element, which he never mentions, and this was the only part of "Ol' Man River" that anyone ever found objectionable.

Back in 1927, Jerome Kern paid a call on Edna Ferber at her apartment, bearing a copy of a new song for the score that he wanted her to hear. Kern was a mediocre pianist (although unlike Cole Porter, who wasn't much better, Kern never made any commercial recordings) and an even worse singer, but no matter, "Ol' Man River" achieved its intended effect on Ferber: "The music mounted and mounted and mounted and I give you my word, my hair stood on end, tears came to my eyes. I knew this wasn't just a musical comedy number. This was a great song. This was a song that would outlast Kern and Hammerstein's day and your day and my day."

BONUS TRACKS

Best and Most Outrageous Version of "OMR" after Jerry Kruger

Perhaps "Ol' Man River" and "Summertime" were ideal targets for ladies who liked to combine swing with silliness. For whatever reason, three highly outrageous divas (two very good [Kruger and Barnes], one very bad [as we'll soon see]) included both of these songs in their short discographies. Mae Barnes's 1958 "OMR" is a howl, a wildly irreverent and swinging treatment from a period when the song was no longer being done in that fashion. Backed by an all-star group that includes trumpeter Buck Clayton, pianist Ray Bryant, and drummer Jo Jones (who gets a snare solo), Barnes switches from fast to faster halfway through, throwing in manic scat breaks and wild lyric changes: "Get full of juice and land in jail," and instead of the familiar lifting and toting bit, she exhorts, "Where's that mop? / Get that pail!"

Worst and Most Outrageous Version of "OMR"

Elizabeth Lands was a Harlem-born soprano apparently recruited by Clyde Otis of Mercury Records in the early years of the twelve-inch LP to compete with the sensation being caused by Yma Sumac on Capitol. On her album *Untamed,* Lands indulges in the same kind of multi-octave, semi-operatic screeching and wordless exhibitionism. Except for a few standards ("Summertime" is another helpless victim, naturally), the bulk of the tracks lean toward folk-jungle exotica. All of which wouldn't be so bad except that Lands attempts to do "OMR" and "Summertime" in a swing tempo, and the weight of these conflicting elements is more than even this material can bear. She attempts to blend the Sumac bit with a light, scattering sense of rhythm more inspired by Rose Murphy or Nellie Lutcher. Too bad the lounge movement of the nineties never stretched far enough to find this one; it's one of the most hysterical performances you'll ever hear.

BODY AND SOUL (1930)

music by Johnny Green

lyrics by Edward Heyman, Robert Sour, and Frank Eyton

L ET'S BEGIN WITH AN OUTRAGEOUS STATEMENT: "Body and Soul" is probably the most-played melody in all of jazz. In the twenties and thirties, the most frequently heard tunes in "hot" music were undoubtedly "Tiger Rag" and "St. Louis Blues," both of which had been around practically from the beginning of jazz—and were certainly part of the music long before jazz was documented on recordings. But like "Star Dust" (in its pop permutation, anyway) and "I Got Rhythm," both also first heard in 1930, "Body and Soul" was introduced during the immediate pre-swing period and thus got in on the ground floor of the big band era. All three songs, not coincidentally, became instant jazz classics, immediately picked up on by countless musicians, thanks to Louis Armstrong. Yet even more than "Star Dust" (or, for that matter, the melody to "I Got Rhythm"), "Body and Soul" did not lose ground among jazzmen in the modern age, while "Tiger Rag" and "St. Louis Blues" gradually faded away. Instead, it became ever more popular among modern jazzmen. On the other hand, "Body and Soul" has been somewhat less treasured by pop singers; as with "Star Dust," its melody is clearly more special than its lyric.

It's true that "I Got Rhythm" and "How High the Moon" (and, to a lesser extent, "All the Things You Are") were, in some way, shape, or form, played even more often than "Body and Soul" in the forties and fifties. Musicians, in fact, didn't need to spell out the songs' full names: the mere mention of the single word "Rhythm" or "Moon" was all that was needed to clue the band as to what to expect next. Yet, as Gary Giddins has pointed out, the actual melodies to these two songs were generally jettisoned—musicians were only interested in their chord progressions, and their tunes often went unheard. By contrast, it was the melody to "Body and Soul" that jazzmen (and -women) adored, and while they also relished the challenges of its daunting harmonic makeup, it was rare for musicians to play those changes without some noticeable trace of the melody on top of them. (Ironically, Coleman Hawkins, who did more than anyone else to establish "Body and Soul" as an all-time jazz standard, was one of the few who actually played variations on "Body and Soul" under another title, the same way the boppers did for "Rhythm" and "Moon.")

Rhapsody in Blue (quoted by Nat King Cole in one of his piano solos on "Body and Soul") is the concert work that most suggests the processes of improvisation. "Star Dust" is the song that most feels like a trumpet or saxophone solo, something that some particularly brilliant brass player like Bix Beiderbecke might have concocted. "Stormy Weather" uses ingenious repeats, and in that sense supplies its own obbligato, like Louis Armstrong behind Bessie Smith or Lester Young with Billie Holiday. Similarly, "Body and Soul" doesn't exactly have the feel of an improvised solo; it feels more like a pop tune that already has its jazz ornamentations built into it. Its melody is strong, simple, and extremely catchy, its structure rudimentary, and those chords—"harmonic sequence" is a better term for them—are amazingly rich, providing unendingly fertile soil for growing a jazz solo.

On the strength of the Coleman Hawkins record alone, composer Johnny Green exerted a strong influence on the history of jazz. As Giddins has said, it's almost impossible to imagine jazz without "Body and Soul." Yet although Green was a virtuoso pianist, he would never have described himself as a jazz musician. "I was never a great jazz player, and nobody ever confused me with Horowitz," he once said, "but I was a very, very damned good piano player." Green came from a school of piano playing that flourished in the 1920s, the genre of novelty piano wizards exemplified by Zez Confrey, Rube Bloom, Phil Ohman, and Victor Arden. This tradition would be obliterated in the thirties by the rise of such purely jazz keyboard virtuosi as Fats Waller, Earl Hines, Teddy Wilson, and Art Tatum. By the second war, with Nat Cole and Bud Powell about, no one wanted to hear "Kitten on the Keys" anymore.

Yet in the twenties and early thirties, these *Tantalizing Ticklers* (as Ross Laird's definitive discography of twenties piano recordings is titled) flourished in hotels, nightclubs, and radio and recording studios. They made no apologies about not being jazz, yet they employed elaborate melodic ornamentation and a rich harmonic sense, and, after a fashion, they swung. Players like Green, Confrey, Bloom, Ohman, and Arden played a kind of pop piano that was closely related to ragtime, stride, and even blues, yet couldn't quite be called jazz. Arden and Ohman embodied the essence of musical-comedy piano: as historian Roger Sturtevant has noted, theaters had no mikes in those days, and a pair of two-fisted pounders like Messrs. A. and O. could fill a whole house with their twin pianos, to the point where the rest of the orchestra was almost unnecessary. Confrey is best remembered for his ragtime-like "novelty" compositions, some of which were given lyrics and performed as vaudeville turns (who can forget Felix Unger's rendition of "Stumbling"?), while Rube Bloom wrote exquisite piano solos like "Soliloquy" and, later, pop standards like "Don't Worry 'Bout Me" and "Day In—Day Out." Yet although many of these men left some sort of permanent imprint on the long-term development of American music, the achievements of all of them pale in comparison to the legacy that Green left to the world with one single song, "Body and Soul."

Most songwriters will tell you the question that they are endlessly asked is which comes first, the words or the music? Johnny Green, however, reported that the question he most frequently heard was, "When you were writing 'Body and Soul,' did you realize that this was to be the most recorded torch song of all time?" Early on, he formulated a set response: "No, all I knew was that it had to be finished by Wednesday."

Apart from the quality of his music, Johnny Green is also notable for being one of the first pop-jazz composers to graduate from Harvard— although, not surprisingly, considering the attitudes of the academy at the time, his degree wasn't in songwriting, or even classical composition, but in economics. It's fascinating to consider how an economics major from Harvard could write something that would inspire so many black jazz musicians in Kansas City, Texas, etc., who were essentially blues players. (In the same way, a composition by the son of a neurologist from Brighton, England, became part of the foundation of bebop—I'm speaking of Ray Noble and "Cherokee.")

JOHN W. GREEN WAS BORN in Far Rockaway, New York, October 10, 1908. His father was a successful realtor and builder, and both his parents played the piano. And although he described his mother as a prodigious sight reader, "neither one of them was a particularly good musician," he said. He remembers them playing four-handed duets of Beethoven and Schubert pieces ("not very inspiredly"). The family passion for music extended beyond his parents' generation. "At the age of four and a half," recalled Green in the late 1980s, "my maternal grandfather, whom I idolized, took me to a Saturday matinee of Gilbert and Sullivan's *The Gondoliers.* I was hooked, but totally, completely hooked: No heroin addict was ever as hooked as I became on the theater. I was four and a half years old. I have stayed that way to this day."

In addition to piano, he studied banjo and guitar, as well as several reed instruments. At the age of fourteen he organized a juvenile dance orchestra, dubbed the Harmonians, that played on local New York radio. While still in high school, he attracted the attention of the British musical comedy star Gertrude Lawrence, who was impressed enough by this "musical boy wonder" to hire him as her accompanist for an American appearance. The following year, he took the entrance examinations at Harvard University and passed, enrolling there at the age of fifteen. Apart from his studies in economics, his activities at Harvard seem to have been primarily musical: he served as chief arranger for the University Military Band and as co-leader of the school's dance band, the Gold Coast Orchestra. Even while he was still at school (and in his teens), Green's orchestrations for this group (which, he said, recorded for Columbia) attracted the attention of such established bandleaders as Jacques Renard, Roger Wolfe Kahn, Hal Kemp, Leo Reisman, and others.

It was a somewhat less established leader, however, who gave Green his first chance to write for a professional band: Guy Lombardo, then a relative newcomer to the business, brought Green out to work for him in Chicago during the summer of his junior year at Harvard. (On the occasion of Lombardo's twentieth year in show business, Bing Crosby remarked, "It just goes to show that if you have talent, dedication, and *one* good arrangement, you can go on forever!") It was through the Lombardo family connection that Green landed his first notable copyright. This was for "Coquette," which Green submitted to his bosses, the Lombardo brothers, to see what they thought of it. Carmen Lombardo, the trumpet-playing, vocalizing, lyric-writing, fun-loving member of the clan, liked the song but was unhappy with the bridge; he thought it too "unconventional" and offered to rewrite this section. Green agreed, and that would be the only time he would share composer credit on a tune. The lyrics were written by Gus Kahn, Chicago's resident pop poet. The song was a widely recorded hit, and in later years something of a jazz standard (performed memorably by Jimmie Lunceford's orchestra, among others, and even heard in the film *Fritz the Cat*). Green was then nineteen years old.

After graduation, Green was pulled in three directions. First, he began working on a master's degree program in English literature. Second, his father convinced him to chuck both songwriting and book-reading and accept a position on the stock market—so he took a day job on Wall Street, with Asiel & Co. And then there was the music, always pulling him back. Within a few months of his graduation, Green was soon contracted by Jean Goldkette to produce orchestrations to be used on the Detroit-based bandleader's Atwater Kent radio program. As a pianist, Green landed his own show on local New York statio WOR. As a composer, he wrote a song with Sammy Lerner ("I Owe You") that didn't go anywhere. Soon he had it out with his father on the subject of music, which the elder Green regarded as a completely inappropriate vocation for a respectable young man. But between "Coquette" and his Monday night radio series, Green was already a respected young man of music, and such celebrities as bandleader Roger Wolfe Kahn, critic Deems "Fantasia" Taylor, and no less than George Gershwin himself tried to convince Green, Senior, to let his son work at music full time. Said Taylor, "A man's calling is not so much the work that he likes to do best as it is the work that nobody and nothing—not even his own inclinations—can keep him from doing."

Green left his Wall Street day job after six months, switching from high finance to low-down harmony, a decision his father would not forgive for many years to come. Fortunately, the father of his fiancée, Carol Falk (whom he married in April 1930, the first of three marriages), was somewhat more tolerant and allowed Green to bunk under their roof on East Seventy-seventh Street. Around this time, he landed a musical day job at Paramount Pictures' Astoria studio, first as rehearsal pianist for early talkies and then as orchestrator and musical director; the gig foreshadowed his multi-decade career with MGM's famous Arthur Freed unit.

At this point, Green began writing songs with two lyricists, Edward

Heyman and Robert Sour; Heyman later told Peter Mintun he imagined they'd become the world's second most famous three-man songwriting team, after Buddy DeSylva, Lew Brown, and Ray Henderson. Then came a call from Gertrude Lawrence, in need of new material. As Green later told Fred Hall, they quickly came up with four tunes for Lawrence: a rhythm song, a ballad, a comic song, and a "torch." "The question arose," Green later recalled, "what was going to be the torch song?" It turned out to be "Body and Soul."

The title had been suggested to Heyman by a friend. The expression had been around for years: "Keeping body and soul together" was a popular way of saying "making a living," or "staying alive." It was somewhat already part of the black experience, vis-à-vis Uncle Tom's speech to Simon Legree: "My body may belong to you, but my soul belongs to God." In 1925 *Body and Soul* had also served as the title for an all-black silent movie melodrama starring Paul Robeson. (This was one of at least a dozen movies to bear this title—four being from the silent era alone.)

"We wrote every day," Green recalled, "so Eddie came in one morning and he said, 'Listen, for the torch song, what do you think of the title "Body and Soul"?' I said 'Holy Christmas, that's sensational!' He was thrilled that I liked it, because so did he." While both of them knew the title was something to work with, they were aware that the direct use of the word "body" might provoke censorship problems in the climate of early 1930. (Indeed, the NBC network would initially refuse to play the song except instrumentally or even to mention the title, while in Boston it would be banned altogether.)

Even so, the three collaborators were so pleased with the title that they decided to press on with it. "The big discussion went on for two days," Green related. " 'Where does the title come? Is it going to come at the beginning of the phrase, is it going to come at the end of the phrase? Are you going to say "Body and soul, my life belongs to you; body and soul, my days begin and end with you" or is it going to be "So and so and so and so and I belong to you, body and soul" at the end?' " For the answer, Green took inspiration from the future great lyricist E. Y. ("Yip") Harburg. The composer and the lyricist already were friends; later that year they would write the standard "I'm Yours" together. How would Harburg approach it, they asked? "We decided that communications-wise, that impact-wise, that feelings-wise, going back to the Harburg ethic in philosophy, that the point could be driven home more clearly by setting up premises and tying them off with a wallop, with that powerful title."

Green noted, "Yip was a martinet about fluidity and the propriety of syllabic emphasis. You don't put the word 'w-o-n-d-e-r-f-u-l' where the music causes you to call it won-DER-ful or won-der-FUL. You put it where the music dictates that it's WON-der-ful, right? So, the fluidity of the triplet structure was something that both Eddie and I decided belonged at the end." Green came up with a triplet phrase that seemed a perfect place for the title phrase. "I said, 'We've got that wonderful triplet leading to a long note. And the relationship of vowel to consonant sound of the end line makes a comfortable lingual transition to the *s* of 'soul.' The line 'Body and Soul' is a very felicitous thing to sing with that rhythm [i.e., a triplet followed by a long note]. That was the first decision." Having agreed that the title would come at the end of the phrase, Green then made a point of letting Heyman come up with the lyric on his own, resisting the temptation, as he put it, to "box him in" to a preset pattern. "It kind of kills me to say this, because I would like to be able to say, and say honestly, that I made up the architectural schematic of the front phrase, but I did not. History has proven that there's something magic about it, or it wouldn't be a classic. And I didn't make it up, Eddie did."

As for the remarkable bridge of "Body and Soul," about which more shortly, Green did not write it specifically for this song; he simply reused his original *B* section from "Coquette," the one that Carmen Lombardo had rejected two years earlier. (Green didn't feel comfortable admitting this in interviews until years after Lombardo's death. The British producer and historian Chris Ellis tells the story that at one point Green left the only copy of the original "B&S" manuscript in a cab and the three collaborators had to reconstruct the song from memory.)

Once the four songs, including "Body and Soul," were finished, they were demonstrated for Gertrude Lawrence, who was taken enough with "B&S" not only to sing it but, in Green's words, to buy "an interest in this song at a low but welcome figure." Lawrence introduced "Body and Soul" in her act, and although she didn't record it, she did sing it on the radio and brought it back to London with her. In 1930, the two top bandleaders in Britain were Bert Ambrose, who was billed simply by his last name and was then in residence at the Mayfair Hotel, and Jack Hylton, probably England's most popular bandleader. One evening, while dressing for his broadcast, Ambrose turned on the radio and happened to hear his friend Gertrude Lawrence singing the most marvelous new song. It turned out that he already knew Green from "Coquette," so when Lawrence told the bandleader the name of the composer, he said something to the effect of "Our Johnny? 'Coquette' Johnny?" Lawrence sent over the music, Ambrose immediately put one of his orchestrators to work on it, and the tune was included on his broadcast of the following evening. Thanks to the wireless, "Body and Soul" was soon the sensation of London, as Green learned shortly thereafter when Henry Spitzer of Harms, Inc., placed a trans-Atlantic call to secure the English publishing rights to it and to sign up Green and his team. "Body and Soul" would not be published in the States until some months later.

On February 18, 1930, "Body and Soul" was copyrighted in England, and it now bore the names of four songwriters: Green, Heyman, Sour, and one Frank Eyton. Curiously, Sour later told Giddins that Eyton's name was added later, when the song was brought back to New York; yet all four names are on the original British copyright. The names of Sour or Eyton are not exactly household words, even among pop song aficionados. Sour went on to write several minor hits, and Eyton was a fairly prominent librettist in London's West End in the early thirties. His name turns up on, among other shows, two productions by composer Arthur Schwartz, *Three's a Crowd* and *Nice Goings On*. Yet for whatever reason his name wound up on "Body and Soul," Sour, whose recollections should be taken with a grain of salt, insisted that Eyton "didn't change a comma" in the text.

One thing that Eyton did do for the song, however, was pull strings to have it recorded in London. Although Ambrose introduced "Body and Soul" to English society and on the radio, it was his rival, Jack Hylton, who, thanks to Eyton, was the first to record it, which he did on February 7, 1930. On the twenty-fifth of that month Hylton waxed the song again, this time in a twelve-inch concert treatment. Meanwhile, three days earlier, on February 22, Ambrose recorded his version; the song proved a big seller for both leaders, and Ambrose would return to it three years later.

Within weeks, the song was also recorded by popular vocalist and commedienne Elsie Carlisle (later to become Ambrose's girl singer) and by Carroll Gibbons, an American pianist and later a close friend of Green's. The Gibbons disc did not employ the pianist's famous band, the Savoy Orpheans; instead, he did it as a piano solo with violin and clarinet accompaniment. In April, Britain's most famous novelty keyboard wizard, Billy Mayrl, published a special arrangement of "B&S"; and in June, the Australian pianist Gil Detch recorded it. It had also been recorded by the bassist, musicologist, and composer Spike Hughes. Although he was later to abandon hot music for the academy, Hughes at that time was leading what was generally regarded as the first pure jazz ensemble in England, as opposed to a dance band with jazz flavoring. This may well have been the first of several thousand jazz recordings of "Body and Soul."

WHEN WE START TO ASK what jazz musicians might find attractive in Johnny Green's composition, we get a valuable clue in the very first note: the song begins on a rest—a dotted eighth rest, to be precise. In order to get something to swing, you have to know what to leave out as well as what to put in, when to cut off a note and when to hold it. To open with a silence, a jazzy pause before the first note even strikes, is an indication that rhythmic as well as harmonic and melodic possibilities are in store. Green's preferred key for the song was D flat, which is how the song is published today, although the earliest sheet music (the 1930 English edition) was in C. Green's insistence on D flat is in itself informative: the ambition of most composers is to make a song as simple as possible for the nonprofessional musician and singer, and most amateurs (myself included) rest easier with as few accidentals as possible. Said Green, "I wrote it in D flat, where all the jazz guys played." In D flat, almost every note is flatted.

The tune is nothing if not catchy: the first two bars go back and forth between two notes, a pattern that's elaborated on in the next two bars; then the original pattern is paralleled several steps higher in the fifth and sixth. Most songs open with the one (I) or two (II) chord; "Body and Soul" commences with the two in minor (ii). The song is predominantly major, yet it opens in minor, which gives it a decidely unresolved feeling. We finally achieve something like resolution in the third bar, when we arrive at the one major chord of D flat—this is where most other songs typically begin.

The construction of the song is deceptively unremarkable, a standard thirty-two-bar A-A-B-A. But consider what's going on in the bridge: we start by modulating from D flat (five flats) to D natural (two sharps) for four bars, and then modulate again, this time to C natural (no accidentals) for its remaining four bars. The first four bars end on D major, the second four begin on the D minor seventh chord (Dm7), and the whole bridge winds up with three descending chords: C7, B7, Bb7. Each of the three *A* sections is identical, and in a nice little twist, Green flats the "and" note of the title phrase. Each *A* section ends with the title phrase, "Body and Soul," descending to the tonic note in major, D flat.

Green once spoke at length about the bridge, which he denied had any kind of "intellectual structural purpose." Green argued that he wrote the bridge this way because "It couldn't go anywhere else."

> I wasn't at the piano when I put that on there. I was sitting in a comfy chair with a pad of manuscript paper in my hand, and biting on a pencil. I knew that the tonic became the leading tone of D major. It couldn't go anywhere else. Then I started to think, "Well, I'm gonna have to take a different tack on the middle strain, and I would like to endow the middle with a rhythmical similarity to the front strain, and then get away from it." . . . As you know, you have a dotted eighth rest, a sixteenth note, a dotted eighth, and a sixteenth note. So I thought I would make it of a piece, with the first three notes and then get away from it. I jotted some ideas, and the one I stuck with was the A seventh lead into the D major chord. Then comes the dotted eighth rest [in first measure of the bridge]. It's the same pattern as the beginning ["I can't believe it . . ."]. Now, I said, I'll change it ["It's hard to conceive it . . ."]. As a matter of fact, I didn't come back to the dominant [at the eighth bar of the bridge, when the key changes from D major to C major]. Do you want to know what gave me that idea? [He plays the opening passage of Beethoven's "Moonlight" Sonata, which has a similar "lead" to the next strain.] You never had a composer talk more honestly. I figured it was good enough for Beethoven, it was good enough for me.
>
> Now I'm in a hell of a fix, because I'm in C major, but I gotta get back to E flat minor seventh. If I was gonna get back to D flat, there's no problem. I just do it enharmonically again. But that's not where we're going. The front phrase does not start on the tonic; it starts on E flat minor seventh. Now, how am I gonna get to E flat minor seventh?

Well, the best way to do that is to get to the B flat seventh somehow. So I wonder if I'll ever forgive me for being chromatic. Everybody else thought that was such a stroke of genius, that series of chromatic sevenths, with which I get back to E flat minor seventh. Do you know who never did forgive me? Vernon Duke. He said, "You ought to be ashamed of yourself. For God's sake, that's taking the easy way out. Anybody can do a descension of chromatic dominant seventh chords." Everyone else was calling me a genius and he was vilifying me. Now the difference between Harold [Arlen] and me—he would have found a major change to make in the last eight bars. I thought the front strain was so strong that all I had to do was repeat it. At least I've been telling myself that since 1929. Maybe I was just lazy.

Strong as the chord sequence is, it has rarely been reemployed with alternate melodies. As we briefly noted earlier, "Body and Soul" is not a jazz composition like "I Got Rhythm" and "How High the Moon," in which new melodic "heads" are created on top of its familiar harmonic pattern—Giddins has identified Percy Heath's 1978 "In New York" as one of the few original jazz melodies based on "B&S" changes that are strictly headless sets of variations on the melody and chords.

Brian Priestly has argued convincingly that the the 1931 "Prisoner of Love," music by Clarence Gaskill (cocredited to Russ Columbo, who might have been a mere cut-in but who did make the song a hit) and words by Leo Robin, should be considered something of a sister song to "Body and Soul": the chord changes are quite similar and the tune is practically a countermelody. Tenor guru Budd Johnson quoted "Prisoner of Love" in the middle of his 1968 reading of "Body and Soul," done with Earl Hines's quartet. (Oddly enough, while Perry Como was able to make "Prisoner of Love" a hit and a pop classic all over again fifteen years later, Como's "Body and Soul" is somewhat disappointing.) There are many versions of "B&S" that don't use the melody, and rather than come up with new "heads" for the piece, these basically just dive into harmonic improvisation—for example, most of the Hawkins versions, Lee Konitz's 1999 "Soddy and Bowl" (clever title, that), and Lucky Thompson's "Deep Passion," from his 1956 *Tricotism*.

"Body and Soul" also has a verse, which, like most of its kind, is sixteen bars. What's not typical is that it starts in E flat minor (six flats) but stays there only for the first four bars, switching, at bar five, to E flat major (three flats). On the line "I look for the sun," Green puts the word "the" on a C flat (which is the enharmonic equivalent of B natural), and the "sun" on Bb. Each of the last two lines of the verse also opens on a rest. It's altogether a worthy verse that, sad to relate, has been sung on precious few recordings after 1930; Ruth Cameron's recent (2000) album *Roadhouse* is one of the few that includes it. Counting the verse, then, the song travels through five keys: E flat minor, E flat, D flat, D natural, and C natural.

As suggested, however, a number of the earliest vocal recordings of "Body and Soul" do contain the verse, including Elsie Carlisle's and Annette Hanshaw's (respectively, March and October of 1930). Though Carlisle was slightly older than Hanshaw, the two singers were roughly Anglo and American equivalents of each other. Unlike most of the better femme chirpers of the era, they were neither "torch" singers nor "blues" singers, in the lexicon of the day, but fine, straight-down-the-middle pop singers with a touch of jazz and fine taste. The Spike Hughes recording does not contain the verse, and would have been better off without the chorus as well—lyrically, that is. The text is sung by the band's drummer, one Val Rosing, and, as with the vocals on ninety percent of those early jazz records that include them, the singing here detracts more than it adds to the overall proceedings.

BY THE SUMMER OF 1930, plans were being made to export "Body and Soul" back to its native country. On June 15, *Film Daily,* an American trade publication, noted the European success of "Body and Soul" and added that the song "will be introduced in America next month." That notice proved a little premature, but it presumably indicates that Chappell and Co. had already offered to publish the song Stateside, and, possibly through Chappell's connections, the American rights to it were snapped up by producer Max Gordon for his forthcoming Broadway revue, *Three's a Crowd*. It was to star a new discovery named Libby Holman, who had made a favorable impression the previous year in *The Second Little Show*. The bulk of the score was to be by Arthur Schwartz and Howard Dietz, with only this one song coming from the Green team. On October 14, 1930, "Body and Soul" was copyrighted in America, with Heyman and Sour listed as the only lyricists, and on November 20, 1930, a French version "Corps et âme" (with French lyrics by André Mauprey) was also copyrighted.

Even though the song was a proven hit in Europe, its success on Broadway was far from assured. The best source of information on the pre-opening trials of *Three's a Crowd* is Jon Bradshaw's biography of Libby Holman, *Dreams That Money Can Buy.* Supposedly, the number was not going well during the tryouts in Philadelphia. Miss Holman did not like the lyric and asked Howard Dietz to rewrite it for her, while, as Sour later told Giddins, he and Heyman were also scrambling around and coming up with alternate lyrics. Sour also claimed that Schwartz and Dietz lobbied to keep "Body and Soul" out of *Three's a Crowd,* an accusation not substantiated in any other account.

The song's chances of making it into the final show were looking bleaker and bleaker; not only did the lyrics have to be continually rewritten, Holman wasn't satisfied with the orchestration, and the staging wasn't working, either. Director Hassard Short had devised an elaborate but impractical number in which the audience saw only Holman's face as she sang the song (a "Body" number without a body) as she was gradually moved forward by a series of pulleys and her face appeared to grow larger and larger. (It sounds a lot like what Busby Berkeley later did in "Lullaby of Broadway" in *Gold Diggers of 1933.*) After spending a thousand dollars on the pulleys, it turned out that they didn't work—and they made so much noise that no one could hear the music. What's worse, when Green conducted the orchestra his podium was too high, so that the audience saw Green's shoulders instead of Holman's face. The star was so upset that she started to walk out, yelling, "Instead of calling it *Three's a Crowd,* you can call it *Two's Company!*"

While the company was still in Philadelphia, Dietz was home in Manhattan, where he had the good fortune to run into composer and orchestrator Ralph Rainger. Far from wanting "Body and Soul" out of the show, it appears that Dietz was doing everything he could to make sure it stayed in. He corralled Rainger into taking the train down to Philadelphia and writing a new arrangement for it. In Rainger's outline, Holman sang the verse with just piano, and then the orchestra arrived "in *tutti*" with the refrain. At the last minute, the director came up with a new staging, in which Holman simply entered from stage left and sang "Body and Soul" in a slinky black dress with a plunging neckline. That was all that was needed to make her a star, and the song and the show an immediate hit, when on October 15, 1930, *Three's a Crowd* opened at New York's Selwyn Theater.

Strangely enough, even though the song went over spectacularly, there was one major dissenting voice among the New York critics:

Miss Holman's voice is even more far-reaching in its effect than last year and her elevation to stardom has given her a new quietness and poise which do nothing to detract. I do not think that her big number, "Body and Soul," is a very good song (it was imported from England quite a long time ago [sic] and has had its edge worn off by several hundred saxophones); in fact, none of her numbers is as good as "Moanin' Low" or "Can't We Be Friends?" [both from *The Second Little Show*, 1929], but Miss Holman herself makes up for whatever unfavorable balance there may be.

Or so opined Robert Benchley in *The New Yorker* (October 25, 1930).

BETWEEN THE ENGLISH and American publications, and between the four different lyricists involved (Heyman, Sour, Eyton, and Dietz, who may or may not have actually contributed to the lyrics), sorting out the different sets of words to "Body and Soul" is a tricky task. The following is intended as a rough guide to the various permutations of the "B&S" lyric:

The original English version (with Eyton's name on the credits, as recorded by Elsie Carlisle) published in C major:

Verse one: "You're making me blue, / All that you do seems unfair. . . ."
Refrain: "My heart is sad and lonely, / For you I cry, for you, dear, only. . . ."
Bridge: "I can't believe it, / It's hard to conceive it. . . ."
The final A of this refrain starts with the risqué line: "My life a hell you're making, / You know I'm yours for just the taking. . . ."
Refrain one ends with: "My life revolved around him, / What earthly good am I without him. . . ."
Verse two: "Life's dreary for me, / Days seem to be long as

years. . . ." (This particular verse was used by Ruth Cameron in her 2000 recording of "B&S.")

The best known American version, presumably the one copyrighted on October 14, 1930, has the chorus in E flat and the verse in E flat minor. It uses the following text, which is roughly the same version as recorded by Annette Hanshaw and Ruth Etting, as well as by Bobby Short (on a 1991 recording made live at the Cafe Carlysle).

> *Verse:* "I'm lost in the dark, / Where is the spark for my love? . . ."
> *Refrain:* "My days have grown so lonely / For I have lost my one and only . . ." (the second eight bars of this refrain contain the line "My house of cards had no foundation").
> *Bridge:* "What lies before me, / The future is stormy. . . ."

Note that while the English version has two verses and one refrain, the American version has one verse and two refrains. The second refrain, which I don't think I've ever heard anyone other than Peter Mintun perform, begins as follows:

> *Refrain two:* "I can't have his kisses / And no one knows what torture this is. . . ."

There are several slight differences in the lyrics recorded by Holman; for instance, in the bridge she sings "No use pretending" instead of "Are you pretending." As Mintun notes, the standard published version of the song, which first began appearing in the mid-1930s, represents an attempt to cobble together a comprehensive text out of all the various versions.

IN THE WAKE OF HOLMAN'S success with it, the song was originally the property of female singers like Etting, Carlisle, and Hanshaw. This tune seems to have caught them in a torchier mood than usual. A version highly favored by Green himself was by Helen Morgan, then regarded as the mother of all torch singers, and one of the great Broadway personalities of the interwar era.

No one today regards Holman as being in the same class as Morgan, Carlisle, or Hanshaw. Hers was not a great or particularly phonogenic voice, like Carlisle's or Hanshaw's, and she doesn't have the unique charm or "brave little voice" of Morgan. Today she's mainly remembered for the quality of the songs she introduced ("Moanin' Low," "Find Me a Primitive Man," "Something to Remember You By," "You and the Night and the Music") and for a scandal in which she married a megarich tobacco heir and, many then believed, shot him, in 1932. The most notable aspect of the Holman recording is, Mintun notes, a particular obbligato to the main melody that appears only in a few recordings made around the time of the 272-performance run of *Three's a Crowd* on Broadway.

Before you could say "My heart is sad and lonely," American dance bands had snapped up the tune. By mid-September 1930, with well over a month to go before *Three's a Crowd* was set to open, Paul Whiteman (on his last date for Columbia) cut what must be the premiere recording of the new American lyric with a vocal by Jack Fulton. Soon, Victor's Leo Reisman, a leader who was particularly close to the Broadway beat, had "B&S" in the can. (Five months earlier, Reisman's band, featuring pianist Eddy Duchin, in residence for many years at the Central Park Casino, had provided the dance music when Green and his first wife celebrated their wedding there in April 1930.) Reisman recorded three different masters of the song, with three different vocalists, two of which (by the male Frank Luther and the female Frances Maddux) were actually issued at the same time, presumably so that listeners could have their choice of genders. All three Reisman recordings feature trumpeter Bubber Miley, who had surprised the jazz world by turning up in a white society show band after making his mark as practically a cofounder of the original Duke Ellington Orchestra. One might even say that Miley was the first great trumpeter to tackle the tune, beating Louis Armstrong by a few weeks. Other bands who recorded "B&S" in September and October of 1930 include Smith Ballew, Ted Black, Lou Gold with Irving Kaufman, Fred Rich with Dick Robertson, and Ozzie Nelson in the second recording session of what would become a showbiz dynasty.

All the early white dance bands play the song in a similar tempo, slow for the time but fast by the ballad standards of the post-Sinatra era. These are terpsichorean tempos unknown to dancers of the post-1935 world (and especially post-1945), which isn't a complaint about the nature of these recordings, most of which come off as having a lot of vivacity and verve. In all, the "hot" dance bands of the pre-swing era deserve a lot more attention than they've traditionally received from music historians.

When *Three's a Crowd* opened on Broadway, Green had turned twenty-two five days earlier—his writing "Body and Soul" at twenty-one seems as precocious an accomplishment as Billy Strayhorn writing "Lush Life" at roughly the same age. Although Green recorded his most famous song as part of piano medleys laid down in 1933 (London) and '34 (New York), he didn't record a full-length (nonmedley) treatment of it until late in the thirties. However, there's a 1935 aircheck featuring vocalist Virginia Verrill, in which the obbligato from the 1930 Libby Holman treatment returns, this time played by the orchestra and not sung.

Around 1939, Green recorded it (this time in D natural) as part of an excellent series of dance-band sides he directed for the Royale label: it's largely a piano-with-orchestra treatment, although there's a fine vocal by Louanne Hogan (billed simply as "Louanne" on the label). Green recorded it again on several other occasions, generally in albums of his own compositions, the best of these being an early postwar collection on Decca featuring Barbara Ames, another good unknown singer, with a briefer piano interlude by the Maestro. If the 1939 Royale sounds like a first-rate hotel band, the 1946 Decca sounds like a first-rate movie soundtrack orchestration: which matches the trajectory of Green's own career, from songwriter to name bandleader on radio to orchestrator and composer of movie music. By the late thirties, Green seems to have lost interest in writing popular songs.

AS GREAT AS THE SONG'S STATURE has been, there aren't as many vocal recordings as one might find of a comparable work like "Night and Day" or "My Funny Valentine." It's the melody and chords that attract the most interpreters, not the words. As "I Wanna Be Loved" ("I wanna be touched until I tingle . . .") and "I Cover the Waterfront" prove, Edward Heyman was an excellent lyricist, one of the underrated (though hardly unsung) heroes of pop love lyrics, but "Body and Soul" doesn't rate as one of his best efforts. If the song had been Heyman's work all the way through, instead of being such a mishmash, with so many lyricists having a hand in it, the words might have been as much of a classic as the music.

As it stands, the lyric includes many professionally rendered rhymes, but there are no brilliant images, no moving metaphors, no stimulating similes. There's not much of a story to it, just vague phrases describing longing and wronging, and a lot of somewhat cumbersome backward constructions ("It's you I long for"; "It's me you're wronging"; and "My life a hell you're making"—with "wreck" generally substituted for "hell" in most pop versions). Great singers have done wonders with this text—or, rather, these texts. For instance, the sentiments are general enough for Tony Bennett to be able to make them into something more cheerful than the song usually sounds. He sings as if he's longing, but also as if he feels he has every reason to believe that his longing will soon be satisfied.

Among straight-down-the-middle pop singers who've done it, there's an admirable treatment by Tony Martin. Frankie Laine also recorded it (appropriately, on a twelve-inch LP titled *Torchin'*), and it's among the more subtle, least overdone, and most listenable things this usually manic belter ever recorded. Morgana King's 1958 reading, with the verse (the "I'm lost in the dark" one), is also remarkably introspective, and is a career highlight for her. (King rerecorded the same chart thirty years later, but the original is the winner.) The oddest pop version is by Marguerite Piazza, a minor-league opera singer who went Vegas in the fifties and cut an album *Marguerite Piazza Sings Torch*. Her "B&S" sounds like Dinah Shore with more chops.

Della Reese and Dakota Staton utilized "B&S" as a means to get big and soulful. Reese, who sings it on a string album called *Softly* (I guess all things are relative), sings with her distinctive pronunciation, "I spend my days in long-GING," while Staton is scaldingly accusatory. She really lets you have it, bellowing "My life, my life, my life!" until she reaches the point where the listener feels compelled to apologize. It's also exceptionally well sung by Helen Humes.

The recordings by Billie Holiday (1940) and Frank Sinatra (1947) are of a piece: neither one is a heavy, torchy, or tortured treatment; they both succeed in being serious without being overly sentimental. Both are graced by their accompaniments. Benny Carter directed the band on Holiday's, and Bobby Hackett plays one of the greatest obbligatos in the history of the cornet (or even trumpet) on Sinatra's. The Holiday record stands out not just in the way she sings the lyrics but in those lyrics that she chooses to sing: for one thing, she goes back to "a hell you're making" instead of "a wreck," but even more astutely, she combines the best aspects of several sets of lyrics. When reaching the bridge the first time around, we hear the familiar "I can't believe it, / It's hard to conceive it . . ." and then the "My life a hell. . . ." However, after Bill Coleman's trumpet solo, Holiday returns with a whole new set of words for the bridge ("What lies before me . . .") and final *A* ("My life revolves about you . . ."). The overall result is that the words resonate more strongly as a story than they ever had before. Holiday would record the song twice more, both times in concert, in 1945 and 1956. (Perhaps following this example, Mel Tormé sang both of the most famous lyrics to the final *A* section in his 1958 reading on *Tormé*.) Sinatra, regretably, didn't readdress "B&S" in the fifties or sixties but came back to it in 1984 in an unissued master intended for his album *L.A. Is My Lady*—and it's a considered, mature performance, far better than the dismal title track on that otherwise fine package.

Helen Morgan notwithstanding, nearly all of the great vocal versions, including those by Helen Humes, Ernestine Anderson (with George Shearing), Anita O'Day, the Brazilian Lenny Andrade, and the many by Sarah Vaughan, are by jazz singers. Billy Eckstine's 1950 treatment is a highlight, not only in the development of the song but in the great singer's career. Rife with melodic and harmonic variations, it's one of the jazziest and farthest-out examples of singing that the great Mr. B. ever gave us. Betty Carter cut it in 1969 on *Finally Betty Carter* and then a year later on *At the Village Vanguard;* both treatments are live, and both place the song in the company of the similarly named "Heart and Soul," a 1938 collaboration by Frank Loesser and Hoagy Carmichael. Carter's "B&S" is almost painfully slow, and the album title *Finally* may refer to the time it takes to get through it, but it's ultimately very moving.

Sinatra was also involved in another of the great treatments of "Body and Soul," that of Ella Fitzgerald. The song had always brought out the best in her, starting with three superb live versions with rhythm-section accompaniment: 1953 in Tokyo, 1957 in Newport, and 1965 in Hamburg. In 1962, she introduced her orchestral treatment on *Ella Swings Gently with Nelson* (meaning Riddle, of course). All of these treatments are slow, sultry, and extremely bluesy, while the original 1953 taping is especially intense. By 1965, "B&S" was one of the ballad highlights of the Fitzgerald canon, but in 1967 she did it one better, appearing on Sinatra's third annual *Man and His Music* TV special, for which she reprised her Riddle orchestration. It would be hard to find two friends and fellow colossi of the pop music world who inspire, goad, cajole, and egg each other on (in their solo performances here as well as in their duets together) more than Fitzgerald and Sinatra do throughout this entire hour.

To all you blasphemers who misguidely accuse La Fitzgerald of not knowing what she was singing about or not being able to sing a ballad, I say rent this video and experience this track. Obviously inspired by the proximity of the greatest ballad singer of all time, Fitzgerald digs in and connects deeply with her soul—and ours—in such a direct, passionate manner that I doubt that even Holiday or Sinatra could do it more movingly. Johnny Green himself concurred: "I would think even though Ella Fitzgerald goes off into other spheres, she really states the song and she sings the lyric. I think maybe that's my favorite recording." (Although on other occasions Green would name Helen Morgan's and Sarah Vaughan's as his favorite, this is still high praise.) In 1960, Fitzgerald cut an album known today as *The Intimate Ella;* her rendition of "Body and Soul," particularly the 1967 TV version, deserves to be released on a collection titled *The Passionate Ella.*

FAR MORE THAN THE WORDS, the music gives a performer something to really sink his teeth into. An indication of the song's popularity amongst jazzmen can be gleaned from the massive jazz discography compiled over a lifetime by the Belgium-based Walter Bruyninckx. This is the most ambitious catalogue of jazz recordings extant, and has been published as a series of thirty or so paperbacks, as a file cabinet full of unbound sheets, and is at last gradually being issued on CD-ROM. As it happens, the first band listed in this massive work, which is an ensemble dubbed, capriciously, A Band in All Hope, has recorded only one album (extending the *infernal* pun, it's titled *Ye Who Enter Here*). And there, within the very first entry of this oceanic, Proust-sized work documenting the entirety of recorded jazz, you will find a version of "Body and Soul."

I haven't had the energy to count how many subsequent versions of "Body and Soul" appear in Bruyninckx, but between page A1, and page A514, when the listing for Louis Armstrong begins, my estimate is about forty recordings. Among those forty, we find that two excellent modern pianists, Joe Albany and Monty Alexander, have recorded the song three times each. The former played "B&S" most famously on his best-known album, *The Legendary Joe Albany,* the latter with his "Ivory and Steel" band, one of the Kingston-born keyboardist's many attempts at merging jazz with his native Jamaican music. We also find that it is the only tune that the young swing tenor saxist Harry Allen, the Australian dixieland multi-reedist Pete Allen, the great New Orleans trumpeter and vocalist Henry "Red" Allen—in three versions spread over thirty years—and TV's famous Clark Kent–lookalike Steve Allen all have in common.

As we've already touched on, it was Louis Armstrong who sold the song to jazzmen, just as he had done for "Star Dust," "I Got Rhythm," and, to venture beyond this book, "When You're Smiling," "Rockin' Chair," and many others. In fact, there aren't many titles that Armstrong recorded in his first big band sessions, from 1929 to roughly 1931, that didn't become instant standards (even the unlikely likes of "Song of the Islands"). Recorded in Los Angeles with Les Hite's orchestra, with which he was currently fronting at Frank Sebastian's Cotton Club, Armstrong's "B&S" opens somewhat on the sweet side, stating the melody on muted trumpet backed by the Lombardo-like reeds he adored. As Dan Morgenstern has noted, the capable arrangement is by Russ Morgan, then a studio trombonist and orchestrator, who would later go on to lead one of the most nondescript big bands in history.

Still, when Armstrong enters there's no mistaking that voice, particularly that telling "oh babe" he throws in after the first eight bars, and the way he attacks the last four notes, growling them out and ending with a gasp, as in "Body and soullll . . . *ah!*" Following the vocal, trombonist Luther Graven takes the first half of the bridge—the record is in E flat, so the opening of the bridge is in E natural—the only part of disc where Armstrong gets to take it easy. He then reenters with the second part of the bridge (here in D natural), and, playing glorious open horn, he ends on a dynamic high note, preceding his coda with a phrase of his own invention every bit as memorable as the original Green melody. Armstrong returned to the song in his postwar "All-Stars" phase, although the many live late-forties versions, especially the one from Boston's Symphony Hall in 1947, are disappointing in that they're inevitably features for Barney Bigard's glissando-heavy clarinet work. By 1951, fortunately, the tune had become a feature for Jack Teagarden (documented superbly from a concert in Pasadena). Better still, Armstrong himself recorded the song twice, in rapid-fire succession, on two albums in two years, *A Musical Autobiography* (1956) and *Louis Under the Stars* (1957).

In 1935, two of Armstrong's greatest heirs, Benny Goodman and Red

Allen, picked up on "B&S." Goodman's trio version comes from the first-ever Goodman small-group date, and is largely a duet by the clarinetist with pianist Teddy Wilson—Wilson plays the bridge the first time around, Goodman takes it on the second—and drummer Gene Krupa in support. Goodman's solo is especially Armstrongian, and at the same time incredibly cool, enough to suggest that he might be considered an progenitor of the postwar cool school, while Wilson's various interludes stray adventurously far from the melody. Goodman's 1938 Carnegie Hall version has the added spark of having been performed in front of a live, cheering audience and, for all of BG's alleged egomania and insecurity, on this occasion he seems to have no qualms about letting Wilson shine. On both versions, Goodman's solo is the essence of swing, particularly in the way he adds notes at times, as in the third bar when he turns a two-note phrase into a triplet and lingers on a trill between E flat and D flat, while in other cases he takes them away, as in bar seven, when he drops the "bod-" note, leaving just the "-dy and soul." Krupa's drumming is louder, faster, and more forceful in the Carnegie version (heavy on the snare), with the result that Goodman and Wilson finish earlier, leaving time for a more florid coda at the end.

After Armstrong, Red Allen seems to have been the first major instrumentalist-vocalist to both play and sing "Body and Soul," and his informal "arrangement" of the tune would be echoed in many subsequent versions. Allen starts with a guitar intro, then plays the tune in double time; unlike what happens in Armstrong's version, in this one the trumpet is more the point than the vocal, and Red is up and down and all over his horn. He ends by sweeping up to a soaring high note that's almost more Pops-like than Armstrong. Live versions have been released of Allen doing the tune in 1952 and, quite spectacularly, in 1965, at the famous *College Concert* at MIT (recorded on Impulse! records), at which Allen and Pee Wee Russell co-fronted a postmodern rhythm section featuring Steve Kuhn and Charlie Haden. On both versions, Allen sings the less common bridge ("What lies before me . . ."); however, in going for the line "My house of cards had no foundation," Henry Red makes it into "My heart was caught with no foundation." (Mel Tormé sang it in 1958 as "But now my love has no foundation.")

The classic Chu Berry–Roy Eldridge reading, made for Commodore in 1938, seems directly inspired by the Red Allen reading, a logical outgrowth as tenorist Berry was present on the 1935 Allen session. Like the Allen, the Berry-Eldridge opens with a guitar intro that eventually gives way to a hot trumpet playing the tune in swingtime. There is, however, one substantial difference: between guitar and trumpet, we have a whole chorus of Berry playing the tune on tenor, a stately ballad reading that gets kind of perky at the end of the bridge. This tempo change is quite rare in the annals of jazz; there aren't many examples of a small-group jam-session format in which the same piece is heard both as a ballad and a swinger—and, in both cases, as a danceable fox-trot all the way.

As Giddins points out, Eldridge subsequently became, after Coleman Hawkins (though beginning before Hawkins), jazz's most devoted exponent of "B&S," and many live and studio recordings exist of his various interpretations. There's an outstanding commercial transcription (a studio recording for radio use), a big band treatment from 1946, and a solo on Billie Holiday's 1940 version, to name just a few. The 1938 Berry-Eldridge reading shows that the melody had become a point of honor for tenor giants even before Coleman Hawkins—however, as we'll see, Hawkins never did exactly play the melody of "Body and Soul."

In 1940, pianist Jay McShann took six men from his Kansas City–based orchestra into a radio studio in Wichita and made a series of private transcriptions on LP. They cut seven tunes, two of them by Johnny Green—"Coquette" and a reading of "Body and Soul" that is directly indebted to Berry and Eldridge, and, indirectly, to Allen. After McShann's piano intro (substituting for the guitar), Charlie Parker plays the melody as a ballad for the first chorus before trumpeter Orville Minor swings it into double time, in the manner of Eldridge and Allen. The piece slows back down to ballad tempo at the end, like the Chu and Roy version, but one move that catches us off guard is McShann's unexpected piano coda (suggestive of Art Tatum, who in 1937 had already recorded "B&S" on the first of nearly a dozen occasions). It almost sounds as if the pianist-leader suddenly realized that there was space left on the recording acetate and hastily decided to improvise a little something to fill it up. Although this is only the second document that exists of Charlie Parker, it was neither Bird's first nor his last performance of "Body and Soul."

Between the Commodore session and the Wichita transcription, history had been made in the form of the watershed Coleman Hawkins Victor recording of 1939. Perhaps all this talk of who-heard-whom and what-influenced-what may sound speculative, but we do know that Hawkins was a fiercely competitive artist who listened to everything and "had big ears," as musicians like to say. Although away in Europe for the second half of the thirties, Hawkins was well aware that a number of younger saxmen in his own image were emerging back home, among them Ben Webster, Chu Berry, and Herschel Evans. The battle-ready Hawk couldn't wait to get home to challenge his progeny, and surely he would have heard the Berry disc of "Body and Soul." (Sadly, Evans had died earlier that year of a heart condition, before reaching the age of thirty, and Berry would die in a car crash in 1941, at age thirty-three.)

Perhaps it was because Hawkins knew that Berry had already laid down a masterful reading of "Body and Soul," one very much in the Hawkins manner, that he himself chose not to play Johnny Green's melody. He recorded "Body and Soul" for the first time on October 11, 1939, for Victor. (It was only the great tenor's second session after returning home, the first, under Lionel Hampton's leadership, paired him with Webster and Berry.) On this classic version, Hawkins and the tune are friendly for about two bars, getting along marvelously, before they unexpectedly part company. Hawk may be thinking about the tune here and there, maybe even stealing a glimpse at it, but he never looks straight at it.

This was, along with Armstrong's "West End Blues," one of the most celebrated improvisations of all time, and a key influence on the emergence of modern jazz, in that it profoundly illustrated the possibilities open for improvising on a harmonic sequence rather than a melody line, as had been the norm in jazz up until that point. Hawkins obviously was a master of harmony, one of the few horn players until then who really knew his way around the changes, and he helped lead the way from melodic to harmonic improvisation, which was to become standard practice in the modern era. But to a great extent, this solo isn't about harmony. It's about drama, grabbing the listener and pulling him in, making him follow every little twist and turn of this increasingly intense, even convoluted, improvised melody line. Hawkins knows when to get loud and when to get soft, when to back off and when to play with overwhelming intensity. The whole record is only two choruses, with Hawk getting more and more frisky, popping out through the top of his horn on the C natural section of the bridge, especially on the second time through.

Even more so than the other standout reed improvisation of that year,

Sidney Bechet's "Summertime," this was a record that everybody in the music industry had to have. It wasn't exactly a pop hit, but it became so well known that Hawkins was able to finance his own big band on the strength of it—and the band's theme song, naturally, was "Body and Soul." Most of Hawk's later performances of the tune were from the concert trail, around a dozen of which were recorded and have been made available commercially. He continued to play the first two bars as if to announce to listeners he was now going to play "Body and Soul," but each improvisation, apart from a few pet phrases, was completely fresh. One particularly exciting reading, done for Jazz at the Philharmonic in 1945 (although not released until 1998), has Hawk playing a glorious near-screeching repeated phrase in the final *A* as he winds down to the coda. There's also a kinescope of him playing the tune on European TV, shortly before his death in 1969.

Whenever Hawk brought "B&S" back into the studio, it was usually to do something different with it: in 1944, he retitled his "B&S" variations "Rainbow Mist," and included them on the second of his Apollo sessions, the same dates in which he helped introduce bebop to the world (Dizzy Gillespie, Oscar Pettiford, and Max Roach were all in the band). One of the most interesting treatments can be found on Benny Carter's classic 1961 album *Further Definitions,* for which Carter took the opening of Hawk's 1939 solo and orchestrated it for four saxes—himself, Hawkins, and two outstanding younger players, Charlie Rouse and Phil Woods. (Carter, who also led the band on Billie Holiday's 1940 version, recorded it himself on trumpet at Montreux in 1977.) In a similar vein, singer Eddie Jefferson once wrote a vocalese lyric to the original solo, which began with the line "Don't you know he's the king of saxophones. . . ." It wasn't particularly poetic (the Heyman-Sour lyrics sound like Shakespeare by comparison), but at least it was accurate. The Manhattan Transfer later adapted Jefferson's text for four voices, and added their own commentary on top of his.

There are several remarkable later variations on "B&S" which find Hawkins with maximal and minimal accompaniment. In 1956, he recorded the tune once again for RCA Victor, this time in an extended, full-blown near-symphonic orchestration by Billy Byers. The presence of strings, perhaps, inspires Hawkins to play more of the original Green melody—all of the first sixteen bars—but after the violins take the bridge and then the woodwinds grab the last eight, Hawk returns with a vengeance, digging in on the second chorus with one of his best "B&S"s ever, climaxing in a long a cappella cadenza that foreshadows Sonny Rollins (who also recorded the tune in an unaccompanied treatment).

Contrastingly, in the mid- to late forties, Hawkins made two recordings that were entirely a cappella (although strictly speaking a solo saxophone cannot be considered a cappella since the term means without any instruments at all, only the human voice) that are generally considered the first important unaccompanied horn recordings in jazz. The first of these, titled "Hawk's Variations (Parts One & Two)," was a two-sided ten-inch 78 pressed in limited quantities by the Selmer saxophone company; the second was a single-sided "Picasso," produced by Norman Granz and released on the anthology album *The Jazz Scene*. (Coincidentally, Charlie Parker had earlier made an unaccompanied recording—playing "Body and Soul" no less—but that was a private disc, not made for general release, and not heard by the public until the 1990s.)

For a while, it was purported that "Hawk's Variations" may have been a rehearsal for "Picasso," an assertion possibly supported by Granz's recollection that Hawk spent hours and hours preparing "Picasso" in the studio, working out ideas on both his tenor and a piano. However, it's currently believed that the "Variations" come from 1945 and "Picasso" from 1948. Scholar Brian Priestly believes that "Picasso" actually takes the 1931 "Prisoner of Love" as its basic harmonic point of departure, though in saying this he acknowledges that "Prisoner" is harmonically quite similar to "B&S." Dan Morgenstern feels that although "Picasso" is a free improvisation that doesn't necessarily follow any set progression, somewhere in the back of Hawk's mind, the "B&S" changes were so ingrained that "Picasso" couldn't help having a little body and/or soul in it. For example, there's something like a major to minor shift at what might be the start of each of its *A* sections. Hawkins recorded another unaccompanied piece live in Brussels in 1962, and on this performance, which was eventually titled "Dali" when the concert was issued in 1991, he sticks noticeably closer to the "B&S" changes.

As it happens, the man who was the biggest fan of Hawk's many variations on the piece was Johnny Green himself. As Green told radio interviewer Fred Hall:

> Coleman and I were good friends and you know, that recording, that treatment of "Body and Soul," is a classic and I loved it. On the

other hand, it is a jazz treatment and the very essence of jazz is improvisation; that's the heart of jazz, that's its motivation, that's its genre,
that's why it exists. So what you have on the Coleman Hawkins
record is very little of the theme and an awful lot of the variations, if
you want to use the nomenclature of the classic form of theme and
variation. It's Coleman Hawkins superimposed on Green, if you will.

On another occasion Green added, "Everything that Coleman did was
somehow or other within the pattern of the song, within the composer's
intent. If I had been a first-class jazz player on the piano, what Coleman did
on that tenor saxophone is the kind of thing that I would have done with my
own song. So I loved it from the word go. I also loved the royalties."

FOLLOWING HAWK'S EXAMINATION of Green's harmonies, "Body and
Soul" became one of the most recurrent themes in all of jazz, particularly
among saxophonists. Charlie Parker cut it four times privately before
anyone had ever heard of him: in an unaccompanied solo in 1940, on
which it is preceded by a set of variations on "Honeysuckle Rose" (caus-
ing some scholars to refer to this disc as "Honey and Body"), with a gra-
cious nod to Hawkins in his opening two bars; with Jay McShann in
Wichita; with guitar, drums, and three tempo changes in Kansas City, in
1942; playing tenor with a different guitarist in a hotel room in Chicago
in 1943. Parker never recorded the piece officially, but it turns up on live
recordings he made with Howard McGhee's quintet in Los Angeles in
1947, playing behind a goofy vocalist in Chicago in 1950, and later that
year leading a group of Swedish all-stars on a jam session. References to
Hawkins and Berry abound in nearly all these performances.

However, Parker's example notwithstanding, in the forties and fifties
the tune was less the property of boppers than of big-toned tenors in the
Hawkins mold: Don Byas, Ben Webster (under drummer Cozy Cole's
leadership in 1944), Charlie Ventura (with Gene Krupa), Houston Person
(with Dakota Staton), Buddy Tate, George Kelly (taped live at a Highlights in Jazz concert), while Budd Johnson cut a superlative reading in
the Webster tradition with Earl Hines's Quartet on *Live at Johnnie's,* taped
in Lausanne in 1968. It's also been played by such early and late modernist tenor titans as James Moody, Dexter Gordon (who left behind
many outstanding readings, including one on a Danish concert issued

on an album entitled *Body and Soul,* and a rather harsh, albeit exciting treatment from the Keystone Korner in 1978), Sonny Stitt, and Teddy Edwards, as well as the two reigning reed giants of the post-bop era, Sonny Rollins and John Coltrane.

Sam Butera, the great Italian tenor whose work straddles the fence between jazz and rhythm and blues (he's best known for his work with Louis Prima), played it on a live date in New Orleans with Paul Gayten's band in 1951. Privately recorded (in rather low-fi) and recently issued on CD, the date also features Little Jimmy Scott; it would have been even greater had Scott and Butera performed together on this one track. Other tenors who took "B&S" into other genres include Stan Getz (in 1952, very early in his career); Zoot Sims and Al Cohn on their last major album together, the 1973 *Body and Soul;* Warne Marsh with *The Legendary Pianist* Joe Albany in 1957; and Ted Brown with Lee Konitz, in 1999. Paul Gonsalves cut it with one of jazz's major composer-pianist-arranger-bandleaders—no, in this instance I don't mean Duke Ellington but John Lewis. There's also an impassioned reading by Serge Chaloff, who plays baritone but comes more out of the tenor tradition.

The 1944 premiere concert of the Jazz at the Philharmonic series includes a ten-minute "Body and Soul" that spotlights a duo-tenor homage to Hawkins in the persons of Illinois Jacquet and Jack McVea. (Concert producers would soon conclude that it was better to have each musician play his own tune separately in a ballad medley rather than have all the guys try and get warm and romantic on the same melody.) Even beyond the saxists, the rest of the JATP ensemble has plenty of stars, starting with J. J. Johnson. Already displaying the tone and technique that would make him the first great trombonist of the modern age, JJJ here exhibits phrases that derive more from Hawkins than from bebop. The rhythm section features two jazz virtuosi who would become better known as pop stars, Les Paul and Nat King Cole.

Paul's electric guitar solo comes out of the guitar tradition of "B&S," which properly begins with Django Reinhardt's two versions and continues up through Wes Montgomery's 1960 recording on bass guitar. Despite the homage to Django (who never quite stated the melody on either of his recordings of "B&S," a '37 with Stephane Grappelli and a '38 with Larry Adler), Paul still sounds as if he's goofing around.

Cole is another matter: even though Art Tatum and Teddy Wilson had already recorded multiple versions of "B&S," Cole was probably the

pianist most identified with it. By 1942, when he recorded in a trio format with Lester Young and bassist Red Callender, he had already been
developing his celebrated chorus of variations on "Body and Soul," and
this was the first of four recordings he would make of this famous routine
between then and 1946. Cole would also record the solo with his own
King Cole Trio, for a Capitol commercial 78 (from earlier in 1944) and
again for a Capitol transcription in 1946. The Cole solo, as heard on all
four recordings, is a combination of variations and quotations from various pieces of music as far afield as "The Peanut Vendor," *Rhapsody in Blue,*
and Grieg's "Hall of the Mountain King."

Cole follows a predetermined but loose routine, and the only section
of the chorus that stays absolutely the same is the second *A* section,
which, in all four versions, is a jazz treatment of "Mountain King"; Cole
could have gleaned it either directly from Grieg or from Fats Waller, who
quoted it liberally in "The Viper's Drag." On the record with Young, Cole
includes a snatch from "My Kinda Love" in the first *A,* which is not heard
in the opening *A* sections of the other three versions. Also on the Young-
Cole, the bridge of the second chorus becomes Callender's bass solo. The
bridge on the 1944 Capitol is a set of bluesy original phrases in which
Cole really leaps on the modulations. Cole's JATP bridge contains a quote
from *Rhapsody in Blue,* whereas the 1946 trio bridge is all block chords
and octave playing—not to mention "Peanut Vendor." The final *A*s of all
four are different: with Young, it's all original; on the 1944 King Cole
Trio disc, the King takes a parting shot at the Green melody before making his bow; with JATP he throws in a little bit of "Lullaby in Rhythm"
and then "Humoresque." (Cole had actually recorded the Dvořák composition under the title "Mabel, Mabel." If you want to know how
"Humoresque" became "Mabel, Mabel," you'll have to ask lyricist Ervin
Drake.) The 1946 retains "Lullaby" and then ends on a snippet of "London Bridge."

The Lester Young–Nat Cole version is doubly remarkable. First, for
Young, in the very fact that for his first-ever recording under his own
name, he takes on Hawkins's signature tune. Second, for Cole, his rendition here is much more spontaneous and less of a set piece than the three
later versions. As Loren Schoenberg points out, Cole is considerably
more playful here and harmonically and metrically further out—even
turning the beat completely around at one point.

Cole's two versions with his trio are especially noteworthy: playing together night after night for a decade, Cole and guitarist and costar Oscar Moore developed a marvelous series of intricate and involved routines on all manner of material, both originals and standards. Yet their "B&S" chart is simplicity itself. Moore plays a wonderful solo that places him somewhere in Reinhardt's league as far as class is concerned, though not in his specific style, and then Cole comes along and plays a solo that's even better. And that's it, that's the whole breakdown. When you have solo improvisations, or even semi-set routines, that are this strong, you don't need fancy charts. More usually, though, Cole's trio arrangements were a combination of both. In 1954 and then again in April 1965 (a month after Cole's death), Moore and onetime KC3 bassist Joe Comfort recorded "B&S" as part of a tribute album in the pianist's memory; although these two recordings used two of the best jazz pianists on the West Coast, Carl Perkins and Gerald Wiggins, the remakes without Cole are surprisingly lifeless. There was just no substituting for the King. In the same vein, guitarist Mary Osborne recorded "B&S" very much in the Oscar Moore manner.

The interplay between Art Tatum and Cole in terms of "B&S" is also fascinating: Tatum recorded the song for the first time in 1937 and would document over a dozen versions between then and 1955, when he laid it down with Lionel Hampton for the set eventually released as *The Tatum Group Masterpieces*. Of all the master pianist's many recordings of the song, the strongest is probably his twelve-inch trio version of May 1944, four months after the Cole trio version on Capitol. Cole had popularized the trio format of piano, bass, and guitar to the point where Tatum adopted it for a time. Tatum also borrows Cole's rough outline, though said outline is very rough; it's essentially just guitar solo (Tiny Grimes, who quotes "I Got Plenty o' Nuthin'") and then piano solo.

Like Cole, Tatum quotes "Humoresque" in the last *A*. Even though the Cole disc was recorded first, the interpolation of the Dvořák melody was more likely Cole's homage to Tatum than the other way around. Tatum (1909–1956) exerted a profound influence on Cole (1919–1965)—not to mention virtually every pianist ever to work in the jazz idiom—and "Humoresque" had long been a Tatum signature piece. The extended playing time (four and a half minutes) of Tatum's May '44 disc allowed him to throw in something Cole couldn't: before the piano solo gets under way, the whole deal goes from ballad time to double time in absolutely no time, and it's one of the hardest-swinging statements of Tatum's career. When pianist Al Haig recorded "B&S" with his trio in 1954, he played it like a kinder, gentler Tatum, and he also threw in the "Humoresque" quote, obviously as a nod to both Cole and Tatum. Charles Mingus did the same when he incorporated a variation on "B&S" into his long-form work *Epitaph*. (Tatum's most irreverent quote on the 1944 disc is "Oh Where, oh Where, Has My Little Dog Gone?")

As we've mentioned, the Tatum disc was a twelve-inch 78, which provided extra (well, for *that* era, anyway) playing time, and some of this was allocated to bassist Slam Stewart, who gets a half-chorus solo (bridge and final *A*) of his own. In 1944, Stewart was following the lead of Jimmy Blanton, who in 1940 had done for bassists what Coleman Hawkins had done for saxophonists with "Body and Soul" the year before. In a duo recording made with Duke Ellington, in whose band the great bassist was playing, Blanton announced that the jazz bass had now come into its own and was capable of sustaining extended solo statements. In 1948, Charles Mingus, obviously inspired by Blanton and Stewart, orchestrated "B&S" as a feature for himself with Lionel Hampton's orchestra (not commercially recorded but preserved on an aircheck), decades before he would work in a reference to it in *Epitaph*. In 1977, a quartet co-led by Al Haig and bassist Jamil Nasser included "B&S" on an album titled *Expressly Ellington*. Obviously, Nasser, like Mingus, was taking his lead from Blanton and Ellington in utilizing "B&S" as a bass feature. Although not an Ellington song, Haig and Nasser apparently considered "B&S" part of the Ellington experience.

In the twenty years or so after Hawkins, "Body and Soul" remained most strongly identified with the tenor saxophone. However, between Cole, Tatum, and Earl Hines, who cut a strong solo reading in 1940, a tradition was established for making it a showcase for keyboard virtuosity, and this approach has come to dominate how the tune has been heard in the last thirty or so years. In recent times there have more versions of "Body and Soul" that focus on the piano—solos, pairings with other instruments, and four-handed keyboard matchups—than in any other format.

Just among strictly solo versions, there are two in the series of Maybeck Recital Hall recordings presented by Concord Records: Gerry Wiggins, who features Tatum-like ruminations with lots of tempo changes, and Jim McNeely, who drifts into "Mountain King" in a nod to Nat Cole. Thelonious Monk's 1962 solo encapsulates the whole history of jazz piano, from stride to whatever it is that lies beyond bop. (Monk's treatment is considerably stronger than Bud Powell's disappointing trio recording from 1950.)

Like Tatum and Cole, Oscar Peterson recorded it many times, most notably in two very different, yet equally personal, readings. In 1951, early in his American career, Peterson cut an extended improvisation with his quartet that opens with Barney Kessel stating the melody (in the Cole and Tatum tradition of starting with guitar) before Peterson takes over with a long set of variations. There's also a 1954 quartet version with Herb Ellis instead of Kessel, and a 1957 session where Peterson plays behind violinist Stuff Smith. In 1967, he recorded a solo treatment at the home of a friend in Germany that was originally released only privately. Like Ella Fitzgerald, Peterson used "Body and Soul" as a vehicle to reveal his more intimate side.

Erroll Garner laid down a typically romping and stomping trio treatment, and Dorothy Donegan recorded a version of "B&S" that suggests Garner on Benzedrine. By the time I saw Donegan, late in her life, she had gone off the deep end and her performances seemed as if she was receiving signals from Mars more than playing jazz on the piano. But in 1958 she still had it, and her Capitol version of "B&S" frantically syncopates the tune, splitting every beat in two and flying into "Airmail Special."

The famous Dave Brubeck Quartet with Paul Desmond doesn't seem to have recorded the song, but each of them did it individually, the altoist on his string album, *Desmond Blue*. Brubeck recorded it with his trio, and while he isn't exactly the most light-fingered of pianists, he certainly makes those notes move, no matter how heavy they may be. (Coincidentally, "B&S" leads off Brubeck's latest CD, *Double Live from the USA & UK*, an outstanding live concert treatment with his current quartet featuring Bobby Militello on alto, which crossed my doorstep just as this was being written.) Other bop-based masters who've addressed the tune include Hampton Hawes, whose treatment has something of a swing-era feel à la Hines, and Ronnie Mathews, who opens by cleverly recycling a snatch from the bridge as an introduction. There's also a fine piano and alto duo by George Cables and Art Pepper from 1982. Pepper had recorded "B&S" twenty-five years earlier in a sweet-toned statement reminiscent of the way Parker played with strings. The later duet, made about two months before Pepper died, is much more personal.

Hank Jones and Barry Harris recorded it individually, and Harris also played it with Eddie Jefferson and as an extended two-piano treatment with Kenny Barron. Harris and Barron phrase the tune, which they recorded live (on *Confirmation*), in a way that's florid in a rhythmically spare kind of way that allows us to focus more closely on their melodic embellishments (to the obvious delight of the crowd). Harris takes the first chorus himself, proving the worth of the track even before Barron joins in and makes it even better. They're not just doodling, they're really getting into the meat of "Body and Soul," exploring it thoroughly. Harris ends his segment by slipping into his Thelonious Monk mode with a few "loco-motive"–style repeated notes. Likewise, Fred Hersch's treatment is at once probing and playful. His phrasing of the melody is, as we'd expect for this most lyrical of contemporary keyboardists, very introspective and withdrawn. The improvisation is fairly free, linked only to the chords in a very subtle way, and the lines he constructs are almost classical-sounding. It's very much a concert performance, while at the same time the whole thing is very tender and intimate.

THE LESTER YOUNG–Nat Cole recording is noteworthy obviously for more than just for the piano solo. Young's tenor statement, with all his graceful and laconic majesty, is no less masterful than that of Hawkins, and Prez does almost as well in a live version of "B&S" from Chicago in 1950. His is a far more relaxed, yet no less dramatic, affair than any of the Hawk's heavier and more operatically intense run-throughs. The 1950 treatment is three and a half minutes of Prez all the way through, with no other solos, and he knocks us completely off balance when he throws in a deep, bellowing, bone-shaking low B flat (the kind of sound Sonny Rollins later got when playing a calypso) as he approaches the coda.

Young was also present, but not actually playing, sadly, when Sarah Vaughan performed the song at a Town Hall concert in 1947, released on CD in 1996. This would be the second of seven documented performances of "B&S" by the Divine One, the others being 1946 for the Musicraft label, 1954 for Mercury (on *Swingin' Easy*, her first album for that label), 1978 for Pablo (a duet with Ray Brown), in addition to three other live and radio versions. One aircheck, from Birdland in 1953, has Vaughan showing her sassy side and being especially playful with the melody, taking it to all kinds of crazy places and getting into some very strange abstractions on the bridge. To listen to all seven of them in a row is to hear one of the most well-appointed sets of chops in all music growing ever lusher, ever fuller, ever richer over the decades.

All of Vaughan's "B&S"'s have her tinkering with the intervals and liberally reshaping the melody. Which makes it all the more surprising that Green named her as one of his favorite interpreters. "She won the contest at the Apollo Theater," he recalled. "That's how she got her start, up in Harlem. And the song she sang to win that contest was 'Body and Soul,' so there's a warm affinity between Sarah and me." As a musician of solid taste, Green knew enough to appreciate equally Ella Fitzgerald, Coleman Hawkins, Helen Morgan, and Sarah Vaughan. What is surprising is that in that same interview, Green reveals that he doesn't regard "Body and Soul" as his favorite among his own songs. He bestows that honor, instead, on the very obscure "Song of Raintree County," a good movie theme song that had the misfortune to be linked with a dreadful Civil War epic, starring Elizabeth Taylor, which quickly flopped.

THE ARTISTS WHO DID the most for "Body and Soul"—and vice versa— in the final decades of the twentieth century were Lee Konitz, instrumentally, and Tony Bennett, vocally. Konitz recorded it at least five times in the nineties—I say "at least," because not only do I make no claim to have heard all of the great alto saxist's recordings of this or any other era, but also because Konitz is so prolific, I can't even imagine a professional discographer keeping up with him. "B&S" turns up as a duet with Peggy Stern on *Lee Wise,* done in Denmark in 1992, then there are two performances of it (the first more melodic, the second more pointilistic) on *Rhapsody II,* both in a trio setting with pianist Kenny Werner and Belgian harmonicat Toots Thielemans, taped the following year. In 1997, Konitz returned (as if he had ever been away) to the tune in a slightly more conventional trio with Charlie Haden and Brad Mehldau on *Another Shade of Blue.* Then, in 1999, he recorded *The Sound of Surprise* (a phrase to describe jazz that has been credited to Martin Williams), which was billed as the first album of the great saxist's long career to consist entirely of his own compositions. However, Konitz's own tunes are generally based closely on standards, and he makes no bones about his sources of inspiration—for instance, the "original" titled "Soddy and Bowl." Even without the title, it would have been easy to identify the source, because while Konitz and company (including the fine, little-known tenor Ted Brown and the fine, well-known guitarist John Abercrombie) don't exactly play the melody, they do stay within the song's general orbit. Unlike Percy Heath's "In New York," this is not a new tune based on "B&S" changes, but rather a decapitated set of improvised variations. Taken together, these five tracks come to roughly fifty minutes of improvisations on Green's chords.

When Tony Bennett sang "Body and Soul," he typically tapped his head on the line "It's hard to conceive it," as if to illustrate the act of thinking. After featuring "B&S" for many years in concert, Bennett finally recorded his treatment in 1989 on *Astoria* with a sumptuous string orchestration by Jorge Calendrelli. Like Sarah Vaughan and Lester Young, Bennett continually paraphrases the tune, reinventing it as he goes along, even to the point of changing the whole intention of the final four notes. He now makes them go up instead of down, ending on a high A flat, although this melodic motion is somewhat obscured by one of the singer's dramatic "belt" endings, in which he climbs slowly up, as if to suggest a jet airplane taking off. Coincidentally, Bennett once told me it was a lifelong dream of his to do an album with Lee Konitz—just voice, alto, and rhythm. If they ever do it, I don't doubt that the first cut will be "Body and Soul."

The Bennett recording makes a fitting coda to the "Body and Soul" saga, because shortly after he had finished his take on the song, one of the engineers in the studio got his attention. "By the way," he said, "did you hear? Johnny Green died today." That was May 15, 1989. Green's body may be in the ground somewhere, but his soul endures.

BONUS TRACKS

Most Surprising Version

John Lewis, pianist and mastermind behind the Modern Jazz Quartet, is generally regarded as one of the leading advocates of prewritten form in jazz. However, on his 1960 album *The World of Jazz,* Lewis presented a fifteen-minute super-version of "Body and Soul" with no form at all. It can't even rightly be described as a jam session, it's just three marathon solos on the tune, by Ellington tenorist Paul Gonsalves, modern guitar genius Jim Hall, and Boston trumpeter Herb Pomeroy. Gonsalves, who perfected the art of the extended solo on "Diminuendo and Crescendo in Blue," is the star here, playing on and on without ever seeming to run out of energy or ideas, yet Hall and Pomeroy are no slouches either. Not only does Lewis decline to assert himself as leader or orchestrator, this most reticent of stars doesn't even feature his own piano, except for a very brief coda at the end. There's plenty of body here, and no shortage of soul either.

Dueling Violins

Stephane Grappelli first played the tune with partner Django Reinhardt and their Quintet of the Hot Club of France in 1937, and the twosome readdressed it a year later behind harmonica star Larry Adler, and then again in Rome in 1949 on their final session together. Grappelli's other (non-Django) versions are all notable for their collaborations: with his quartet featuring George Shearing in 1941; in a duet with Kenny Clarke, on piano instead of his customary drums, in 1970; and in one session in 1972 he cut it twice, once with French guitarist Jimmy Gourley and once with French jazz organist Eddy Louiss (both takes with Clarke on drums). Another outstanding, extrovert swing violinist, Stuff Smith, recorded "B&S" with Oscar Peterson in 1957, an extended ten-minute improvisation not issued until 1994. Still, the grabbin'est hot violin version is Joe Venuti's quintet treatment of the mid-fifties (with Mundell Lowe, Buddy Weed, Ed Shaughnessy, and Jack Lesberg). This starts out like the warmest and most romantic ballad treatment you ever heard, but soon Venuti starts swinging like a demon, with so much vigor that he threatens to reduce the whole place to a pile of rubble and ravioli.

The Tenor Tradition Is Alive and Well

Nineteen seventy-eight may seem like a long time ago, but it's the relatively recent past as far as the tenor tradition of "Body and Soul" is concerned. That's the year Joe Farrell cut "B&S" (available on a 1997 Galaxy CD, *Ballads by Five*), a doubly amazing performance in that this short-lived player spent much of his career doing jazz-rock and other forms of fusion. Perhaps he laid down this virtuoso performance to show the world that he could play the hell out of a standard when he wanted to: the major part of the track is a conventional albeit excellent jazz treatment of the melody, but it's the way Farrell begins and ends that remains in our memory. He opens the piece with what can only be described as the grandfather of all a cappella cadenzas, the a cappella cadenza from hell, the a cappella cadenza of the gods. He seems to be playing all the notes in every chord all at once, not just the chords that Green used in the song but every chord ever written by anyone.

The other most unlikely tenor of the times to interpret "B&S" is David Murray, generally thought of as a postmodernist whom one would not expect to hear playing any standard. Yet Murray has recorded it at least twice. The second time, with his quartet on a 1993 album titled *Body and Soul,* isn't at all bad as far as the leader's own playing is concerned; the only thing that drags it down is vocalist Taana Running, whose singing is fine but whose decision to sing an entirely new set of lyrics to this venerable old tune is, to say the least, questionable. It's on Murray's 1990 "Body and Soul" that his passion for the jazz tradition becomes palpable. Recorded in Barcelona, it's a duet with local bop piano star George Arvantis on a CD with the unwieldy title of *George Arvantis Presents . . . The Ballad Artistry of . . . David Murray—Tea for Two.* "B&S" marks its centerpiece and longest track (nearly thirteen minutes) and finds Murray exploring all the nooks and crannies of the melody in a kind of Ben Webster–Don Byas big-toned tenor vein. Knowing his penchant for outside playing, we keep expecting Murray to get goofy and start squeaking and squawking. But, no. He gets frightfully abstract, and does pop into the mysterious notes above high F natural (the so-called false fingerings used to produce notes that aren't properly on the horn), but he never leaves the chords behind. It's a brilliant solo (Arvantis, who takes a couple of choruses in the center, doesn't do badly either), filled with Hawkish arpeggios and the kind of lovingly rendered ornamentation used in both the swing and the bop eras. It's also a great blindfold test, and proof that "Body and Soul" lives on.

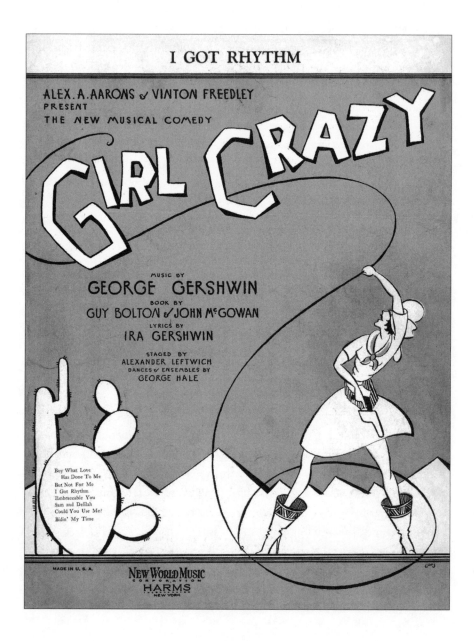

I GOT RHYTHM (1930)

music by George Gershwin

words by Ira Gershwin

Gershwin's appetite for innovation was insatiable. One evening, upon learning that "Stuff" Smith, the phenomenal "hot" violinist, was perform-ing with his band at the Onyx Club at 53rd Street [actually, 52nd Street] in New York, we took off to hear them. Soon after a waiter had placed us at our table, "Stuff" and his orchestra went into a maze of intriguing and intricate convolutions of sounds and rhythms. When they finished, "Stuff" came over to greet a puzzled George, who asked them what they had been playing. "Why, Mr. Gershwin," he chuckled, "don't you recognize 'I Got Rhythm'?"

——KAY HALLE, socialite, writer, and longtime friend of George Gershwin (from *Gershwin Remembered*, Ed Jablonski, ed.)

"IT CANNOT BE MERE COINCIDENCE that when jazz and popular song parted company, in the 1960s," the British writer Dave Gelly has observed, "they both degenerated into pretentiousness and absurdity." The judgment may be severe, but Gelly does have a point. Still, I find it more productive to focus on a place and time in which the interests of jazz, the popular song, and musical theater all coalesced into a single spectacular event. A prime example occurred with the opening of *Girl Crazy,* produced by Alex Aarons and Vinton Freedley and with a score by George and Ira Gershwin, on October 14, 1930. That night two of its cast members, Ginger Rogers and Ethel Merman, became stars, *Girl Crazy* itself became a classic American show (to be filmed by Hollywood no less than three times, and very successfully revived on Broadway, in a much-altered form, in 1992), and at least eight of its songs became hits, a few even becoming classics. And with "I Got Rhythm," a great moment in the history of American song could be said to have occurred.

It was Ethel Merman who, at the climax of the first act, introduced "I Got Rhythm," with all the subtlety of a tornado descending on a trailer park. A few minutes earlier, she had come out and sung "Sam and Delilah." "The audience yelped with surprise and pleasure," she later recalled. "To be honest, I thought my garter had snapped or something." Then, at the close of act one, she lunged into "I Got Rhythm," and the crowd's mood shifted from mere "surprise and pleasure" to total hysteria. When Merman finished the first chorus, instead of reprising the melody for a second time through, she simply belted a single note (a high C) for an entire thirty-two-bar chorus—or so the legend goes. The show was officially stopped, and both a great standard and a great star had been born.

But, as I have suggested above, this wasn't a major event for show music only but for jazz as well. The Gershwins had insisted on using a genuine jazz orchestra in the pit, and to that end had hired Red Nichols, the ambitious trumpeter and bandleader (who had already fulfilled this function on their well-titled *Strike Up the Band*), and he put together a doozy: among the players were Benny Goodman, Gene Krupa, Jimmy Dorsey, and Glenn Miller, all of whom would be superstar leaders, far eclipsing Nichols, within a few years. Less than a week later, the Nichols orchestra (still being billed as the "Five Pennies," a moniker which for the previous few years had seriously understated the size of the ensemble), recorded what was surely the first of an uncountable number of jazz treatments of "I Got Rhythm." Virtually all the sidemen listed above would be returning to this song again and again, for the rest of their lives. At the millennium, it's impossible to imagine one composer writing material for, say, both Bernadette Peters and David Murray, but on October 14, 1930, you could summarize the best of jazz, Broadway, and the popular song in a single word: Gershwin.

IN A SENSE, *Girl Crazy* was a follow-up to *Whoopee,* a Ziegfeld musical of 1928 (with a score by Walter Donaldson), in that the plots of both shows involved depositing an unlikely, comic leading man in the wild and woolly West: in *Whoopee,* it's a slightly effeminate and hypochondriacal Eddie

Cantor; in *Girl Crazy,* the lead is one "Danny Churchill," a Broadway playboy, skirt-chaser, and irrepressible tippler. (Dudley Moore, doing his *Arthur* shtick, would have made a good choice for an eighties revival.) His dad forces him to go West to an all-male town to get his mind off women, but he nonetheless manages to find the only female in the county and get next to her. Ginger Rogers (in only her second show) was the female lead in 1930; and Judy Garland, playing a character named "Ginger," would embody the role in the best of the three film versions. Originally, Bert Lahr was set to play the comedy lead, but he was reluctant to leave *Flying High,* his hit show that had opened in March and was still running in October. (Coincidentally, Kate Smith, Lahr's long-suffering costar in *Flying High,* would be one of the first singers to record "I Got Rhythm.")

Whoopee is also worth mentioning because Gershwin had been Ziegfeld's first choice, back in the spring of 1928, to write its score, but Gershwin was too busy at the time composing *Treasure Girl* for Gertrude Lawrence. But George promised "Ziggy" that he would work on another project for him. Ziegfeld had an idea about adapting a 1918 play titled *East Is West* into a musical, and put the Gershwin brothers to work on the songs. Then he decided that this particular property would be too expensive to mount, so he dropped the whole project, but not before George and Ira had written half the score, including a little something called "Embraceable You." The brothers didn't fret, though, because shows and songs were so interchangeable in those pre-*Oklahoma!* days that they knew they could always find an agreeable spot for a good song.

In fact, the Gershwins were able to place a number of the *East Is West* songs in *Girl Crazy,* the show they started working on in the spring of 1930 for Freedley and Aarons. Around that time, Ginger Rogers, already cast as the show's ingenue, happened to catch Ethel Merman in a vaudeville theater in White Plains. Impressed, Rogers recommended "the girl from White Plains" to Vinton Freedley. The producer, who needed a second female singer for *Girl Crazy,* took the time to check out Merman, who was already playing some of the top houses in vaudeville, and brought the twenty-two-year-old former stenographer in to sing for George at his splendiferous penthouse apartment on Riverside Drive.

It would be nice to report that at his first hearing of the soon-to-be-famous Merman choppers, the Gershwins were so impressed by her overwhelming clarity, energy, and projection that they were immediately inspired to write "I Got Rhythm." But, no; Merman later reported that Gershwin had all three of her numbers ready at that first interview, "Sam and Delilah," "What Love Has Done to Me," and "I Got Rhythm." Indeed, "Rhythm" actually goes back two years earlier: when George had been working on *East Is West,* he thought about writing a love song in which the melody went up and down the pentatonic scale (roughly F-G-Bb-C), which is somewhat similar to the melody one gets out of just playing on the black keys on the piano (C#-D#-F#-G#). At some point between *East Is West* and *Girl Crazy,* this pentatonic, black-key ballad melody was transformed into "I Got Rhythm," the most celebrated rhythm song of all time.

It's not known if Ira had written any lyrics for it during its love-song phase. It is known, however, that the older brother had a dickens of a time finding the right words for the up-tempo incantation of the melody. By this point, the tune had settled into its familiar pattern: four bright, staccato lines—more like bursts—for each *A* section. Early on, Ira seems to have hit on the brilliant idea of leaving the fourth line out of the rhyme scheme. However, in the beginning he was trying to rhyme all of the first three lines in a complicated triple-rhyme scheme. When asked years later how that sounded, he ad-libbed the following as a demonstration:

> *Roly-poly*
> *Eating slowly*
> *Ravioli*
> *Better watch your diet or bust.*

In some accounts, this piece of poetry is described as a "dummy lyric," a little bit of nonsense used by Ira Gershwin, who had a hard time reading musical notation, to help him remember the tune. (Susannah McCorkle tells the story and sings this lyric in her Gershwin album.) Ira was aware that he hadn't yet come up with the right syllables to allow the notes to "throw their weight around." The rhymes, he felt, gave the song a "jingly, Mother Goose quality."

The Gershwins also decided to make the song ever more staccato, expressing its message in short words, short phrases, and short ideas that rarely went on beyond three or four words, and soon enough they decided that rhymes in general were too hoity-toity to work in this context. Eventually, they did away with the rhymes altogether for the chorus except for "mind him" and "find him" in the bridge. As Ira later wrote, "Though there was nothing remarkable in this, it was a bit daring for me, who usually depended on rhyme insurance." The finished text would also eschew conventional rules of proper grammar for a slanguage all the Gershwins' own.

Ira must have felt that he had struck pay dirt when he came up with the phrase, "Who could ask for anything more?" (It became a TV commercial jingle in the nineties.) He used it four times in the song, once at the end of each of the first two *A* sections, and twice at the end of the third. The brothers toyed with the notion of titling the tune "Who Could Ask for Anything More?" but they soon chucked that option, since the phrase Ira had come up with for the first line, "I Got Rhythm," was so powerful, it simply had to be the title. But "I Got Rhythm" wasn't just an opening line or even a song title; it was a statement of purpose, a rallying cry, a declaration of everything that the Gershwins, and for that matter, all of American music, were about.

And when George Gershwin heard Merman singing in his apartment, he knew he had the perfect voice for the song. "I'll never forget the opening night," the composer said four years later. "I got a real thrill out of the audience's reaction to Ethel Merman singing 'I Got Rhythm.' " Merman herself recollected, "As I went into the second chorus, I held a note for 16 bars while the orchestra played the melodic line—a big tooty thing" (perhaps not the thirty-two bars of legend, but still one hell of a note). Unfortunately, she didn't get the opportunity to make a commercial recording of "Rhythm" until 1947, although there's an early location film clip of her singing it around 1931 live at a benefit in a New York theater. By the time of the 1947 Decca, which opens with a cymbal pattern, rather like a swing band, Merman was holding her big tooty notes for only six bars (in the second chorus). In all three *A* sections, the orchestra plays the melody to the first three lines while she holds the note, going verbal again only to sing "Who could ask for anything more?" on the fourth line. In 1961, Merman rerecorded "Rhythm" in the company of Frank Sinatra's longtime collaborator Billy May for Sinatra's own label, Reprise Records. Merman does her set routine, and May does his usual stuff, at once whimsical and hard-swinging, and somehow between the two of them, it works.

Merman's account of opening night continued: "By the time I held that note for four bars, the audience was applauding. It seemed to do something to them. Not because it was sweet or beautiful, but because it was exciting." In fact, in Merman's hands the song might well have been called "I Got Excitement." For her, as for most Broadway singers—both the belters, of whom Merman was by far the most powerful, and the more romantic types—it was always more about energy than rhythm. That's why so many musical comedy divas, such as Judy Garland (in the 1943 film) and Mary Martin (in Columbia's 1952 studio cast recording), have been able to put "Rhythm" over so convincingly, even though rhythm is not their strongest point.

When one considers the musical makeup of "I Got Rhythm," the song seems predestined to become a jazz classic; Gershwin, an improviser himself, almost seems to have designed it as a template for improvisation and variation. The structure of the song is supremely modular, being entirely built up in two-bar patterns that form a comfortable springboard for all manner of interpretations. The melody, published in B flat, is basically variations on a four-note progression: over two bars, we go up from F to G to B flat to C (skipping A); then for the next two bars, we do the same thing in reverse (C to B flat to G to F). The third set of two bars reiterates the first two, and then the last two bars offer a wholly new musical phrase that jumps around between the high E flat, D, and C before concluding on the tonic, B flat.

Syncopation and swing are, even now, difficult concepts to write into a piece of sheet music, and they were more so in Gershwin's day. He doesn't write in triplets, as many composers do when trying to notate swing, but he does use a lot of dotted notes, and what's more, he begins each *A* section on a rest—which here creates a kind of jazzy pause—before leaping in with the staccato melody. The bridge is practically pure rhythm, with almost no melody to speak of: for the first two bars, D is repeated three times, followed by a sustained E natural, then repeated again three times, dropping down to a held G. The remaining four bars use the same pattern down one step, with one variation: three short C's, then a long D, and, lastly, three short C's followed by a long C.

The central melody may be catchy, but it takes a backseat to the rhythm; the tune might even be described as pure rhythm. Essentially, we have the same sequence of notes over and over, and the important thing is not how they're ordered or the intervals between them, but the pure rhythm of the notes, how long they're held and where they're cut off. "I

Got Rhythm" is generally held up as a perfect example of Tin Pan Alley construction, being thirty-two bars in the *A-A-B-A* form. If you want to be picky, it's actually thirty-four bars, since the final line ("Who could ask for anything more?") is supposed to be stated twice, but it's not always performed that way.

The song also has a verse, with the unusual length of twenty-four bars, which is performed almost exclusively in musical-comedy contexts (as by Merman, Garland, and Martin, and by Ella Fitzgerald in her *Gershwin Songbook*). The verse is comparatively rubato, although it can be said to possess more conventional melody than most verses. It sets up the refrain like a straight line before a punchline: first unfunny, then funny—or, as in this case, first slow and in a minor key, then fast and in a major key. The verse stays in minor until about two thirds of the way through, changing into major on the words "I'm chipper." (Where did Ira get that? Was he being deliberately Brit, or is that something Americans used to say back in 1930?) The minor section uses a lot of D sharps, then after our last high D sharp, there's a rest before we drop down an octave and change to a low D natural, and the D sharps are replaced by D naturals for the remainder of the verse (the major section).

The melody of the refrain is irresistible and the lyrics are a supremely witty display of slanguage (Ira had to endure stick-in-the-muds who insisted on correcting the "I Got" even as they did "S'Wonderful"). Yet it's the harmonies that have done the most to attract musicians to this song. Like most popular tunes, "I Got Rhythm" uses the II, V, and I chords; yet it's not the chords themselves, but rather the specific way these harmonies are laid out that became the basis for so many jazz "heads."

The first bar of each central refrain (each *A* section) is always the I chord, the second bar always goes from II to V. The third and fourth repeat the same pattern (I in bar 3, II and V in bar 4). Bars 5 and 6 continue the pattern, although the sixth bar spices things up a little with some extra chords. Bar 7 ("ask for anything . . .") moves between I and V, and then the last bar to each section essentially gives us one note (the tonic, B flat) and one word ("more").

The simple, playful melody and well-constructed chord sequence also seem designed to encourage improvisation. By beginning and ending on the I chord, Gershwin makes the song, in harmonic terms, feel more like a blues. Indeed, some variations on "Rhythm," like the King Cole Trio's "Hit That Jive, Jack," emphasize the bluesier aspects of this set of changes. Most popular ballads start someplace harmonically and then go someplace else, giving an impression of harmonic ambiguity, leaving things incomplete and unresolved. But by ending where he began, Gershwin gives the piece a feeling of resolution, and as a framework for improvisation the piece is telling the soloist that here is everything you need. In other words . . . who could ask for anything more?

CERTAINLY NOT GERSHWIN HIMSELF. Unlike many composers of his generation such as Irving Berlin and Jerome Kern (whose melodies, no less than Gershwin's, were foundations for much of jazz and the jazz age), Gershwin not only wrote melodies that encouraged improvisation but was a virtuoso pianist and no mean improviser himself. In 1932, *George Gershwin's Song-Book* was published by Simon and Schuster. Instead of being, as the title suggested, a standard collection of sheet music, this was in fact a gathering of extended piano solos that purported to be transcriptions of Gershwin's own improvisations. I don't know if these transcriptions were performed by subsequent pianists, but it would make a helluva recording project for a contemporary keyboardist like Peter Mintun, who works in that genre.

Two years later, the composer took things a step further. While preparing to undertake a concert tour, on which he was to be accompanied by Leo Reisman's orchestra, Gershwin felt the need for another showpiece for his keyboard virtuosity. For perhaps the only time in his career, he decided to combine three aspects of his musical self in a single piece: his reputation as a keyboard wizard, his success as a writer of popular and theater songs, and his experiments in the field of longer-form works—rhapsodies, concertos, and ballets. He composed the piece that became *Variations* on "*I Got Rhythm*" in record time, and it premiered on January 14, 1934, at Boston's Symphony Hall, with Charles Previn (father of André) conducting the Reisman orchestra and the composer at the piano.

Perhaps because it was written for a dance band, the *Variations* is the lightest of Gershwin's concert works. Fittingly, considering the city where it was introduced, this is Boston Pops kind of music (Arthur Fiedler did indeed record it for Victor, with Earl Wild on piano). As biographer Charles Schwartz notes, "The 'I Got Rhythm' tune serves as the basis for six spindly, powder-puff variations, none of which would hurt a fly." Gershwin originally outlined the work as follows:

1. simple
2. orch melody—piano chromatic variation
3. orch rich melody in 3/4 piano variation P
4. Chinese variation interlude
5. modal variation
6. Hot variation finale

Gershwin's own attempt at jazzing up "I Got Rhythm" was oddly disappointing, particularly when compared to what Lester Young and Duke Ellington would do with the same material. However, his *Variations on "I Got Rhythm"* served one crucial function, in that, for the first time, the main man in American popular music was sanctioning the practice of using his melodies as a point of departure for variations. Perhaps Gershwin can be seen as a transitional figure between older colleagues Berlin and Kern (not to mention the old-at-heart Richard Rodgers), who wanted their music played exactly as written, and slightly younger ones, like Hoagy Carmichael, Johnny Mercer, and Harold Arlen, who were in and of the jazz world. (In 1995, pianist Marcus Roberts attempted a modern jazz treatment of the *Variations* that combined the original orchestral framework with piano variations of his own devising. It was not an improvement.)

"I GOT RHYTHM," in its many guises, whether as show tune or jazz anthem, whether with its melody intact or its chords recycled, is probably the most widely heard piece of music that Gershwin ever wrote. Undoubtedly this would have surprised the composer himself—that more people should know him by this humble, ungrammatical pop song than by the ambitious concert works, the early revues, the musical comedies, the film scores (for Fred Astaire and others), the three political satire shows (*Of Thee I Sing,* etc.) or his amazing opera, *Porgy and Bess.* Indeed, this little song would exert more influence on what we could call art music than all of his "serious" works put together. Both the swing era and the modern era of jazz were astonishingly dependent on this one sequence of chords, as contemporary players in those idioms still are. Indeed, the whole movement of jazz from melodic improvisation to harmonic improvisation—from prewar to postwar jazz—was largely made possible by "Rhythm."

As with "Body and Soul" and "Star Dust," it was Louis Armstrong who, in 1931, sealed the fate of "I Got Rhythm" as a jazz classic. However, although his record was tremendously important, today it seems more as if Armstrong merely sped the song on its way toward jazz standard status rather than truly launching it. Not that his record is anything less than great: he opens with a spoken intro, with which he exhorts the band to go into "Rhythm" and give it all they've got ("All right, you cats been talkin' 'bout you got rhythm. You got this and you got that. *I* got rhythm! I'm gonna see what you all got"). He continues spieling, even as the band plays a quick chorus of the melody, and then encourages each individual soloist to strut his stuff in brief, eight-bar turns. "Every tub there," as Armstrong says, meaning that every man gets to solo, and all the while the leader is calling out their names and urging them on like a football coach: Preston Jackson (trombone), Lester Boone (alto sax), Zilner "Old" Randolph (Pops's "second trumpet man"), George James (clarinet), Mike McKendrick (guitar), Charlie Alexander (piano), Al Washington (tenor).

When the leader's turn comes, it's not a solo in the customary big band manner the way it happens in most Armstrong records from this period, with his trumpet clearly distinguished from the rest of the ensemble, who are playing background figures in unison. Rather, there's more of a New Orleans heterophonic feel to this solo-and-background, in which the sidemen play their own own semi-improvised lines. The piece ends with a Bronx cheer–like ensemble figure that sounds as if it could come from a Laurel and Hardy two-reeler.

The only thing wrong with the record is that Armstrong, for all of his *compère*-ing and carrying on, never does actually sing "I Got Rhythm." Of course, there would be plenty of people who would sing it in the Armstrong mode, such as Leo Watson with the Spirits of Rhythm in 1934. The great man's major European disciple, Nat Gonella, would play and sing in a spirited recording with his own band in 1940. Armstrong himself would come back to the song and sing it briefly, though beautifully, as the finale of an absurd 1965 Hollywood remake titled *When the Boys Meet the Girls.*

As brilliant as Armstrong's record was, it was hardly necessary for him to tell the jazz community how perfect a song "I Got Rhythm" was, as so many of the music's seminal figures and future leaders of the swing era had been staring up at Ms. Merman's garters, snapped or unsnapped, from the orchestra pit on opening night. Red Nichols's recording, the first jazz version, features Benny Goodman playing a throaty clarinet solo in his Pee Wee Russell phase, Glenn Miller playing a bluesy solo in his Jack Teagarden phase, as well as Gene Krupa, Jimmy Dorsey, and Charlie Teagarden all meaningfully present if not soloing. There's also a vocal by studio singer Dick Robertson that's the quintessence of twenties pep. Like virtually every other period vocalist, Robertson sings the refrain fairly straight, but he does throw in a slight but significant variation on the bridge by singing "'Round my front or back door," as if to indicate that no sooner was the song introduced on Broadway than musicians and singers couldn't wait to start jazzing it up.

As mentioned above, all the instrumental stars in the *Girl Crazy* band would return to "Rhythm" again and again. Both Jimmy Dorsey, who played alto in the pit, and his trombonist brother, Tommy, had a long history with the song. Both brothers were on hand when Ethel Waters beat Ethel Merman to the punch, by seventeen years, when she recorded "Rhythm" in November 1930. That Waters did justice to the song surprised no one, but what really was a shocker was that two weeks earlier, Kate Smith (with a trombonist who sounds like Tommy Dorsey, although this record is not listed in *TD on the Side,* the definitive Dorsey discography) cut an astonishingly good, hot version.

For most of her career, no one would accuse Miss Smith of even remotely having rhythm, but this record (and a few others from the twenties, as well as her great 1934 Deccas) shows what a formidable swing singer she could have been. Smith gets especially frisky on the out-chorus (after an instrumental break that opens with sixteen bars of trombone), all but growling in the black blues tradition, and her final eight bars are full of zesty syncopations. (In a similar vein, the song inspired the most rhythmical performance in the career of London musical-theater star Bobby Howes, earning the entertainer his only entry in Rust's *Jazz Records.*) Within a matter of weeks, the Dorseys would also record the tune with Columbia house-band director Fred Rich, who would cut at least three different masters of "Rhythm" for release under various pseudonyms.

Jimmy Dorsey also cut a superior instrumental with his own orchestra in 1937. While the band plays the melody, Dorsey noodles all over the place in double time (in a manner similar to Gershwin's chromatic variations), frantically darting up and down and all but daring the rest of the ensemble to catch up with him—and tenorist Herbie Haymer and drummer Ray McKinley answer his challenge. Tommy Dorsey was apparently not a member of the *Girl Crazy* band, but the younger brother had a long association with "Rhythm" just the same, climaxed by his participation in the epic Busby Berkeley production number of the song that closes the 1943 MGM film of *Girl Crazy.*

The honor of playing hot trombone in the *Girl Crazy* pit went to a man whom no one would associate with that role seventy years later: Glenn Miller. Already known as much as an arranger as a trombonist, Miller is also said to have assisted orchestrator Robert Russell Bennett with scoring some of the hotter numbers in the show. With his own orchestras, Miller formulated at least two completely different approaches to the song. The first was an up-tempo, half-swing, half-schottische treatment from 1937 loaded with solos (Hal McIntyre on clarinet, Jerry Jerome quoting *Rhapsody in Blue* on tenor, trumpeter Sterling Bose). This was a capriciously swinging, whimsical treatment, succeeding nearly as well on both counts as drummer Chick Webb's small-group version from three months later, in which Webb's remarkable drumming propels a front line of clarinet and flute. Miller's other treatment was very unusual in the annals of "Rhythm"-mania, a loping, almost balladic rendition from 1942, arranged by Billy May but never recorded commercially by the band.

Of the instrumental "cast" of *Girl Crazy,* the star musician who had the longest relationship with Gershwin and his music was Benny Goodman. According to a story the clarinetist related to his young associate Loren Schoenberg (who first worked in the Goodman office and eventually put together the clarinetist's last band), Gershwin happened to hear the twenty-one-year-old Goodman at a rehearsal and from that time on singled him out. The composer wrote a brief solo feature for the clarinetist for the instrumental music that was later dropped after Goodman eventually left the show. It obviously pleased Gershwin when Goodman made his famous breakthrough in 1935, launching not only his band but the entire swing era: the year later, Gershwin wrote a song in Goodman's honor titled "King of Swing." The song was introduced in a Radio City revue, but possibly because it had lyrics by Al Stillman (later famous for writing for Johnny Mathis) rather than by Ira Gershwin, "King of Swing" remains one of the more obscure items in the Gershwin canon.

Over the decades, Gershwin became easily the most-performed composer in Goodman's repertoire; BG recorded at least sixteen different Gershwin tunes for Columbia Records alone. While Dorsey and Miller (not to mention the Casa Loma Orchestra in 1932) played "Rhythm" with their big bands, Goodman seems to have regarded the tune strictly as a jam-session vehicle for his small groups. Although radio versions proliferate from 1937 onward, it wasn't until 1945 that Goodman cut "Rhythm" commercially. But long before that great sextet version, Goodman had conceived the tune as a vehicle for his classic quartet, with Lionel Hampton, Teddy Wilson, and Gene Krupa.

In 1937, the quartet performed "Rhythm" in the A-minus feature *Hollywood Hotel,* and for Warner Brothers to devote a whole two minutes of screen time to instrumental, small-group jazz was, at the time, considered a giant step forward for hot music. The tune is titled "I've Got a Heartful of Music," and although it's credited, along with the rest of the score, to Harry Warren and Johnny Mercer, the piece is indeed our old friend "Rhythm" wearing a false mustache. There's a full, thirty-two-bar "head" melody, heard after a dazzling intro from Hampton, but it's nothing to speak of, and Goodman dispenses with it summarily. Goodman's improvisation, which follows Wilson's, is the main thing here, and a thing of beauty it is. Even better is a rapid *accelerando* passage in which all four instruments are allegedly playing in unison, though it really sounds as if they're all trying to beat each other to the finish line. Within the story of the film, this is supposed to be a rehearsal of the Goodman band, and at the end of the track the leader says, "All right, boys, that's all. Don't forget, let's be on time."

As fine as the *Hollywood Hotel* version is, it's only a warm-up for the still superior treatments to follow. The tune was the highlight for the quartet at the famous Carnegie Hall concert in January 1938. Twice as long as the film version (four minutes versus two), it gives us the Gershwin melody plus extended solos from Wilson and Goodman, and a full solo by Hampton as well (who only plays the intro on the soundtrack) as well as that great unison passage, although the *accelerando* is harder to make out under the surface noise and applause on the concert reading (the movie sound-track, by comparison, is sonically superb).

But wait, that's not all. Goodman's 1945 commercial reading, which is also four minutes long (or roughly a minute longer than 90 percent of all 78s of the period), done with his sextet for Columbia, is even stronger. By the end of the war, Wilson and Hampton have remarkable replace-ments in Mel Powell and Red Norvo, while guitar (Mike Bryan) and bass (Slam Stewart) have also been added. Powell and Norvo are clean, fresh, and swinging, and Goodman's two choruses are among the liveliest of his career. The unison passage has been updated and upgraded with another spirited horse race for the ensemble in which stop-time breaks play a more important role. The real surprise is a bowing and humming chorus by Slam Stewart, a career-long trademark of the great bassist (in which he improvised a line *arco*—with the bow—rather than the usual jazz pizzi-cato, at the same time scatting the same notes vocally an octave higher).

In 1981, Stewart expanded his chorus with Goodman into a whole track; on one of the few recordings he made as a leader (or co-leader in this case), *Duologue,* a series of duets with guitarist Bucky Pizzarelli, Stewart has virtually the whole enchilada to himself, getting to play the main "Rhythm" melody in the slapping-and-scatting style.

Lionel Hampton's Victor version, issued as "Rhythm, Rhythm (I Got Rhythm)," juxtaposed black swing stars, most notably Buster Bailey and John Kirby from the latter's Fifty-second Street group, and Ellington *über*-altoist Johnny Hodges, along with Goodmanites like the vibist him-self. (Clarinetist Buster Bailey gets into some rapid up-and-down motion here similar to both Goodman and Jimmy Dorsey.) It's an unusual oppor-tunity to hear Hodges jam in a non-Ducal context, reminding us that if it weren't for Ellington, jazzmen would perhaps have relied on "Rhythm" changes even more extensively.

Nineteen thirty-seven proved to be something of a banner year for "Rhythm": Goodman, Dorsey, Chick Webb, Hampton, Miller. There's also an aircheck by Count Basie and the second of Django Reinhardt's many versions. The guitarist recorded it in 1935 under Stephane Grap-pelli's leadership, then in 1937 with Basie-associated trombonist Dicky Wells and the jubilant expatriate trumpeter Bill Coleman, then two takes in 1938 with mouth organist Larry Adler. On the guitarist's 1949 Roman transcription session, he cut "Rhythm" yet again, this time with both Grappelli and a pianist in place of the usual multi-guitar Hot Club of France line-up. Grappelli's original inspiration on the violin, Joe Venuti, had cut "Rhythm" as early as 1934, but that was on a radio transcription with guitarist Frank Victor that was probably not heard in France. Venuti played it again in the 1970s in a violin-sax battle with the formidable Zoot Sims on soprano, and, unlike the two-violin version by Grappelli and Yehudi Menuhin, this really is a hard-swinging fight to the finish.

NINETEEN THIRTY-TWO HAD also been a banner year for "Rhythm." By then, the song was firmly established as a jazz and pop standard, meaning that it was one of the very few non-current tunes that bands or singers were likely to do. That year saw a fantastic recording by the Casa Loma Orchestra, which, like Nichols and Armstrong, further helped establish the song as a future fave among swing bands. There's an intriguing trombone hocket passage near the end, similar to what Ellington was already doing and would perfect with the later "Braggin' in Brass." But what everybody really remembers the Casa Loma "Rhythm" for is the two hard-swinging choruses by Clarence Hutchenrider, usually the band's star clarinetist, here playing baritone sax. The year 1932 also saw Sidney Bechet's breakthrough recording, about which more later.

The first film of *Girl Crazy* was also released in 1932 (by RKO), although this event may have hurt the song more than it helped. It was a dreadful movie, even by the standards of us happy few who enjoy the shenanigans of Bert Wheeler and Robert Woosley, a comedy team forgotten by everyone except obsessed cable viewers of American Movie Classics. Chief among the film's many sins was to all but throw away "I Got Rhythm," by which I mean it was given to the appallingly bad Kitty Kelly (no relation, apparently, to the egregious journalist of the same name), instead of star Dorothy Lee, due, it's rumored, to Miss Kelly's supposedly more than professional relationship with producer William LeBaron. Not only is she a lousy singer, but Kelly commits what Ira Gershwin considered the cardinal sin of "correcting" his English and singing "I've Got Rhythm." Fortunately, RKO Pictures atoned a few years later by commissioning the Gershwin brothers to write the score for *Shall We Dance,* one of the greatest of the Fred Astaire–Ginger Rogers epics.

The last remake of *Girl Crazy,* the 1965 *When the Boys Meet the Girls,* starring an utterly unlovable Connie Francis, was even worse. Alternating between contempop stars doing their hit singles and lukewarm musical-comedy treatments of the *Girl Crazy* score, the picture is pretty much a waste of time. In the film's own terms, its major occasion must be when the two strains—sixties pop and Gershwin—come together in a Herman's Hermits "Bidin' My Time," which is surprisingly sweet (rather like the Beatles' take on "Till There Was You"). The picture's two saving graces are Liberace (doing a delightfully fey mambo, grunts and all) and Louis Armstrong, who at least sends us happily on our way by concluding the proceedings with a resounding treatment of "Rhythm." It's been a lousy meal, but Pops at least allows us to leave with a pleasant taste in our mouths.

It's the middle version of *Girl Crazy,* from MGM in 1943, that's the charm. In Hollywood fashion, they tampered with the book, but then the plot of the 1930 original was easily improved, and the story now works so well as a Judy Garland–Mickey Rooney vehicle (the very best, in fact, of their many movies together) that one can't help wondering if this might be what Aarons and Freedley had in mind in the first place. Also, as happened with most movie treatments, they didn't stick to the letter of the score, but at least MGM retained most of the big numbers and added Gershwin classics from other shows (such as "Fascinatin' Rhythm" from *Lady, Be Good!*). It was a foregone conclusion that a great film of *Girl Crazy* would climax with "I Got Rhythm," and this is the "Rhythm" production number to end all, utilizing the combined talents of Garland, Rooney, Tommy Dorsey (and his entire orchestra), Roger Edens (pianist and accompanist for Merman on the 1930 show and now a musical director for Metro), and a large singing and dancing chorus (including leggy cowgirls in short skirts), with Hollywood's manic master of the terpsichorean surreal, Busby Berkeley, pulling the strings.

Berkeley's "Rhythm" number makes the point that the relationship between theater and jazz was deeper than anyone suspected. We know that jazz gives musical comedy its rhythm and energy, and musical theater by and large gives jazz and pop its repertoire. But the best of Berkeley's numbers are visual jazz, theme and variations. This concept exists in European music, but the way Berkeley applies it, it's distinctly American and perfectly suited to Tommy Dorsey and His Orchestra. Some dancers go this way, others go that way, the banners fly, the line wheels around, we see them from the front, the side, overhead—the camera dances as much as the showgirls. Berkeley's number could be described as *Visual Variations on "I Got Rhythm"*—visual variations that make a perfect counterpoint to the melodic and harmonic variations of the Dorsey crew.

Garland, too, has never been more irresistible. At the start of her recording career, Decca had attempted to promote their new find as a teenage swing singer. In retrospect, this seems quite a misjudgment, since in no way was Garland ever competition for Ella Fitzgerald—nor the other way around. But by the time of Garland's recording of "Rhythm," that whole faux-swing thing was behind her. Likewise, Mary Martin, in her 1952 *Girl Crazy* studio recording, does a whole extended chorus with just drums, à la Goodman's famous interlude with Gene Krupa on "Sing, Sing, Sing." Neither Garland nor Merman nor Martin has rhythm in the same way that Benny Goodman has rhythm, but they more than put the number over. An added delight to Garland's 1943 Decca is that someone was obviously very much enamored of the chromatic chorus in Gershwin's 1934 *Variations,* as the intro and instrumental portions of Garland's record are packed to the brim with chromatic piano variations, and they're more effective here than they are on the original concert piece itself.

As one of the composer's best-known songs, "Rhythm" was de rigueur for Gershwin pastiche productions, like *Rhapsody in Blue,* the Warner Bros. 1945 biopic, and another MGM epic, the 1950 *An American in Paris* (and forty years later, on Broadway, *Crazy for You*). Taking its title from Gershwin's 1928 ballet, *An American in Paris* was the first of three Arthur Freed productions that could be called "catalogue musicals," which built a story around songs by a single composer or team without resorting to the overdone (even *then*) biopic format. (The other two major catalogue musicals were based on the output of songwriters who held down day jobs as executives at Metro: *Singin' in the Rain,* which took off on Arthur Freed and Nacio Herb Brown, and *The Bandwagon,* built around the catalogue of Howard Dietz and Arthur Schwartz.)

For the "Rhythm" number, star Gene Kelly took advantage of the song's childlike simplicity: playing the titular *American in Paris* (with the character name of Jerry Mulligan—now where have I heard that before?), he uses the song to give a bunch of French kiddies a lesson in English. Once he gets them to say the two words "I" and "got," he figures

that he's already taught them enough for one day, so the bulk of the number gives us the little *enfants du paradis* chanting "I got" while Kelly fills in
the "rhythm," "music," and everything else.

"Rhythm" turns up yet again in Broadway's 1992 *Crazy for You,* itself a
variation on *Girl Crazy,* in which the new plot was unexpectedly lousy
(worse than any of the Gershwin films, even) and the orchestrations
unexpectedly authentic and true to the 1930s. The "Rhythm" number,
placed, as in *Girl Crazy,* at the end of act one, tried to out-Berkeley Busby
Berkeley in its length and in the fertility of its ideas, and in the end gave
him a respectable run for his money.

AS WE'VE SEEN, 1932 was the year of Sidney Bechet's variation on "I Got
Rhythm," which the great New Orleans reedman titled "Shag," a piece
sometimes described as the first instance of what would soon become
exceedingly commonplace in jazz: a musician taking the chord sequence
to "Rhythm" and putting a new melody of his own on top of it." That isn't
exactly what Bechet does on "Shag," though; he starts with the last line of
the original melody ("Who could ask for anything more?") and then
immediately tears into his improvisation. Jazzmen generally refer to the
initial chorus of a performance as the "head," and in most small-group
jazz this is the major place where the prewritten melody is heard, be it an
original by one of the musicians or a standard. By that same anatomical
metaphor, one would expect the closing chorus, in which the melody is
played again, to be called the "tail," but it's just thought of as a repeat of
the head. The majority of jazz heads are based on the chord changes to a
familiar standard, and often as not it's "I Got Rhythm."

"Lester Leaps In" (Lester Young) and "Anthropology" (Charlie Parker)
have great heads, tunes that are just as memorable as the original Gershwin "Rhythm" line. One can't say the same thing about the opening choruses on Benny Goodman's "Heartful of Music" or Bechet's "Shag";
they're just very passive melodies, meant to be dispensed with as quickly
as possible. In fact, the opening chorus melody of "Shag" is so nondescript one wonders if it, in fact, even qualifies as a head. After the opening
"Who could ask for anything more?" the band lays out the "rhythm"
changes while Bechet plays a variation melody on top of those changes.
It's accompanied by the same kind of predetermined background figures

that accompany a head, and it occurs at the start of the disc, where the head is supposed to happen, but it's not songlike enough to rate as a genuine head.

It matters not. The improvisations themselves are wild enough to make one forget the opening. After the first chorus, trombonist Teddy Nixon and pianist Henry Duncan share a chorus before bassist Teddy Myers flies into a wild scat solo that anticipates the Leo Watson version of two years later. When Bechet takes over, things really get crazy: after a brief quote from "Buddy Bolden's Blues," he leads the ensemble in a frantic series of stop-time breaks, in which the rest of the group rather vociferously signifies their approval.

The 1932 Bechet makes a perfect follow-up, even a B-side, to the 1931 Louis Armstrong: by starting with the final two bars of the song, Bechet seems to be beginning exactly where Pops left off. Was "Shag" the first new head to be devised over the "Rhythm" changes? The question is moot. Even if we were to hear every jazz record made between October 1930 and September 1932, we still wouldn't know which variations on "Rhythm" may have been conceived and played in clubs but never made it into the recording studio. Still, the Bechet record is a good indication that musicians were starting to think of things to do with the tune apart from its melody.

As we get closer and closer to the bop era, the "Rhythm" variations start coming ever more frequently. The two best known entries in the "Rhythm" stakes arrived in 1939 and 1940, Lester Young's "Lester Leaps In" and Duke Ellington's "Cottontail," respectively. Both are masterful moments in the history of jazz, although, as it happened, the Lester Young record would anticipate a lot more of where the music would go in the forties and fifties than the Ellington record. The two recordings also make a point about the nature of composition in jazz. "Lester Leaps In" has a great head, the tune is substantial; it stays with you, and is far more hummable than the paper-thin openings of "Shag" and "Heartful."

"Cottontail," however, is something more than a head, though relatively simple by Ellington standards (it's closer to his jam session vehicles like "C-Jam Blues" than his more ambitious works, even the short-form ones). Unlike most jazz composers, Ellington only occasionally wrote his melodies to fit on top of preexisting chord patterns: in the twenties and thirties, he came up with all manner of variations on "Tiger Rag" ("High

Life," "Daybreak Express," etc.), and from time to time he went to work on the "Rhythm" changes. Generally, these "Rhythm" variants were jam-session vehicles, often for small groups: "Frolic Sam," written by Cootie Williams and introduced by Barney Bigard and His Jazzopaters in 1936; "The Jeep Is Jumpin' " by Johnny Hodges and His Orchestra two years later; "The Bridge to Perdido," by Juan Tizol, from 1941; "Trombone Buster," by Cat Anderson, from 1965; and "Battle Royale" from the Ellington orchestra's 1961 encounter with Count Basie.

Essentially "Cottontail" is an opening chorus by the whole ensemble, boasting the catchiest of all "Rhythm"-inspired heads. This is followed by one of history's great tenor solos, a two-chorus K.C. masterpiece by Ben Webster. The next chorus is sixteen bars by the ensemble, mostly brass, then baritone saxist Harry Carney gets the bridge, and Ellington takes the last eight on piano. Then we have a sensational thirty-two bars of the whole sax section going to town, in which all five reedmen become a sort of super-colossal, collective Ben Webster. (While some scholars believe that Ellington had a hand in the basic content of Webster's solo, it's also widely held that the sax-section episode really is what it sounds like—that is, an improvisation by Webster that had been transcribed and orchestrated for five reeds.) After the sax piece, the full ensemble, mostly brass again with some reed underpinnings, comes back for still another chorus, highlighted by an ascending bridge that sounds not only as if the melody is shooting skyward but that the bandsmen themselves are leaping into the air. After this bridge, Ellington returns, for the first time, to the original opening line—the "Cottontail" melody, as it were. It's worth stressing that this is the only time that the soon-to-be-famous "Cottontail" melody has been heard since the opening sixteen bars of the disc—and "Cottontail" is so rich with music and ideas it barely has time to reiterate a snatch of its central melody at the close.

There are other big band compositions that do this with "Rhythm," that intertwine prewritten variations with the improvised (or semi-improvised) individual statements by the soloists: "Your Father's Mustache," written by Neal Hefti for Woody Herman's First Herd (the definitive recording of which is an extended six-minute V-Disc), while not as ambitious as "Cottontail," shows how it can work. There's an opening statement (in this case, a lot of it is background for leader Herman's clarinet), and then a long series of solos.

Why is this different from the head/string-of-solos/head format of most small-group jazz? It's that the background behind the solos is constantly changing; there are all kinds of figures and patterns by various combinations of the horns behind them, and some solos that, small-group style, have only the rhythm section for accompaniment. Then, at the end, there's a whole bunch of ensemble happenings—still more variations, stuff to do with the "Rhythm" changes that we haven't yet heard here or anyplace else, even a brief, a-"Rhythm"-ic section launched by the leader chanting "Glee club!" and the gentlemen of the ensemble, led by falsetto-voiced bassist Chubby Jackson, chanting the words "Your father's mustache" over and over. That's hardly the end of it, either; there are still more ensemble variations and a tenor break before Hefti and Herman take it out.

Although "Lester Leaps In" (performed in C on both of Young's major commercial recordings) is far simpler, it's no less catchy. This jazz standard was introduced by a small group from the Count Basie Orchestra billed as the "Kansas City Seven." Paradoxically, when you consider that this was the most famous melody Lester Young would ever devise, the tune is played first by the full ensemble; in virtually every subsequent Young performance, the melody would be played by the tenor saxist himself with just a three-piece rhythm section. Again, the improvisation is the thing, and Lester Young's solo here is one of the greatest that any jazzman would ever put on record, a declaration of artistic principles every bit as monumental as Coleman Hawkins's earth-shattering rendition of "Body and Soul," recorded a month later (or, for that matter, Webster on "Cottontail").

The only thing lacking in "Lester Leaps" is a worthwhile bridge; the original Kansas City Seven version, in fact, had no bridge to speak of, just eight bars of noodling by Basie and bassist Walter Page. The tune became such a staple of Young's repertoire—the best-known tune in it, in fact—that he eventually had to devise a stronger bridge for the tune. In that respect, the 1946 remake, which was done for Aladdin Records and retitled "New Lester Leaps In," is even better than the 1939 Columbia-owned original. His playing has gotten a tad heavier, and he hangs around the lower register of the horn more than in the almost ethereally light original, but the newer version cannot be said to suffer by comparison.

In the mid-forties, Young also participated in still more remarkable recordings of "Rhythm": with trombonist Dicky Wells's band (December 1943), with Basie in another edition of the Kansas City Seven (March 1944); and on two live versions by Young with Jazz at the Philharmonic (April and June 1946). The very first ever JATP concert, in 1944, had opened with "Lester Leaps In," but when Young participated in the two concerts from 1946, they elected not to use the famous Lestorian head. Instead, as Prez scholar Loren Schoenberg has observed, they use the head credited to Cootie Williams as "Frolic Sam," which, to risk confusing matters further, was also recorded by Young in November of '46 under the title "Sax-O-Be-Bop." Of the two JATP concert tracks from that year, the first is particularly valuable as it consists of perhaps the only occasion when the three greatest saxophonists of all time—Lester Young, Coleman Hawkins, and Charlie Parker—are playing on the same stage. The JATP format tended to treat everything like a competition, sort of a jazz wrestling match, and to my mind, Young, the most introspective of the four saxes (the other alto is swing star Willie Smith), is unquestionably the winner. Prez doesn't honk like Illinois Jacquet in the JATP tradition, but he wins over the crowd via some thrilling low notes and in general comes off as much more of a showman than the reluctant, self-contained innovator he is generally portrayed as.

In the 1930s, nonsense songs, jive songs, and novelties were all called "rhythm songs," and quite a few of these were based on "I Got Rhythm." Some jam vehicles grew into more fully realized heads and then, with the aid of lyrics, full-blown pop songs. The King Cole Trio, who were to rhythmic novelties what Esther Williams was to bathing suits, were especially fond of these, particularly "Hit That Jive, Jack!" written by clarinetist and alto saxist Skeets Tolbert, who led a six-piece jump band in New York in the late thirties and early forties. His band, Skeets Tolbert and His Gentlemen of Swing, was somewhat similar in feeling to Louis Jordan and His Tympany Five, but as all three groups were under contract to Decca, only one could record it, and that wound up being the Cole Trio. The jivey lyric is even more minimal than Ira Gershwin's original, mainly repeating the title over and over, but rhythm it has more than got. (Later on, Slim Gaillard worked "Hit That Jive" into his *faux*-extended work, *The Avocado Seed Soup Symphony.*)

Cole's own "Straighten Up and Fly Right" also has more than a touch of "Rhythm" changes in it, particularly in the bridge—indeed, "Cotton-

tail," "Hit That Jive, Jack!" "Straighten Up and Fly Right," and many others all repeat similar motifs in the bridge. And most of these swing and
bop variations on the "Rhythm" chord sequence also emphasize those
aspects of Gershwin's harmonies that have the most in common with the
blues. For instance, from Bechet on, the bridge always seems to encourage stop-time breaks; they're especially prevalent in "Lester Leaps In"
and "Your Father's Mustache," and it's not hard to see where they could
be worked into "Jive Jack."

Thus, by the early forties, "Rhythm" was already the most-played
chord sequence in all of jazz, and its popularity with musicians only
increased as the modern era dawned. Charlie Parker and Dizzy Gillespie, the founding fathers of bebop, were both especially in tune with
"Rhythm" as a compositional framework. Parker was a master of the
blues, and Gillespie helped make Latin music a regular part of jazz, but
both of them played an awful lot of "I Got Rhythm." At least eight
"Rhythm" variations may be found among the cornerstone tunes of modern jazz, starting with "Red Cross," which Parker had introduced at the
end of a 1944 Savoy session built around guitarist and singer Tiny Grimes
(and widely regarded as the first full-blown recording of either bop or
Bird). The next two major milestone sessions in the development of bop,
both featuring Parker and Gillespie, were done for the Guild label (which
made Savoy look like a huge conglomerate by comparison), and between
them introduced three more major "Rhythm" variations. The February
1945 date produced "Dizzy Atmosphere" (in A flat), while "Shaw 'Nuff"
(B flat) and "Salt Peanuts" (F) came from May. The latter tune has a two-
word novelty vocal, sung usually by Gillespie but also performed by
Parker on a Royal Roost aircheck.

Parker's February 1946 Savoy date, the first to feature Miles Davis,
yielded "Thriving on a Riff" (B flat), which was also known as "Thriving
from a Riff," but which eventually evolved into the better-known bop
standard "Anthropology" (also B flat). One of Parker's most memorable
"Rhythm"-a-nings was "Moose the Mooche" (B flat), introduced at his
first Dial date, in March 1946. From May 1947 (and back on Savoy),
"Chasin' the Bird" (F) has Davis trailing Parker by exactly one bar, sort of
a round harmony effect that provides the "chase" referred to in the title.

The bridges of these "Rhythm" variants are particularly revealing: the
bridge to "Red Cross" is, like that of the "Rhythm" melody, essentially

the same basic lick repeated four times. The bridge to "Dizzy Atmo-sphere" starts with part of the sax-section *soli* bridge from "Cottontail." The bridges to "Salt Peanuts" and "Moose the Mooche" are probably the most alike. The pieces don't always start straightaway with the "Rhythm" changes: Parker, and Gillespie even more so, were adept enough as com-posers to devise interesting introductions of their own ("Shaw 'Nuff" has a particularly arresting opener, a wild, quasi–Middle Eastern motif). In 1949, pianist Bud Powell composed and recorded an original blues enti-tled "Dance of the Infidels," and though it's a fine tune, somehow I've always felt that this title more accurately describes "Shaw 'Nuff" than Powell's piece. Surely, the "Shaw 'Nuff" intro and main melody put one immediately in mind of dancing infidels.

After Parker and Gillespie, tracking the ebb and flow of "Rhythm" variations in the jazz world becomes impossible. One of the major devel-opments in the evolution of jazz through the thirties and into the forties had been an ever-increasing shift from melodic improvisation (that is, playing variations on the tune itself) to harmonic improvisation—spin-ning wholly new lines based on the chord changes of the original tune that have nothing to do with the original melody. And, as we have seen, the chord progressions they were playing were most often those of "I Got Rhythm." Groups like the Bebop Boys, who recorded for Savoy in 1946, featuring Bud Powell, Kenny Dorham, and Sonny Stitt, all star players in the next generation of boppers (the ones who came immedi-ately after Bird and Diz), recorded entire sessions of nothing but "I Got Rhythm" changes, with an occasional blues thrown in for good measure. Dizzy Gillespie writes in his memoirs, "Of course, there are ten million tunes based on the changes of 'I Got Rhythm.' " One of Gillespie's own more typical later variations was "Clappin' Rhythm," a novelty vocal vehicle for himself and entertainer Joe Carroll, taped live in Paris in 1953.

Veteran bassist Milt Hinton has elaborated how "Rhythm" changes became so prevalent that he and Gillespie became besieged at jam ses-sions at Minton's by amateur musicians, who would "just jump in" and "foul up the session." Continued Hinton:

> So Diz told me one night, "Now look, when we get down to the
> jam session, we're gonna say we're gonna play 'I Got Rhythm,' but
> instead of using B flat and D flat, we're gonna use B flat, D flat, G flat,

or F and then we change." After working out these changes in various unfamiliar keys, Hinton and Gillespie would tell the "kids" hanging around the bandstand that they were going to play "I Got Rhythm." Then we'd start out with these new changes and they'd be left right at the post. They'd be standing there, and they couldn't get in, because they didn't know what changes we were using.

The melody, or a semblance of it, was still being heard in the bop years. In 1945, the dawn of the modern age, Don Byas performed a remarkable workout on the "Rhythm" melody and changes in a live concert at New York's Town Hall recorded by Commodore Records. Accompanied only by bassist Slam Stewart (who takes another strumming-and-humming chorus in the center), Byas is all over "Rhythm," fragmenting it, abstracting it, stretching it out, and compressing it in a treatment that's more fresh and up-to-date than anything I've ever heard at the Knitting Factory. As a result of this imaginative, not to say astonishing, treatment, Byas might well be dubbed the Tatum of the tenor.

Sonny Stitt took on "Rhythm" on an LP appropriately titled *The Hard Swing.* While his treatment isn't quite as melodically imaginative as Byas's, it's still pretty terrific. Stitt stresses pure, breathtaking speed, spinning his rhythmic variations at an unbelievably fast clip, producing more notes, it seems, than the human brain can comprehend. His improvisation is incredibly complex, yet he gets in and out in a tidy, clean fashion. Gerry Mulligan played "Rhythm" in all manner of fashions, such as "Bweebida Bwobbida," first recorded in 1951; "Who's Got Rhythm?" from his 1959 meeting with Ben Webster; "Bright Boy Blues," at a 1971 concert done in Italy with Hampton Hawes on piano; and on a track under the original title in his 1957 reunion with Chet Baker.

The height of both "Rhythm"-ic awareness and bebop was the mid-to-late forties. As bop evolved into other musics, "Rhythm" gradually became less and less a part of the territory. West Coast cool jazz stressed composition over marathon jamming on familiar changes, East Coast hard bop was more about the blues than anything else. Eventually, Ornette Coleman came along with what he called "free jazz," which, to perhaps oversimplify his theory, returned everything to the idea of playing on "the line" (the melody) rather than the chords. And although not all of post-Ornette jazz followed this new approach with rigor, harmonic variations and "Rhythm" changes never quite regained their prominence, even in the bop and hard-bop revivals of the seventies, eighties, and beyond.

Still, "Rhythm" changes appeared here and there, if not nearly so frequently as they had in the high bop era, as when Sonny Rollins introduced his "Doxy" at a 1954 Miles Davis date with Horace Silver. By far the most famous of the later "Rhythm" variations is John Coltrane's "Giant Steps," recorded in Spring 1959 (the first take, from April, was issued years later on the Japanese LP *Alternate Takes;* the famous, originally issued version, came from May). Even more than most of the Parker-Gillespie variations, it's a fully realized melody, just as catchy as "Lester Leaps In," but with a stronger, more clearly defined bridge. Along with Wayne Shorter's "Footprints," "Giant Steps" became one of the most memorable tunes of an era in which the role of the composer had declined and the soloist reigned supreme. Virtually everyone who has ever picked up a horn in the last forty years can play "Giant Steps."

MOST OF THE JAZZ GUYS who have played the "Rhythm" melody in the last forty or fifty years have been pianists and, as with "Body and Soul" and "Night and Day," the general inspiration seems to be Art Tatum. Tatum recorded "Rhythm" many times, including an eight-minute all-star jam from the Metropolitan Opera House (with Louis Armstrong, Red Norvo, Jack Teagarden, Coleman Hawkins, Roy Eldridge, and others). However, it's Tatum's 1944 trio version that most other pianists grew up with. Nat Cole played it often, but never for commercial release: there are treatments for two different transcription firms (MacGregor and Capitol), plus an extended jam from a Just Jazz concert (front line: Charlie Shavers, Stan Getz, Willie Smith, and Red Norvo, again). There's also an appearance in an all-black feature film, *Killer Diller,* in which the Cole Trio plays a thinly disguised "Rhythm" variant titled "Breezy and the Bass" as a feature for bassist Johnny Miller.

There are no less than four piano treatments on Mosaic's *Master Jazz Pianos* collection, almost all of which start by playing the verse as slowly as they possibly can and then turn on the heat and the speed and play the chorus as fast as humanly possible, if not faster. (Dick Hyman and Derek Smith deliberately avoided that familiar slow-then-fast pattern for "Rhythm" in their four-handed treatment, by playing it at a singularly odd, loping tempo.) From the beginning, the song was something special for pianists: in 1935, Fats Waller played and sang it not with his familiar small group, his Rhythm (which, now that I think of it, would have been especially appropriate), but on a special big band date, which could have been billed as "Fats Waller and His Rhythm De Luxe."

Oscar Peterson played it in at least two outstandingly exciting Gershwin collaborations, one a meeting with clarinetist Buddy DeFranco and full orchestra, the other a quartet setting with Zoot Sims. "I Got Rhythm" was also the first song Peterson ever recorded, back in his native Montreal. At the age of nineteen, he has already synthesized the best of Cole, Hines, and Tatum—with a few Fats Waller licks thrown in for good measure—not to mention all the dexterity of the two-piano team of Albert Ammons and Pete Johnson (the influence of Bud Powell would come later). Hampton Hawes recorded "Rhythm" both with his trio (an especially dense keyboard treatment) and behind tenorist Warne Marsh in a Los Angeles area location recording from 1952; Marsh wasn't always strictly identified with the bop school, but his treatment of the "Rhythm" changes shows that he was more than up to the genre's challenges.

Pianist Fred Hersch and guitarist Bill Frisell, like a sort of postmodern equivalent of Bill Evans and Jim Hall, devised a rather pointillistic set of variations that minimizes both the melody and the chords; the piece keeps circling the airport without feeling the need to land. The Dwike Mitchell–Willie Ruff piano and bass did an especially convincing slow treatment. Teddy Wilson, on his album *Mr. Wilson and Mr. Gershwin,* delivered up a satisfyingly swinging Hines-like treatment. Erroll Garner swung it like the most with his classic quartet featuring bongo drums.

Apart from pianists, the "Rhythm" melody itself had also become the province of singers, now more from the worlds of jazz and related pop (Ernestine Anderson, Lena Horne, Helen Merrill, and Chris Connor). The bop duo Jackie and Roy recorded "Rhythm" first in 1964 as part of a suite of songs from *Girl Crazy,* then redid the same chart on the 1982 Concord Jazz LP *High Standards.* "Rhythm" amounts to one of J&R's more durable works, particularly the verse, which is so thoroughly reharmonized that it's practically another song. Bop singer supreme Joe Carroll also recorded a wild vocal version of "Rhythm" on his own (without Gillespie), although it's not as polished as his later treatment of the Gershwins' "Oh, Lady, Be Good!" Mark Murphy did it at the very beginning of his career, a treatment that takes the familiar slow-to-fast trajectory to thrilling extremes, starting excruciatingly slow and winding up very fast and exciting indeed.

Sarah Vaughan cut hers in Chicago in 1963, accompanied by Lalo Schifrin, the arranger best known for writing the *Mission: Impossible* theme. Her "Rhythm" is blindingly fast and to the point, sixteen bars with just fingersnaps, the orchestra announcing its presence at the start of the bridge but not coming in completely until the second chorus. For a later chorus, Vaughan gets a bizarre quivering sound going, almost singing two notes for every one written, and then improvising over the cacophonous sounds of the orchestra for the fade-out coda.

More recently the song has shown a tendency to return to its roots. Larry Adler, who might be dubbed the Oscar Levant of the harmonica, in terms of both his virtuosity and his special relationship with Gershwin, had recorded it with Reinhardt and Grappelli in 1938 and then again fifty years later in a live album done at the Ballroom, in New York. Essentially, Adler is more of a classical virtuoso than a jazz improviser, but with the help of pianist Ellis Larkins he pulls off a capable solo, one with a surprising visit from chicks and ducks and geese from "Surrey with the Fringe on Top"—not to mention "Louise," "The Sailor's Hornpipe," "Anything Goes," and Liszt's "Hungarian Rhapsody number 2." Cabaret artiste Laurie Beechman did a very musical-comedy treatment in 1990 that effectively serves to remind us that "I Got Rhythm" can still function superbly as a showtune and not only as a chord sequence.

It would be hard to find a better reading than Ella Fitzgerald's, on her 1959 *George Gershwin Songbook*. She is perhaps the first performer from the jazz spectrum to address the verse. Fitzgerald and arranger Nelson Riddle start achingly slow, after a tone poem of an introduction, then abruptly rev into tempo when the piece goes into major on "I'm chipper." Chipper it is, with Fitzgerald singing the first sixteen bars largely a cappella but with biggish orchestral fills at the end of each line. It's a rare example of a performer alluding to a scat time sequence in the central refrain rather than the bridge. For the second chorus, we're treated to the glorious sound of Fitzgerald scatting over a Riddle string background, which is as close to paradise as most of us are likely to get. Singer and arranger end with a fast recap of the lyric, sung over what amounts to a whole new melody.

And this was neither the first time nor the last that those changes had been used in support of a new tune. It would be impossible to name a melody or a set of chord sequence that has withstood more interpretations and variations, while Ira Gershwin's lyric has become part of our common cultural consciousness. Performers looking for an inspiring piece of material may "ask for anything more," but they're not very likely to get it.

BONUS TRACKS

Most Romantic Treatment

Cornetist Ruby Braff is one of the few musicians to show that "Rhythm" has romance. In a live set of Gershwin tunes done with the fine quartet he and guitarist George Barnes co-led in the early seventies (two guitars, bass, and cornet), Braff plays "Rhythm" as if it were a love song. They do break into swing time in the second chorus, but it's the slow treatment of the opening thirty-two bars that stays with you. Forget about Marcus Roberts, this really is Gershwin for lovers.

The Hidden History of Thelonious Monk and "I Got Rhythm"

It's no secret that many of Charlie Parker's most famous original compositions were variations on the "I Got Rhythm" changes. What isn't as well known is that quite a few original compositions by Thelonious Monk also use a "Rhythm" foundation; Monk, as biographer Peter Keepnews has pointed out, was more careful to cover his tracks. According to Keepnews and musicologist Bill Kirchner, all of the following compositions by Monk are based—to some degree—on Gershwin's chord progression. "52nd Street Theme" (in C) and "Little Rootie Tootie" both use the "Rhythm" chord changes for their main melody while the bridge is based on those of Fats Waller's "Honeysuckle Rose." "Thelonious" and "Humph" are "Rhythm" variants that use altered chord changes. "Think Of One" uses altered "Rhythm" changes and a "Honeysuckle Rose" bridge, while "Shuffle Boil" combines an altered "Rhythm" for the A section with an altered "Honeysuckle Rose" bridge. Contrastingly, "Work" uses an original A section but its bridge is based on "Rhythm." In "Bemsha Swing" (which is, technically, an "altered partial A section of

'Rhythm' ") and "Nutty," Monk uses "Rhythm" for both the main melody and the bridge—when he gets to the B section, he simply modulates up a fourth (in "Nutty," the leap is from B flat to E flat). The most complicated case, however, is "Rhythm-a-ning," which is essentially "Rhythm," as the title indicates. However, as Keepnews has determined, the kernel of the "Rhythm-a-ning" melody line also turns up as part of Mary Lou Williams's "Walkin' And Swingin' " (not the main part), Lawrence Brown's trombone solo on Duke Ellington's "Ducky Wucky," and as a location recording from Minton's Playhouse—during the Monk–Charlie Christian "birth of bop" period—entitled "Meet Dr. Christian."

Benny Goodman Award for Most Different Versions of "I Got Rhythm" in Completely Different Contexts

Surely no one did more different versions of "Rhythm" than Stephane Grappelli, and that's not even counting his three or four recordings with Django Reinhardt. In 1958, the violinist recorded an ambitious treatment with a symphony orchestra, and then another with visiting American star plectrist Barney Kessel in Paris in 1969. There are three separate recordings with a British guitar star, Diz Disley, and a rhythm section sometimes billed as "The Hot Club of London," taped in 1970, 1973 (on an album called *I Got Rhythm*), and 1975, the '75 done on the road in Australia. Disley also turns up with Grappelli and Martin Taylor doing "Rhythm" in San Francisco in 1982, while Grappelli next cut it with yet a third Euro-guitar-star, Philip Catherine, back home in France a decade later. Plus there's a meeting with Danish jazz violinist Svend Asmussen (the Grappelli of Scandinavia) in Paris in 1988; an all-star tribute to Grappelli—and featuring Grappelli—at Carnegie Hall, 1993; and a live set at New York's Blue Note with Bucky and John Pizzarelli in 1995. Grappelli's silliest recording is a two-violin treatment with Yehudi Menuhin and a full orchestra. Grappelli plays melody, Menuhin hammers out a bass line, but the thing is more evocative of a barn dance than a stomp at the savoy. The best may well be two meetings with postmodern pianists who supply both lyricism and swing to complement Grappelli's own—one with McCoy Tyner (who had already participated in one of the most famous "Rhythm" variations of all, John Coltrane's "Giant Steps") in 1991, and one with Michel Petrucciani in 1995. Postscript: violinist Didier Lockwood, along with guitarist Birelli Lagrene, included it on his 2000 *Tribute to Stephane Grappelli*.

AS TIME GOES BY (1931)

words and music by Herman Hupfeld

IT WAS OF ONLY SECONDARY IMPORTANCE that the fog enveloping the airport where Rick and Ilsa say goodbye at the end of *Casablanca* happened to look romantic. The director's primary concern was that the fog nicely shroud the airport set and the plywood airplane, to obscure, as much as possible, their cheap, phony-looking façades.

Which helps to explain why Ingrid Bergman was supposedly either puzzled or downright annoyed when, later in her life, fans old and young would approach her to say that *Casablanca* was their favorite movie. *For Whom the Bell Tolls,* which she made immediately after *Casablanca,* was much more to her liking: a famous, well-established property, a role that was, at the time, a famous one, and one much contended after by the leading actresses of the day. (No one fought over playing the female lead in *Casablanca,* because the property was completely unknown and the character of Ilsa was the last major figure in the script to be developed.) *For Whom the Bell Tolls* was meticulously developed by a producer with Oscars in his eyes, who was trying to make high-profile, high-prestige pictures that would knock the Academy on its ear. *Casablanca,* in Bergman's view, was just ground out by the Warner Brothers factory, with a screenplay by a veritable assembly line of writers, and the production as a whole was as cobbled together at the last minute as was that slab of plywood that was trying to pass itself off as an airplane.

Great art, Bergman's Scandinavian mind must have thought, is the work of careful planning and meticulous consideration. Art doesn't just happen; even when you throw the most talented group of people in the world together, they can't be expected to sit down and bang out something that will endure. And yet, the American popular arts, especially jazz and the movies, frequently depend on the element of spontaneity— things just happening on the spot. On some other day, with the same people and the same circumstances, something completely different might take place. There's no predicting it, no depending on it; you just throw it all together and let the magic happen.

Serious artists also have proven track records: great art is not produced by men who have a single stroke of inspiration and then disappear; if you're a great artist, you can hit the mark more than once, you can make it happen time and again. If you can come up with a classic only once, then perhaps you're not a major artist but a guy who just got lucky. Maybe *Casablanca* isn't great art after all but just the product of sheer, random luck.

BEARING THIS IN MIND, let's take a look at the three men who are responsible for the creation and the enduring appeal of "As Time Goes By":

Herman Hupfeld: Wrote a couple of songs that caught on in their day, but for the last six decades has been known, if at all, exclusively for this one tune, which only became a major hit a dozen years after it was introduced.

Murray Burnett: Wrote (or rather co-wrote, with Joan Allison) the play *Everybody Comes to Rick's,* based partly on his own experiences in prewar Europe. After failing to interest a producer in mounting the show theatrically, he sold the script to Warner Brothers for twenty thousand dollars. Not only did he never again write anything of note, Burnett had to go to court to be recognized as the creator of *Casablanca.* Incidentally, he is also the one who thought of using "As Time Goes By" in the original play and was adamant that it be used as the central love song of the film.

Dooley Wilson: Appeared in the Broadway shows *Cabin in the Sky* and *Bloomer Girl,* and made a few movies, like *Higher and Higher,* with Frank Sinatra and Mel Tormé, but nothing outside of his role in *Casablanca* is remembered by anyone except Trivial Pursuit specialists. It's almost as if fate doesn't want anything to interfere with his identity as Sam, the pianist and singer who performs "As Time Goes By," first for Ilsa and then for Rick, in the Café Américain.

EXCEPT FOR PUTTING OVER this one song in this one film, none of their careers amounted to a great deal. Were they major talents, or just lucky?

Does it matter? All three obviously had something important to contribute to the collective cultural pool, or they wouldn't have been able to join forces and create a film and a song that mean so much to so many. Which is not to imply that *Casablanca* is strictly the work of one-shot talents who had only this effort to show for their entire careers. On the contrary, Humphrey Bogart and Ingrid Bergman were among the most revered actors ever to work in Hollywood, and director Michael Curtiz and producer Hal Wallis were responsible for a remarkable string of hits that extended long before and long after the making of *Casablanca*. You could remove *Casablanca* from their credentials and they would all still be legends.

Casablanca is rightfully held up as an argument in favor of the now long-departed Hollywood studio system. Aljean Harmetz's definitive history of the making of the film, *Round Up the Usual Suspects,* convincingly establishes that art isn't always the result of a single artistic vision; that, particularly in the performing arts, it can be the result of collaboration. Shakespeare, DaVinci, Eugene O'Neill, and François Truffaut didn't create art by committee (or by assembly line, as we might say of Warner Brothers), but old Hollywood did. Surely, one of the reasons the script of *Casablanca* is so excellent is because at least three of the greatest writers in movie history, Howard Koch and Julius and Phillip Epstein, put their best efforts into what was already a strong story outline by Murray Burnett and Joan Allison.

"As Time Goes By," on the other hand, makes the opposite argument. The words and music are both by a single writer who didn't seem to require a gaggle of fellow composers standing around telling him to make line seven more sentimental or go to minor in bar 9 instead of using an augmented fifth. The truth is that both methods of artistic creation can work, depending on the people and the circumstances.

Even those only slightly knowledgeable about old movies are fond of citing the misconception concerning *Casablanca*'s most famous line, "Play it again, Sam"—or, rather, the most famous line that never was. (According to critic Peter Filichia, a friend of the late Murray Burnett, the line in the original script was "Play it, you bastard!") Like Cary Grant's "Judy, Judy, Judy" (probably a phrase that some impressionist dreamed up) and Mae West's "Come up and see me sometime" (the title of a popular song that she inspired but never sang), the line is never spoken exactly that way anywhere in the film. Woody Allen probably cemented the misunderstanding by making *Play It Again, Sam* the title of a play (and subsequent film) about a movie fan—played by himself, naturally—obsessed with Bogart and *Casablanca*. But, as everybody knows, Bogart's character, Rick, never said it.

It's a similar fallacy that Herman Hupfeld never had another hit song. Actually, he had two that, in their day, did considerably better. "When Yuba Plays the Rhumba on the Tuba" was a widely heard number in 1931, lots of bands and singers performed it, and almost anyone who listened to the radio with any regularity during the Depression (and that was *every-body*) would have instantly known who "Yuba" was. Likewise, "Let's Put Out the Lights and Go to Sleep" was almost as well received, and was also performed by many stars both in America and England. Compared to those two, "As Time Goes By" was a distant third. Even so, during the years 1931–32, when Hupfeld had at least three songs with fairly exten-sive recording and radio coverage, his would never be a household name.

In fact, the name *Herman* Hupfeld was known to almost no one, not even to the composer's friends and relatives, since from boyhood on he was always called "Dodo," or, more often, just plain "Do" (pronounced "Doh," like Homer Simpson's favorite monosyllabic expletive). Even when Rudy Vallee announced one of Hupfeld's songs on the air—and, at least once on a commercial record ("Savage Serenade")—he referred to the composer as "Dodo Hupfeld." Born on February 1, 1894, Dodo was raised in Montclair, New Jersey. He seems to have been something of a musical prodigy, as his parents sent him to Germany to study the violin while he was still in short pants. He served Stateside during World War I as a musician in a Navy band, without having to leave his native New Jersey.

Dodo had no brothers or sisters, and his father died when he was still a boy. Family members say he was overly attached to his mother, and that he had a drinking problem. (Major Strasser: "What is your nationality?" Rick: "I'm a drunkard.") When his songs began providing royalties, he built a house which contained sets of rooms for himself and his mother, adjacent to the one he lived in as a little boy. He never married and it's not too much of a stretch to infer that Hupfeld was gay. A longtime friend, actress Bernice Claire, suggested as much to pianist and scholar Peter Mintun: "Do had many friends of both sexes, but women never had to feel threatened around him. He wasn't interested in them 'that' way."

Aljean Harmetz notes, "Hupfeld wrote over a hundred songs"—not much to show for a lifetime of work (Sammy Cahn wrote that many in one good season)—"but he never wrote a complete show." It's true enough, yet we should view this fact in its historical context: many musical productions in the 1920s and thirties were revues of the loosest possible sort, and very few of these featured the work of only one composer or songwriting team. For instance, although on *The Little Show* and *The Second Little Show,* the "core" songwriters were Arthur Schwartz and Howard Dietz, Hupfeld contributed songs to each. And some other shows that Hupfeld worked on employed so many different composers that it wouldn't make sense to describe any of them as a core writer.

Hupfeld produced so little in his career that we can map the bulk of his output fairly easily. Edward Jablonski's valuable *Encyclopedia of American Music* lists Hupfeld's first notable song as being an unnamed piece for the *Ziegfeld Midnight Frolic* of 1912, but I can't confirm this, nor even that there *was* a *Ziegfeld Midnight Frolic* in 1912. He did, however, write a song ("Two Quick Quackers") for the same producer's *Ziegfeld 9 O'clock Frolic of 1921* and this seems to have been his first production of note. Here is a show-by-show breakdown of his work:

Ziegfeld 9 O'Clock Frolic of 1921: "Two Quick Quackers."

Merry World (1926): Two songs by Hupfeld, "Come Over to Deauville" and "Don't Fall in Love with Me."

A la Carte (1927): Hupfeld is listed as the core composer here, but there are lots of songs by other writers. One of his songs, "Baby's Blue," did catch on briefly. "The Calinda," a parody of twenties dance crazes, was recorded at the time by Paul Whiteman's orchestra, featuring a young Bing Crosby as one of the vocalists.

The Little Show (1929): As noted, the bulk of the score was by Schwartz and Dietz, but Hupfeld supplied "A Hut in Hoboken" (never recorded by Frank Sinatra).

The Nine Fifteen Revue (1930): A legendary flop that ran just seven performances, but Hupfeld is in good company, as the other songwriters included Rodgers and Hart, Harold Arlen, Kay Swift, and even Rudolf Friml and the late Victor Herbert. Hupfeld's song: "Two Gat Gertie."

The Second Little Show (1930): This is the show that actually introduced "Sing Something Simple" (which was written for *Artists and Models,* a revue from earlier that year, although the song was cut while the show was trying out in Newark). "Sing Something Simple," a very wry commentary on Tin Pan Alley, is one of Hupfeld's best songs. It was recorded by several bands at the time, including Leo Reisman (who included the verse), but has been woefully neglected ever since, except by June Christy (on the classic *The Misty Miss Christy*), although even she overlooked the verse.

Experience Unnecessary (1931): This was a nonmusical play which utilized one song, Hupfeld's "We Were Waltzing."

Everybody's Welcome (1931): The basic score here was by Sammy Fain and Irving Kahal; Hupfeld's sole contribution was "As Time Goes By."

The Third Little Show (1931): Unlike the first two, this used too many songs by too many different writers to qualify Schwartz and Dietz as the core composers. The score for this production included the work of Burton Lane and Noel Coward, who introduced several of his most famous songs to Broadway audiences here. Hupfeld's only contribution was "Yuba," his biggest hit of the period.

George White's Music Hall Varieties (1932): This revue introduced the hit listed in the program as "Let's Turn Out the Lights and Go to Bed," soon a hit as "Let's Put Out the Lights and Go to Sleep."

Hey Nonny Nonny (1932): This production has the distinction of being even more obscure than most other Hupfeld-associated ventures, and it boasts three songs by the composer, "Be a Little Lackadaisical," "Would That Be Wonderful," and "Let's Go Lovin'."

The Passing Show of 1932: Passing is right; it closed out of town. Hupfeld's only contribution: "Sing a Little Song."

Murder at the Vanities (1933): Hupfeld wrote the very clever "Savage Serenade" for this one, and though it caught on to some degree it didn't quite challenge "Yuba" or "Let's Put Out the Lights" for popularity.

There also were two films in 1933:

Take a Chance: In which Cliff Edwards introduces the beautiful "Night Owl," a stunning song also recorded at the time by the beloved Ethel Schutta, and more recently by Barbara Lea.

Moonlight and Pretzels: A delightful, underappreciated *42nd Street*–style backstage musical, with Roger Pryor as a pushy songwriter-producer and two of "Dodo's" best songs, "Are You Makin' Any Money?" and "Gotta Get Up and Go to Work," which were only two of the several directly Depression-oriented songs in the piece. Paradoxically, Jay Gorney, who had already written (with Yip Harburg) the anthem of the era, "Brother, Can You Spare a Dime?" was the core songwriter on the film, yet here Hupfeld's songs were considerably more topical.

That was the bulk of Hupfeld's work. He seems to have written even fewer songs away from Broadway. The most notable of these is "Goopy Gear," a 1931 opus along the lines of "Piccolo Pete," a twenties and thirties convention among songwriters of describing musicians of mythical ability: whereas Pete could play "tweet, tweet" on his piccolo like "a bird in disguise," Goopy Gear "plays piano and he plays by ear." An extended "art song" with lots of verses and choruses, "Goopy Gear" (which inspired a 1931 Merrie Melodies cartoon) was also recorded by Britain's Al Bowlly. Of all Hupfeld's songs, "Goopy Gear" was the only one that the composer himself recorded, a Brunswick 78 with Victor Young's orchestra.

After 1933, Hupfeld turns up again on Broadway in several more revue-type productions:

The Show Is On (1936): Starring Bert Lahr. HH's only song is "Buy Yourself a Balloon," but, again, our man is in good company: Rodgers and Hart, Harold Arlen, Hoagy Carmichael, Schwartz and Dietz, even George and Ira Gershwin ("By Strauss"). "Buy Yourself a Balloon" would also be heard two years later in the London revue Happy Returns.

Two Weeks with Pay (1940): This one also closed out of town, but featured choreography by the young Gene Kelly and what seems like another Hupfeld commentary on the nature of the popular song, something called "June Moon Spoon." Unrelated to this show, in 1939 both Cab Calloway and Ted Weems and His Orchestra, with a vocal by the young Perry Como, recorded a pop song credited to Hupfeld, "Ad-De-Day (Song of the Cuban Money Divers)." It's another oddity in a career filled with oddities; perhaps the composer intended this return visit to Cuba as a follow-up to "Yuba."

Dance Me a Song (1950): Wotta cast—Wally Cox, Bob Fosse, Bob Scheerer (then dancer and future director of Sinatra and *Star Trek*)— but wotta flop! Only thirty-five performances on Broadway. Hupfeld's sole song here is one for the books: something called "My Little Dog Has Ego." I'd like to hear Michael Feinstein sing *that!*

And so it would appear that in 1931, *Everybody's Welcome* just represented another little show to place another little song, "As Time Goes By," in. There was always the possibility that it might go somewhere, but more likely it wouldn't. Unlike most Hupfeld-oriented productions, *Everybody's Welcome* had a clear-cut plot, being based on an older comedy entitled *Up Pops the Devil*. Harmetz states that the plot concerned "an unmarried couple who lived together in Greenwich Village." (But, then, Harmetz also states that the Ritz Brothers appeared in the show, something I can't verify.) The production starred Frances Williams (who sang "As Time Goes By"), Oscar Shaw (a very stiff leading man of the period best known for playing straight man to the Marx Brothers in *The Cocoanuts*), Ann Pennington, comic Jack Sheehan, and leading lady Harriette Lake. The last-named actress later became a star at MGM under the name Ann Sothern, but in retrospect, the two biggest names in this production were not on stage but beneath it: Tommy and Jimmy Dorsey, who led the pit band during the show and played dance music during the intermission.

Even before the show opened, on October 13, 1931, at the Shubert Theater, "As Time Goes By" had been heard on records and radio. The first recording seems to be the Rudy Vallee Victor version, which had been waxed back on July 25. There was also a September tenth recording by Freddie Rich's orchestra, vocal by Smith Ballew, as "The Columbians" (on Columbia, naturally). The major recording from the American Recording Corporation (ARC), which owned Brunswick, was by Jacques Renard and His Orchestra, with a vocalist not listed on the label or in any of the reference books but identified by thirties vocal authority John Leifert as session singer Frank Munn; this track was laid down on October 12, 1931, the day before the Broadway opening.

After the premiere, there were recordings by a two-piano combo called "The Piano Twins" (on Banner, December 1, 1931), while the first international recording was apparently by the American-born English bandleader Carroll Gibbons and the Savoy Orpheans (February 5, 1932, on the British Columbia label). The first female vocal version is by the English musical-comedy star Binnie Hale (also on British Columbia, February 5, 1932), a member of a British theatrical family that included her brother, Sonny Hale, and sister-in-law, Jessie Matthews. Miss Hale places the verse in the middle and talk-sings most of her second chorus, sighing a bit too enthusiastically after the phrase "a sigh is just a sigh." Although Vallee's is by far the most widely heard of the original "period" versions of "As Time Goes By," the best early version is not a recording at all but an aircheck of one of Bing Crosby's early radio performances, from November 7, 1931. (Frances Williams also sang the song on an early radio broadcast, while *Everybody's Welcome* was still running on Broadway, although no aircheck is known to exist.)

At 127 performances (Harmetz says 139), *Everybody's Welcome* was far from a blockbuster, but back then that was long enough to turn a profit for the investors, and it was one of the longer-running shows Hupfeld was involved in. The recording industry seems to have been ahead of the other cultural institutions of the day in realizing the song's worth. One unnamed critic for *Time* magazine wrote: "Frances Williams sings three good songs, one funny ('I Shot the Works'), one tuneful ('As Time Goes By'), one both ('Is Rhythm Necessary?'). Oscar Shaw and Harriette Lake sing a silly song ('You've Got a Lease on My Heart') so well that it will probably be a minor hit."

Another item, written by one Wilela Waldorf (discovered by Peter Mintun, who wasn't able to pinpoint the publication) made the point that the early exposure of the song might not have been such a good thing. "Mr. Shaw and Harriette Lake, the leading lady, plunge through a number of limpid ditties, making each word clear, alas!" says Miss Waldorf, if that was indeed her name. "Miss Williams seems to have brought along one of her favorites in 'As Time Goes By,' or did we only think we'd heard that before?" Meow!

Ann Sothern was billed as the ingenue leading lady of the show, yet it was Williams, then an established singing star, who sang "As Time Goes By." The song "was the big hit of the show," Sothern later recalled for Harmetz, "and Frances Williams sang it wonderfully. I always wished I could be the one to sing it." (Yet twenty-five years or so later, when Sothern recorded an LP of her own, she didn't include it.) "As Time Goes By" was heard twice in the show, sung both times by Williams, the first time close to the end of Act One, the second in act two as a duet between Williams and comedian Jack Sheehan.

It's a major loss that Williams was between recording contracts in 1931; she had recorded earlier for Brunswick in 1928–29 and would record later in '33 for Columbia, but the timing was wrong for her to make a record of "As Time Goes By." She was a fine, jazz-influenced singer, one of the best of the era, with a deep sultry voice—"a long, skinny lady with a low husky voice" is how Sothern described her—not strictly a torch singer like Libby Holman, and somewhat more mannish but perhaps less mannered than many femme singers of the era.

As mentioned above, Williams also sang "As Time Goes By" on a radio broadcast that is not believed to have survived. Indeed, it's a fortunate fluke that Bing Crosby's great November 1931 aircheck exists, or we should say half-survives, because it exists only as a fragment. We get the verse and a full chorus, and then it cuts off, leaving us to wonder whether it was just about to end or did Crosby actually sing another half or full chorus. The Crosby aircheck has been in the hands of Crosbyphiles for some time but has only been issued semiprivately on LP.

Thus, the most widely heard of the early versions is that of Rudy Vallee, which is appropriate as Vallee seems to have been a personal friend of Hupfeld's. He certainly recorded more Hupfeld songs than any other artist, among them "Yuba" (which he cut on at least three different occasions), "As Time Goes By" (which was released as "As Time Goes On" on the English HMV record label), "Let's Put Out the Lights," and "Savage Serenade," the last of which begins with a spoken introduction wherein Vallee mentions "Dodo Hupfeld, composer of 'Yuba.' " Eventually, Vallee's faith in Hupfeld's work would pay off for the Vagabond Lover, and in a very big way that no one could have imagined back in 1931.

Among Hupfeld's other friends was George Gershwin, who invited Dodo to perform on his radio series, *Music by Gershwin,* in 1935. Another was Bernice Claire, best known for her work in several early talkie musicals, such as the rare original film of *No, No Nanette* (1930) and Hupfeld's own *Moonlight and Pretzels* (1933). Claire also came up with a nugget of information that challenges, though mildly, the idea that "As Time Goes By" was written by one man. Claire suggests, in fact, that she herself had some input. "He said he couldn't get the penultimate line the way he wanted, so I suggested 'The world will always welcome lovers. . . .' "

Claire once showed Peter Mintun a vintage photograph of the composer with the inscription: "To my very good friend, Claire. And thanks for the last line! [signed] Do Hupfeld."

REGARDLESS OF WHO WROTE the second-to-last line, "As Time Goes By" is an outstanding song, both musically and lyrically, philosophically and melodically. The current edition is in C, although at different times it's been published in E flat—that's the way it appears in various fake books, including a collection of reharmonized treatments of popular songs by piano wizard Dick Hyman, as well as in an earlier edition of the sheet music reproduced in the 1997 Rhino CD release of the *Casablanca* soundtrack.

The song is basically in *A-A-B-A* format. Some songs ("I'm in the Mood for Love," "Night and Day") place the title phrase at the beginning of each *A* section; "As Time Goes By," like "Body and Soul," positions it at the end. In both of the first two times that we get to that "As time goes by" phrase, the first three notes (in the key of C) are always the same: G ("As") C ("time") D ("goes"). But then the fourth and last note ("by") is placed differently: at the end of the first *A* section it's an E; in the second, it's the low tonic C. The title phrase gets four different notes: "As" (E) "time" (G) "goes" (G), ending on the high tonic C on "by." In the third and last (after the bridge), it's the high tonic C. That's not usually how it's sung, however. Often singers perform it in two choruses (or a chorus and a half), and they generally end the first chorus on the low tonic and the second on the high tonic. Therefore, we might say the structure of the song is thirty-two bars, A-A^1-B-A^2, preceded by a twelve-bar verse.

Harmonically, the song is neither as interesting as "My Funny Valentine," as challenging as "Body and Soul," or as useful to musicians as "I Got Rhythm." The chords are no more interesting than they need to be. (As with many songs, the tonic chord isn't heard at all in the bridge.) The harmony is sufficient but not spectacular, which explains why "As Time Goes By" hasn't received as much instrumental jazz attention as the above three songs. No, it isn't the harmony that makes "As Time Goes By" a great song, it's the melody and the lyrics. As with most songs, the tune basically proceeds step-wise or scale-wise.

Hupfeld also holds notes for emphasis, the last note of each *A* section

("As time goes *by* . . .") being held for either two whole measures or close to it. But more frequently he uses rests for the same purpose: there's a pregnant pause between the second and third lines, and between the fourth and fifth lines—the first two lines set up a conflict and the second two resolve it. Then there's another pause before we start the next section (and new conflict).

The verse, like many of its kind, consists mainly of repeated notes—it's a spoken introduction almost as much as a musical verse. Indeed, the music is little more than a very basic background for the lyric; but, again, that's all that's required. The verse sets up the song's outstanding lyric, and gives us a clue as to what we're in for by starting with the quadruple rhyme of "apprehension," "invention," "dimension," and "tension." Both Vallee and Crosby include the verse in their 1931 performances, although since it was not heard in *Casablanca,* only a few post-1942 treatments use it (Lee Wiley and Mark Murphy are two). Crosby omits it in his 1943 aircheck.

Vallee's and Crosby's early versions illustrate the difference between the two singers, as do those of Frank Sinatra and Vic Damone thirty years later. There's no denying that Vallee's is romantic—he was the big crooning heartthrob of the the late 1920s. Vallee's is also the most important version to use the countermelody, possibly written by Hupfeld but conceivably by an in-house arranger at Harms, Inc., the song's publisher. That countermelody can be found in the piano accompaniment to the vocal line in the sheet music as published today. But if Vallee is mildly tender and almost charming in a fey way, Crosby is considerably more modern-sounding, not to mention more jazzy and darkly sensual. He personalizes the melody far more aggressively, starting with an Armstrongian "Ah," before the first line of the refrain, "You must remember this. . . ." His treatment of the verse is especially interesting: more than any other singer, at least up until Mark Murphy (1972), Crosby *sings* the verse rather than talking it in recitative style, and he does it at a uniquely fast and clearly defined tempo.

Where Vallee is warm, Crosby is hot, lingering on the word "mate" and slowing down enticingly at the end of the bridge. Crosby also makes one important lyric change: as written by Hupfeld, the verse makes reference to "speed and new invention / and things like third dimension." One wonders what the big deal is about the third dimension; surely, the idea of three dimensions in physical space had been around for a while. Crosby, however, sings "things like *fourth* dimension," which is rather more apt, as the fourth dimension, time, was a concept that was turning up in physics and science fiction of the period.

Whether it was about the third or fourth dimension, Hupfeld's message was that no matter where progress takes mankind, certain things will always still say the same. This was an era of scientific achievement; the changes that had taken place in transportation and the reproduction of music in Hupfeld's own lifetime alone were staggering, yet his song's lyric is fundamentally skeptical of technology, lightly pooh-poohing the whole idea of scientific progress. Hupfeld denigrates human "speed and new invention" while at the same time praising human emotion. Small wonder that Murray Burnett fought to keep the song in the movie: Hupfeld's lyric could be the unspoken mantra for Bogart's Rick Blaine. In forty-four bars, the song completely captures *Casablanca*'s leading man, the cynical idealist, the tough guy with a sentimental streak.

Hupfeld was thinking in terms of what was then considered to be "progress"—he couldn't know where the world was heading in the next decade. Thus, in 1931 Hupfeld was saying that no matter how mankind "betters" itself in things like technological progress, hearts will always be "full of passion, jealousy, and hate." By 1942, the song had taken on a different meaning, or, rather it meant the same thing from a different perspective. Instead of saying that no matter what new gadgets we invent, love and romance will always be the same, the lyric now suggested that no matter how many brutal wars we start, no matter how many millions of innocent people we slaughter, no matter how close mankind comes to blowing itself up, love and romance will always be the same. Indeed, the war imbues the message with a spiritual slant: in the face of World War II, even as Major Strasser informs Ilsa that "in Casablanca, human life is cheap," love is still the only thing that can redeem us and make us whole, and that will never change, as time goes by.

Naturally the verse wasn't used in the film; it would have been completely unnecessary to remind people of "speed and new invention" when the song had by 1942 assumed a much greater significance. The "progress of what may yet be proved," as Hupfeld's verse somewhat awkwardly though endearingly put it, somehow no longer amounted to a hill of beans in this crazy world.

MURRAY BURNETT HAD LOVED the song since 1931, when he was a senior at Cornell University and had played it over and over. He later remembered playing Frances Williams's recording (so he told Aljean Harmetz), which was impossible, since Williams never recorded it. *Everybody Comes to Rick's* was inspired by La Belle Aurore, a nightclub on the French Riviera that Burnett visited during a trip to Europe in 1938, where people of all nations, including both French and German officers, sat and talked and listened—or didn't listen—to a black pianist and singer performing the old chestnuts. In Ronald Haver's article "The Truth about *Casablanca*," it's even suggested that the pianist there actually played "As Time Goes By," already Burnett's favorite song. The most important character in both the unproduced play and the subsequent movie was the venue itself, Rick's Café Américain, and now Burnett had that as well as his "Sam," whose piano was at the center of it all.

So there was Sam and there was "As Time Goes By" before there was Bogart's Rick, Claude Rains's Captain Louis Renault, Paul Henreid's Victor Laszlo, Peter Lorre's Ugarte, Sydney Greenstreet's Signor Ferrari, even Cuddles Sakall as Carl the waiter. At one point, producer Hal Wallis came up with the masterstroke of making Sam into "Samantha," turning Rick's piano-playing sidekick into a woman. He had been to Cafe Society in Greenwich Village to hear and see Hazel Scott, a fine pianist and occasional singer, who was even more impressive as a stunning presence and the epitome of the superelegant, ultraclassy sophisticated lady of color, circa 1942. In addition to considering Scott for the part, Wallis debated using Lena Horne or Ella Fitzgerald. ("Play it again, Ella!") Luckily, the sex change idea was abandoned and the screenwriting team returned to Burnett's original conception of Sam as Sam. (Fitzgerald herself did sing a corker of a treatment of "ATGB" in 1970, however.)

In 1941, Arthur "Dooley" Wilson (1884–1953) was known only for having originated the leading role of "Little Joe" opposite Ethel Waters's "Petunia" in the 1940 Broadway musical *Cabin in the Sky*. In a career that began around the turn of the century, Wilson had experience in every aspect of black show business, from singing in church as a child in his native Texas to working in nearly all the early attempts at creating a legitimate theater showcase for "colored" talent, from the Pekin Theater in

Chicago in 1908 to John Houseman's Negro Theater Wing in the 1930s and Orson Welles's all-black production of *Macbeth*. Wilson also made music, playing drums and singing, most notably in a band that entertained American troops in Europe during World War I.

Thanks to *Cabin*, Wilson earned a contract with Paramount Pictures (though not the chance to repeat his role of Little Joe in the lavish MGM film version, in which the role went to Eddie "Rochester" Anderson), where he primarily played servants and frightened "darkies" in ghost stories. Oddly, none of his memorable movie roles were at Paramount: he gets some notable comedy in Fox's *Stormy Weather* and snatches of a song in RKO's *Higher and Higher,* in addition to the Warners' *Casablanca*. Although he was an actor, drummer, and singer, one thing Wilson didn't do was play the piano. After *Casablanca* briefly made him a big name, he was hired to entertain at a nightclub in San Francisco. Bay-area newspaperman Herb Caen reported that when Wilson showed up at the club, "he horrified the naïve café owner by asking, 'Where's my accompanist?' " Obviously, they didn't know they were hiring Dooley Wilson, the actor. They thought they were presenting Sam, no last name given, the singing pianist and best bud of Rick and Ilsa.

Just as Wallis had nearly blundered by giving Sam a sex change (and Ilsa was the one from Sweden!), Max Steiner, the film's musical director, similarly schemed to shortchange history. "As Time Goes By" set Steiner's teeth on edge, and he insisted on replacing it with a love theme of his own composing. The story goes that after shooting was completely finished, Steiner actually convinced Wallis of the need to use this new original melody, even to the point of reshooting the scenes in which the love song was played on the set, and redoing the dialogue, with "As Time Goes By" replaced by "Maxie's Melody," or whatever the new theme was to be called.

Fortunately, the story continues, Ingrid Bergman had already cut her hair killer-short for *For Whom the Bell Tolls* and there was no way to make the new footage match the old. So the right song was preserved, and all for the want of a few follicles. Now, I'm no expert on wig crafting, but it seems to me that by 1942 the state of hair technology had progressed to the point where some inventive hair stylist could have devised a mop to resemble Bergman's hair of just a few weeks earlier. The story about the locks not matching is probably something they dreamed up to pacify Steiner, while in reality the budget-minded Wallis and Jack Warner wouldn't have dreamed of undertaking costly retakes merely to assuage their music director's ego.

It was Steiner's orchestrator, Hugo Friedhofer, who eventually convinced the great man of the song's worth. "I know that [Steiner] didn't have the feeling that 'As Time Goes By' would work in the orchestra at all," he said in a 1974 interview, "because he had a concept of it being kind of a square tune, which requires translation from what's in the printed piano part to a more relaxed version. . . . I said, 'Max, think of it this way, with broad triplet phrasing.' He kind of thought about it and that's the way it came out. But it's a good tune, let's face it, and it's the kind of phrasing that jazzmen fall into naturally."

Once Steiner was convinced, he stayed convinced. He made it the leitmotif of the entire movie, not just the love theme. It's heard straight-ahead, it's heard ironically, it's heard romantically, it's heard stirringly (as a quasi-march), it's heard in major, it's heard in minor, it's heard fast, it's heard slow, it's heard exuberantly, it's heard tragically, it's heard to communicate things to the audience that they are not being shown and that the dialogue is not saying. It provides the first clue we have that there is a love story between Rick and Ilsa, and then it provides a bridge to the flashback, dissolving into "La Marseillaise" from the Casablanca of the present (December 1941) to the Paris of the past (June 1940), the day she wore blue and the invading Germans wore gray.

As people who have never even seen the movie know, "As Time Goes By" is their song—Rick and Ilsa's, that is. It's the symbol of their love together in Paris, before they were separated not only by the war but by Ilsa's discovery that her husband, Victor, was still alive, despite reports of his death at the hands of the Nazis. Wilson sings it at two points in the film: first, when Ilsa comes into the café to see Rick and asks him to play it (encouraging the reluctant Sam by humming it in her Swedish accent, thus marking the first time we hear the melody in the film), a performance that is cut short by Rick's storming in angrily with "Sam, I thought I told you never to play that!" The second time occurs when Rick is getting plastered, waiting for Ilsa to return. Now it's Bogie's turn to demand that Sam play the song: "You know what I want to hear. You played it for her, you can play it for me. If she can stand it, I can!"

Wilson never sings it all the way through; in fact, the second time he doesn't sing it at all; he (or rather, the off-screen "sidelining" pianist,

Elliot Carpenter) plays a few bars of it before we fade into the Paris montage. Wilson did record a complete vocal version, which has been released on the *Casablanca* soundtrack CD, and in 1943 he also cut a commercial 78 of the song for Decca. Both of Wilson's versions are in D flat; in the movie he gets the first line slightly wrong when he sings "a kiss is *just* a kiss" instead of "a kiss is *still* a kiss," as it should be, but he gets the lyric right on the Decca. Wilson also plays a bit with the notes: he begins the bridge on a high B flat, a sixth above the tonic (where Hupfeld intended it to start) and, curiously, ends both of his choruses on the fifth (as Crosby had in 1931 and Sinatra would in 1961), instead of the high or the low tonic.

Although *Casablanca* would earn Oscars for nearly all the behind-the-scenes talent—best picture, screenplay, direction, a Thalberg Achievement Award for Wallis, and best score—Hupfeld, sad to say, was not eligible to win one for best song from a motion picture because of another Oscar. In 1940, Oscar Hammerstein and Jerome Kern, emotionally moved by the fall of the France, wrote a song called "The Last Time I Saw Paris." It was composed independently of any show or film score, but a year or so later, MGM worked it into *Lady, Be Good,* a musical starring Ann Sothern of *Everybody's Welcome* fame. It won an Oscar for best song, but Hammerstein and Kern were sore winners, so devoted to the higher ideals of musical drama that they petitioned the Academy to change the rules so that only songs written especially for the movies they were in could be considered for the Oscar. Thus, two years later, "As Time Goes By" wasn't even in the running. Did that annoy Hupfeld? One assumes that the long-neglected composer, who hadn't landed anything on Broadway or in Hollywood in years, was nothing short of ecstatic over the reception his dozen-year-old song was getting, even if the Academy could not honor it. In the spring of 1943, the song began turning up on *Lucky Strike Presents Your Hit Parade,* where the resident crooner was Frank Sinatra, then in an emergent mode roughly analogous to where Crosby had been when "As Time Goes By" was new, in 1931. The song was all over the radio that year, and Crosby, on his long-running *Kraft Music Hall,* returned to it in a gentler, less intense reading than he'd given twelve years earlier.

Would that Crosby or Sinatra had recorded it in 1943. But Hupfeld had the ill luck (once again) of landing his biggest hit during the infamous American Federation of Musicians recording ban of 1942–44, in which no union instrumentalist was allowed to so much as walk into a commercial studio. Virtually no recordings at all were made during that two-year period, and most of those that were made are best not mentioned in polite company. However, because this was an old song, the companies did have vintage 1931 waxings that they were able to take out of mothballs, most notably the Jacques Renard–Frank Munn dance version (reissued with a bright green Brunswick label), which made it to the number-three spot on the *Billboard* chart, and Rudy Vallee's Victor, which shot all the way up to number one and stayed there for four weeks. Vallee himself had long since switched from being a stiff romantic leading man to being a very funny comic supporting player (most winningly as John D. Hackensacker III in *The Palm Beach Story*), yet when "As Time Goes By" returned to the charts, the song briefly made him into a crooning idol all over again. (Vallee was, coincidentally, present for another memorable "ATGB": in November 1943, he was the guest on a Lifebuoy-sponsored broadcast starring Spike Jones and His City Slickers. On that occasion, the Slickers cut their goofball version of "ATGB" for a V-Disc, replete with gunshots, breaking glass, and assorted shrieks and grunts punctuating their bizarro dixieland treatment plus a female singing duo, the Nilson Twins, who didn't neglect the verse.)

HUPFELD DIDN'T SUFFER because of the recording ban. In fact, it gave "As Time Goes By" an advantage over new songs; it sold far more records in the spring of 1943 than, for instance, the new songs from the Broadway superhit *Oklahoma!* simply because there were no *Oklahoma!* recordings by dance bands or by singers with proper orchestral accompaniment. The individual who was probably most hurt by the ban was Dooley Wilson. If he had been able to record the song in January of 1943, he might well have beat out Vallee and landed a number-one hit. Wilson undoubtedly agreed to record the song for Decca because that was the first of the major labels to reach an agreement with the musicians' union, which happened in October 1943, beating Columbia and Victor by a year. But, alas, by October it was too late: the rereleases had hit the charts seven months earlier and the song had been on *Your Hit Parade* from February to May. When Wilson's record came out at the end of the year, it failed even to dent the charts. By the time the labor action ended, few of the major labels even bothered to record "As Time Goes By"; Crosby re-revived it on a New Year's Eve radio recap of the year's hits, but Decca didn't ask him to record it.

THE SONG WOULD become a classic, but it was not yet a standard, just a revived hit that would come and go like other hits. As the forties wore on, a minor precedent would be set for reviving the occasional older song such as "Little White Lies" (1930 and 1948), "Guilty" (1931 and 1947), every now and then. As already mentioned, Sinatra sang "As Time Goes By" a number of times on *Your Hit Parade* and elsewhere on the air, the most interesting version in circulation being a rehearsal take featuring a stunning arrangement by his longtime musical director Axel Stordahl (at that time, radio rehearsals were extensively recorded for possible use by the Armed Forces Radio Service and the V-Disc program). Sinatra is feisty and lively here, not only singing but talking back jokingly to some technicians who seem to be standing around, ribbing him. As written, the bridge is a telegraphic list of phrases and ideas and not a complete grammatical sentence: "Moonlight and love songs / Never out of date" it goes. The young Sinatra, however, singing it in B flat, is one of several singers who inserts the verb "are" between the two lines. Sinatra also holds the last note ("by . . .") for four measures. It would have made a classic Columbia record for him.

Billie Holiday, probably on the advice of her producer, Milt Gabler, was the rare singer who had the smarts to record the song after it was off the charts and the picture out of the theaters. On her 1944 Commodore Records version, she rewrites the melody quite liberally. Taking it in G, she goes up a fourth (to D) at the end of the first two bars, where it's supposed to go down, and then repeats the motion where the phrase occurs again at the start of the second eight bars, as if to show us that this is not a random decision or merely a case of getting the melody wrong. She starts the bridge on E instead of the expected low G, going down chromatically from B to B flat to A on the words "man must . . . ," then back up to the high B on "have," and down once more by half-steps on "his [B flat] mate [A]," A being the note where it would have ended anyhow, without these melodic alterations. The ending is classic Holiday: instead of merely holding the last note for a measure on the tonic, she starts to sing "by" a whole step above the tonic, on A, and then slides down chromatically to the tonic, from A to A flat to G. It's the kind of mannerism she would overuse in her later years, but it seems fresh and new here.

The song and the film also caught on again in England, where there was no recording ban to impede its progress. Back in February 1932, Carroll Gibbons and the Savoy Hotel Orpheans recorded "ATGB," and then in March 1943, the song was recorded again by Gibbons. Adelaide Hall, the black American songstress (and early Ellington canary), who spent most of her career in London, recorded a fine treatment, virtually in dance tempo, in 1943.

With the success of the song and the movie, Hupfeld is said to have petitioned Warner Brothers to give him a regular salary as an on-staff songwriter, but the studio turned him down. Luckily, though, the song's burst of fame in 1943 assured that Hupfeld wouldn't require any other income. Little, if anything, is known about his later songs. As mentioned above, in 1950 he contributed one song ("My Little Dog Has Ego"— thank you, Sigmund Freud) to the flop revue *Dance Me a Song;* his most recent show had been an entire decade earlier. There was a *Ziegfeld Follies of 1957* (it lasted for 123 performances at the Winter Garden) that featured a song by Hupfeld with still another odd title, "Miss Follies of 192 . . . ," although by this time both the producer and the composer were long gone. Herman Hupfeld had died on June 8, 1951, at the age of fifty-seven, still living in the house he shared with his mother, who survived him by many years.

IN THE LONG RUN, however, it was none of the 1943 or '44 performances that made "As Time Goes By" into a standard; it was more of a cumulative effect that began in the fifties, when *Casablanca* began to appear regularly on TV and singer after singer began including "ATGB" on long-playing albums. While "Body and Soul" was mainly the province of jazz singers, "As Time Goes By" was primarily the property of pop stars: Vera Lynn, Britain's most popular songstress of the Blitz years and beyond, cut this greatest love theme of the war. Perry Como cut a low-key and thoroughly convincing version in 1955 (on *So Smooth*). Barbra Streisand, on her 1964 *Third Album,* gave it all she had back in the days when she still knew what a good song was (and was able to convince us that she also knew what things like sighs and kisses were). Joni James rendered it in that slightly pinched voice that sold eight zillion singles in the years when everybody liked Ike. Julie London's seductive style wasn't exactly suited to "ATGB," as she sounds more as if she'd rather be making love than singing about it, but she gave it her best shot.

Smoky-voiced Lee Wiley recorded it on what might be the best of her LPs, *West of the Moon* (1956), on which she was accompanied by a no-less-smoky-sounding ensemble of woodwinds, strings, and rhythm under the baton of Ralph Burns. For a jazz singer, Wiley is surprisingly faithful to the written melody, and her inclusion of the verse gives the piece more of a thirties feel than Burns's lightly dissonant orchestration might suggest. One of Wiley's artistic progeny, Peggy Lee, recorded an equally misty treatment (on *If You Go,* 1961), slow and sensual and starting without any introduction or verse, opening straightaway with Lee on the first note of the refrain. With Quincy Jones conducting, Lee does it so hypnotically slowly—almost as if she were swimming in Jell-O—that there's no room for much of a second chorus, just a repeat of the final line. Lee's voice is not the only one heard on the track: a haunting, Oliver Nelson–like alto saxophone follows her throughout, soloing briefly in the instrumental break.

Two of the deeper-voiced "black baritones" of the 1950s, Al Hibbler and Billy Eckstine, gave it a go. Hibbler doesn't indulge his tendency toward bizarro sonic distortions here, but croons it as romantically as he knows how, in a fashion that makes him sound like the Barry White of his generation. Eckstine's recording, done with Billy May (two Billy's from Pittsburgh) on the excellent *Once More with Feeling* album, is outstanding. Starting with the verse, Mr. B. sighs very movingly on the word "sigh" and personalizes the melody throughout, sounding remarkably tender.

There's a fine, straight-as-written reading by Tony Martin on Mercury, and a Jack Jones treatment (on *Our Song*) that uses a light bossa nova backing in an easily danceable tempo that keeps the thing sounding like Prom Night 1966. Surprisingly, Billie Holiday's treatment did not make the song a fave among jazz singers. Carol Sloane made an album called *As Time Goes By;* now, lots of folks do their impression of Bogart uttering his apocryphal famous line, but Sloane is that rare artist savvy enough to bite off Ingrid Bergman's actual film line: "Play it, Sam; play 'As Time Goes By.' "

Vic Damone recorded a singularly beautiful treatment in 1958 on his album *Closer Than a Kiss,* on which he had the benefit of one of the finest orchestrations ever credited to Frank DeVol (whose arrangements for Tony Bennett, unfortunately, were never quite this good). There's a nicely throbbing countermelody throughout, and the tempo picks up slightly after the first chorus, at which point Glenn Miller–like reeds appear just when we expect strings. Damone starts his out-chorus at this tempo, but slows down after a few bars. For a coda he brilliantly blends into the reoccuring countertheme. Damone sings it like the master he is, but, as is true of most Damone performances, while he obviously knows what the words are about and sings them beautifully, he also leaves them bereft of irony or the deeper meaning that Sinatra always finds.

Sinatra's 1961 treatment (from his final Capitol album, *Point of No Return*) is, like his 1943 radio version, done in B flat and also has Axel Stordahl conducting. There the similarity ends. As with Peggy Lee, we start with only the voice at the refrain, first with just Bill Miller's piano and no tempo, just rubato; both the strings and the tempo arrive at the end of the first *A* section. Stordahl sprinkles a little celeste here and there, one of his favorite tonal colors since the forties, and the sustained strings rising chromatically behind the vocal (which are extremely effective on the first bridge) are more reminiscent of Nelson Riddle. Every note Sinatra sings is rife with meaning, and he makes us hear all kinds of things we've never noticed in the lyric before. A line like "On that you can rely" might come off as almost Runyonesque in someone else's hands, but Sinatra makes it sound supremely logical and natural. Just before his out-chorus, the whole thing modulates up a half-step to B natural, and the singer ends the piece as it began, with just voice and piano. Just as Holiday ended with a classic Holiday tonic slide, Sinatra concludes with a classic Sinatra understated, postclimactic "quiet" ending.

In an enthusiastic write-up of the film *Sleepless in Seattle,* critic Leonard Maltin wrote that "repeated allusions to the old tearjerker *An Affair to Remember* make you wonder if the only way to generate old-fashioned romance in a '90s movie is to invoke a product of Hollywood's golden age." *Sleepless in Seattle*'s primary reference was to the 1957 *Affair to Remember,* but by opening with "As Time Goes By," filmmaker Nora Ephron also clearly evokes *Casablanca,* a love story with an adventure angle, a tear-jerker that could be enjoyed by men as well as women. Ephron used a 1965 recording of Jimmy Durante singing "ATGB" with Gordon Jenkins's lush, heavy string orchestra (from the album *Jimmy*

Durante's Way of Life). When he was singing "straight"—that is, when he wasn't doing things with titles like "Inka Dinka Doo" and "Umbriago"— Durante could get fairly sentimental. Sentiment was Jenkins's stock-in-trade, and here the old left-handed conductor is especially baroque. Fortunately, the comically raspy tonal quality of Durante's voice was enough to balance out the potentially over-schmaltzy tendencies of both men. Jenkins also recorded Hupfeld's hit a decade or so later with the young singer (and songwriter) Harry Nilsson. Though Jenkins's work hasn't declined, Nilsson's voice makes us yearn for Durante.

Tony Bennett always named Durante as one of his key influences, and his voice might be described as similarly raspy. He didn't record "As Time Goes By" until 1975, but in 1969 he recorded a new song by Larry Gross-man (future *Muppet Show* composer) and Hal Hackaday (the team responsible for the legendary Broadway flop *Good Time Charley*) titled "Play It Again, Sam," apparently inspired by the Woody Allen play. Rather like Allen's play, the song "Play It Again, Sam" echoes both *Casablanca* and "As Time Goes By"—a jaded ex-lover repeatedly returns to a saloon and entreats the reluctant pianist to indulge him by playing the tune that was "their song" (presumably that song is Hupfeld's classic). Convincingly sung by Bennett (on his album *I Gotta Be Me*), with a warm trumpet solo by Marky Markowitz, "Play It Again, Sam" is a valuable contribution to the "As Time Goes By"/*Casablanca* mythology. Bennett's recording of the Hupfeld song itself (from his 1975 *Life Is Beautiful*) is equally beautiful. Both arrangements are by Torrie Zito, who gave Bennett's "As Time Goes By" (in C) a solidly Basie-esque feel, not only in the tempo (here you can even dance to the verse), but in the reed-section writing. Bennett does go up at the end, but it's not quite one of those big Tony Bennett blockbuster belt-strain endings he's known for.

A very young John Pizzarelli came up with his own variation on the "As Time Goes By"/*Casablanca* double-play in "Here's Looking At You, Kid," on his first album, the 1983 *I'm Hip*. It's a lovingly rendered homage from an aspiring songwriter and includes several catchphrases from the original song and movie, though, curiously, he renders it in a quasi-folk fashion rather than the Tin Pan Alley–jazz-triplet style associated with saloon songs and torch songs.

Mark Murphy's 1972 recording (on *Bridging a Gap*) is the Hupfeld words (although he changes "trifle" to "little") and music, but it sounds so different that listeners may well feel he's written a whole new song, or even that he's entered the fourth dimension (although he sings "third," as written). Murphy doesn't actually change too many notes or chords, he just makes changes to the temporal framework: in other words, he sings it killer-fast, even the verse, and the whole track sounds groovier still, thanks to a funky-sounding electric organ. The chart ends with a long, jazzy fade-out coda in which Murphy "rants" observations on the nature of time and space going by. It almost sounds as if he's inventing the entire career of protégé Kurt Elling in a single coda.

Other recent recordings have been more traditional. Chris Connor's 1991 reading (released only in Japan) is quite exquisite, although it's perhaps better identified as the Chris Connor–Hank Jones–George Mraz version, since both the pianist and the bassist take long and worthy solos. Connor sings it slowly but in tempo in her classic, understated style, letting the power of the words speak for themselves, without any unnecessary additional heaviness on the part of the singer, while Jones is his usual shimmering self on the keyboard. Rosemary Clooney has recorded the song twice in what could be called recent times, once at the start of the modern era of Rosiedom (1977), on her first Concord Jazz album, *Everything's Coming Up Rosie,* and more recently on *Dedicated to Nelson* for the same label in 1995. The 1995 CD uses an expansion of an arrangement Nelson Riddle wrote for Clooney for her TV series, and features a sax solo by TV's most famous tenor, Tommy Newsom. Yet although Riddle arranged the song for Clooney in the mid-1950s, the tempo and voicings are more suggestive of the big band era, gradually modulating upward and ending in a subtle yet exciting climax.

It's more of a song for singers than anything else, and as strong as the melody is, most of the instrumentalists who play it (and, as noted, there are far fewer of them than have played "Body and Soul" or "Funny Valentine") do so in a manner that recalls the lyrics. Erroll Garner, in his 1964 *At the Movies,* not only evoked the movie by staying in roughly the same tempo as the film version but sounded like Sam on steroids. His intro contains more of the familiar melody than is usual for "The Elf," giving us a hint that he won't stray much from it throughout the whole chorus and half—and he doesn't. He doubles both the time and the intensity of the chords in his out-chorus, and lovingly recaps the opening melody in the coda, which fades out like an old movie. (So does Mark Murphy eight years later, but the singer uses a board fade and Garner employs only the piano.)

Whereas Garner keeps his wit about him, other pianists seemingly can't resist the temptation to indulge in schmaltz. Teddy Wilson recorded "ATGB" at least three times—in a solo, a trio, and with string orchestra conducted by Glenn (real name Abe) Osser—and the song, unfortunately, never failed to bring out the cocktail keyboard side of Wilson. The same is true of Joe Bushkin, who also cut it with a rather Muzaky, Jackie Gleason–like orchestra. Still, there is a swinging, Tatumesque treatment by pianist Herman Chittison for a 1944 transcription, using a Cole-style trio with guitar and bass.

Which raises the question: Why didn't Cole himself ever play or sing "As Time Goes By"? For some reason, none of the leading pianist-singers seem to have done it, not Buddy Greco, Bobby Short, Nat or his talented younger brother, Freddy. It could be that they, especially the black artists listed here, regarded Dooley Wilson's Sam as an Uncle Tom–like figure, and wanted to avoid that stereotype. One prominent singer-pianist who went for it was the white Hugh Shannon, who embraces both the song and his status as a lounge lizard supreme *con mucho gusto.* He's very much in the spirit of Wilson as well as the movies' leading singing keyboardist, Hoagy Carmichael, and at one point hums the melody for a stretch.

It may well be that the best singer the song has found in the 1990s is tenor saxist Flip Phillips, who croons it with great sensitivity on *Try a Little Tenderness,* a '92 outing with strings and rhythm arranged by Dick Hyman. Phillips doesn't only render the melody lovingly, he phrases his improvisation as if he were crooning a love song. So does Ruby Braff, who recorded it with his New England Songhounds in 1991 (a group featuring pianist Dave McKenna, who himself recorded a worthy solo treatment), and again in 1999.

The oddest version of "As Time Goes By" is far from the worst (I made a point of not listening to recordings by Liberace and Johnnie Ray). Herbert Khaury, aka Tiny Tim—don't snicker—made two brilliant pop-comedy concept albums in the late 1960s, *God Bless Tiny Tim* and *Tiny Tim's Second Album.* These LPs would be notable if only for the range of their material, incorporating everything from hard rock to folk songs to Tin Pan Alley classics to country-western with steel guitar, some done completely straight, some done as affectionate parodies, with Tiny Tim and his orchestrators drawing on pop icons ranging from Gene Austin to Jerry Lee Lewis to Bob Dylan. Indeed, it's hard to know much of the time whether TT is being sincere, pulling our legs, or some combination of the two. As far as his own falsetto singing voice is concerned, Khaury may have been the first vocalist to make the connection between the androgynous pop stars of the long-haired, psychedelic sixties and the high-pitched, androgynous pop crooners of the twenties. If one bypasses the more aggressively masculine singers of the Crosby-Sinatra continuum, this is what remains. When Sinatra was trying to appeal to kids, he put pictures of himself with George Harrison and Tiny Tim (both long-haired, androgynous types) on the back of one of his albums. On TT's album, cut for Sinatra's own Reprise label, the singer positions a picture of himself with Rudy Vallee.

Tiny Tim is best remembered for his falsetto-and ukulele retread of "Tip Toe Thru' the Tulips," the signature song of twenties headliner Nick Lucas. Actually, his squeaky-high voice was no more or less an obvious gag than the voices of most of the male singers of the immediate pre-Crosby era. At the end of his *Second Album,* he closes with a parodically unctuous announcement in his goofy over-the-top high-pitched voice ("As all things must end, so must our little album, and I can think of no better way to leave you than with the words of this song . . ."). TT does the verse rubato with just piano accompaniment, singing the whole piece with the famous Tiny tremolo but in more of a baritone register. Darneill Pershing's lush arrangement sounds like forties movie music, and, like TT's singing, is nothing if not steadfastly earnest. TT makes a gaffe when he repeats "on that you can rely" in the bridge instead of "that no one can deny," but earns points with some Crosby-like whistling. (The label gives credit to one Herman Hupfield, which isn't as bad as a prominent discography that lists the name as Herman Hirschfield.) Such interjections as "Why, they're never out of date" and "But remember, my friends, woman still needs man," make the point that the biggest influence on TT's phrasing may be the vaudevillian-tragedian Ted Lewis. TT sings Hupfeld's verse as written, with its reference to "third dimension," but with his artful blending of various genres and eras of pop culture, Tiny Tim seems to have found a way to conquer things like the fourth dimension as well. For all of his audacity, TT may be the most successful of rock-era pop stars to tackle the tune. Others who have tried include Carly Simon and Roxy

Music's Bryan Ferry, but unlike certain other classic songs, "ATGB" doesn't lend itself easily to these kinds of voices.

Tiny Tim and Spike Jones were not the only performers from what we might call the spectrum of novelty music to address "As Time Goes By." The Warner Bros. cartoon division was keen to capitalize on "ATGB"'s hit status, especially since their parent company already owned the rights to the song. It appears in one form or another in almost a dozen Looney Tunes and Merrie Melodies, but gets its best moment in *Unruly Hare* (1944). That's the one where Bugs Bunny sings a generous chunk of Hupfeld's lyrics on screen, and, upon reaching "Woman needs man / And man must have his mate," the philosophical rabbit turns to the animation camera and directly addresses the audience with the affirmative observation, "Ain't it the truth?"

Bugs is right, and so is Hupfeld. It's been seventy years since "As Time Goes By" was first unleashed, and, old-fashioned as it sounds, the world is still welcoming lovers. They may not be traditional lovers circa 1931, they might be men with long hair and women in pants, or they might even be of the same sex, as Hupfeld's own loves seem to have been. But love goes on, and it's still the only thing that will redeem us all. And that, my friends, is something that no one can deny.

BONUS TRACKS

Most Moving Version

Here's our first of two treatments by great jazz ladies who apparently only sang "ATGB" when they were very far from home. Carmen McRae, on a 1973 album alternately titled *As Time Goes By* and *Live at the Dug,* recorded live at a club of that name in Tokyo (it's a rare LP, one never widely available in America), finds a perfect balance between speech and song in both the verse and the chorus. This ranks as one of the most touching and personal performances of McRae's entire career, made even more intimate because it's virtually the only album, live or studio, where McRae accompanies herself on piano. She uses a greatly altered set of lyrics in the verse ("No matter what the outcome / Or what might still be had, / The dearest things in life are free / So how can that be bad?"), and while they aren't necessarily an improvement on Hupfeld's, they do serve to make McRae's performance even more personal.

Most Surprising Version

Who knew that Ella Fitzgerald ever had anything to do with "As Time Goes By"? It's never been listed in her discography, but in 2000, four years after the great lady's death, Pablo (Fantasy) released a live concert from Budapest taped thirty years earlier. And lo and behold, there is the mother of all "As Time Goes By"s. Somehow, Fitzgerald manages to be aggressive and tender at the same time, consoling and swinging with a firm but gentle, rocking rhythm. We all know she's capable of taking either the melody or the changes and running rampant with them; instead, here she tactfully chooses to embroider the music only mildly, for instance stretching vowels on "no one ca-aa-aa-aan deny." She takes the song to a place it's never been, before or since. Maybe she wouldn't have been a bad choice to play "Sam" after all.

Most Intriguing Possible Version

Researcher Ivan Santiago has uncovered a clipping from *the New York Daily News,* May 10, 1953, which mentions that Peggy Lee was, at this time, shooting a Warner Bros. picture titled *Everybody Comes to Rick's.* There were many *Casablanca* rip-offs (such as *Singapore* with Fred Mac-Murray, and its remake, *Istanbul,* which featured Nat King Cole as a six-foot Sam who could actually play the piano), but judging from the title, this one seems to have been an authorized remake of *Casablanca,* using the title of the original play. Perhaps the Swedish-American Lee (born Norma Dolores Engstrom) was cast in the Ilsa role? What's especially odd is that the story doesn't say that Warners was merely contemplating a remake of the story—it says they were actually shooting it with Miss Lee. Nothing else is known about this project.

Most Touching Presentation

On December 6, 1979, the American Film Institute presented a special tribute to Ingrid Bergman via a TV special. At one point, in a sort of "This Is Your Life" bit, they arranged for Miss Bergman to sit in a replica of the Rick's set, and, to her apparent surprise, she was greeted by Frank

Sinatra singing "As Time Goes By." (Making it doubly delightful, Sinatra was accompanied by piano great Teddy—not Dooley—Wilson.) I don't doubt the stories that Bergman was lukewarm about both the song and *Casablanca,* but if she's not incredibly moved by it here, she's doing the best damn acting job of her career.

Zaniest Version

Even more zany than Spike Jones, Tiny Tim, or Bugs Bunny, the wildest reading is easily that of Louis Prima. The great New Orleans wildman recorded it, probably live, for his own label in the early seventies (on one of his last albums, *The Prima Generation '72*), using his soul-and-rock combo of the period, featuring funky electric organ and Sam Butera playing what sounds like amplified or Varitone sax. Prima is just out there, frantic and frenetically swinging the tune like crazy and just plain goofing on the words. In all of showbiz, there's no one funnier or more entertaining than Louis Prima, on that you can rely.

NIGHT AND DAY (1932)

words and music by Cole Porter

I can't leave you alone with a strange Italian. Why, he might turn out to be a tenor!

—GUY HOLDEN, *The Gay Divorcee*

CERTAIN SONGS HAVE TRADITIONALLY served as gateways to particular cultures. For instance, when dance bands in interwar Europe played "Stormy Weather," they wanted to evoke the world of the American Negro, jazz, and the blues. (Ironically, of the three major songs from the period associated with the black experience, "Stormy Weather," "Summertime," and "Ol' Man River," not one was written by an African-American composer.) "Night and Day" summons up an entirely different world—a world where crowds at El Morocco punish the parquet and where gay divorcées (not to mention jaded roués) leave the cherry, the orange, and the bitters out of their old-fashioneds and drink straight rye. When bands and singers wanted to go high-hat, they went into "Night and Day." Both its composer, Cole Porter (1891–1964), and the performer he wrote it for, Fred Astaire, were regarded as the very epitome of elegance.

The main idea isn't merely to be rich, but to show true sophistication—that is, to be cool, to act as if you have millions of smackers but couldn't care less. To register happiness, unhappiness, or any kind of emotion at all is to risk uncoolness. Singer-songwriter Jon Hendricks goofs on his lack of sophistication when he describes himself as "suave" and "blasé" but comically mispronounces these words as "swayve" and "blaze." Duke Ellington, in his famous "finger-snapping bit" performed during the closer of thousands of concerts in the sixties and seventies, showed an audience how to snap their digits to the backbeat. Snapping them on the beat, he explained, was "considered aggressive," whereas the whole point of the bit was to show the world that "you really don't care."

Cole Porter was the quintessence of cool. In the verse to "I Get a Kick Out of You," he describes himself as "Fighting vainly the old ennui," and according to Charles Schwartz, the best of his many biographers, this was indeed often the case.

> If the going became slightly tedious, he became almost another person: nervous and withdrawn, the glow gone, the eyes clouded. . . . His low boredom threshold could hardly be disguised. In a room full of elegantly dressed people, chattering away, he would turn inward if he was bored and became completely oblivious to the crowd.

As Porter's colleague Noel Coward put it in "A Bar on the Piccola Marina," "Nobody can afford to be so lahdy-bloody-da. . . ."

Coward may have given us the faux-blasé protagonist who claimed to be "so weary of it all," but in song after song, it's Porter who savages his own kind and himself. He starts "Well, Did You Evah?" with a verse (almost never sung) that cautions against the showing of one's anxiety. He then presents us with a room full of society types, the men looking like the Monopoly man or Mr. Esquire, the women looking as if they were drawn by Peter Arno or John Held. Then these dowagers and diplomats are given the news that a succession of members of their circle have perished in a variety of astonishing accidents—avalanches, lightning, empty swimming pools, and faulty parachutes (even worse, one "Mimsie Starr" was actually pinched in the Ass . . . tor bar). Instead of reacting in horror, the most these sophisticates can muster is a stifled, "Well, did you evah?"

In this respect, both Porter's comedy songs and his love songs have a common subject: emotion. The comic numbers tend to ridicule stone-faced upper-crust types who are too stiff to show any, even as the entire human race is about to be pulverized when, come next July, we collide with Mars. Conversely, Porter's love songs openly celebrate the few among us who have the guts to come out and express honest emotion and show the world what we feel. These are the unnamed, first-person heroes and heroines of such classic Porter songs as "I've Got You Under My Skin," "I Concentrate on You," "I've Got My Eyes on You," "I Get a Kick Out of You," and chief among them, "Night and Day."

The idea of making fun of the swells is at the heart of Porter's 1932 Broadway show *Gay Divorce*. The very mention of the word "divorce" in the twenties and thirties constituted sexual sophistication. This was, of course, well before the so-called sexual revolution of the post-Kennedy years, when divorcées (what was the male equivalent of this term, divorceurs?) and widows were the only women legally entitled to have had more than one man in their lives. Even though "gay" hardly suggested then what it does now, the idea of a Broadway romp on the subject of divorce was, nevertheless, intended to raise a few eyebrows. When the story was filmed a year later—alas, without most of the songs—"Such are the ways of the Hays office," Porter's friend Garson Kanin pointed out, that the picture had to be titled *The Gay Divorcee*.

Cole Porter had had hit songs and even hit shows before, but with *Gay Divorce* he was now a force to be reckoned with. In a period when many top Broadway writers, like Rodgers, Hart, Hammerstein, and Kern had been experiencing tough sledding on the Great White Way at the height of the Depression (the above four spent most of the early thirties hiding out in Hollywood), Porter was now firmly established as one of the top two or three songwriters working not only in the theater but throughout all of American pop. *Gay Divorce* did the same for Fred Astaire, who had previously been known as half of the dancing Astaires (with his sister, Adele), a terpsichorean team that had made good in vaudeville and then on Broadway and in London's West End. *Gay Divorce* was the vehicle with which he established himself not only as a solo leading man, but as probably the greatest of all dancers to fox-trot, waltz, and tap his way through the American imagination. And, last but not least, *Gay Divorce* gave us "Night and Day," a song that Frank Sinatra, who should know, once described as being even more rarefied than a standard—a "standard classic" was how he put it.

Porter and producer Dwight Wiman apparently came up with the basic idea and plot for *Gay Divorce* together. It's roughly the same as the movie: The leading man, already in love with the leading lady, who is about to dump her nogoodnik husband, is mistaken by her for the professional "co-respondent" in her divorce case. (That few people reading this after the millennium will know what a professional co-respondent is shows how much things have changed.) In any case, complications and hilarity ensue. What's amazing is that Porter and Wiman came up with this plot, such as it is, first, and only later thought of Astaire for the lead, because it certainly seems tailor-made for Astaire's talents as comic, actor, singer, and dancer.

As it happened, Porter already had his number-one song for *Gay Divorce,* according to Richard Rodgers, who believed that Porter might actually have written "Night and Day" as early as 1926. Porter and his wife, Linda, were living in Venice at the time, and Rodgers and Hart, fresh from their earliest Broadway triumphs, had schlepped over to Europe. Both Rodgers and Hart were younger than Porter (Rodgers, born in 1905, especially so), but it took considerably longer for the Indiana-born songwriter to establish himself on Broadway. Before the Venice visit, Rodgers and Hart had assumed that Porter was some kind of dilettante expatriate—he had, in fact come from a rich family and then married the ex-wife of an even richer man. To such an industrious, bourgeois type as Rodgers, Porter must have looked like a playboy who between polo matches and tea parties sat down at the old baby grand and knocked off innocuous baubles for the amusement of his society playmates.

Rodgers was in for a shock. As he remembered it, he was simply blown away by the quality of Porter's songs, and immediately pegged him as a tunesmith of the highest order. When Rodgers wondered aloud why Porter's work wasn't better known, Porter responded that this wouldn't be the case much longer, for he had just discovered the formula for writing hit songs: he was going to write "Jewish music." It was an audacious remark, referring, as it did, to how Jews dominated songwriting much the same way blacks dominated instrumental jazz. There were great goyish songwriters (the Italian Harry Warren, the midwestern Hoagy Carmichael, the southern Johnny Mercer) and great white jazzmen, but the focus in these fields seemed nevertheless to be on Jews and blacks. Rodgers and Hart, both Jews, were more surprised than offended. (No less an authority on Jewishness and pop music than Mel Brooks recently wrote: "When I discovered to my amazement that Cole Porter wasn't Jewish, I was taken aback for a moment but then quickly forgave him. I'd become a practicing Episcopalian, too, if I could write songs like his.")

By "Jewish music" Porter meant that he planned to make more use of minor tonalities, including allusions to the five-note pentatonic scale, although these sounds are not exclusively Jewish—in fact, they're found in just about every music of the world except Western European classical music. Various amounts of pentatonicism can be found in Spanish music, African music, and traditional Jewish–Eastern European klezmer music.

As Rodgers explained, "Just hum the melody that goes with 'Only you beneath the moon and under the sun' from 'Night and Day' or any of 'Begin the Beguine,' 'Love for Sale,' 'My Heart Belongs to Daddy' (that song in particular has an overtly klezmer-ish wailing 'scat' section), or 'I Love Paris.' These minor-key melodies are unmistakably Eastern Mediterranean." Concluded Rodgers: "It is surely one of the ironies of the musical theatre that despite the abundance of Jewish composers, the one who has written the most enduring 'Jewish' music should be an Episcopalian millionaire who was born on a farm in Peru, Indiana."

Rodgers got almost everything right, except that Porter had never been anywhere near a farm. Instead, he met the Indians on the Amazon, saw the fleas that tease in the high Pyrenees, owned a silly little chalet in the Interlaken Valley. In 1921, Cole and Linda Porter made their most exotic trip of all: they chartered a large private boat and spent two months chugging up and down the Nile, guided by no less an Egyptologist than Howard Carter, who would discover the tomb of King Tut only a year later. In 1930, the Porters visited Europe again and from there headed to Japan and the Far East. Presumably, it was on one of these excursions that Porter passed through the Middle East and there heard an Islamic chant, the call to the faithful. In later years, Porter would claim that this chant was one of the inspirations for "Night and Day"; Semitic, certainly, though not specifically Jewish.

NO MATTER WHAT THE ethnic makeup of "Night and Day," it is a remarkable song on every level. To start with, there's the structure. We can all agree that it's forty-eight bars long, and that it roughly conforms to the familiar A-A-B-A pattern. The song has been diagramed as A-B-A-B-C-B, but for our purposes here we're going to chart it as A(16)-A'(16)-B(8)-C(8), the C section being the same as the second eight bars of A. As noted, each of the two opening sections, A and A', are sixteen bars long, while the two closing sections, B and C, are eight bars each, thus the first "half" of the song is thirty-two bars and the second "half" is sixteen bars.

Most editions are in C. Some versions open with the flatted fifth; others, including the official Cole Porter edition, do not. This is heard on the third note, "Night and *day*. . . ." (Some versions, but not all, open with a pickup chord, usually the tonic, C, which is heard on the first two notes (words), but many simpler editions leave the first two notes without any harmonies at all.) Along with the blue note that opens "What Is This Thing Called Love?" the flatted fifth here goes a long way toward explaining why modern jazzmen kept so much Porter in their repertoires, as these devices were important building blocks in the foundations of bebop.

The chord changes to "Night and Day" are fairly straightforward, using the basic II-IV-I pattern. The lyric is written as five lines, and each of the first two lines utilizes this II-V-I progression. Then, on the third line ("Whether *near to me* . . ."), Porter starts a series of downward chromaticisms. The lyric is unusual in that three of the four sections begin and end on the phrase "Night and day" (although the second section, the *A¹*, reverses it as "Day and night, why is it so . . ."). When we come to the ending title phrase, Porter backs it with the V (the dominant, G) and the I (C).

The second A, the *A¹*, is harmonically identical to the first. The idea of the *A¹* section is a favorite of Porter's—he likes the idea that you can bring back your opening melody but do it in a way that's not entirely a strict reiteration. When you hear the "Night and Day" melody again, it's the same, but it's different. Porter would employ this device again later on in, among other songs, "I Concentrate on You," and particularly "I've Got You Under My Skin" (in which the melody goes into a series of raised fifths in the *A¹* that are not present at all in the *A*).

In "Night and Day," the differences between the *A* (bars 1–16) and the *A¹* section (bars 17–32) appear six bars into the second section, roughly around "that this longing for you follows. . . ." At this point, the tune becomes a lot notier and wordier, possibly to convey the increasing anxiety of the song's "voice"—he's now getting so caught up in what he's singing and, more importantly, what he's feeling, that he can barely get his thoughts out. Not only are these lines more passionate, but by putting the phrase "follows wherever I . . ." on two triplets, Porter is tipping his hat that he wants the melody to swing, since triplets, are, in effect, a kind of composer's shorthand for swinging rhythmic feeling.

The bridge (two lines) alternates between the I chord (C) and the flatted III chord (E flat). Loren Schoenberg feels that in doing so, the bridge actually sets up two separate tonal areas, alternating from the major tonality of the tonic and the minor tonality of the mediant. It is, in fact, a shift of modes on C, varying between C major and C minor.

Although certain aspects of the song were conceived without anything to do with *Gay Divorce*—the Islamic inspiration and as we'll see, Mrs. Astor's drip-drip-drop—the melody and rhythm of the finished song are inextricably bound up in the person of the performer for whom the song was written. Astaire thought of himself primarily as a dancer, not a singer, but with the benefit of hindsight, he emerges as one of the great vocal artists of his time. He didn't have the chops of a Nelson Eddy or Vic Damone, but, with no disrespect to those gentlemen, I doubt that there's anyone reading this who wouldn't prefer to listen to Astaire, whose vocals were rife with rhythm and personality.

When Porter wrote the melody for Astaire, he gave it a very strong rhythmic impetus. One characteristic of verses to songs written for Astaire is that they tend to be more consistently in tempo than those for your average song of the period. Sometimes they're in rubato, like the verses to most other songs, but more often they have a definite pulse, as does the verse to "Night and Day." This sixteen-bar verse is made up essentially of two notes: the first two lines are all sung on the note G, the third is all sung on A (except for one bar, in which all four A's are flatted), and the last line takes us back to G.

The repeated notes are mirrored in the lyric. Supposedly, the idea for the verse came at a moment when Porter was working on the song and not getting anywhere with it. Monty Woolley, his friend since Yale days and a longtime coconspirator in carnal pursuits, encouraged him to take a break and spend a weekend with their mutual friend Vincent Astor at the latter's cottage in Newport. It happened to be raining, and a drain pipe was broken, which caused a dripping noise that threatened to drive Mrs. Astor crazy, but which eventually made another fortune for Mr. Porter. According to Charlotte Breese, writing in *Hutch,* her biography of the entertainer Leslie Hutchinson, Mrs. Astor exclaimed, "I must have that eave mended. This drip-drip-drip is driving me mad!" The story goes that Porter raced to the Astors' piano and instantly finished the song. (This account doesn't necessarily contradict the stories about the song's Middle Eastern origins; the chorus could have been written in the late twenties and the verse in the early thirties at the Astor piano.)

The verse is one of the strongest parts of the premiere recording of "Night and Day," which was done by Leo Reisman's orchestra with Astaire on November 22, 1932. As Astaire sings "the beat, beat, beat,"

and "the tick, tick, tock," and "the drip-drip-drip," Reisman's unidenti-
fied orchestrator underscores them with appropriate rhythmic effects: a
little plinky-planky percussion to illustrate the raindrops, and whooshing
wind effects and pizzicato strings for "When the summer show'r is
through." It's an obvious idea, but it works. Significantly, when the musical director of Ella Fitzgerald's *Cole Porter Songbook* tried the same idea
nearly twenty-five years later, the device now sounded stale and hack-
neyed. (The rather corny writing for three trombones, swinging this-
a-way and then that-a-way, didn't help any.) The arranger here takes it
even more literally than Reisman, opening with—you'll never guess—
beat-beat-beating tom-toms. Fortunately, Fitzgerald's always astonishing
singing more than saves the day. Better still, she came back to the tune in
1971 in an outstanding live recording from Nice, with, at last, the suitable
accompaniment of Tommy Flanagan's trio. This is a more driving "Night
and Day," so much so that at the end of the number, the French crowd
refuses to let her leave the stage until she reprises a portion of the song,
with the Gallic audience clapping resoundingly on every beat.

Like Astaire and Fitzgerald, Tony Bennett also makes notable use of
the verse. (He recorded the song on his 1992 tribute to Sinatra—though
he could just as easily have waited and done it the following year on his
tribute to Astaire.) Bennett is the only singer in pop who's made a specialty of whispering loudly, which he does on the opening line about the
tom-toms and beat-beats, accompanied by drums only, in a manner that
recalls the famous Benny Goodman–Gene Krupa exchange on "Sing,
Sing, Sing." He gets so into that beat-beat-beat thing that he repeats the
line twice, and when he gets to the line about the raindrops, pianist Ralph
Sharon comes in with a shimmering shower of raindrop-like notes.

Both Astaire and Bennett have taken advantage of the way that Porter
uses repetition, in the verse as well as the chorus. In a Cole Porter song,
repetition is a musical concept that ties into the emotional concept of
obsession. In fact, most of Porter's "serious" love songs are about obsession: "I've Got You Under My Skin," "I Concentrate on You"—they're all
about how the speaker-protagonist is completely obsessed with the
objection of his/her affection, how he/she can't get her/him out of
his/her mind no matter what he/she does (you get the idea). Night and
day I think of you, no matter what I do, I can't stop thinking about you.
Porter pushes emotions as far as they'll go, sometimes even over the
edge; were the first-person speaker of any of these three songs to take

things much further, the object of this obsession might have to go to court to file for a restraining order.

Melodic repetition effectively underscores this kind of obsession: the repeated single note represents the object of desire, and by repeating that note Porter illustrates the extent of the protagonist's preoccupation. Naturally, the refrain of "Night and Day" uses much more melodic movement than the verse, but there are still a lot of repeated notes. The song is certainly the only one in this book in which the three words of the title phrase are all on the same note—in this case, G. As we've seen, Porter also uses a string of G's to open and close every section of the song (with the exception of the final A). By repeating these dominant G notes over and over in this fashion, he gives "Night and Day" a melodic and a rhythmic imperative. At the same time, he makes it easier for Astaire. By giving him only one note to worry about, he now can devote more energy to the rhythm and the feeling, as well as the overall drama of his interpretation, without having to concern himself with the intonation of a lot of tricky notes or to sustain a long pitch.

This isn't meant, however, to imply that Astaire can't sing, or that he doesn't have vocal range. Astaire himself raised such fears when Porter first demonstrated the song to him. Asked whether or not he sensed it would be a hit, Astaire answered: "I was more concerned with whether or not I could sing it. Well, it was a long range, very low and very high, and it was long—and I was trying to figure out what kind of dance could be arranged for it. This all went through my mind, I just went blank, and then I asked him to play it again and again, and after four or five times, I finally got with it."

Astaire was right: the song is long, forty-eight bars, and though it might have seemed very rangey, the span is actually less than an octave and a half, from the G below middle C to the C above middle C. Each of the first two A sections drops way down to that low G on the phrase "I think of you," and then shoots up to middle G for the title phrase "Night and Day." (Unlike Harold Arlen in "Over the Rainbow" and "Stormy Weather," however, Porter doesn't put his octave jump in mid-phrase but gives the performer a chance to breathe before making the leap.) The range alone makes it a song that an unskilled voice would have a tough time with.

Throughout, Porter stresses the G, both as a chord and as a note. By emphasizing the fifth (the dominant) so strongly, he gives the song an unresolved feeling; when you hear the dominant, you know you're going somewhere; the tune still seems unfinished. We don't achieve resolution until the very end of the song, the final three notes, the last utterance of the words, "night and day." Now, at last, the title phrase is put on the tonic note, three high C's. Resolution has come at last as the hero declares that his "torment" will finally be through when "you let me spend my life making love to you." He doesn't want to hold her hand or walk his baby back home around the block, take her for a cup of coffee, a sandwich, or another piece of pie or tea for two, take her for a ride in the surrey, take a stroll down the street where she lives, bring her home to Mammy, dunk her in his coffee or spread her on his bread. Porter rarely indulges in the kind of metaphors favored by other lyricists, and he saves his double entendres for the comedy songs. When Porter is making love, he just lays it all flat out.

As Alan Jay Lerner put it, "Cole was the only composer and lyric writer in the entire musical world who ever knew how to write a passionate song. To this day, that's the truth. Everybody else could—when we're fortunate—write a tender song or a romantic song or a wistful song or a nostalgic song, but only Cole could write passion." I don't think it's indulging in psycho-babble or reading too much into something to describe the ending of "Night and Day" as a sexual, even orgasmic, release.

"IT'S A KNOWN FACT THAT 'Night and Day' made the show," Astaire said in 1966, two years after Porter's death. "The show really was in an awful lot of trouble when we first started on the road and got to New York. Finally, it was known after that, after it caught on—and it ran for a pretty good run in those days, 38 weeks (248 performances)—it was known as the 'Night and Day' show."

Astaire elaborated on the kind of "trouble" that he meant:

> It turned out to be a run, but we had a rather rocky first night. The swells were really out that night, very elegant, at the Ethel Barrymore Theater, nothing but white ties, chinchillas, jewels. . . . They were very obnoxious! They were very nice in a funny kind of a way, they ran up and down the aisles (talking to each other), that upset the critics and us on the stage, and it was a little tough to get the plot of this show across. But when it came to the numbers, ["Night and Day"]

erupted, and there were all kinds of standing ovations and sitting ovations, and anyhow we got through that night. But then the notices
came out and they were not so good. There was one I remember, it
came out in *Time,* a miserable little column down the side that can
really fix it for you, he said he didn't like the play at all, but that there
was a "certain amount of enthusiasm that came forth from the
brandied roarings of Cole Porter's friends."

Gay Divorce opened on November 29, 1932. Within a month the song
had become one of the biggest hits in years, a signature event in the early
days of the Depression and the late days of Prohibition. In January 1933,
Variety billboarded the song as the nation's leader in both sheet music and
record sales. Astaire and Reisman's debut recording had been made a
week before the show opened.

A former violinist, Leo Reisman directed bands and recorded from the
early twenties through the early forties but best captured the musical
moment during the years 1929–33, when he recorded for the Victor
label. No one put together the three major strains of mainstream pop at
the time—jazz, show music, and dance music—into one supremely listenable package with the same verve that Reisman did. He was responsible for the final recordings by trumpeter Bubber Miley (among them,
Porter's "What Is This Thing Called Love?"), as well as for the the first
recordings by future great jazz singer Lee Wiley. In an age before original
cast recordings were commonplace Reisman brought in Broadway stars
like Astaire and Clifton Webb to record songs they were doing nightly on
the boards as "vocal refrains" with his dance band. All of that, however,
mattered less than the smooth-as-silk quality of the band itself, which, for
all its finesse, was surprisingly jazzy. Jerome Kern once called Reisman's
orchestra the Budapest String Quartet of dance bands.

Reisman's last session of 1932 occurred on November 22, and his first
session of 1933 on February 28. On these two dates, Reisman introduced
what may well have been the two most popular songs of the entire
decade, Fred Astaire singing "Night and Day" and composer Harold
Arlen doing his own "Stormy Weather." On December 7, pianist Eddy
Duchin made his own recording of "Night and Day," and that treatment
reveals what's so remarkable about Reisman's. Duchin's is a perfectly serviceable dance band treatment, opening, in an unusual move, with the
vocal (by one Lew Sherwood, who also served as Duchin's manager and

was later portrayed by James Whitmore in *The Eddy Duchin Story*). In addition to the leader's always elegant piano chorus, there's a tightly muted trumpet solo in the manner of Henry Busse. It's smart and it's peppy and it accomplishes what one expects of it.

Reisman's treatment, on the other hand, does all kinds of things that no one expects: it may be set in a major key (E flat), but Reisman begins with a minor chord, starting with a faux-primitive intro (more suggestive of Africa than the exotic East), and stresses the minor mood throughout. He voices the melody on alternating sections—which is in the jazz tradition—but they're alternating sections of woodwinds and strings. He brings the full ensemble to bear on the bridge and then the last eight bars to make ready for Astaire's entrance. Astaire comes in with the verse, and for the remaining two minutes it's his disc. You could describe it as a vocal record with an elaborate intro. Astaire not one of the all-time great singers? Not on your top hat and tails! The verse, in particular, has never been sung better.

Astaire's two-thirds of the Reisman disc are distinguished by more than the verse. He handles the dip down on "I think of you" very effectively, and no less so the climb immediately back up to "night and day." He sounds unbelievably young, at thirty-three, though he'd been starring on Broadway and recording for almost a decade, with a voice closer to a tenor range than we're used to hearing. And he has chops enough to go all the way down to low B flat and up to high E flat. He makes the rhythm his first priority (it moves along at a fairly fast clip), no surprise there, yet he gets more than enough emotion and drama into his reading.

Indeed, apart from Crosby and Al Bowlly, there weren't many singers recording in the dance-jazz-show-music world of 1932 who could do even half as well. Frank Sinatra often spoke of how he first came upon his original inspiration, Bing Crosby, in a darkened movie theater; I'm not convinced that Sinatra wasn't equally inspired by these performances of Astaire's. One doubts that the sixteen-year-old Sinatra made it much to Broadway in 1932, but he would have had his chance two years later, when RKO Pictures released *The Gay Divorcee*.

In the interim, on November 2, 1933, *Gay Divorce* opened at the Palace Theatre in London, where it played a healthy 180 performances. The song already had had a year in which to capture England and Europe, having been recorded by such outstanding favorites among British audiences as cabaret *chanteur* Leslie Hutchinson (billed as "Hutch"), "crossover" superstar Richard Tauber, popular crooner Al Bowlly, and bandleaders Harry Roy and Ambrose. (Incidentally, none of the three singers listed here was actually born in England, though all were an important part of the interwar British experience.) Essentially, all these recordings are dance performances in the Astaire tempo. The Ambrose disc need not take a backseat to any American dance band; it's a very strong, rhythmic reading that makes good use of call-and-response patterns and a satisfying vocal by the fine baritone Sam Browne, the most accomplished band singer of the time and place after Bowlly. Bowlly himself cut "Night and Day" in one of his rare "solo" sides, meaning that for once he was presented not as a band vocalist but as featured attraction. Though he drops the verse, he turns in a solidly intimate and romantic treatment, done in a comparatively slow tempo, with an especially laconic trombone in the bridge and the South African crooner going for an impressive high note in the coda.

Hutch offers something completely different. We've seen that Porter wrote the song with Astaire's voice and style in mind, but to my mind, Hutch performed the song the way Porter would like to have done it himself. By professional standards, Porter was a mediocre singer and only an adequate pianist. Hutch seems to have presented the song exactly the way the composer wanted it to be done—the combination of the masculine baritone and the slightly effeminate mannerisms, the balance of sentimental sound and incessant drip-drip-drip rhythm, the well-placed background pattern that so effectively complements the main melody (in fact, it anticipates the melody to "Anything Goes," a Porter hit of two seasons later), the well-crafted piano solo, the distinctly Hutch-like juxtaposition of the formal and the casual.

After Broadway in 1932 and London in '33, Astaire and the production made it to Hollywood (the following year). Although the *Gay Divorce* score included such Cole Porter gems as "I've Got You on My Mind," "After You, Who?" and "Mr. and Missus Fitch," these were all scrapped. In fact, the only thing that was saved was the mistaken-identity plot and the song "Night and Day." That song, after all, had saved the show, and it was too big a hit to leave out. This was the second of Astaire's film appearances with Ginger Rogers, and although they had danced together in *Flying Down to Rio* (which fortunately had more dancing than flying), this was the movie that established them as the greatest dance team of modern times. The song "Night and Day" thus can be said to be a doubly major song in the Astaire career: in *Gay Divorce* it was the tune that allowed him to establish himself as a solo artist—rather than half of a brother-and-sister act—and in *The Gay Divorcee* this same song "consummated," as it were, the union of Fred and Ginger.

"Night and Day" also established a particular pattern in the series: the dance of seduction. He's already in love with her and wants to dance; she wants nothing more than to get away, but gradually the combination of the beat, the melody, and the man's irresistible charm conspire to overpower her. By the end of the four-and-a-half-minute number, she's not only in his arms, but the look she gives him (Rogers does much of her best dancing with her eyes) is one of the defining moments of the entire series of Fred-and-Ginger film pairings. Incidentally, the first soundtrack version is the reverse of the Reisman, in that it opens with the vocal (verse and chorus at about the same tempo) and then goes into a long instrumental. The rhythm is made doubly strong by what seems like a combination of both brass bass (tuba) and string bass.

From that point on, the song was part of Astaire's permanent canon. He had recorded a solo treatment for the British market in 1933 that begins and ends with Astaire, yet is no less a dance disc than the Reisman (with the same tempo); the only moment it goes out of dance tempo is when the time stops for dramatic emphasis on "oh such a hungry yearning. . . ." There's an instrumental break in the center, with brief solos by trumpet and subtone clarinet. Even better is Astaire's 1952 recording, which is a highlight of his career retrospective *The Astaire Story.* This innovative package found the great song-and-dance man rerecording three LPs worth of his signature songs of the twenties and thirties, although in a startlingly new context. As Astaire himself put it, he became sort of an unofficial member of the Jazz at the Philharmonic troupe, which starred Oscar Peterson (and his trio with Barney Kessel), Charlie Shavers, and Flip Phillips. This treatment is also in E flat, and thus Astaire once again returns and rereturns to the much repeated note of B flat, the fifth in this context. (The Peterson trio also recorded this arrangement, minus Astaire and the horns, as an instrumental, which features the same guitar countermelody behind the verse.) Shavers plays the subtlest muted trumpet imaginable behind Astaire's main vocal. Peterson's trio, at the core of the production, is still very much in thrall to the more famous King Cole Trio, especially in the use of block chords—a trademark of Cole (Nat

King, that is, not Porter). (In addition to those with Astaire and his own trio version, Peterson recorded yet a third disc of "Night and Day" in 1952, also produced by Norman Granz. This was an unusual big band date built around the great saxist Charlie Parker, and Peterson solos prominently here as well.)

Although Astaire had already enjoyed two amazing careers by 1952, his spoken intro indicates that he had much of his best work ahead of him. Not only does he admit to being "especially intrigued" by the JATP accompaniment, but he describes *Gay Divorce* as the only stage show of his that subsequently became a picture. The next few years would see two more, *The Bandwagon* and *Funny Face*.

Astaire is widely acknowledged as having introduced more standards into the great American songbook than any other vocalist; even the most-recorded and best-known voices of the twentieth century—Bing Crosby, Ella Fitzgerald, Frank Sinatra—don't come close. Cole Porter is listed as one of the writers closest to Astaire, but in truth they worked together on this one show only, and Porter did not write for any of the subsequent Fred-and-Ginger RKO masterpieces. They did do three films together in Astaire's post-Rogers phase. The first was *Broadway Melody of 1940,* a surprisingly low-energy outing that had only two major new songs, "I've Got My Eyes on You" and "I Concentrate on You" (although it did use Cole's five-year-old "Begin the Beguine" for the spectacular climactic dance). In 1942 came *You'll Never Get Rich,* which produced no hits or standards but had several tunes enjoyed by song cognescenti such as "Dream Dancing" and "Since I Kissed My Baby Goodbye." And, finally, 1955's *Silk Stockings* was a late-career triumph for both Astaire and Porter. Numerically speaking, Porter lags behind the Gershwins, Irving Berlin, and even Johnny Mercer in terms of the number of vehicles he crafted for Astaire. Still, if any one tune can be said to have established the Astaire aesthetic—his combination of elegance, rhythm, and pure passion—it's "Night and Day."

ASTAIRE SANG THE TUNE yet again under very different circumstances in 1967, on the occasion of the dedication of the Cole Porter Library at the University of Southern California. There was a formal dinner, and a symposium-cum-impromptu-concert very thankfully recorded featuring

Astaire, Frank Sinatra, Ethel Merman, Gene Kelly, Jimmy Stewart (who had introduced "Easy to Love," although no singer he), and Alan Jay Lerner. Prodded by moderator Garson Kanin, this veritable Olympian gathering of showbiz living legends exchanged anecdotes about their late "chum," who had died two and a half years earlier, in October of 1964; most also sang a quick chorus or two with Roger Edens at the piano. Astaire sings a brief but hardly cursory two-minute verse and chorus of "Night and Day" that's by the far the most intimate he ever laid down. The verse is the closest to rubato that he ever sang it, although there's still a definite tempo. He had mostly given up dancing by then, pushing seventy as he was, but it's a pity he didn't have more respect for his talents as a vocalist and continue to make recordings at this stage of his life. He did cut a few albums in the sixties and seventies, but not nearly enough.

In his speech at the Porter symposium, Gene Kelly, Astaire's heir as the screen's most famous dancer-choreographer, mentions casually that while "coming down in the car with Fred tonight, we both [remarked on how we] envy singers so much, how they can handle songs." Most music lovers would agree that Astaire had no reason to be jealous of any vocalist.

Sinatra sang five songs that night—"I've Got You Under My Skin," "Let's Do It," "It's All Right with Me," "I Love Paris," and "I Concentrate on You"—but he kept his hands off "Night and Day," leaving it to Astaire, as it was the major Porter song associated with him. Between songs, Sinatra, Astaire, and the other participants gave voice to a few pithy observations regarding the late Mr. Porter. Sinatra was particularly impressed that in marked contrast with certain other composers, whose initials were Richard Rodgers, Porter never voiced objections when performers came up with interpretations of his songs that might have differed, perhaps even dramatically so, from his own original conception. "Mr. Porter was a very liberal man in that sense," said Sinatra. "He really didn't care how you arranged [the tune] as long as you did the song in its entirety, even if you changed the tempo from a slow four to a 12/8, it didn't make any difference to him."

By 1967, when Sinatra said this, he had already put this theory to the test. "Night and Day" was never a hit song for him (well, almost never; the original Bluebird version made it to number sixteen on the *Billboard* chart for two weeks), nor was it a song identified with him to the point where fans would scream for it at concerts, the way they would for

Rodgers and Hart's "The Lady Is a Tramp" or Porter's "I've Got You Under My Skin." However, he did include the song on his first commercial recording session as a soloist, made while he was still on the payroll of the Tommy Dorsey Orchestra, in January 1942. And he selected it as his only number in his first post-Dorsey film appearance, later that year, *Reveille with Beverly.* He went on to sing it at every turn of his career, in every phase he would pass through, and as part of every recording affiliation he was ever involved in.

He also sang it in every way that it was conceivable for Frank Sinatra to sing any song, and that was quite a few. You want it fast and swinging? There's the great Nelson Riddle orchestration from November of 1956, first heard on *A Swingin' Affair.* (There are also amazing variations on the Riddle versions, such as a sextet reading from Japan in 1962 and one from Australia, three years earlier, which teams Sinatra with the Red Norvo Quintet and a full local orchestra.) You want it slow and romantic? There's the original Axel Stordahl arrangement, which Sinatra sang in various, ever-evolving forms from the time he introduced it on that first solo session for Bluebird in 1942. You want it Latin style? There's the 1954 treatment from his last major radio series, *To Be Perfectly Frank,* a swinging treatment with bongos and flute that anticipated subsequent Pan American treatments by Steve Lawrence and Vic Damone. You want it big and dramatic, with, like, a thousand violins? Try the 1961 *Sinatra and Strings* chart by Don Costa, in which it's rendered with considerable passion and power, not to mention some of the slowest singing that Sinatra ever did. You want it small and intimate? Lots to choose from: the tune was one of Sinatra's favorites for one-to-one duos with such instrumentalists as pianist Bill Miller and guitarist Al Viola, who assisted Sinatra with a stunning interpretation performed nightly in the latter part of the singer's 1962 world tour.

You want the verse? He used it in the beginning, where Porter intended, in the *Sinatra and Strings* reading, although that heavy ballad version was most decidedly not in Porter's designated dance tempo. While Porter didn't exactly have the mambo in mind, the 1954 Latin version (which is definitely danceable) uses the verse, although here he puts it in the middle of the song. You say you don't even like Sinatra? Well, after you get your hearing and your head checked, you might enjoy a 1998 recording of the Riddle arrangement for Sinatra by Erich Kunzel and the

Cincinnati Pops Orchestra, in which it's adapted into an instrumental, with slide trombonist Jim Pugh in the spot originally written for valve trombonist Juan Tizol.

You want more versions? "Night and Day" is an especially rewarding tune for Sinatra scholars, in that hitherto unknown performances always seem to be turning up. There's a concert version from Buffalo, in 1982, that uses a Norvo-style instrumentation, stressing vibes, piano, and guitar. As on the 1954 Latin-style version, Sinatra sings the verse in the middle, and some of his phrasing on said verse is very similar to that much earlier radio treatment. After Sinatra's death, one enterprising fan put together an entire sixty-eight-minute homemade CD of Sinatra treatments of the song that included a few surprises: a 1944 reading of the Stordahl chart from a radio adaption of *The Gay Divorcee* in which Sinatra essayed the Astaire role, portraying "Guy Holden" as a singer rather than a dancer; a 1950 *Light Up Time* performance of the Stordahl—on which, presumably because the Lucky Strike people were too cheap for a string section, woodwinds, reeds, and soft brass scramble to take its place; several treatments from early in the 1962 world tour (including a promo film for the Perugina chocolate company, done in Rome), before the duo approach evolved, when FS was still doing it as an up-tempo with the full sextet; and a truly remarkable reading from an appearance on Italian radio nine years earlier, a duet with Bill Miller. This final item lodges itself exactly halfway between the Stordahl approach of the forties and the Al Viola duo of the latter part of the world tour, and also falls nicely between the Stordahl (1942) and Costa (1961) approaches.

Indeed, "Night and Day" occupies such a large subset of the Sinatra canon that it could also be said to incorporate some of the worst of Sinatra's output: the film performance, from *Reveille with Beverly,* in which some Hollywood hack got the goofy idea of filling the screen and the soundtrack with a bevy of broads pounding away on pianos, is surely no Sinatra classic. Then there's the dread disco record of 1977. To be sure, FS gives it all he's got, and invests himself as thoroughly in this Joe Beck arrangement as in everything else he's ever sung. Unfortunately, the disco background, to use a colloquialism from the period, sucks. Mr. Beck himself would surely agree; Beck was a respectable jazz guitar player on the New York scene, and his association with Sinatra occupies a proud spot on his curriculum vitae, yet he's understandably reluctant to brag about this particular chart.

Then there's an early concert recording from roughly the same time as the above-mentioned 1953 Italian version. This was the low point of the Sinatra career. In the summer of 1953, Sinatra trotted out the classic Stordahl chart of "N&D" for possibly the last time, saving it for the finale of a concert in Blackpool. Although the very positive and supportive attitude of the British audiences made this stop one of the few high spots of an otherwise unfortunate European tour, the performance itself—at least of this final number—seems hardly worth the crowd's kind indulgence. The tide was already beginning to turn in terms of Sinatra's career, but since the primary vehicle of his comeback, the film *From Here to Eternity,* had not yet been released, nobody but Sinatra knew it at the time. "We really have to close it up now," he announces at the windup, "because I have to sweep up the place for the next performer." Apart from a lovely "Don't Worry 'bout Me," this is a largely dispensable Sinatra concert. Which is regrettable, because Blackpool may well be the earliest full-length concert of his which survives in its entirety via a location recording.

By the time he gets to "N&D" at Blackpool, FS is in an extremely pissy mood indeed, and seems to be merely going through the motions. However, any kind of singing is welcome, since he spends less of his Blackpool time vocalizing than indulging in a rambling monologue that is roughly divided between making fun of the audience (with an annoying mock-British accent and weak Churchill impressions) and self-deprecation. He starts "Night and Day" (with Bill Miller playing the string passages on piano), but only gets up to the start of the second eight bars before he bizarrely sidetracks into a series of vocal exercises and grunted pedal notes. He then abruptly decides to conclude both the tune and the concert, begging off with, "Thank you for putting up with my nonsense."

And yet, most Sinatra versions of "Night and Day" give us the singer at his very best. His 1947 version (which exists in two takes, one released in 1993 and a slightly shorter one that has thus far circulated only unofficially) shows that both the singer himself and the 1942 Axel Stordahl chart have evolved considerably since both debuted on Bluebird. The tempo is slower, the mood grander, the size of the string section larger, and the singing is considerably more intimate. Sinatra has gotten significantly better (and would get better still in the fifties and sixties) at using what could be considered jazz devices—for example, the impression of a spontaneous melodic alteration to make the mood more informal and intimate, the words more believable.

Part of the inspiration for this comes, obviously, from Billie Holiday, who recorded the tune herself in 1939 (in A flat). As with most of Holiday's great recordings, she sings hardly any portion of the tune exactly as written; in this particular case, she changes the lyric on the last line: instead of the expected, "Day and night, night and day," she reverses those two phrases at the end of the first chorus. (It's almost as if Holiday had learned the song from the German translation, "Tag und Nacht," in which the sequence of times is given the other way around. She does correct their order at the end of the side.) Sinatra was influenced not only by Holiday but by her own inspiration, Louis Armstrong, the man who virtually invented the idea of using jazz as a tool for animating the Great American Songbook, and by two other Armstrong disciples, Mildred Bailey and Bing Crosby, who followed suit.

Sinatra's melodic alterations are not as dramatic as Holiday's, but they're no less effective: on the second line, "You are the one," the notes as written, for the key of D, should be G-F#-E#-F#; instead Sinatra sings G-E-G-F#. Then, on "[I] think of you," where Porter wrote B-A#-A, Sinatra sings B-C#-A, going up a third from where Porter put the "of." Both choruses end with Sinatra refusing to sing the title phrase as written, on three repeats of the tonic note. Instead, he ends on repeats of the dominant (V), and even there he jumps the middle note a third higher, giving us A-C#-A instead of where the written D-D-D ("night and day"). And this is still 1947, the Columbia-Stordahl era, when the tempos are generally much less swingy and the mood less jazzy than they would be ten or twenty years hence. The 1959 Australian concert version of "Night and Day," which uses the 1956 Riddle chart as its starting point (complete with the modulation), is among the most rhythmically supercharged performances that Sinatra ever laid down. He has never swung harder or been more at the top of his game.

If Sinatra's proclivity for melodic alteration is what links him most closely to Holiday, his slight embellishments of Porter's lyrics provide concrete evidence as to who was listening most closely to him. In the second chorus of the 1942 Bluebird, Sinatra sings "There's an oh such a hungry yearning / Burning *way down* inside of me" and then "and its torment won't *ever* be through." One doubts that Steve Lawrence and Vic Damone were familiar with Sinatra's 1954 Latinate radio transcription, but both their treatments are at least lightly Latin. Lawrence's recording hitches its wagon to the mambo craze of the fifties and early sixties. Although the track was included in a collection of "lounge music," there's nothing the least bit campy and dated about it; wild and swinging would be a more appropriate description. Lawrence includes the verse, for which the orchestra supplies dramatic "stings" after each "You! You! You!" on the last line, and syncopates the chorus further by throwing in "I think *about* you." He modulates higher for the second chorus, and as he gets to the end, alludes to one Sinatra variation ("there's a yearning burning *down deep* inside of me") and directly quotes the next one ("won't *ever* be through").

Damone recorded "N&D" on his 1997 two-CD package *Greatest Love Songs of the Century;* it's probably the most interesting chart on the program, many of the others being rather Muzaky. He takes the song in a less flagrant Latin tempo, a gentle bossa nova. It opens more menacingly with low-voiced guitar and baritone saxophone and includes a soprano sax between his two choruses, the second of which includes both the Sinatra signatures, the "*way down* inside" and the "won't *ever* be through." Which isn't to suggest that either Lawrence or Damone is consciously aping Sinatra, even though the basic voices of both singers do happen to sound a lot like his. They can't help singing like that—it's part of who they are—a certain amount of Sinatra style is inbred in them, and for them to exorcise Sinatra's spirit from their work would be a squandering of time and talent. Both use Sinatra as a starting point, but both found their own way early on, rooted in Sinatra but not chained to him.

Still other singers who can be described as part of Sinatra's general orbit have made "N&D" their own (as did Bud Shank and Lou Levy in an instrumental tribute to the Chairman), also with lightly Latin beat-beat-beats. Jo Stafford sings it wonderfully on *Broadway's Best,* starting with a rendition of the verse that's about as close to out-of-tempo as it can be. Unfortunately, the arrangement gets a tad purple in spots, particularly with its bolero background and the completely unnecessary presence of the vocal group the Starlighters. (Like Stafford, Doris Day did a superb reading, on *Hooray for Hollywood,* although the background is a trifle stiff and overdecorated.)

Sammy Davis, Jr.'s, "Night and Day" is particularly strong in the swing department: he does the verse just with bongos, and before the verse is through he louses up royally by singing "evening shadows *through*" instead of "fall." Decca apparently issued this take because it swings so solidly, whereas a retake might have gotten the words right but not the feeling.

(Decca also issued a version by Al Hibbler with Jack Pleis and His Orchestra, in which the singer and the conductor seem to be heading off in two different directions, the second trying to find and stay behind the first.) Davis works mostly with just drums and bass, ending with an improvised scat coda. (Likewise, the contemporary jazz singer Karin Allyson has sung the verse with just drums and the chorus as a bossa nova.)

OTHER MASTER MUSICIANS HAVE USED "Night and Day" as a career milestone, interpreting the Porter classic both as a ballad and as a swinger, even merging the two approaches in a single performance. Unlike many pop songs, "Night and Day" is a ballad that's not easily rendered in an overtly sentimental or melodramatic fashion; something about the melody, and especially the lyric, with its straight-ahead statement of passion, makes it near impossible to use "N&D" as a vehicle for excess sentiment. As Alan Jay Lerner put it, "You'll never find any self-pity in a Cole Porter song." Perhaps for that reason, many jazzmen—particularly top tenors like Don Byas (in a straight-ahead, medium-tempo treatment from 1951) and Zoot Sims, both of whom were recording in Porter's beloved Paris, as well as Joe Henderson, Sonny Rollins, and most of all Stan Getz—use it as a fast or semi-fast ballad, a love song with a strong rhythmic drive. The song has passion as well as that beat-beat-beat.

Getz and Bill Evans both developed treatments of "N&D" that can be considered definitive by any yardstick except for the fact that the word "definitive" has no real place in this discussion. There are so many approaches to the canonical works of the Great American Songbook that no single recording could be considered definitive, even ones by the likes of Getz or Evans, or even more remarkably, by the likes of Getz *and* Evans.

Evans played "Night and Day" as part of a series of sessions produced by and starring clarinetist Tony Scott in 1957 (the leader's playing on the instrument here is close to Jimmy Giuffre or a slightly more boppish Pee Wee Russell), and then included it in his second recording as a leader, *Everybody Digs Bill Evans*. In general, the Evans trio treatment (in E flat) is not in the unendingly lyrical, deeply romantic style we associate with him; indeed, it opens with the sound of sticks and wood—via drummer Philly Joe Jones—bringing to mind Dave Brubeck and Joe Morello on such specialties as "Pick Up Sticks" and "Unsquare Dance." The intro is all drums and bass—rather than being tempoless, the intro is all rhythm and no melody; the tune only arrives with the entrance of Evans himself. I can't recall Evans ever sounding more like Lennie Tristano than he does here, fragmenting the melody like crazy, offering a few notes of it here and a few more there, along with some unaccompanied runs that also suggest Art Tatum. Evans was doubtlessly familiar with Tatum's two very striking treatments of the theme, his solo from 1953 and his masterful collaboration with Ben Webster from 1956. Even though Tatum was considered a relentless swingster with a modernist's sense of harmony while Evans was modern jazz's most incurable romantic, the two have a lot in common, including a gift for personalizing any melody without needing to improvise on it.

Evans's 1958 track timed out at seven minutes. Stan Getz's first version, from 1960, was even longer, at ten. It could be considered an early example of the marathon solo, à la John Coltrane and Sonny Rollins. Yet Getz is more about relaxation than their kind of intensity—or is he? Just as "Night and Day" is a love song and a swinger at the same time, Getz has figured out how to sound at once relaxed and amazingly intense. He doesn't linger on the melody very long, though he continually alludes to it. And we wonder why critics of the era bitched about European rhythm sections. Getz was living in Sweden at the time, and if the three local lads who accompanied Getz are typical, America could no longer claim a monopoly on great rhythm players.

In 1964, Getz and Evans recorded two sessions together for Verve, one with the core of the tenorist's own group that has never been issued, the second with bassist Richard Davis and drummer Elvin Jones that came out in 1973. Like Getz's first studio meeting with Chet Baker, this is an album that generally gets dumped on. According to the pianist's manager, Helen Keane, "The date didn't go well and we unanimously agreed that the session shouldn't be released." Still, such reservations do not apply to "N&D," the highlight of the encounter. It's a treatment that owes much to both men's past histories with the tune: Getz is at once relaxed and intense, Elvin Jones launching the piece with fancy stick-throwing and a quasi-exotic rhythm pattern, similar to what Philly Joe Jones (no relation) played on Evans's 1958 trio recording, and both Evans and Getz take advantage of the occasional stop-time break. Evans's playing is gentler and more focused on the melody—to paraphrase his friend and fellow pianist Warren Bernhardt, even when Evans didn't play the melody, he always made you hear the essence of it. Elvin Jones also gets a solo here, and while this may or may not be the first time anyone conceived of "Night and Day" as a vehicle for a drum solo, it's certainly one of the best.

And that's not the end of the relationship with the song for either man, both of whom returned to it in unique, "team-up" settings. Evans revisited "Night and Day" in 1977 on *Crosscurrents,* which paired him with the superb saxists Lee Konitz and Warne Marsh. The two reeds open with no rhythm section, playing the melody not in unison but hetero-phonically, more or less the same notes at the same tempo but each embellishing it in his own way, their two lines never actually meeting, in kind of a fast ad-lib, although when Evans enters, bringing the tempo with him, he doesn't lapse into the kind of Tristano impression that the company of Konitz and Marsh would lead us to expect.

Getz also confounds expectations on his final "Night and Day," on *People Time,* a duo concert with veteran pianist Kenny Barron recorded in Copenhagen. (Incidentally, the '58 Evans trio, the '64 Getz-Evans quartet, and the '91 Getz-Barron duo are all in E flat.) This is virtually the only time Getz recorded so extensively in the duo format, and "Night and Day" finds him almost working overtime to prove that he doesn't need the beat-beat-beat of the tom-toms (i.e., bass and drums) in order to outswing everybody on the planet, day or night, night or day. Barron, too, sounds flawless, whether playing with Getz (he can't be said to be merely accompanying the saxist) or in solo, throwing in a Latin pattern here and there, and positively riveting all the way through. Made in March of 1991, this would be last officially released album by the tenor colossus, who would be dead within three months.

THE LYRICS TO "My Funny Valentine" and "The St. Louis Blues" are specifically meant to be sung by a woman, whereas "Ol' Man River" is a male anthem, and any woman who wants to sing it "straight"—that is, not jazz it up—has to work extra hard to keep it from sounding silly. Although most of Cole Porter's comic songs, like those of Noel Coward, are about a very specific time and place (not to mention social set), his love songs achieve one of the ultimate ideals for a popular song in that they're personal and universal at the same time. They express what one individual soul is feeling, yet it's an experience anyone can relate to. He may have written "Night and Day" with one specific, thirty-three-year-old white Anglo-Saxon male in mind, yet the song works for anyone: men or women, swing big bands or bop combos, tenors or sopranos, trumpets or flutes—even, as we've seen, an Elvin Jones drum solo—at any tempo, in any key.

Plenty of swing soloists have essayed the tune, men like Art Tatum and Ben Webster, as well as Webster's fellow Ellingtonians Lawrence Brown and Johnny Hodges on a 1960 session of standards not issued until the new millennium. Trombonist Brown handles the major melodic statement, and his key inspiration seems to be Tommy Dorsey, who recorded one of the most remarkable big band treatments of "N&D." We talk a lot about tempo and mood, how one affects the other until they're practically inseparable, but this isn't always the case. On the classic Dorsey version, each section of the orchestra plays a different chunk of the melody and the mood changes completely from segment to segment, even though the tempo is totally uniform. Each section, too, gets further away from the melody: Dorsey himself plays the tune fairly straight, as if he's singing a love song, with only slight decoration; the saxophones are light and airy, dancing with the melody with lots of variations. Then pianist Howard Smith, admittedly not a familiar name among hot-music exponents, gets away from the tune entirely, with eight bars of harmonic improvisation that are completely removed from Dorsey's statement—positively barrelhouse, in fact—and yet they complement it magnificently. Dorsey and Lawrence Brown are the essence of how "N&D" should be interpreted, with acres of emotion but not a centimeter of sentiment.

I always felt that Mel Tormé was being, well, perhaps disingenuous is too strong a word, when he disavowed the bebop movement. He grew up in the swing era, and always felt that jazz should have stayed a popular music, and to the day he died he resented Charlie Parker and Dizzy Gillespie for changing that. Yet he couldn't help admiring what Bird and Diz had achieved musically, if not sociologically, and there was always a great deal of modern harmony and rhythm in what he did. Interestingly, the two major versions of "N&D" that illustrate the swing-to-bop transition are those of Tormé and Charlie Parker. Both are essentially bop improvisations with swing big band accompaniment, although Tormé's 1946 version, with a studio orchestra conducted by Sonny Burke (the swing band arranger who later became Sinatra's producer) actually has considerably more modern elements to it than Parker's 1950 recording.

The Tormé record is also inspired by Ella Fitzgerald's contemporaneous series of scat epics, things like "How High the Moon," "Flying Home," and "Rough Riding," all wordless vocal improvisations with full orchestral backing. Like Fitzgerald or Sarah Vaughan, Tormé doesn't even wait for the first melody chorus to be over before he starts improvising—he starts rewriting the melody and even the lyrics from the very first line, adding the phase "for me" at end of the first two lines ("you are the one *for me*"). Working in E flat, he starts on a B flat chord, and his new phrase, "under the *sun for me,*" falls on the descending notes G-D-C. Like Sinatra and Bennett, Tormé couldn't help being a crooner, and even in a wild jazz number he can't resist caressing a note in the line "under the *hide* of me." After a chorus of lyrics and much melodic variation, he soars into a staggering scat solo, full of catchy riffs, repeated phrases, squeals and screeches, even quotes from other tunes (including the unlikely "Stars and Stripes Forever")—as far-out a scat as any recorded up to that point. For a climax, he trades fours with the instrumental ensemble, including one phrase that resembles the current hit "Hey Bop a Rebop." Before the scat ends, he gradually brings it back to the written melody, humming the bridge in unison with the band, and then coming back to the lyrics for the final eight bars without so much as having to catch his breath.

In 1959, Anita O'Day recorded a largely scatted treatment of "Night and Day" (which she resisted retitling "Night and O'Day"). Unlike Tormé or Parker, she starts with the verse, her phrasing of which shows her to be a better interpreter of lyrics than she usually gets credit for. As written by Porter, on the third line, "like the *drip, drip, drip,*" the repeated note is supposed to switch from the fifth to the lowered sixth. O'Day, however (singing it in B flat), sings the original note as a high F sharp (a raised fifth) and waits till a bar later, to "*rain-drops,*" where, instead of going a half-step up, she dives down a whole octave, all the way to a low F sharp. After the verse and refrain, O'Day goes into an exuberant improvisation: the orchestra, arranged and conducted by Billy May, plays the first half of each *A* section (the II-V-I part), then O'Day reenters and scats over the second half of each *A* (the chromatic part). It's a delectable, two-minute gem and the highlight of her *Anita O'Day Swings Cole Porter with Billy May* album. She also reused the May arrangement with a smaller band in 1963, on a Japanese TV appearance with Japanese players that's been issued on a Japanese LP, and it still sounds great, and looks pretty good, too.

Tormé, O'Day, and Parker all fuse swing and bop traditions in their big band treatments. Fifty years of hearing a jazz soloist accompanied by orchestra and strings have accustomed us to a set format. As it developed, following Charlie Parker (the first soloist to use the format extensively) and then blossomed in the LP era, the idea was to spotlight a single soloist against an orchestral backdrop. Parker's 1952 "Night and Day" is quite different: the orchestration by Joe Lipman, who wrote for Benny Goodman as early as 1934, is solidly in the big band swing tradition (even if Bird himself certainly isn't). And as with most big bands, there's more than a single soloist here: there are brief bits from trombonist Bill Harris and trumpeter Bernie Privin. Perhaps to make the chart sound more in keeping with Parker's usual bebop mode, the saxist informed Lipman at the date that he wanted the thing played about twice as fast as the arranger originally had in mind. Then, as Lipman later recalled for Phil Schaap, when they speeded up the chart, they raced through it at under a minute and a half. In order to fill up the side, Parker "had a pianist I had never heard of named Oscar Peterson. . . . I said to Charlie, 'Can he blow?' And he says, 'Ya, let him go.' And we gave Oscar Peterson choruses [like] I never heard in my whole life." Peterson's solo is a grabber, and completely different from the ones he played with his own trio and with Fred Astaire. Still, it should be noted that Peterson does not steal the show from Parker (any more than he did from Astaire).

Parker's longtime colleague Dizzy Gillespie recorded it less than two weeks later at the Théâtre des Champs-Élysées in Paris. Billed as "Dizzy Gillespie and His Operatic Strings," this is a more typical use of the soloist and large ensemble format, the trumpeter as featured star playing variations on the tune and everyone else serving as window dressing for the whole three minutes of the piece. Yet this performance is no less satisfying from a jazz perspective than Parker's.

Some of the more notable piano readings include Joe Sullivan's 1955 version, which opens with an intro by clarinetist Archie Rosati that anticipates the Beatles' "With a Little Help from My Friends." Sullivan's recording is more interesting than Earl Hines's solo of 1974, which sneaks the melody in and around an enormous tremolo. Adam Makowicz, one of Tatum's finest modern-day disciples, recorded a treatment that gets more and more intense and complicated as it goes on. The Dave Brubeck–Paul Desmond reading amounts to still another standard cooked to a T by this seminal combination. Lou Levy played the melody in a ruminative duet with Bud Shank (on *Lost in the Stars—Bud Shank & Lou Levy Play the Sinatra Songbook,* 1992). The rarely recorded pianist Joe Albany cut it with his trio. Normally known as a bass player, Red Mitchell had started as a pianist, which is how he recorded "N&D" in a duo with Lee Konitz. (Konitz didn't include "N&D" on his 1996 *Inside Cole Porter,* recorded in Italy, a CD that opens, strangely, with Jerome Kern's "The Song Is You." Go figure.)

Django Reinhardt's 1949 Rome recording of the song is less of a swing-to-bop transition than one might assume from other tracks recorded by the great guitarist during the latter part of his career. He would tackle the Porter song on four separate occasions, most notably with Stephane Grappelli and the Quintet of the Hot Club of France at their pinnacle in 1938, and then again with the violinist on their final reunion in '49. (The other Django "N&D"s come from a rarely heard collaboration with Ellington cornetist Rex Stewart in 1947 and his penultimate appearance on record, in March 1953.) While other, later Django tracks have him using electric guitar and boplike rhythms, the '49 "N&D" seems more like a refinement of the '38. Perhaps it's the presence of Grappelli, who assumes most of the major melody solo, following an intro by the guitarist. The '49 is certainly freer rhythmically, as the original has that slightly sluggish (though often charming) groove often found in prewar Eurojazz (the time feels generally more like 2/4 than 4/4), whereas the Italian rhythm section is eleven years looser. In fact, it's so loose, one often suspects it's not there at all—the cut sounds like just Reinhardt playing behind Grappelli, and the bassist and drummer (who, if he's playing at all, is probably playing brushes) only become slightly more audible behind the guitar solos. Certainly the pianist isn't playing at all, and the combination of the guitar and violin, with only slight string backing, sounds like one of the various attempts from the '49 Rome session to re-create the classic Quintet of the Hot Club sound. (Among other leading guitarists who've tried "N&D," Joe Pass did a rather baroque solo treatment on his 1973 album *Virtuoso.*)

NONJAZZ GUITARISTS WERE NOT quite so fond of the song. It never did catch on in the rhythm-and-blues or rock-and-roll communities the way that "Stormy Weather" and "Ol' Man River" did. The closest thing to an important early R&B version is by Louis Prima, who used elements of that music along with various strains of jazz (not to mention the shuffle beat he'd been using since the thirties) to create a genre unto himself in the mid-fifties. The shuffling countermelody is particularly intense on "Night and Day," the first track of *Louis and Keely,* the trumpeter-vocalist's first album for Dot Records (1959). Although, as the album title suggests, it's a collection of duets with wife and partner Keely Smith, the performance might better be described as a duel than a duo. The two combatants are all over each other, particularly in the verse, wherein the repeated notes take on the rhythm of machine-gun fire hurled back and forth at each other as they trade lines. Prima rewrites the third line, "Like the drip drip drip of the raindrop *as it falls against the dew*" (!), and on the whole their treatment has less in common with Nelson Eddy and Jeanette MacDonald than with Dexter Gordon and Wardell Gray.

There are contempop takes on "Night and Day," but not many, and even fewer that are any good. Two British pop combos, Everything but the Girl and U2, illustrate the pros and cons of rock-and-rollers moving outside their own territory. The first group presents the song in a simple and straightforward fashion, a female voice (Tracey Thorn) intoning the famous melody and lyrics against a samba-ish acoustic guitar background; it's a single that supposedly charted in England and represented the debut of the group. At the windup, Thorn is joined by what sounds like a male vocal group (more likely a single male voice multitracked) intoning the title phrase, while she goes into a new extended coda, repeating Porter's ending lyrics against a new, complementary melody.

Would that the U2 version were quite so copasetic. Theirs comes from *Red, Hot and Blue,* not the 1936 Porter show but a 1991 centennial benefit album in which rock stars offered their generally lame versions of Porter classics in order to raise money for AIDS research. While their hearts were in the right place, their voices, unfortunately, were not. Where the Everything but the Girl treatment is honest and direct, the U2 is a bloated mess, level upon level of synthesized pseudo-orchestration and drum machines, setting the whole thing, starting with the verse (which the lead singer, presumably Bono, sings as "the tick tick tock from *the eye of the clock*"—I guess if clocks can have faces, they can also have eyes), to a wretched disco-like rhythm. Now, there's nothing wrong with attitude, and Bono, who has praised this aspect of Sinatra's music, has plenty of it, but it's a shame he doesn't have the vocal chops to go with it. This whole overlong and overbaked treatment seems deliberately designed to camouflage the inescapable fact that nobody involved in the production can sing or play an instrument.

Perhaps the furthest-afield "N&D" of recent years is that by opera (and musical comedy) baritone Thomas Hampson. While I suspect that Louis Prima may have been too outrageous for Porter's own tastes, Hampson risks erring in the other direction, being too straight for a song that was originally a highly rhythmic dance feature. (But, then, who remembers that it was the wooden-voiced, ultra-stiff Douglas McPhail, not Fred Astaire, who introduced "I Concentrate on You" in *Broadway Melody of 1940?*) Yet Hampson is charmingly robust here and the orchestration is outstanding. Unexpectedly, the singer does not try to dominate the proceedings: he merely sings a full verse and chorus at the start of this five-minute extravaganza, with the rest of the piece being given over to a lovely dance instrumental that sounds somewhere in between Robert Russell Bennett and Leroy Anderson.

WHEN COLE PORTER WAS BORN, in 1891, the center of world culture, both high- and lowbrow, was Europe. London, Paris, and Vienna were the hot spots; New York and Boston were then considered the hinterlands (and Los Angeles was not even on the map). By 1932, the nexus had shifted: now New York was the most sophisticated, as well as the jazziest, place to be; it set the trends and the rest of the world followed. When British dance bands and German vocal groups performed "Night and Day," they were paying homage to America's emerging musical dominance.

"Night and Day" was particularly popular in Europe: in France it became "Nuit et jour," whereas the Germans, as noted earlier, with their characteristically sneaky way of saying everything backwards (as one comic commented, a typical German sentence might be "Into Poland march!") called it "Tag und Nacht," which, if my German 101 had it right, is "Day and Night." The best foreign-language version is by the Comedian Harmonists, the innovative tight-harmony vocal sextet that flourished in Weimar Berlin before Der Führer objected to their polyreligious lineup. The Harmonists start with a foreboding hummed intro, then do the chorus in harmony before a soloist starts again with a full verse and chorus over a wordless background by the remaining members. He doesn't come anywhere near the jazz universe (although there is something like a stop-time passage), but he is, nonetheless, a crooner, delineating the song in an intimate singspiel with a personality that travels across the language barrier. More recently, the King's Singers recorded this arrangement in tribute to the Harmonists, although they restored it to English. Not so the Jesters, who also made an outstanding treatment of the Harmonists' arrangement in modern (1993) fidelity, and who chose to use the French lyric, rendering the chart with only three voices instead of five.

In a sense, lovely as the Thomas Hampson treatment is, deliberately evoking the past, "Night and Day" is the wrong song for such an approach. It has been with us for too many years, and we've heard it in too many different formats, from bossa nova to acid rock, for the song to be a cue to the thirties. It's been in more films than almost any other song—from *The Gay Divorcee,* to the 1937 *Rosalie,* to *Reveille with Beverly* with Sinatra to *Lady on a Train* (1945) with Deanna Durbin, to the supremely ludicrous biography of Cole Porter himself that the song titled in 1946. There's also a short subject made for American GI's in the early forties in which Dinah Shore sings a specially penned lyric about how the folks back home are thinking about the guys at the front. (Faced with news of this development, Germany retaliated by commissioning its own, an Axis version of "Night and Day" from Nazi bandleader-crooner "Charlie," for once without propaganda lyrics.) If you want to make people think of the thirties, try "Happy Days Are Here Again," or "Cocktails for Two," songs so embedded in that era that it's impossible to revive them without conjuring up mental images of breadlines and art deco dance palaces. "Night and Day" has been a part of our lives and our musical universe for so long that its history is essentially immaterial—you can't imagine the song being chained to any specific era, even the one that gave birth to it.

BONUS TRACKS

The Odd History of Bing Crosby and "Night and Day"

As Rosemary Clooney and other keen observers have pointed out, songs that required a frank and open expression of passion were not exactly Bing Crosby's strong suit. (Clooney explains that Crosby was more comfortable with an indirect expression of love, the perfect example being the phrase "If I say I love you . . ." from Burke and Van Heusen's "Moonlight Becomes You.") Thus it's surprising that Crosby even attempted "Night and Day" in 1944. Ken Barnes, pop-culture scholar and producer (who worked with Crosby on some of his final sessions) has been especially unkind to this disc, declaring, "Clearly he was in poor voice on this session and the performance should not have been issued. If there is a worse version of this wonderful song in existence, I have yet to hear it." It seems to me that the problem isn't Crosby's voice, but that he's just not the right artist to sing about that yearning burning inside of him—at least he wasn't in 1944. Crosby later recalled that this was the first time he ever recorded a Porter song (possibly true, if you don't count several Porter pieces he sang while with Paul Whiteman's band) and that he "waited too long." That might be closer to the point. Crosby could have and should have recorded "Night and Day" in 1933, when it was new and Crosby himself was a hotter, lustier crooner than he had evolved into by the war era. However, the 1944 session yields a bonus: a breakdown take has survived, in which Crosby gets through a chorus before something goes awry. It was generally the singer's policy to keep going when something like this happened, and then to ad-lib a goofy, sometimes slightly blue, set of lyrics as he went along. In this case, Crosby starts improvising and says, "And here comes Cole Porter on my ass!" He then goes into a maniacal laugh and concludes with what might be the only example of Father O'Malley uttering the F-word on microphone: "Fuck off!" It's safe to say that, even counting Sinatra's screwed-up live version from Blackpool in 1953, there's no recording of "Night and Day" quite like this one.

The Single Most Wonderful Version of "Night and Day," Instrumentally at Least

One doesn't necessarily think of Art Tatum as "cerebral," yet you wouldn't describe him as "emotional," either. On the other hand, while Ben Webster is probably the most passionate player who ever lived, his style is rooted more in the blues than in burning yearnings à la Cole Porter. On paper, neither would seem an ideal interpreter of Porter's ballad, but together, in 1956, they crafted one of the most exquisite readings of "N&D" ever recorded. The balance between the two is similar to that achieved by John Lewis and Milt Jackson in the Modern Jazz Quartet:

both are thinking about the piece melodically, but where Tatum's approach is more abstract, boiling the material down to a series of fragments he can speed up and play with, Webster is more visceral, delivering a from-the-heart crooning of the tune that introduces Porter's Broadway swells to the feeling of Kansas City blues.

A "Night and Day" That's As Different As Night and Day From All Other "Night and Day"s

Richard Tauber, the great opera and operetta tenor, was a German Jew who settled in England during the Nazi era. As you might expect, he doesn't get it exactly right on "Night and Day"—the melody is perfect, but the phrasing remains somewhat operatic—yet his voice is so beautiful and his acting so convincing that one more than forgives his rhythmic shortcomings. It's a powerful treatment, particularly when he inserts a little cry on "*think* of you," and emphasis on "yearning *burning* inside of me." This is certainly the most beautiful voice ever to address Porter's melody, and ample evidence as to why Tauber's reputation and popularity were roughly the equivalent of Caruso's and Jolson's combined.

STORMY WEATHER (1933)

music by Harold Arlen

words by Ted Koehler

IN THE LAST FEW YEARS of the life of Harold Arlen (1905–1986), the composer was at the center of a revival of interest in the black music and culture of fifty years earlier. (Unfortunately, he was too much of a recluse in those years to enjoy it or perhaps even be aware that it was going on.) The Cotton Club, where Arlen had labored as an in-house songwriter in the early thirties, served as a focal point for much of this activity: there was a book, several documentary films, and all manner of recordings (both reissues and new productions, the best of which was Maxine Sullivan's very specific *The Cotton Club Songs of Harold Arlen and Ted Koehler*). It all culminated in a major motion picture, Francis Ford Coppola's ghastly *Cotton Club,* which opened on Christmas Day 1984. No matter that this monstrosity quickly tanked, the very fact that it was produced demonstrated that Hollywood was willing to bet millions of bucks that people were interested in the Cotton Club and the great black singers, dancers, and bands of the interwar era.

During these years, it became fashionable to suggest that although Arlen had spent the bulk of his career writing for Broadway and Hollywood, he was in fact a jazz composer, a member of the hot community. Martin Williams, dean of jazz critics, had already boldly declared that there was more jazz in Arlen than in any other face on Tin Pan Alley's Mount Rushmore, even George Gershwin.

But not everyone was convinced. According to Arlen's longtime friend and biographer Ed Jablonski, the composer himself was somewhat annoyed by this particular kind of attention, in a manner that recalls the quasi-embarrassed, quasi-aggrieved way that Fred Astaire used to feel when Mel Tormé went around telling people that the song-and-dance man was also a great jazz singer. Hard to believe, yet Jablonski knew

Arlen better than anyone else, both as a friend and as a scholar—when he owned and operated the Walden Records label, Jablonski even produced a collection of Arlen songs featuring the composer himself singing—and one can't easily discount his conclusions.

There can be no doubt that throughout his life, from his earliest days as a bandsman up until the era when his name was up in lights on Broadway, Arlen had an acute affinity for black performers and what Duke Ellington called "the Negro musical idiom." As a young Jewish music-maker growing up in Buffalo and playing the piano, singing, arranging, and composing, he was attracted to the world of bands as well as to that of musical shows. Not that there was anything so unusual about harboring such twin aspirations in the 1920s and thirties, when jazz was closer to mainstream show business, and Swing Street and Broadway represented not only intersecting avenues but adjacent universes.

Arlen's career was launched by the dance bands, and it was the world of jazz and bands that continued to nurture him through the early years of his song successes. But even on the Great White Way, Arlen continued to think in terms of black performers: surely no other major writer, black or white, worked on so many shows for what they used to call "all-colored casts" or with black themes, from the many editions of the *Cotton Club Revues* in the early thirties up through *St. Louis Woman, Jamaica, House of Flowers,* and *Free and Easy.* Virtually the only Negro-centric show of the period that was not written by Arlen was Vernon Duke's *Cabin in the Sky,* and when MGM decided to make a film out of this production, they went to Arlen for a couple of additional songs.

Arlen (born Hymen Arluck) grew up in a two-family house in Buffalo. One of those two families was the Cantor Arluck and his brood, including his two sons, Hymen and Julius (who, as Jerry Arlen, later sang with Johnny Green's band); the other family was black. It would be hard to name another white Tin Pan Alley heavyweight who was raised under the same roof as a family of African-Americans. This fact puts one in mind of Ethel Waters's oft-quoted description of Arlen as "the Negro-est white man I ever knew."

Jablonski quotes a lengthy statement from Roger Edens, the composer's longtime friend, who elaborates:

> It was great excitement for me to go with Harold to the rehearsals [at the Cotton Club]. I shall never forget the sight and sound of

Harold with the cast. Singing with them, dancing with them, laughing and kidding with them. He really was one of them. He had absorbed so much from them—their idiom, their tonalities, their phrasings, their rhythms—he was able to establish a warm rapport with them.

All well and good, but Edens then goes on to say that black people then were not as sensitive about themselves "as they are today" (the book, *Happy with the Blues,* was finished in 1960). He explains that even then, however, "they resented the so-called 'professional southernism' that was rampant in New York in those days. I was always amazed that they completely accepted Harold and his super–minstrel show antics. They loved it and adored him."

Still, it was hardly Arlen the Negro-est white man who wrote "Over the Rainbow," undoubtedly the composer's most famous song. Many a jazzman has recorded "Rainbow," but Arlen hardly wrote it with the hot community in mind. The singer for whom it was written, Judy Garland, who showed the good sense to make it the signature song of her career, revealed equally good taste in never opting to make a claim for herself as a jazz artist. (This was only the start of a career-long professional relationship between Garland and Arlen, which also included *A Star Is Born, Gay Pur-Ree,* and *I Could Go On Singing.* Between "Rainbow," "Get Happy," and "The Man That Got Away," it certainly seems no songwriter did as right by Garland as did Harold Arlen.)

Were one to go solely on the evidence of this 1939 song, which opens, famously, with an octave leap, one might conclude that Arlen was a songwriter not with jazz leanings but with operatic tendencies. His 1934 "Last Night When We Were Young" would lead us to the same conclusion. Might it be that this direction was encouraged by Yip Harburg, the lyricist on both "Last Night" and "Rainbow"? Obviously, in addition to such other factors as the nature of the show, the performer, and the story, the taste of the lyricist is a major influence in determining the specific musical quality of the melody.

If Harburg steered Arlen toward the concert hall, then Johnny Mercer drove him back to Harlem. With Mercer, he wrote more jazz standards than with any other collaborator: "My Shining Hour," "Blues in the Night," "That Old Black Magic," "Come Rain or Come Shine." With Ted Koehler, his first extended partner, it was a bit of both: they wrote primarily for all-black Cotton Club revues, but their output was not intended to be exclusively jazzy. Indeed, it seems more likely that Arlen was the dominant jazz influence in this particular collaboration, especially since Koehler away from Arlen didn't write nearly as much with a hot slant. (That is, except for his collaborations with other similarly oriented composers, like Rube Bloom and Jimmy McHugh.) Not everything written for the Cotton Club was fodder for Cab Calloway; for instance, there's the lilting "'Neath the Pale Cuban Moon," which seems more directly intended for some sort of faux tropical nightclub.

Arlen also enjoys the distinction of having written the signature songs for two of the great singers of our time—Garland's "Over the Rainbow," and Lena Horne's "Stormy Weather." Not that signature songs are always great works: both Bing Crosby's ("Where the Blue of the Night Meets the Gold of the Day") and Frank Sinatra's ("Put Your Dreams Away") are pleasant but fairly undistinguished (Sinatra gradually phased his out and never used it even as bow music in his later appearances). But it would be impossible to imagine a Garland show without "Rainbow," or a Horne appearance minus "Stormy" (the titles even share a certain meteorological imperative). That's because they're not only theme songs, they're great songs, masterful products of the songwriter's art. For all of its success, from the Academy Award onward, "Rainbow" is to this day inseparable from Garland's memory; if ever a song were chained to a single great performer, this is it. "Stormy," on the other hand, had a whole history before Horne ever sang it, and it goes on being performed by artists who are self-confident enough to go up against a personality with the raw firepower of Lena Horne.

WHEN YOU HAVE SOMETHING as great as "Stormy Weather" inside you, it doesn't take very long for it to come out. Supposedly, "Stormy Weather" was written in about half an hour. Arlen and Koehler were at a party when the idea struck them. They were contracted to do the score for the twenty-second edition of *The Cotton Club Parade,* which was to open in April of 1933. At this point, probably around January, it had been announced that Cab Calloway and His Orchestra were to be featured in the forthcoming *Parade,* so Arlen and Koehler began trying to write a number that would show off that flamboyant bandleader-singer's jazzy, scat-oriented style. With Calloway specifically in mind, they came up with the very dramatic first three notes of the song ("Don't Know Why"), which Arlen dubbed "the front shout," and then proceeded from there. Thirty minutes later, the story goes, they were finished and left to get a sandwich. (That part of the story has always puzzled me: it couldn't have been much of a party if there was nothing around to eat.)

Arlen was, at that time, in the habit of spending weekends with his friends the Roger Edenses at their house in Nyack in New York State, along the Hudson River. Edens later told Jablonski that Arlen spent one of those weekends polishing the song that became "Stormy Weather."

> He had already found the melody, and, I believe, Ted had a first rough lyric. And on this weekend, he sang it for us many times— each time with an added note, or a different phrase, or a possible change in the lyric. I do think he possibly found the "repeat phrase" [more about that later] as he was playing it. Undoubtedly, he polished and perfected it to his satisfaction, for it went into rehearsal at the club several days later.

It was soon after that, while they were demonstrating "Stormy Weather"—and noting the reaction of the dancers and other Cotton Clubbers—that Messrs. A. and K. began to realize that they had written something out of the ordinary. To the great good fortune of everyone concerned, instead of Calloway, fine as he was, the club management signed Duke Ellington and His Orchestra, who had made their initial rep at the club, working there for most of the late twenties, and for the first time the club landed Ethel Waters as the headline entertainer. Waters was apparently on the fence about whether or not to do the Cotton Club show until she heard "Stormy Weather." That made up her mind for her—she just had to sing that song.

Some accounts insist that Waters was then in the midst of a career lull. The evidence, however, argues otherwise: she had already starred on Broadway in three all-black revues (1927 *Africana;* 1930 Lew Leslie's *Blackbirds;* 1931 *Rhapsody in Black*) and was practically unique in the black showbiz community of the time in that she had even been featured singing in a major Hollywood motion picture, *On with the Show* (1929).

Waters apparently had input into the song beyond the way she interpreted it. According to some accounts, Arlen and Koehler originally took their weather-oriented title quite literally, and included some kind of falling-rain sound effect in the melody. With A&K's permission, Waters took the music home with her one night and went over it, and the next morning all the stormy weather effects were gone and "Stormy Weather" emerged in the form we know it today. At some point Arlen and Koehler added a special patter section, and it makes sense that this would have been written expressly for Waters, since it's hard to imagine Cab Calloway singing it.

Waters was quite excited about "Stormy Weather": she was willing to sing it, she was waiting to sing it, she was wanting to sing it, but she made one proviso. She wanted to put everything she had into it, but she knew she could handle doing that only once a night. Therefore, even though it was the club's policy to give multiple shows, Waters stipulated that she would sing "Stormy Weather" only once per evening.

By 1933, Arlen's career as a performer was receding with each song hit he scored as a composer, although he still occasionally recorded his own songs, usually with Leo Reisman's orchestra. Although Reisman played dance music, his was the dance band with the strongest ties to Broadway and the band most likely to feature the new showtunes, often in elaborate medleys devoted to the key pieces from an entire score, and the band most likely to feature a Broadway star (such as Fred Astaire) or a singing songwriter (such as Arlen) as guest vocalist. On February 28, 1933, Arlen recorded "Stormy Weather" with Reisman's orchestra. The band takes the first chorus and, interestingly, the first instrument ever to introduce this melody, tinged with the blues and forever associated with the black experience, is not a growling trumpet or a wailing saxophone but a solo violin. A trumpet does lead the ensemble during the bridge, but the whole first chorus is pretty much the violin's show.

Arlen takes the second chorus himself, singing in a low, bluesy moan. His vocal is a matter of taste: in a set of liner notes to Ella Fitzgerald's *Harold Arlen Songbook,* critic Benny Green describes another of Arlen's vocals from this period (the Joe Venuti–Eddie Lang disc of "Little Girl") as a "desecration" of the otherwise fine jazz record on which it appears, and adds that Arlen's singing style "may best be described as eccentric." However, on another set of notes to the same double-album, deejay Gary Shivers opines that the Arlen vocal with Lang and Venuti reveals the composer to be "a singer of tremendous instrumental sophistication, a jazz singer rivalled among white vocalists of the day only by Bing Crosby and

Cliff Edwards." Roger Edens, who had a lot to do with formulating the styles of both Garland and Ethel Merman, once said that Arlen himself "could sing his own songs better than any man or woman." High praise indeed, considering that Frank Sinatra and Judy Garland fall into those latter two categories, but all hyperbole aside, we know what he means. My own opinion is closer to Mr. Edens and Mr. Shivers than to that of Mr. Green: Arlen's few recorded vocal choruses are quite charming and especially appropriate when heard on one of his own songs. As a singing songwriter, Arlen is exceeded only by his longtime collaborator Johnny Mercer and by one of Mercer's other partners, Hoagy Carmichael.

Whatever one's opinion of Arlen's abilities as a vocalist, in 1933 the public responded enthusiastically, whether because of the nature of the song or because they liked the band and the singing composer. Both record and song were an overwhelming success. *Variety,* which noted that in May 1933 "Stormy Weather" was selling an average of 8,000 copies a week, went so far as to proclaim it "the biggest song hit of the last ten years." ("Night and Day," which is often described as the biggest hit of the thirties, had been introduced only six months earlier.) Whatever the actual figures, "Stormy Weather" was a blockbuster: within a very short time, other record labels rushed versions out to compete with Victor and Reisman.

Columbia's premiere band version was by Ted Lewis, "the high-hatted tragedian of jazz," who in the twenties and thirties led a very credible hot dance outfit. Like the Reisman, the Lewis disc is essentially two choruses—one vocal, one instrumental. The first is taken by muted cornetist Muggsy Spanier, with obbligatos and other support from wailing trombonist George Brunies. The second is at first a disappointment in that it's not sung by Lewis himself, whose over-the-top singspiel style could be most endearing. However, the singer they did get, the quite obscure Shirley Jay, turns out to be a dark-toned contralto with an appropriately bluesy style. In those days, when a white woman attempted to sing something like the blues she was generally labeled a "torch" singer, and Miss Jay, who seems to have been otherwise unrecorded, is as torchy as they come.

Similarly, Columbia's major vocal version was by Frances Langford, who at this early stage of her career (she's just about twenty), was a dark-haired torch singer; she hadn't yet become the blond, sunshine-voiced costar of a million Bob Hope USO tours. Langford's treatment is surprisingly—for her—bluesy; she takes it in a slow, languorous tempo, opening with thirty seconds of very sensual scatting, humming as if she's lounging about her boudoir, expecting company. It sounds worlds removed from the squeaky-clean image she would convey in her heyday, ten years hence.

Brunswick Records had a big-selling version by Guy Lombardo, which, as with most attempts by the Royal Canadians to get hot or blue, almost seems like a parody. Like the Reisman and the Lewis, it's in two semi-slow choruses, the first of which is given over to a single soloist, with the exception of the bridge, taken by Lombardo's throbbing reed section. The first chorus features brother Lebert Lombardo's growling trumpet, which has more in common with such cornmeisters as Henry Busse and Clyde McCoy than it does with Cootie Williams. The second is brother Carmen Lombardo, who sings in a clipped fashion that perfectly matches the band's staccato (in the forties they would have said "Mickey Mouse") rhythm, with prominent guitar "plings" after each line that sound almost like a celeste. Because they play it slightly faster than Reisman and Lewis, the Lombardo chart has room for an instrumental half-chorus following Carmen's contribution.

Victor's Bluebird subsidiary came out with a far more copasetic dance-band treatment by the little-known Paul Tremaine (who also sings). Where Lombardo was still using a tuba, very old hat within two years of the swing era, Tremaine opens with a countermelody played by the bass sax, a highly unusual sound for any era, and lays out the melody considerably faster than we've heard it up to now, making it even more danceable. Two different trumpets, muted in different ways, share most of the first chorus. After the leader's high-pitched vocal and a dramatic transitional passage, a sweet-toned alto dominates the last eight bars.

Tremaine recorded his version on April 13, a week after the opening of the twenty-second edition of the *Cotton Club Parade*. By then, "Stormy Weather" was already a bona-fide hit, being heard all over the airwaves, so audiences thought they knew what to expect when they filed into the club to see the production that had already been tabbed "The Stormy Weather Show." Normally, the Cotton Club shows were ornate, even spectacular, affairs with lots of beautiful, light-skinned young black girls parading around in all manner of costumes and varying states of dishabille. It was something of a surprise, then, when the curtain came up on scene two, and there stood Waters, looking beat, leaning on a lamppost, under a blue follow spot.

She sang the song simply, honestly, and devastatingly. " 'Stormy Weather' was the perfect expression of my mood and I found release in singing it every evening," said Waters, who had just broken up with her second husband. "When I got out there in the middle of the Cotton Club floor, I was telling things I couldn't frame in words. I was singing the story of my misery and confusion, of the misunderstandings in my life I couldn't straighten out, the story of wrongs and outrages done to me by people I had loved and trusted." On another occasion she added that if she was indebted to her ex-husband for anything, "It's that he enabled me to do a helluva job on 'Stormy Weather.' "

If the song was already a hit, the show itself and Miss Waters were together a sensation. This would be probably the most successful revue in the long history of the club's reign as the premiere showcase for black talent (and white audiences). By spring of 1933, Ethel Waters and "Stormy Weather" were the talk of show business. More than ever, white celebrities made the trip uptown to Harlem to see and be seen, among them Irving Berlin, who immediately cast Waters in his forthcoming revue, *As Thousands Cheer,* thus affording her the most prominent role an African-American performer had yet enjoyed in anything outside of an all-black production.

Waters readily acknowledged "Stormy Weather" as the turning point in her career—in her autobiography, *His Eye Is on the Sparrow,* and whenever anyone asked her. She recorded the song on May 3, and on the eleventh appeared with Rudy Vallee on NBC's *Fleischmann's Hour,* which led *Variety* to predict that she might become the first black woman to have an impact on radio. This prediction came true in June, when NBC made her "the first Negress to win a network sustaining build-up," thanks to a twice-weekly, fifteen-minute sustaining spot. Two early airchecks survive of Waters performing the song. One of them is from the Fleischmann show. The other, included on a recent CD of live performances of Arlen songs, finds Waters segueing directly into "Raisin' the Rent," another Arlen-Koehler song from the same edition of the *Cotton Club Parade.* For a while, the singer was even billed as Ethel "Stormy Weather" Waters.

Although some of the radio broadcasts actually originated inside the club, Waters's airwaves activity was a sign of the song's acceptance beyond the Cotton Club itself. Further confirmation came from another of New York's legendary showbiz venues, Radio City Music Hall. Robert Wachsman, a promoter and advertising man who had apparently heard the Reisman-Arlen recording, got the idea of building a vaudeville-like spot around the song and its composer, complete with wind and weather effects. Arlen was into the idea, but before they could proceed, they had to convince the Cotton Club's owners that the song's being heard at Radio City wouldn't keep crowds from coming uptown to hear it at the club. As Arlen later told Jablonski, Wachsman made an impassioned plea to the club's boss, the notorious gangster "Big Frenchy" DeMange, whose only response was the rather cryptic, "I t'ink it's de nuts." This they took as permission to proceed.

WATERS HAS SPOKEN OF HOW "Stormy Weather" reflected her mood at the time she sang it, at a moment when she felt particularly dejected. Indeed, part of the reason for the song's success was that it came at a time when the whole country was feeling down and depressed, economically though hardly culturally. It was, as Frank Sinatra later introduced it (on a 1944 V-Disc), "a song that tells of the blues," which is an appropriate description, since "Stormy Weather," though not in the standard twelve-bar blues form itself, certainly has a blues feeling to it.

Arlen has spoken of how he chose to begin with what he called a "front shout." There would be no verse (although Maxine Sullivan used the song's twelve-bar interlude in its place). Arlen, who was thinking at the time that Cab Calloway would be the one to introduce it, wanted the song to get underway in the most dramatic fashion possible: to begin with an arresting declaration of unhappiness, opening with a blue note (the flatted third), then going up to a fourth, and then up a third to a sixth on the words "Don't know why. . . ."

The song is roughly in thirty-two-bar A-A-B-A form, though not exactly, and there's a twelve-bar "interlude." Each of the three A sections is eight bars of essentially the same melody, except for those two remarkable "repeats." The first repeat occurs at the end of the second A, which has three extra bars in which part of the melody is reiterated ("The time, / So weary all the time"). The second repeat is in a four-bar segment heard at the end of the third and final A section ("Keeps rainin' all the time"), concluding the song. Arlen saved a little space melodically by beginning each of the *A* sections in the middle of the preceding bar, or, in the case of the first *A* section, with a couple of pickup notes that occur before the first bar officially starts. Therefore, the chorus might more accurately be described as thirty-eight bars in a format of *A-A¹-B-A²*.

These repeat tags are unique in the annals of popular song, in that they represent an attempt to codify in the written melody the kind of spontaneous variations that a jazz or a blues singer would add naturally in performance. They're particularly suggestive of the way Louis Armstrong would phrase a song. It's ironic that "Stormy Weather," unlike "I Got Rhythm," "Star Dust," and "Body and Soul," is *not* one of the songs made into a jazz standard by Armstrong, who waited until 1957 to record it. (It was, however, done at the very beginning in an assuredly Armstrongian style by Nat Gonella, the Cockney answer to Pops, in London in 1933, with Harlemite Garland Wilson on piano in a duet obviously inspired by the Pops–Earl Hines "Weather Bird.")

The song is published in G, but many fakebook versions are in A flat, presumably because that's the key employed by Lena Horne, the song's best-known interpreter. It was no less an authority on the popular song than George Gershwin who pointed out to Arlen that the melodies of the *A* sections were unique in that they were each through-composed; that is to say, no part of the melody is repeated until the start of the next *A* section. Harmonically, however, there is a repeated pattern. The first two notes are meant to be done with no chordal accompaniment, and then we get our first chord on the third note, on the word "why." From there it goes as follows (keeping in mind that we're in the key of G):

G major chord (I) on "why"
G♯ diminished chord (I♯dim) on "there's no"
A minor seventh chord (IIm7) on "sun"
D seventh chord (V7) on "up in the sky"

The above two-bar pattern is essentially repeated throughout the *A* sections, with some variations. The harmony is generally major except for those spots where the minor seventh chord appears, for instance, on the word "weary." This is the portion, incidentally, that's repeated at the end of the *A¹* section.

For the bridge, we go to the IV chord (as in "As Time Goes By"), and for all eight bars we bounce back and forth between the IV and the I (the subdominant and the tonic), ending on the V chord (dominant). This one-to-four (I-IV) movement occurs in other songs ("Summertime" and "Ol' Man River") that affect a black folk feel. It's not specifically evocative of the blues, but it instills a distinctly spiritual mood into the bridge, which is quite apt, considering the references to prayer and "The Lord above" in the third line.

Anticipating "Over the Rainbow," Arlen employs an octave leap between the two syllables of the key word "wea-ther." There's another such leap, high G to low G, halfway through the interlude, on the repeated word "love" (the first "love" is high G, the second "love" is low G). However, this twelve-bar interlude, which begins with the line "I walk around, heavy-hearted and sad," is only infrequently performed: it seems to be the exclusive property of divas—Waters, Horne, Fitzgerald, Garland, Sullivan. Arlen himself, on his mid-fifties Capitol album, and Billy Eckstine (on *Once More with Feeling*) are among the few major male singers to use this section, which is identified in the sheet music as "The Interlude." The interlude starts in minor, but early on shifts to major. Throughout, the melody makes a keen distinction between minimal movement (for instance, the line "Since my man and I ain't together," which is essentially all performed on repeats of the same note), more dramatic intervals, such as on "I'm weary all the time," which moves by thirds, and really big jumps, like those octave leaps.

Although Arlen doesn't employ what we think of as blues harmony, as in "The St. Louis Blues" (the standard I-IV-V progression), he does use a fair amount of blue notes. As we've said, the melody starts on a blue third with "*Don't* know why," and continues to employ them on "*There's* no sun up in *the* sky, / *Storm*-y weather. . . ." All the italicized syllables fall on B♭ natural (or A♯, if you prefer), which in the key of G is the flatted third, with the exception of "the," which lands on a flatted fifth (in this case, a passing tone).

Koehler's lyric also freely alludes to blues subject matter. The traditional blues uses a twelve-bar form and a lyric setup that we can loosely describe as "conundrum" and "resolution." For example:

First line: "Sent for you yesterday, here you come today."
Second line: a repeat of that "Sent for you yesterday, here you come today."

Third line: either a response or some kind of resolution—"If you can't do better, then just stay away."

Each line is four bars, and together they total twelve. Although he doesn't keep kosher with the twelve-bar form and the repeated second line, Koehler does use constructions that refer to typical blues lyrics, particularly with regard to the blues tradition of the virtue of omission. In correct English, Koehler might write "I don't know why / There's no sun up in the sky, / It must be stormy weather," Koehler eliminates the "I" and the "it must be" and skips straight to the conclusion. It's both a blues and a folk convention to imply the missing verb. (Al Hibbler, it should be noted, puts the word "I" back before the opening "Don't know why.") Although the repeated line is gone, Koehler finds his own approach to the blues model of conundrum/resolution and manages it within the eight-bar format of Tin Pan Alley, repeating parts of the words and music for emphasis, as we have seen.

In terms of specific references within the text, it's worth mentioning that Koehler pays homage to Hoagy Carmichael by summoning up the icon of the ol' rockin' chair, Carmichael's 1930 song of that title having already established that piece of furniture as a symbol of defeat, or at least of resignation, in the black/blues lexicon. Koehler also inaugurates what would become a career-long tradition for both Arlen and Yip Harburg (although Harburg had nothing to do with "Stormy Weather") of songs about atmospheric conditions and phenomena: "Over the Rainbow," "Look to the Rainbow," "Little Drops of Rain," "Come Rain or Come Shine," "Right As the Rain," "Rainbow," "Like Clouds Up in the Sky," "Hanging Out a Rainbow (Over the U.S.A.)," "Oh, It Looks Like Rain," and A&K's own "Ill Wind." It seems perfectly fitting that it would be Koehler—not Harburg, not Mercer—who would reunite with Arlen in 1941 to write "When the Sun Comes Out," the song that comes closest to serving as a sequel to "Stormy Weather."

UNTIL 1940, THERE WAS no chart of best-selling records in *Billboard* or any other trade publication in the modern sense, one that covered all record labels in all areas. In the thirties, sales coverage was broken down by label and geographical order. (Although not many people realize it, the

early years of Joel Whitburn's *Pop Memories* are essentially an educated estimate as to what those totals might have been.) Brunswick's national top-
selling record in the spring of '33 was Lombardo's "Stormy Weather," and
number two was the same song. Interestingly, in two major markets this
number-two seller was a "race" version: in New York it was Duke Ellington (recorded April 16) and in Chicago it was Ethel Waters (May 3). Both
of these should also be regarded as original cast recordings, since Waters
and Ellington had jointly introduced the song in *The Cotton Club Parade*.
Although the singer and the band, who were probably the two leaders in
their fields, had collaborated on an all-star cast album of songs from *Blackbirds of 1928* only a few months earlier, unfortunately Brunswick president Jack Kapp did not think to combine them again, even though they
were working together nightly. A combined Waters-Ellington disc surely
would have been an even bigger seller, but then each had an ego and perhaps did not want to play second fiddle to the other.

Then, too, it was decided to make the Ellington version an instrumental, even though, apart from Waters, the band employed Ivie Anderson,
who (along with Mildred Bailey with Paul Whiteman) was the finest
female singer working with a band at that time. But what an instrumental
it was! This greatest of all jazz orchestras opens with a most classical-
sounding introduction, a dramatic concerto grosso–like cadenza on the
first two bars, followed by a Ducal piano flourish and some mellow reeds.
The melody proper starts with an object lesson in Ellingtonian muted-
trumpeting, as the first eight bars are given to the straight-toned Arthur
Whetsol before the second *A* becomes a fiesta in blue growling for Cootie
Williams. The last half of the first chorus then goes to trombonist
Lawrence Brown; the most hymnlike player in the aggregation, Brown
brings out the churchy qualities of the bridge and final *A*. What the brass
did for the first chorus, the reeds do for the second, which is only the second half of the song, resuming at the bridge with baritonist Harry Carney
and then letting Barney Bigard take it out on clarinet, right up to the
coda. The whole piece is essentially these five solos, with no ensemble
playing other than in the background, yet the hand of Ellington the
orchestrator, setting the mood, charting the course of the melody, is
unmistakable.

Waters claimed that "Stormy Weather" made her a star, but it also did
a lot for Ellington—and he for it. They started out together with a hit

record, and over the decades Ellington came up with at least six different treatments of it, more probably than of any piece of music other than one of his own compositions. The second version came almost immediately: the combination of the band and the song was such a hit that Irving Mills, who was in the serendipitous position of being the manager of the Ellington band as well as the publisher of "Stormy Weather," persuaded Paramount Pictures to film a short subject of the band and the song. The tune is at the center of Paramount's one-reeler *Bundle of Blues,* filmed in Astoria on May 23, even while the twenty-second *Cotton Club Parade* was still packing them in.

Ellington's spoken intro is brief and to the point: "We will now give you our conception of the most popular composition in recent years, that haunting melody, 'Stormy Weather.' " This five-minute cinematic opus differs considerably from the April recording. Yes, it again opens with the dramatic intro, and the first eight bars are again given to Whetsol. But Ellington then condenses the rest of the first chorus down to another *A* section; and since the remaining *A* that he does play has more of a tag on it, we could say that he skips the *A¹* and the bridge and goes straight to the *A²*, in order to hasten the entrance of Ivie Anderson. The superb singer then sings a full chorus, which may not sound like much, since all band vocals then were essentially one chorus, but this is hardly another band vocal. Instead of just singing in tempo and trying to keep with the fox-trot rhythm, the whole thing is phrased very slowly and sexily, the band complementing Anderson's every nuance. It's almost more of a vocal record (as the art of arranging for singers was then developing) than a standard dance band performance.

Anderson starts out very low-key, extending the last note of the bridge into a trill ("once mo-o-re") and then builds up to Waters's pattern of reaching a near-hysterical peak of emotion on the final "*Keeps* rainin' all the time." Following her impassioned statement, Lawrence Brown's trombone chorus, which finishes the number, is mournful but comparatively reserved. Unfortunately, the camera does not remain on either Anderson or Brown for long, treating us, instead, to "arty" shots of falling rain and puddles. The performance, having come in like a lion, goes out like a lamb, with Brown moaning the final notes.

From June to August 1933, Ellington played a triumphant first tour of Europe, where the whole band was well received, especially Anderson.

Sixty years later, Ellington associate Stanley Dance still vividly recollected the band's performance at the London Palladium at which Anderson, "dressed all in white, sang it and broke hearts galore." At the time
(July '33), *Rhythm* magazine reported that "Ivie Anderson is a coloured
lady who sings 'Stormy Weather' as you'll never hear it again." Unfortunately, unless you caught *Bundle of Blues* or saw the band live—outside of
the Cotton Club, where Ethel Waters, understandably, owned the song—
you never heard it at all, since Ellington's big-selling Brunswick disc was
strictly instrumental. Seven years later, in February 1940, closer to the
end of Anderson's eleven years with Ellington (1931–42), Ellington rerecorded "SW," this time featuring Anderson. Gone is the concerto grosso
opener; the "front shout" has now become a whisper. The piece opens
subtly, with Cootie Williams playing the first part of the *A* very straight,
almost like Arthur Whetsol, then jarring us by switching gears into one of
his most exaggerated growls ever. The rest of the disc is pretty much a
vocal feature for Anderson all the way, being joined by some serious
obbligato work from the band's new tenor star, Ben Webster. That's
pretty much it in the way of an outline, Webster accompanying Anderson
and the rest of the band laying out (except for some wah-wah fanfare
behind the twosome on the bridge and very subtle brass and reeds in the
last *A*). The ensemble joins her for the coda, in which she hits a high note
on "*all* the time," but it's a far cry—literally—from the over-the-top last
line of seven years earlier. (Elisabeth Welch, a black American who spent
most of her career in England, recorded "Stormy Weather" when she had
become a grand old lady of song, and hers may be the most recent treatment to retain that high, semi-hysterical yelp on "*Keee-eeps* rainin' all the
time.")

And this was hardly the end of Ellington's association with "Stormy
Weather." As with "Ol' Man River" and "Summertime," those other
songs by white songwriters that were constantly associated with black
performers, there always seemed to be some permutation of "Stormy" in
the Ellington band book. In 1950, a group billed as "The Ellingtonians
Featuring Al Hibbler" recorded it for Mercer Records, the label operated
by Duke's son (who also plays E flat horn on this date). This particular
session consisted roughly of fifty percent Duke's men, including baritone
colossus Harry Carney and bassist Wendell Marshall, in addition to studio
virtuosi Benny Carter on alto and guitarist Dave Barbour, while Ellington

himself alternated on the piano with his customary keyboard deputy, Billy Strayhorn. Hibbler's singing is at its churchiest here, and he taps into a prayer-like vein of inspiration similar to that which he achieves on the Ellington single "It's Monday Every Day." The simple orchestration (whose?—Ellington's, Strayhorn's, or Carter's?) makes effective uses of the three horns, having the younger Ellington phrase (on his rather unusual brass instrument) in unison with the alto and baritone, making for a most sonorous reed sound, somewhat akin to those charts of the thirties in which valve trombonist Juan Tizol would blend his own unusual horn with the saxes.

Carney has a more prominent role in the 1953 Capitol recording of "Stormy Weather" by the full Ellington big band as arranged by Strayhorn. Like the initial version from twenty years earlier, it's essentially a string of soloists who stick fairly close to Arlen's melody. After a brief Ducal flourish, Carney bookends the first chorus by playing the first A and the last A^2. In between, the rest of the tune is divided up between open-bell trumpeter Willie Cook (on the A^1), and another trumpeter, Ray Nance (on the bridge), who growls and moans on his horn like the once and future Ellingtonian Cootie Williams. What's interesting is that the 1950 Hibbler and the 1953 full-band versions are the only two treatments to allude instrumentally to the patter section: on the Hibbler, the opening of that portion is played very briefly by Carter in the short instrumental section approaching the end before Hib returns with the "Keeps rainin' all the time" coda, and on the 1953 it's played in full by yet a third trumpeter, Cat Anderson, who goes from the interlude back to the bridge, reserving his high-note showboating for the out-chorus, during which he returns to the A^2 to the accompaniment of an orchestral *tutti* and some organ-like chords from the reeds. Ellington closes with a few well-chosen plunks.

And even that isn't all for Ellington and "Stormy Weather." There's a live version listed in the discographies from Minnesota in June of 1954 (presumedly it's the Strayhorn Capitol arrangement), and in 1965 the band played the song again, this time in tandem with Dinah Shore, as part of a special TV tribute to Arlen. Furthermore, outside the Ellington fold several Ducal dudes recorded it on their own: Johnny Hodges on his 1965 *Blue Pyramid,* costarring organist Wild Bill Davis, and Ben Webster during a live concert in Copenhagen from that same year, which was recorded and posthumously released on a CD titled *Stormy Weather*. For a time I regretted that the Maestro did not include it on *Ellington Indigos,* his major collection of romantic treatments of non-Ellington standards (which includes "Where or When" and "Autumn Leaves"). But, then, considering that he had already recorded so many different treatments of "Stormy Weather," it might have seemed redundant.

"STORMY WEATHER" WAS ALMOST immediately accepted by the black community, and it continued to be recorded by artists far beyond the walls of the Cotton Club. It turned up on a lot of European recordings: Larry Adler; Nat Gonella with Garland Wilson; Herman Chittison; a black band in Paris led by Maceo Jefferson with a vocal by Elisabeth Welch; and Adelaide Hall in Copenhagen. Don Redman also tackled it with his big band (1937), as did the New Orleans–based Joseph Robichaux and His Rhythm Boys, in a wild treatment that commences with an original intro with slide whistles, presumably meant to simulate wind effects, and a habit of rendering the bridges in just about the unchurchiest fashion imaginable, with the tempo being doubled rather than halved on the *B* section of each chorus.

The early recorded legacy of "Stormy Weather" is especially rich in piano players, starting with Ellington and proceeding to Chittison, Garland Wilson, Willie the Lion Smith, and Art Tatum. (Later, Earl Hines recorded it solo on the 1974 *One for My Baby: The Music of Harold Arlen.*) Tatum's 1937 solo recording is especially noteworthy. It's one of the keyboard master's great ballads, revealing a more expressive, even introverted Tatum than we're used to hearing. He tones down most of the characteristic Tatum mannerisms, such as his habit of stopping the melody and breaking out in a series of chromatic runs. Here Tatum sounds more like a classic blues pianist, like Pete Johnson or Albert Ammons, though without the boogie-woogie effects.

But finally it was the 1943 film, titled *Stormy Weather,* that made the song into an all-time classic, and also firmly established it as the property of Lena Horne. According to the late jazz filmographer Dr. Klaus Strateman, when the song was a new hit in 1933, Paramount Pictures had the idea of using "Stormy Weather" as the title for a film. At one point, they considered using it as the name of the one-reel short subject starring the

Ellington band (released as *Bundle of Blues*) which used the song as its musical centerpiece, but publisher Irving Mills held out for a feature. He got his wish ten years later, and at another studio, starring an artist who was a mere slip of a girl in the Cotton Club chorus line back in 1933.

Thus *Stormy Weather* was produced by 20th Century Fox in 1943, starring Lena Horne, on loan from MGM, where, in her role as the female Jackie Robinson of showbiz, she was Hollywood's first black glamour girl and occasional leading lady. It seems to be a complete coincidence that Horne, who had been encouraged to sing by Ethel Waters, had first recorded "Stormy" two years earlier, in 1941. She would eventually make at least five recordings of the song, all of them in A flat. The 1941 is conducted by RCA Victor house director Lou Bring, and both it and Horne's movie version seem inspired by the idea of treating "Stormy" as what "Summertime" was also fast becoming, a sort of bridge between the musical worlds of high art (classical) and low (which, at that time would have meant jazz and pop music). Horne's 1941 record opens with arty effects such as a sharp contrast between tinkling, pizzicato strings over low-and-slow groaning bass clarinet, followed by growling brass. To a degree, the Horne-Bring arrangement seems inspired by the kind of charts Horne performed on *The Chamber Music Society of Lower Basin Street*, an NBC radio series that specialized in mock-classical arrangements of jazz standards. Throughout, the Bring version labors hard to contrast its classical textures (a small string section) with such jazz elements as an exaggeratedly rendered growling trumpet.

The 1943 soundtrack takes that same contrast and milks it even harder—although more in a visual than a musical way. The big 20th Century Fox orchestra, however, isn't pushed to go classical, though it easily could have. Particularly in the out-chorus, the orchestra sounds for all the world like Glenn Miller's Army Air Force band of the same period in its combination of the famous Miller creamy reeds with a big string section. (The comparison is made all the easier thanks to the fact that the Miller AAF orch recorded their own version of "Stormy Weather" around this time.)

On the soundtrack, Horne's opening vocal is almost four minutes long by itself; including a full chorus, the patter section, and then the last eight bars (A^2) repeated. The arty aspirations come less from the singing (which is outstanding) or even the orchestration, but rather from the imagery. It was decided to finish the movie with a spectacular acrobatic dance by the Nicholas Brothers. There could be no topping that, so producer William LeBaron chose to climax the picture emotionally with Horne's big torch song, and supplement it with a dance number of a different sort. Instead of the usual tapfest, this may be the only instance when Hollywood presented a black modern-dance troupe—Katherine Dunham and her dancers, who had recently "broken through" on Broadway in *Cabin in the Sky*—in a turn than has more in common with Baryshnikov than Bojangles.

Horne is shown singing in what's supposed to be her living room, and upon the finish of her four-minute vocal, the camera zooms out her window to a group of jitterbuggers waiting out a thunderstorm underneath an elevated subway station. When one of them (Dunham herself) gazes skyward, she has a vision, a dream ballet, as it were (this was, after all, the year of *Oklahoma!*), in which she and her troupe dance across an abstract background, apparently meant to symbolize clouds and rain; the wind is provided in more concrete form by a machine offstage. Pretentious? Sure, a little bit. How could it not be? Virtually all of Hollywood's attempts to present dance on film, unless it's tapping like Buck and Bubbles, or romantic partner dancing like Fred and Ginger, turn out to be overly serious. But, at the same time, no number ever gets too pretentious as long as the music is good and stays in a jazzy tempo, which "Stormy Weather" in *Stormy Weather* definitely does—this isn't a case of Paul Whiteman trying to symphonize things up by playing them in a concert tempo.

Horne is superb on the 1941 Victor and even better on the 1943 film soundtrack; as already mentioned, the number provides the emotional climax of the picture. The plot is thin but sufficient: she and leading man Bill Robinson (yes, he was forty years older than her, but she was closer in age to Robinson than Shirley Temple, who had been Bojangles's previous leading lady) have been estranged, as they used to say, and when she gets to the line "Since my man and I ain't together . . ." she throws him a knowing glance. However, Horne hardly needs the help the plot along to break our hearts with this number.

The 1941 and the 1943 are considerably subtler than later treatments, although Horne's career has endured long enough for her to pass through many phases. In her Hollywood years, the 1940s, Horne was a considerably more demure singer than she became in the ensuing decade, when she performed primarily in nightclubs and the Broadway show *Jamaica* (with a score by Arlen and Harburg). Horne's next commercial recording came in 1957 (on the United Artists label) and features a much bigger and brassier Horne voice; in the post-Hollywood years she became something of a belter. About ten years later, she recorded the song again, this time for an independent label. Her voice on the sixties reading is bigger still, but there's an appreciable difference in the orchestration, which now relies on the sixteenth-note rhythms and backbeat-style phrasing of rock-and-roll. Horne, as always, sounds great, but otherwise the backing is very much of its era, and in this case that's not a compliment.

The 1981 reading, which provided the climax for both acts of her one-woman show, is a tour de force that neatly encapsulates her entire career. Part one is a no-nonsense, straightahead chorus that's perfectly suited to Horne's big band phase and her MGM years. Part two starts with her informing the audience, "I'm still finding things to think about when I sing this. It's taken me a lot of years to grow into it." She starts slowly, opening with the patter section, which most people in the house do not recognize right away as being part of "Stormy Weather." By this point in her career, Horne has gone from being a belter in the musical-comedy sense (think Ethel Merman) to a belter in the soul sense (think Aretha Franklin), and even before she reaches the chorus she goes off on a soulful-gospel kind of tangent, interjecting, "Don't it hurt when you think about love . . ." To some, Horne's apparent conversion into an R&B diva seemed a little forced—why was she all of a sudden making like Ray Charles or Etta James after all those years when we enjoyed her so much as Lena Horne?—but it's hard not to be blown away by the sheer power of this nine-minute showstopper.

While Horne recorded at least five distinct arrangements of "SW," Sinatra did three, even though it's not a song associated with him and he rarely if ever included it in concert performances. The 1944 version, arranged by Axel Stordahl (or possibly George Siravo), is almost feather-light, not the least bit stormy or tempestuous, although it's in what could be considered a ballad tempo for the day. The Ken Lane Singers, who make like the Pied Pipers, add to the vaguely optimistic nature of the piece even while the extended solo by muted trumpeter Yank Lawson considerably elevates the jazz content of the chart. As with many of his performances of the era, Sinatra takes more liberties with the melody than he is generally given credit for—often they're so subtle as to not call attention to themselves. Sinatra starts in E flat, and in the A^1 section, instead of just going to the written A flat on "gloom and misery every-where," he bends the note down to G flat, which in this case is a blue note, a flatted third. Just by bending the note, he really hits you in the gut with it. Following Yank Lawson's solo, the chorus sings the bridge, and before FS enters with the final "can't go on," the thing modulates up a half-step to E natural.

For all its sunniness, the 1944 "Stormy Weather" is more successful than the 1959 treatment (in F) with Gordon Jenkins on *No One Cares.* The latter version fails to bring out the best in the orchestrator, and while Sinatra tries to get intimate, Jenkins sounds merely morose. *No One Cares* may rank as Sinatra's saddest statement ever, and the combination of the melancholy nature of the material, the over-heavy, semiclassical Jenkins chart, and Sinatra's downer mood add up to too much. Singing "Stormy Weather" with a little more rhythm, however, would give the piece the ironic edge it needs, which is what Sinatra does on his 1985 album *L.A. Is My Lady,* arranged by Sam Nestico and produced and conducted by Quincy Jones. The near-seventy Sinatra finds the sharp blues edge in his voice and slashes his way through the song with it. After a walloping intro, he does most of the first *A* with just Fender bass for accompaniment and with an electric guitar obbligato by Lee Ritenour, in the key of E. He repeatedly hits the high E, an octave above the tonic, on such words as "*gloom* and misery." This chart also modulates up a half-step (to F), and while in that key on the last line, he goes for a high F on the last "*can't* go on." It's an undervalued performance on an underappreciated album—the last great Sinatra album, in fact.

"Stormy Weather" shares a most unusual distinction with "The St. Louis Blues" and "Night and Day": during World War II, it was played by both the Allies and the Axis sides of the conflict in propaganda broadcasts intent on undermining enemy morale. The Glenn Miller Army Air Force band version, which we've already mentioned, was preserved thanks to a series of shortwave transmissions beamed at Nazi troops. The bulk of the Miller propaganda broadcasts were musical performances, and some tracks, like the band's ultra-lush, five-minute treatment of "Stormy," were instrumental. Others had vocals, sung in phonetic German, by Miller's

regular vocalists, Johnny Desmond and the Crew Chiefs. Between numbers, Major Miller, also speaking in phonetic German, would banter with
a German hostess named "Ilsa."

America tried to seduce the Germans with American popular music,
both swing and romantic ballads. Germany responded not with beer-
garden music or Teutonic titwillows in Viking helmets, but with their
own approximation of American swing. Since long before America entered the war, the Germans had been trying to undermine the Allied
effort with Charlie and His Orchestra, a sort of musical equivalent of
Lord Haw Haw and Tokyo Rose. The Miller broadcasts to Germany were
comparatively "commercial-free"; it was implied that the Yanks were
sending this music to the Jerries as an advertisement of the American way
of life, mom, and apple pie. Not so the Charlie recordings: vocalist and
compère Charlie's technique was to demoralize and ridicule the Allied
enemy. On "Stormy Weather," he sings from the perspective of Winston
Churchill, and laments that the reason there ain't no sun up in the sky is
because "Since my ships and the German planes got together / I'm
beaten all the time." Charlie, who comes across like the emcee of the Kit
Kat Club in Cabaret, goes on to list other reasons for Winnie to sing the
blues, among them the news that "now the French are against me," which
would have been news to de Gaulle. Indeed, "Charlie" was the most
politically extreme and hate-filled figure in pop music until Eminem.

Speaking of the French, the great Gypsy guitarist Django Reinhardt
recorded his own treatment of "Stormy Weather" in Rome in 1950, as
part of a session for radio transcriptions—it's one of the most accomplished performances of his later period (he died in '53). In general, the
song was not as popular among postwar jazzmen as it had been with
pre-. In 1957, Henry Red Allen and Coleman Hawkins recorded a treatment originally distributed only for stereo demonstration purposes on an
open-reel tape. It starts with the trumpeter offering a dramatic introduction and sticking to the melody before Hawkins enters and takes it off in
his own directions.

Hank Crawford, an early exponent of what they later called "soul jazz"
and then not long out of Ray Charles's band, recorded an intensely
romantic treatment with a string orchestra arranged and conducted by
Marty Paich in 1962. Roy Eldridge recorded a rather harsh, even abrasive
treatment of the melody, whereas the André Previn Trio (with Ray

Brown and Mundell Lowe) swings it lightly and politely, as if it had nothing to do with the collective sorrows of a million women whose men
done went away and left them with the blues.

The major modern jazzman who really went to town with "Stormy
Weather" was bassist and composer Charles Mingus, who seems to have
been attracted to it for its combination of blues and Tin Pan Alley elements, as well as because of its connection to Ellington. Like the Ellington versions, the two recordings by Mingus are both essentially strings of
melody solos, and both frame those solos, phrased very, very slowly,
against a stark, generally a cappella, background. The three-minute 1954
version for Bethlehem spotlights trumpeter Thad Jones, with a brief bit
of cello by the leader himself. The thirteen-minute 1960 recording is
introduced verbally by Mingus as a feature for "Eric Dolphy, fresh from
California," but rather than mention the tune by name, he introduces it
by plucking out the first few notes of the melody on his bass. In both
cases, Jones and Dolphy stretch the edges of the tune, taking them to the
point where they're almost distorted beyond recognition. The same
could be said for their intonation, which may not be completely sharp but
is certainly on the sharper side of whatever one's personal definition of
"in tune" happens to be. The 1960 also features spots for Mingus (on
bass) and trumpeter Ted Curson, but it's pretty much Dolphy's show the
whole way.

After Sinatra, only a few notable male singers recorded "Stormy
Weather," among them Billy Eckstine with Billy May's orchestra (they
start wild and fast but switch to bluesy and slow before getting down to
business), Lou Rawls, and, most notable of them all, Louis Armstrong.
The great man's treatment comes from two albums, *I've Got the World on a
String* and *Satchmo under the Stars,* he did in 1957 that represent his most
significant attempt at a modern vocal album in the manner of Sinatra or
Ella Fitzgerald—a fitting turn of events, considering the inspiration he
provided for both of those singers, and a great many others, besides. One
wishes Pops had made albums with Nelson Riddle and Billy May (actually,
he did a disc of duets with Bing Crosby accompanied by May), yet Russ
Garcia, his collaborator on these two albums for Verve, is a more than fair
substitute. Garcia contrasts brass and strings, while pianist Paul Smith,
the most prominent voice after both of Pops's, evokes Tatum playing the
blues. Armstrong sings the first chorus and plays the second; the first

bridge is utilized as an excuse for a series of stop-time blues breaks, the second is given over to Smith. As is characteristic of him, Satch is both powerful and mellow throughout. With the song set in the key of D flat, his trumpet builds to a high A flat (the fifth) at the climax.

In the postwar, post-Horne lens, "Stormy Weather" remained primarily the province of the ladies, including a few straight-down-the-middle types like Anita Ellis and Eydie Gorme. Ellis, who recorded "SW" on a transcription in 1945, is not yet the master (mistress?) she would become, and this early treatment captures her in something of a Dinah Shore bag (although Miss Shore occasionally evidenced sympathy for the blues and could have done a fine version, especially early on). Other female singers found other things to do with the song: the Keely Smith–Nelson Riddle version incorporates subtle wind and rain effects, along with a thunderous bass trombone, elemental vamps, and counter-melodies. The Arlen-Koehler song is made to order for Smith's sultry monotone, which she sustains until reaching the windup, at which point she catches us off-guard by going into a little singsongy original coda of her own: "It's rainin', and I'll go on complainin', / until my man comes home again to me, / Stormy weather," singing the latter phrase on four entirely different notes.

Ella Fitzgerald, on *The Harold Arlen Songbook* (her one extended project with Billy May, from 1960), isn't necessarily fast, but she more than swings. Fitzgerald expands many a syllable into multiple notes, as in "sto-or-ormy we-ee-ather," while May's five-minute chart is firmly rooted in swing-era practices and instrumentation (that is, no strings). Still, Fitzgerald's reading, like Keely Smith's, goes through more than the usual share of speed-ups and slow-downs.

The song can be done in a more or less straight pop fashion, as in Judy Garland's 1961 *Judy at Carnegie Hall* reading, and sound great. Yet it was custom-made for women who sang with a touch of the blues, such as Billie Holiday (1952), Peggy Lee (1947), Lee Wiley (1940 and '48), and Kay Starr (1945). Holiday's, done with Joe Newman, Paul Quinichette (both recent Basie alums), and Oscar Peterson, is rendered with her customary razor-sharp tone, playful phrasing, and slow yet intense tempo. Lee Wiley's 1940 commercial recording, surprisingly, isn't nearly as deep as we'd expect. She seems rather resigned to "gloom and misery everywhere" and isn't putting up much of a fight. Done with the great trumpeter Billy Butterfield and an Eddie Condon band, it's almost a masochistic approach to "Stormy Weather." However, an aircheck exists of Wiley performing the song eight years later, and though the accompaniment here (Dick Jurgens's orchestra) is hardly as simpatico as Butterfield and Condon, Wiley herself shows considerably more spirit.

Lee's is the most poppish of this grouping, and the singer's own sound is the softest and most mellow, with husband Dave Barbour not only conducting but dominating the orchestral texture with his guitar. In complete contrast, Kay Starr sings it as if she's never been mellow, with a certain hillbilly twang, but is no less jazzy or bluesy. Starr herself once described to me the circumstances under which she recorded "Stormy Weather," which happened with an all-star group billed as "The Capitol International Jazzmen," so named because Benny Carter, Coleman Hawkins, and Bill Coleman had spent some years in Europe, although all the participants were Americans:

> Originally, I started recording for Capitol just as sort of a guest star on Dave Dexter's jazz albums. When I went down to the studio to do the first one, Dave did not tell me who was going to be there. He just said that he did all-star jazz sessions and he kind of told me some of the musicians, but it never occured to me that I'd actually be singing with them. And when I went into that studio, they had these two big sets of doors there, and you go through one door and then you just gently pushed open the second door, which actually went into the studio, because it was blinking but not red. I knew that I needed to be in there because it was the time Dave had said.
>
> But I just looked in and I saw Nat Cole on piano and John Kirby on bass and Coleman Hawkins, I opened up the door a little more just to be sure of what I was seeing, and in the same breath I thought "This can't be the right studio!" I wanted to dissolve, I didn't want to make any noise so that nobody would know I was there. I must have made a mistake. I started to do what I call a crawdaddy out that door, to walk backwards like the crawdads do when they're afraid, but I heard Dave's voice saying, "Get in here, Okie, you're in the right place!"
>
> I was supposed to sing "Stormy Weather," and I know Nat Cole had done a vocal record of that for Capitol, and I was so nervous I thought I had to ask permission. I asked him if it was okay, and he

laughed and said of course. And Nat later used to kid me about that when we got to be friends. He said, "She can't sing 'Stormy Weather' without my permission!"

The funny thing is, Cole had not, in fact, done a vocal record of "Stormy Weather," for Capitol or anyone else. The great pianist-vocalist never actually sang the Arlen-Koehler song—at least not on records— which would have been so right for him, but he had made a recording in which he accompanies Ida James, former vocalist with Erskine Hawkins, who sings in a tight, pinched little voice that anticipates Eartha Kitt. (Ida James also sounds a bit like the young Betty Carter, who later recorded "Stormy" on her early 1958 album *Can't Help It*.)

Peggy Lee takes more liberties with the melody than most singers, particularly when she accentuates the movement up a third on "Ev'ry- thing I *had* is gone" in the last *A* of the first chorus. She also adds an extra bit of melody to the coda, "Since my man and I, we ain't together, / Keeps rainin' all the time," which could be interpreted either as a Billy Eckstine–like addendum (in the tradition of Mr. B.'s "Cottage for Sale") or merely as an extension of what Arlen had begun by repeating one of his repeats.

Della Reese, Etta James, and, most of all, Dinah Washington cleave even more closely to the letter and spirit of the blues. Washington's voice and style, which could be described as finding the precise halfway point between the blues and mainstream jazz singing (in the sense that, say, Ella Fitzgerald and Sarah Vaughan are "mainstream" jazz singers), were absolutely made to order for "Stormy Weather." Yet neither of her two recordings of the song, both done for Mercury in 1961, lives up to our expectations. The first, arranged by Belford Hendricks, submerges Washington's spirit in a treacly morass of ersatz country-and-western strings. The second, conducted by Quincy Jones, takes the tune a tone lower and has a solid jazz trombone solo, but still includes annoying background voices, and in general leans too far over on the sticky-sweet kiddie-pop side.

Etta James's arrangement also uses a pop-R&B–style rhythm, and some annoyingly high-pitched, piercing strings. Yet while I can't say I wouldn't prefer hearing James in a straight-ahead setting, somehow this poppish background suits her better than it does Washington—at least it doesn't make her impossible to listen to. James builds very convincingly to a big note and a big dramatic moment on "Can't go on. . . ." Keeping the whole thing fairly restrained, she steers clears of the clichéd pratfalls a lesser artist might not have avoided, such as the big, screeching climax. Would that all of them could have sung the arrangement written by Sy Oliver for Della Reese on her album *Story of the Blues*—not that Reese doesn't do a first-class job of singing it. Like Washington and James, she is really right in your face, chomping and biting and snarling her way through the tune, at times sounding like a female Al Hibbler. She does the bridge entirely in blues-style stop-time, and finishes with a very loud final eight.

Another major blues singer who tackled "SW" was Amos Milburn, the R&B pioneer (coming shortly after Louis Jordan), who recorded it for Aladdin in 1952. Milburn's short, one-chorus take (two minutes, twenty-three seconds) is distinguished as possibly the song's most authentically blue version, by virtue both of his moaning voice and of his boogie vamp piano accompaniment—not to mention a fine tenor obbligato. Milburn's may well be the only version that completely drops the opening lines, "Don't know why / There's no sun up in the sky," easily the most famous part of the song. Milburn begins with the lyrics for the final A (A^2) section, "Can't go on, / Everything I had is gone. . . ." He's fine for the A^1 and the bridge, and then resings the A^2 lyric, this time in its proper place.

Over the last forty years, "Stormy Weather" has served as a veritable symbol for genre crossover: from classic pop into the blues and country and back again. Brenda Lee's version is only slightly countrified, utilizing a repetitive electric bass pattern throughout that's common to both kiddie-pop and country, until the bridge, at least, when a real Nashville-style piano tinkler makes his presence known behind her. Her phrasing recalls Kay Starr, who surely set a precedent for a merger of hillbilly and Harlem techniques. Cowboys Willie Nelson and Leon Russell recorded a spare, effectively minimal interpretation, with Nelson singing atop electric piano and synthesized strings (which, to be honest, make it sound as if there's nary a cloud in this particular sky, but the performance is engaging, nonetheless).

George Benson and Lou Rawls both recorded treatments that draw on all the native traditions of the song—blues, Tin Pan Alley, and jazz. Benson's, with his famous sixties quartet featuring baritonist Ronnie Cuber, is one of the best of all the up-tempo treatments, showcasing the then-promising guitarist and singer long before he discovered electronic gimmickry. Lou Rawls is right on the border between blues, soul, and jazz. His singing would also become more mannered, and his choice of material went right down the toilet (which explains how he became a pop superstar), but these early performances are golden.

The Spaniels recorded the definitive doo-wop treatment: double-time rhythm (motivated by a drummer playing brushes), a booming baritone in the background, a beeping tenor soloing up front. It's a shame that Sam Cooke, as far as can be determined, didn't make a record of "Stormy Weather," but one Troy Walker, a more obscure R&B crooner, included it on *Recorded Live* (taped at Hollywood's Crescendo) in a performance more or less in the Sam Cooke style. Jeff Lynne, the British rocker behind the Move and Electric Light Orchestra, left posterity a rather countrified reading, although where Nelson and Russell are engagingly spare, Lynne's version is somewhat overproduced (though not, it must be admitted, as badly overdone as that of sometime jazz pianist Joe Sample), with a wordless choir and a percussion device that sounds strangely like a cowboy boot being stamped up and down on a wooden floor.

The crossovers continue: folk-rock singer-songwriter Joni Mitchell delivered a rendition that surprised me with its depth and effectiveness, but which probably was no surprise for her longtime fans. Mitchell has a burnished voice like the best of the great jazz ladies and a more than persuasive way with a lyric. She obviously grew up with the 1959 Sinatra reading, for her background arrangement seems deeply in debt to Gordon Jenkins. Oscar Peterson recorded it not only on his 1959 *Harold Arlen Songbook* but more recently in tandem with violin virtuoso Itzhak Perlman. Perlman is no Stephane Grappelli (then again, when it came to playing Mozart, Grappelli probably was no Perlman), but he does get around the melody pretty well, leaving most of the hardcore harmonic improvisation to Peterson (who's especially bluesy and barrelhouse here).

Mel Tormé never sang "Stormy Weather," and neither did Barry Manilow, but they referred to it in a 1984 duet on something called "Big City Blues." This wasn't the fine Gottler-Mitchell-Conrad "Big City Blues" of 1929 but a typically forgettable opus by Manilow himself, which includes the deathless couplet, "No more stormy weather, / Love will last forever." There's even a relevant track by a more recent "alternative rock" group called the Pixies. This song is listed (on their third album, *Bossanova,* 1990) as "Stormy Weather," although it's not the Arlen-

Koehler song but an original, the full title of which seems to be "It Is Time for Stormy Weather." I'm pretty sure that's the actual title; I know it's the sum total of the lyrics. Not only is it not "Stormy Weather," it's not even remotely a bossa nova. (On the same wavelength, there's also an unrelated country-and-western song bearing this title that was performed by Dolly Parton and Tanya Tucker, among others.)

I have to confess, I don't particularly care for the Pixies' song. *Bossanova* has been described as the most mellow of their albums, which I suppose is a matter of comparison and taste. It certainly doesn't sound "mellow" to me, just the same screeching guitars and screechier vocals I hear on every other rock-and-roll record. But regardless, the Pixies were onto something. It *is* time for "Stormy Weather," and always will be.

BONUS TRACKS

Lena Horne's Most Feared Rival in the "Stormy Weather" Department

Where Ella Fitzgerald turns "Stormy Weather" into a musical tour de force, Judy Garland, in her epic Carnegie Hall concert of 1961, treats it as an emotional one. She starts small and builds and builds and builds, until by the out-chorus (after the interlude) you can't believe she can sustain anything so large. It's like a little girl trying to inflate a Macy's parade balloon all by herself. No one but Garland could parade emotions at once so large and so subtle—a trick that Barbra Streisand never quite managed to master. Some of her most effective moments are the smallest, as when she's gasping out the words "Ev'rything I had is gone." Surely no other singer has ever painted so complete a picture of spiritual desolation. You feel as if you could look into her eyes and see straight into the abyss. Even after I had listened to sixty or so other versions of "Stormy Weather," Garland's still reduced me to tears.

Eydie Gorme . . . Belts the Blues?

All right, the title may be good for a few laughs, but stop chuckling. Talented as Miss Gorme is, she can no more "belt the blues" than Mississippi John Hurt can sing "Miss Otis Regrets" or Tex Ritter could do the

"Quando men vo" from *La Bohème*. Yet, if you can get past the ludicrous title, *Eydie Belts The Blues* is a fine album of pop standards with a light blue tinge, of which "Stormy Weather" is a perfect example. She may not match Kay Starr for blues feeling or Peggy Lee for jazz invention, but this is a fine, "straight-as-written" pop treatment of the Arlen song, with every note in place and everything exactly where it ought to be.

Best Versions That Never Were

In addition to Nat King Cole and Sam Cooke, three singers who could have sung "Stormy Weather" to perfection were the three major vocalists who graduated from Count Basie's ranks, Jimmy Rushing, Helen Humes, and Joe Williams. Perhaps they considered it redundant, since they were already spending their entire careers on the borderline between jazz, pop, and blues. But any one of them could have sung the hell out of it on any day of the week.

SUMMERTIME

THE THEATRE GUILD PRESENTS

PORGY and BESS

MUSIC BY

GEORGE GERSHWIN

LIBRETTO BY

DuBOSE HEYWARD

LYRICS BY

DuBOSE HEYWARD and IRA GERSHWIN

PRODUCTION DIRECTED BY

ROUBEN MAMOULIAN

GERSHWIN PUBLISHING CORP.
R K O BLDG. NEW YORK N. Y.
CHAPPELL & CO. INC.
SOLE SELLING AGENT
MADE IN U.S.A.

SUMMERTIME (1935)

music by George Gershwin
words by DuBose Heyward

THE INITIAL PROBLEM that faced reviewers concerning the original production of *Porgy and Bess* was the form of the work itself. "Critics at the time complained because it wasn't an opera and it wasn't a musical," recalled director Rouben Mamoulian toward the end of his life. "You give someone something delicious to eat and they complain because they have no name for it." By the mid-1980s, when Mamoulian made those remarks, the question of opera versus Broadway musical had become moot. It's even more so at the millennium, now that both forms seem archaic, meaning that what happens within the walls of the Marquis Theater or the Eugene O'Neill is just as likely to be a revival as anything presented at the Metropolitan or City Opera.

But this was a hot topic in 1935, and the Gershwin brothers and DuBose Heyward, the creative team behind *Porgy and Bess,* did not make the issue any clearer by deciding to stage the work in a Broadway theater rather than in an opera house or a concert hall. Then there was the Theatre Guild's own subtitle for *Porgy and Bess*—"A Folk Opera"—which only muddied the waters further. Even by 1935, few people referred to African-American music as folk music (except in Louis Armstrong's definition that all music was folk music: "I ain't never heard no horse sing!"). Then as now, black music was jazz or blues—or perhaps spirituals or the emerging genre of gospel music.

The problem of categorizing *Porgy and Bess* became even more daunting when it came to describing the most famous song in the score. Act one opens with an instrumental "introduction"—it's usually referred to as that, rather than as an overture, since technically it isn't a musical-comedy overture, containing brief snippets of the tunes that are to follow. The first notes that are actually sung in the opera are those of "Summertime," which a woman (Clara) croons to her baby, cradled in her arms. "Summertime" opens the opera thanks to a fluke. Initially, DuBose Heyward's plan was to start with an instrumental entitled "Jasbo Brown" (the title came from an early poem of his). The piece was cut, however, during the original Boston tryout—not because of length, which was the reason much of Gershwin's material was pruned from the final score, but because of economics. The "Jasbo Brown" number required an entire extra stage set, an expense the Theatre Guild could not justify, so it was cut, except for a few bars of piano between the intro and "Summertime." ("Jasbo Brown" has been restored in several recent revivals and recordings, such as Joe Henderson's). The Guild's budget-consciousness became history's boon, as the way "Summertime" opens the action helped solidify its stature as the single best-known piece of music in the opera and one of the most famous of all Gershwin compositions. "Okay," said Gershwin when he realized that "Jasbo" had to be cut, "that means we start with the lullaby—and that's some lullaby."

As Gershwin suggests, "Summertime" is ostensibly just that, a lullaby. But it's much more. Its lyrics are rife with religious imagery, and then there is the matter of the female choir that joins Clara halfway through her chorus of the song. Clearly, "Summertime" is not only a lullaby but a spiritual as well.

"Summertime" is other things, too: Billie Holiday sang it accompanied by growling, vocalized trumpet and hot clarinet. Her interpretation makes the song sound more like a blues, and that's not all: when she returns after the clarinet solo in the middle section, she reenters at the halfway point. Here, her phrasing of the line about rising up ("One-of-these-mornins") is very declarative indeed, and her broad staccato pattern spaces the notes out in such a way that the song assumes a defiant, almost militant flavor. Billie Holiday not only makes "Summertime" into a blues, in her hands it's almost a civil rights anthem. The entity that will spread its wings and take to the sky is not merely an individual baby but an entire race, and, beyond that, all oppressed peoples everywhere. (For what it's worth, on this most "Afro-" of interpretations of "Summertime," almost all of Holiday's accompanists, including trumpeter Bunny Berigan and clarinetist Artie Shaw, are Caucasian.)

"Summertime" is all these things, but it has two basic identities: as an operatic aria and a Broadway showtune. It's the only piece of music—

certainly the only song from the twentieth century—to enjoy equal popularity with singers of opera and singers of jazz and pop. Nor is it hard to
imagine it being done by country-and-western singers, folkies, or hardcore blues shouters. In short, it's difficult to think of a species of musical
artist that couldn't warm up to "Summertime."

"FOR SOME REASON, he loved my piano," Kay Halle, a socialite and con-
fidante of Gershwin's recalled many years later (as quoted by Robert
Kimball).

> George and I had an arrangement with the man at the desk of the
> Elysee, where I lived, if I was out and George wanted to come in, he
> could always have the key to my room. One night, I came in after a
> dinner about 11:00, and as I walked up the stairway to my apart-
> ment, I heard the piano. I tiptoed in, George turned and saw me and
> said, "Sit down, I think I have the lullaby." I knew he had been work-
> ing hard to get the lullaby and that he had done several versions that
> didn't suit him. And so he sang in this high-wailing voice "Summer-
> time," and it was exquisite. We looked at each other and the tears
> were just coursing down my cheeks and I just knew that it was going
> to be beloved by the world.

Traditionally, the "Tin Pan Alley" type of song is described as one
of the few "serious" words-and-music genres where the melody often
comes first and the lyrics are written to fit. Sammy Cahn, for all his jok-
ing about the phone call being the first element (by which he meant the
call from the studio exec hiring him to write a theme for whatever movie
they were turning out), often said that when he and his partner (from
Saul Chaplin to Jule Styne to Jimmy Van Heusen) had their title, they
would usually lay down the tune before Sam would come up with the
words to fit it. In opera (and in postwar musical comedy), however, the
story is all-important, therefore the libretto comes first and the music is
generally written to fit the words. (Although, for all the primacy of the
text, the composer is still king—no one speaks of Da Ponte's or Beau-
marchais's *Marriage of Figaro,* only Mozart's.) It's taken as a sign of the
increasing seriousness of American musical theater, for instance, that
Richard Rodgers generally wrote his melodies first when working with

Lorenz Hart in the twenties and thirties but almost always wrote his music to fit Oscar Hammerstein's words in the forties and fifties.

Gershwin's ambitions might be measured in the same way. For the bulk of his pop and show songs, he worked with his older brother, Ira. It was Ira's job to take his younger brother's jaunty, syncopated melodies and come up with appropriately slangy and jazzy words to suit them. Thus it may be taken as a sign that Gershwin was aiming for something more serious than a typical musical-theater evening when he set about composing *Porgy and Bess* in the operatic fashion, DuBose Heyward supplying the lyrics first. In fact, we can categorize the nature of the songs within the score according to this yardstick: those numbers in which Gershwin worked to prewritten lyrics by Heyward, for example "My Man's Gone Now," are generally the most like operatic arias; those with a text later added by Ira, such as "It Ain't Necessarily So," and the up-tempo "There's a Boat That's Leavin' Soon for New York," are more like showtunes, and in some cases, more like "rhythm" tunes suitable for hot jazz bands.

"Summertime" was the first of the songs completed for the score. This was sometime near the end of February 1934, and Gershwin would not get around to writing the bulk of the music until that summer, between seasons of his radio series *Music by Gershwin*.

Duke Ellington later performed "Summertime" on many occasions. In the decades following Gershwin's death, in 1937, when he was held up as the gold standard of American music, Ellington reported with some pride that Gershwin had once said that he had wished he had composed the bridge to Ellington's "Sophisticated Lady." When *Porgy and Bess* premiered, Ellington's reaction to the opera was that it was "grand music and a swell play," but he was not above a criticism or two. Chief among these, Ellington charged, was that *Porgy and Bess* "did not use the Negro musical idiom."

No doubt such criticism hurt Gershwin and Heyward, both of whom had set out to depict Negro society and culture as accurately as they could. Heyward was long fascinated with Charleston's Gullah culture as he witnessed it from the perspective of a white southerner, and that included black music as well as speech. His original 1927 nonmusical play *Porgy* (which inspired a memorable song of the same title by Dorothy Fields and Jimmy McHugh), had been the first straight drama based on the concerns of black people (and with a genuine black cast, as opposed to white actors in blackface) to have a major impact on the theatrical scene, and *Porgy and Bess* was the first "serious" dramatic musical work to concern itself with these same issues. The 1927 *Porgy,* though a "straight" play, was not without music: it featured a generous amount of choral singing, although this was all traditional black gospel and folk themes, as opposed to the 1935 *Porgy and Bess,* in which all the songs are original. At one point in Heyward's *Porgy,* Bess, the female lead, sings an old folk lullaby with something of a morbid edge, "Hush, little baby, don't you cry, / Mudder and fadder born to die. . . ." This was undoubtedly the genesis of the idea of using a lullaby in *Porgy and Bess.*

As Hollis Alpert notes, *Porgy* launched a vogue on Broadway for all-black dramas with incidental singing of black spirituals, such as Marc Connelly's Amos-and-Andy treatment of the Old Testament, *The Green Pastures,* and the 1933 *Run, Little Children* with the Hall Johnson Choir. Because authentic spirituals had already been much heard on Broadway by the mid-1930s, Gershwin announced that the music for his production would consist largely of his own spirituals, newly written, but true to the tradition of black religious music.

The extent to which he succeeded can be measured, sixty-five years later, by how several generations have grown up all but unaware that "Summertime" was in fact written by a Jewish New York songwriter for a twentieth-century opera. Most of the millions who have heard it no doubt assume that "Summertime" is a traditional black lullaby, perhaps even a holdover from the days of slavery. The lyric to "Summertime," in fact, reflects a literary antecedent in which poets strove to make their verse capture the cadence and feel of traditional folk ballads.

Porgy and Bess in its initial 1935 run lasted 127 performances, fantastic for any opera, but not enough for a very expensive Broadway production to recoup its investment. One of the reasons not enough people came to see it is because the 1927 original was still fresh in people's mind; it might have been too soon for a musical treatment of that story. There was, however, a more successful revival in 1942; then a sensational production that played every place you can think of, starting in 1952; and a film in 1959; and numerous successful productions since, both in opera houses and Broadway theaters. If in 1935 *Porgy and Bess* couldn't escape the shadow of the original *Porgy,* within a few years the pre-Gershwin play would be completely forgotten (as has been DuBose Heyward's original novel), remembered only as a footnote to theater history.

WHEN WE SAY THAT "Summertime," as a piece of music, has at least two distinct identities, we are not waxing philosophical—the song itself is published in two very different forms, both as part of the official score to the opera and as a stand-alone popular song. The full score is very specific about how everything is to be performed, whereas pop and jazz versions tend to take a lot more liberties. The score is published in B minor at a metronome count of 96 beats per minute ("moderato"). One of many fakebook versions for jazz and club-date musicians puts it in A minor, and it specifies a tempo of 82 beats per minute. The reason for changing the key in pop editions is obvious: the song starts on a high F sharp, a note beyond the range of many amateur singers, not to mention saxophonists. Accomplished, professional sax players can go up that high by means of what they call "false fingerings," but the actual notes on the horn only go up to high F natural.

Structurally, the entire song is thirty-two bars, but it's anything but A-A-B-A. It can be broken down several ways: essentially it consists of two A sections and no bridge, each half being sixteen bars long. However, each of those sixteen-bar sections can be described as being in four four-bar sections, making the song as a whole look like A (A-B-A^1-C) A (A-B-A^1-C). The melody of the opening phrase never recurs exactly: the last half of the first line ("And the livin' is easy") is the same melody as the last half of the third line ("And your ma is good lookin'"), but the opening halves of each of those lines are different. Still, it makes little sense to think of "Summertime" in terms of the As and Bs of a pop song since that's clearly not what Gershwin intended. Nor is it surprising that it should follow no preestablished format.

The piece is in minor pretty much all the way through; and it's one of the few popular songs (if it even is a pop song) that doesn't go into major for any length to speak of. Some pop and jazz versions will go into major briefly near the end of the first half, on the words "hush, little baby" (the only part of the song taken from the traditional lullaby heard in *Porgy*). Perhaps in these cases the major harmony is thought to reinforce the sense of reassurance from mother to baby that this particular passage is meant to convey. "Summertime" relies quite extensively on the tonic chord (B minor), and, to a lesser degree, on the iv chord (E minor). Deena Rosenberg also notes that the melody is connected to "Porgy's Theme," the instrumental leitmotif of the leading man.

One of the most arresting things about "Summertime" is the secondary melody, which starts out as an introductory vamp. At first it is essentially just two notes, but as it goes on—when the main melody begins—this theme recedes into the background and now becomes a countermelody, and the longer it goes on, the more chordal it becomes. The vamp theme reappears on line three, the A^1 section, and also between the two halves. On the A^1 section (the third line), the harmony, likewise, is a one-two proposition, bouncing back and forth between the I and the IV chords.

The purpose of the vamp is self-evident, to suggest the rocking feeling of a baby in a cradle, or in his mother's arms. In going back and forth between two poles, the rhythm, melody, and harmony of the vamp all convey a lightly rocking feeling. For the first few years of the song's existence, the vamp was the most familiar part of the song. Acting with the permission of Gershwin himself, the Bob Crosby band adopted "Summertime" as its theme song. The band would play it at the start of each broadcast, starting with the vamp; however, by the time the ensemble reached the central melody, the announcer would have begun chiming in with "This is Bob Crosby and His Orchestra coming to you directly from the Hotel Sheets in beautiful downtown Parkstown. . . ." Thus, the "Summertime" melody itself would be obscured while the vamp would be heard free and clear. Small wonder that a whole generation of jazz musicians grew up thinking of this song's vamp as a challenge to be met.

If the inspiration for including a lullaby in *Porgy and Bess* comes from "hush, little baby," it's often said that the traditional air that has the most in common with "Summertime" is "Sometimes I Feel Like a Motherless Child." Their melodies and harmonies are similar, and the lyrics of each use the image of a child. The intention of "Summertime" is to reassure a baby so it can sleep, whereas the first-person protagonist of "Motherless Child" is comparing his plight to that of an infant all alone in the world. There's a literary precedent in nineteenth-century poetry, for example the *Lyrical Ballads* of Wordsworth and Coleridge, which were written to sound like traditional folk ballads. "Summertime" could fool anyone into thinking it was a folk song.

In fact, it's in the lyrics of "Summertime" that the song has the most in common with traditional black spirituals. The piece is not exactly a Noel Coward patter piece with acres of triple rhymes; in fact, each of the two halves includes only one rhyme, and it's fundamentally the same in both: "high" and "cry" in the first, "sky" and "by" in the second.

The most overtly religious piece of imagery that Heyward employs is the idea of spreading one's wings and taking to the sky. It could be a literal meaning, as the only time most of us acquire wings is when we go to the great bandstand in the sky. (The multi-instrumentalist Rahsaan Roland Kirk recorded "Summertime" on harmonica as a kind of last will and testament, in his final session, taped two weeks before his death.) That's a morbid thought, but then again the original "hush, little baby" attempted to quiet a noisy infant with the news that the death of its parents was imminent—hardly what one would consider a comforting thought. Also, there's the possibility that Hayward might have meant this image as a metaphor for achieving great things in life, for blossoming like a flower, for coming out of a cocoon like a butterfly and spreading those wings. Which is surely what "Summertime" itself came to mean in the decades after *Porgy and Bess* gave birth to it.

ALL THREE OF THE AUTHORS of *Porgy and Bess* had invested their own cash in the production, most of which they lost. It's said that Gershwin had hoped at least to make some money from recording and radio performances of the songs, but whatever dough he did see barely paid for the time he put in orchestrating the work. The earliest document of the *P&B* score is a sequence of five songs recorded on July 19, 1935, nearly three months prior to the premiere. Released on an LP in the seventies, this recording, which runs about twenty minutes, is allegedly of a rehearsal; that would have been a most unusual move for the period—the very process of bringing recording equipment into a theater would have been difficult (and probably prohibited by the musicians' union). Whatever the circumstances, it's an extremely valuable document: it's the only recording of the material to be conducted by the composer and to feature Abby Mitchell, the original Clara. Mitchell is much simpler and down to earth than later Claras, particularly the many opera divas who've sung "Summertime." She ends economically, rather than on a big, overdone high note, and doesn't use the famous wailing tag that eventually became standard among classical-style performers of the tune.

The first major commercial recording of the *P&B* music was a twelve-inch collection of excerpts on RCA Victor featuring two big-name (i.e., white) classical singers, Lawrence Tibbett and Helen Jepsen, with the Orchestra of the Metropolitan Opera. Alexander Smallens conducted, as he had the original Broadway production, and the disc was released with the legend "Recorded under the personal supervision of the composer." There also were dance medleys made in 1938 by Nat Shilkret and the Victor Orchestra over here, and by Carroll Gibbons and the Savoy Hotel Orpheans in London.

Three years after the death of George Gershwin and two months before the death of DuBose Heyward, in June 1940, Jack Kapp of Decca Records produced the first original cast recording—of sorts—of the work. Kapp was the major American pioneer of the concept of the cast album, a form that would solidify with the release of the Decca album for *Oklahoma!* three years later. In 1940, the idea of using "members of the original cast" was close enough for all concerned. The recording focused on the original Broadway leads, Todd Duncan and Anne Brown, and they sang most of the songs, with hardly any other members of the cast present. In that sense, the project foreshadoweed such celebrity *P&B* recordings as Fitzgerald-Armstrong, Charles-Laine, and Belafonte-Horne. Duncan sang "It Ain't Necessarily So" instead of either John Bubbles or Avon Long, the first two performers to play Sportin' Life; and Brown sang "Summertime," originally introduced by Abby Mitchell as Clara. We tend to think of Clara as a lower female voice, but Brown sings in a high and completely operatic soprano.

Brown reprised the song three years later for the film *Rhapsody in Blue* (she recorded her number in '43, although the picture wasn't released until two years later), the Warner Bros. biopic of Gershwin; this is a considerably more opulent treatment, with even more voices in the choir. This version is also considerably longer than the one on the original cast recording, and adds a second chorus of the song, as rendered by the women's choir. (Brown then returns for a third chorus—or rather, the second half of one.) This was probably the biggest moment in Ms. Brown's career: many more people saw her in this film than in anything else she ever did, and, ironically, it associated her permanently with a song she hadn't introduced.

After Billie Holiday's recording, made only a few months after the original production closed, the next notable treatments were by the

Crosby brothers, Bing and Bob, on two separate occasions for Decca. Bob's version, arranged by Deane Kincaide, was, as noted, a commercial recording of what had already been serving as his theme. The Bob Crosby band's specialty was new treatments of New Orleans and early jazz perennials, and by choosing Gershwin's spiritual-lullaby, Crosby was continuing his band's concept of creatively reworking the roots materials of jazz.

By contrast with Holiday's "hot and anxious" treatment, Bing Crosby's was supremely relaxed and summertimey—with Crosby, the living really is easy. But Bing has one major point in common with Holiday, in that the song is taken far less seriously than it would be in later years, before the opera and its number-one aria would be, in a sense, canonized. People who have grown up thinking of *P&B* as a super-serious opera will undoubtedly consider Holiday's rendition a bit too much on the sexy side, as if sung to a lover rather than a child, and might also consider Crosby's rendition a mite too casual—especially when he interjects "the livin's *so* easy." Crosby's backup is provided by violinist Matt Malneck, an old friend then also recording for Decca whose band included a prominent accordionist. Again, it ain't exactly Catfish Row.

Both Malneck and Crosby had gotten their start thanks to a man who had helped Gershwin as well, bandleader Paul Whiteman. Surprisingly, Whiteman himself didn't record anything from *Porgy and Bess* in the thirties. However, around 1955, Joe Venuti, Malneck's former Whiteman string sectionmate, made a rather outrageous "Summertime" for the Grand Award label, an obscure concern that, at the time, also had Whiteman under contract. According to the LP jacket, the orchestra behind Venuti is none other than his alma mater, Pops Whiteman's band; more likely it was just some pickup group and the company paid Pops for the use of his name. The track begins with a big classical cadenza for an intro, then Venuti enters and plays the melody once through, completely straight. After a pause, the violinist returns, this time swinging—like a demon, no less. His hot chorus seems that much more rhythmically aggressive when compared to the dreary stuff that has preceded it. Finally, the thing changes tempo yet again, Venuti playing another chorus in ballad time before it all winds up with a big symphonic finish.

The most audacious and irreverent early treatment of "Summertime" was recorded in 1939 by a singer named Jerry Kruger, who is one of the more fascinating footnotes on the swing era: from photographic and recorded evidence, Kruger seems to have been a white female singer who used a male name and generally worked with black bands. She specialized in jivey, swing treatments of traditional and standard material—not merely lightly swinging folk songs and treating them with at least a modicum of respect, like Maxine Sullivan, but irreverent, almost zany doubletalk treatments. Kruger made four sides with Ellington trumpeter Cootie Williams and His Rug Cutters (among them, an "Ol' Man River," which has been discussed elsewhere), and with Gene Krupa she cut a swing version of the Scottish folk song "Fare Thee Well, Annie Laurie." Kruger did two dates under her own name, the first with an early version of the John Kirby Sextet. The second, which contains "Summertime," was long believed to feature Lester Young and Buck Clayton on tenor and trumpet and was even reissued as such on a Lester Young collection on French Columbia. Historian Dan Morgenstern eventually divined the truth, that the group was a contingent from the Benny Carter Orchestra of 1939, featuring Carter himself on trumpet (he later said he was honored to have been mistaken for Buck Clayton) and the lesser-known Ernie Powell on tenor—although the group certainly sounds like the Kirby Sextet leavened with more than a touch of your average klezmer band.

Employing a technique principally associated with black entertainers, Kruger was a master of jive doubletalk, and her treatments of "Ol' Man River" and "Summertime" in particular are masterpieces of the style later associated with such vocal groups as Jimmy Lunceford's orchestra ("My Blue Heaven"), the Joe Mooney Quartet ("Tea for Two"), the Sentimentalists with Tommy Dorsey ("On the Sunny Side of the Street"), and the King Cole Trio. The doubletime-doubletalk style is also closely related to the Tommy Dorsey "Marie" cycle. Kruger sings the first chorus comparatively straight, interjecting just a little word or two here and there (". . . harm you, or alarm you . . ."). It's on her second chorus that she really goes to town:

"Summertime, and the livin' is easy—and the chicken is greasy and weather is breezy"
"the cotton is high—where the airplanes fly"
"One of these mornin's you're gonna start singin'—hold tight, hold tight, buddle-y-agasacky"

(That last phrase is an untranscribable scat syllable à la Leo Watson, and the whole line is a reference to the Ink Spots–Andrews Sisters hit "Hold Tight," aka "Seafood Mama.")

We then expect her to go to the third and fourth lines ("But till that mornin' "); instead, she starts again from the beginning, this time with still further variations: "Summertime, / And the livin' is easy / Your daddy is a millionaire and your mama is a contest-winner." She concludes with a dynamic declaration of the title, "Summertime," shooting up winningly for a high note at the end. There's something of a mystery associated with this performance, however: in years to come, at least three other singers interpolated that line about your mama being a "contest-winner" into their recordings, namely, Mae Barnes, Joe Williams, and Mel Tormé. Did this routine originate with Kruger or was it something that was going around black and jazz circles and became part of "Summertime"'s history independent of her? I wish it had occurred to me to ask Joe or Mel while I still could.

"SUMMERTIME" WAS GENERALLY SUNG by jazz-oriented singers. Conversely, jazz instrumentalists have tended to treat it with more respect, even when improvising on it and embellishing it. Sonny Rollins and Coleman Hawkins may completely transform the melody almost beyond recognition on the 1963 *Sonny Meets Hawk*, but they're certainly not doing so flippantly.

In 1942 the opera was successfully revived on Broadway, and in 1945 the film *Rhapsody in Blue* was released, both of which events did much to further the cause of the song. There wasn't exactly a flurry of wartime versions, but there were a few: both Mildred Bailey and Frank Sinatra sang it while the American Federation of Musicians ban was on, she on a V-Disc (distributed to servicemen only), he on a broadcast. Bailey's version is notable: the woman had a small voice (which pundits frequently contrast with her notably un-small body) and didn't always have the proper equipment to sustain notes, and it would have been easy for her to do a jivey, double-time treatment. Yet what she pulls off here is far more remarkable. Through smoke and mirrors, she manages to create the illusion of held notes. It's a feat comparable to the way her husband Red Norvo (who is audible in the ensemble here) could create the illusion of sustained notes on the xylophone which, as Dan Morgenstern has pointed out, is a technical impossibility, considering the sonic nature of that instrument.

Sinatra's turn comes as part of a *Porgy and Bess* medley—not much of one, though, as it consists of a mere two songs. In fact, the medley aspect of the track is the only thing that makes it less than sublime (that, plus the rather awkwardly worded spoken intro at the start). Sinatra opens doing "Summertime" in solo. He alters the melody here and there (he puts a slight spin on "easy" at the end of the first line, a lesser one where the melodic sequence reappears at "livin' "), but not dramatically so, also making one very small change to the lyrics ("You gonna rise up to singin' "). Ira Gershwin, who was notoriously finicky about singers altering so much as a syllable of his lyrics, would have found little to object to here, had he written "Summertime." There is a choir, but it's only heard on the other tune in the medley, "I Got Plenty o' Nuttin'," and it quickly manages to dispel the intimate mood that Sinatra has built up. The choir offers what is certainly as pale a performance of any selection from the opera as anyone would ever want to hear. Sinatra's "Summertime," however, is singularly beautiful; it's a shame he didn't use this arrangement for the flip of his Columbia single of "Bess, Oh Where's My Bess?" two seasons later.

Again on the radio, Sinatra sang a further variation of the medley (which included "Bess") two years later, but he never commercially recorded "Summertime," although it would have fit right into the program of his 1963 *The Concert Sinatra,* as well as some of his other albums. One of the bigger surprises of the later Sinatra career is a 1982 concert in Buffalo in which he unexpectedly launches into an eight-minute *Porgy and Bess* medley, doubly interesting because it's a duet with musical director Vinnie Falcone on piano. "Summertime" is the obvious highlight here, and although Sinatra keeps it in tempo, he sings it with a warm, grandfatherly tenderness that's miraculous even by his standards. (He then proceeds to do "It Ain't Necessarily So," on which he resists the temptation to utilize his trademark "dooby-dooby-do" in the scat sequence, and winds up with "Where's My Bess?")

Even by negative example, Sinatra was again setting the style among pop singers. After the war, the song would only rarely be done by straight-down-the-middle pop singers of the Steve Lawrence and Eydie

Gorme variety, even though some of them—Jo Stafford, for one—could have sung it superbly. This "middle stratum" of pop singers tended to avoid the song. The major proponents of "Summertime" were two other classifications of performing artists who were on entirely opposite ends of the musical spectrum, namely, opera divas and jazz folk.

Among jazz singers who have done the tune in the past fifty years, there are roughly two approaches to "Summertime": tasteful and audacious. It doesn't necessarily have anything to do with tempo, as there are up-tempo performances that are tasteful (Joe Williams) and slow treatments that are outrageous. At the top of the list is a trio of women who represent three of the greatest class acts this music has been lucky enough to know: Mildred Bailey (recording in 1945, two years after her 1943 V-Disc), Maxine Sullivan (1947), and Helen Humes (1974). All three manage the somewhat difficult balancing act of giving "Summertime" a distinct swing feel without compromising its effectiveness as a lullaby—they're intimate and jazzy at the same time. Humes's treatment has a hint of the defiant, militant qualities we've heard in Holiday, but all three are simple, direct, and highly effective.

Nina Simone, whose rendition of the song is not as celebrated as her well-known reading of "I Loves You, Porgy," aspires to that same tradition. She's obviously going for intimacy, but at the same time there's a current—so strong it's not really an undercurrent—of hostility toward anyone who might get in her way. (Likewise, Lena Horne's reading has a threatening feel to it—nobody better harm *her* baby!) Simone first engages us with a long, slow piano solo that sounds like John Lewis on Prozac, and her monotonal vocal, in the classic Simone style, characteristically suggests a bridge between the traditions of jazz, blues, and folk music. By the time she's done, "Summertime" has become more of a call to arms, a rallying cry, than a lullaby. Those interested in other slightly stoned-sounding versions might want to check out Helen Merrill, who recorded it on *The Nearness of You* (1959), *Helen Sings/Teddy* [Wilson] *Swings* (1970, Japan), *Chasin' the Bird* (1979), and *Collaboration* (1987) with Gil Evans, the last being the best.

The treatments by Mel Tormé, Joe Williams (on *Have a Good Time*), and Chris Connor (done with Maynard Ferguson) are fast and swinging, and though there's a hint of irreverence, they're certainly well within the boundaries. Connor was best known for her moody, introspective ballads (her "Lush Life" is a more typical masterpiece), but she could swing, too, as her treatment of the aria with Maynard Ferguson's atmosphere-piercing trumpet and orchestra demonstrates. Again, there's a counter-vamp of the arranger's own devising, played primarily by the bass and emphasized by the drums.

Mark Murphy cut "Summertime" live at the North Sea Jazz Festival in 1971, in a well-assembled (and -sung) arrangement that combines four elements: a bossa nova underpinning, a hard swing feel, a scat episode, and the counter-riff introduced by Miles Davis and Gil Evans.

Mel Tormé also swung the hell out of it (swung the Mel out of it?) as the opener of a first-rate medley he documented via a radio transcription in 1962 (later issued on CD); apparently he had waited six years to give people a chance to forget his part in the somewhat disastrous 1956 complete *Porgy and Bess,* produced by Bethlehem Records (discussion to follow). Tormé had been in love with *Porgy and Bess* his whole life. He saw the original Broadway production when it took briefly to the road, hitting Philadelphia, Pittsburgh, and the World Theater in Chicago (hometown of the then ten-year-old Mel) in February and March 1936, and the show left an indelible impression on him. Tormé later recalled that Avon Long, the preeminent Sportin' Life of all the early productions (except the original Broadway run), had already replaced John Bubbles in that role in Chicago, a fact not corroborated in the Hollis Alpert book. The 1952 Robert Breen production impressed the singer yet again with the beauty of the opera. His love for it remained undiminished even through the only incarnation of it that he distinctly did *not* enjoy, the 1956 Bethlehem recording with himself in the lead.

Tormé's most significant consummation of his love for the opera was a fifteen-minute extravaganza of a medley that was part of his act in the mid-to-late 1970s. Never recorded commercially, this gem survives only in a jittery videotape of an appearance on *The Merv Griffin Show.* It's an extended medley that deals with virtually all the opera's themes, major and minor, at greater length and with more depth than is common to the medley format. (Tormé seems to have earlier arranged still another completely different *P&B* medley, this one performed by Judy Garland and Vic Damone on the former's CBS TV series in 1963, in which Damone and Garland do "Summertime" together.)

Anita Ellis, with her sweet but strong voice, recorded a dramatic

"Summertime" with pianist Ellis Larkins on the 1979 *A Legend Sings*. Dakota Staton, with her deep-voiced, lightly blue approach and a tendency to utter the phrase "Ha! Ha!" at unlikely intervals, recorded a wailing "Summertime" on her breakthrough album, *The Late, Late Show*, with an easy rocking vamp, a growling trumpet following her throughout. Lena Horne did a convincing "Summertime" on her album of the *P&B* score with Belafonte; husband Lennie Hayton's orchestration is busy but effective, and Horne, rather than trying to achieve intimacy, goes for outsized emotions and a big belt ending.

Horne's biggest, loudest ending, though, couldn't compare to those of the many classical divas who've essayed the song. Among the more outstanding operatic versions is a 1984 highlights disc of the opera starring Roberta Alexander with the Berlin Radio Symphony Orchestra conducted by Leonard Slatkin. Alexander is one of the more notable purveyors of the "Summertime" tag, a little extra ascending yelp at the end that's unique to opera singers. The Maori soprano Kiri Te Kanawa, the African-American Barbara Hendricks, and Julia Migenes (another Euro-diva) have all sung "Summertime" on Gershwin collections. Te Kanawa's is pure operatic chops; it's more of a show-off piece for the voice—and what a voice it is—than a lullaby. Hendricks's recording, accompanied by the two-piano team of Katia and Marielle Labeque, is much more intimate, and is also notable for the singer's attractive swoops upward and downward. Migenes, recording with another German radio orchestra, turns in an expecially full-throated rendition. Eleanor Steber recorded it for RCA in 1946, making her one of the first major classical stars to address "Summertime." She, too, sings the coloratura tag at the end, although on the whole she's quite controlled, clear, and direct, true to the story as well as to the notes.

But the opera singer most in the spirit of "Summertime" is Leontyne Price, who played Bess in the classic Breen production of 1952, long before she became a superstar diva on the Viking-helmet circuit. While, surprisingly, there is no complete cast recording of that production, Price and her Porgy, William Warfield, recorded a single disc of highlights for RCA under the baton of Skitch Henderson in 1963. If this disc is any indication, Price was the best of all possible Besses (making it a shame that the 1959 film didn't use her and Warfield instead of its dubbed stars), and her "Summertime" is suitably terrific. This is a reading of extraordinary clarity and in an amazing voice; yet far from neglecting the dramatic aspect of the song, Price makes it sound as if she's living every note. She goes through all the expected "Summertime" pyrotechnics, including the diva tag, but also makes you feel the entire weight of Clara's lullaby. Price has since sung the song hundreds of times in concert, and several of those performances have been recorded and issued commercially, including an outstanding reading from Germany in 1968. I can't claim to have heard every classical recording of "Summertime," but I can't imagine there's any opera singer who's done it more convincingly than Price.

"SUMMERTIME" WAS PERFECT for projects that combined the jazz and classical ideals, such as Charlie Parker's sessions with strings. The great saxist's 1949 "Summertime" helped to establish a tradition for the song that, although it doesn't lack humor, is essentially serious: he confines his improvisations primarily to the fills—the spaces between lines—thereby leaving the actual melody essentially as written. Parker plays Gershwin's melody, and a whole hell of a lot more. The ensemble included two classical musicians who were already in the process of creating pop careers for themselves, oboist Mitch Miller and conductor-arranger Jimmy Carroll (normally an alto saxophonist, Carroll later became Miller's right-hand man when the oboist became a major pop producer). Carroll's low-pitched strings have a dark, operatic sound, and he embellishes the familiar vamp with harp arpeggios. Parker's playing is intense, yet he doesn't cancel out the soothing qualities of the lullaby.

In the wake of Parker, the piece became a favorite of saxophonists, and many titans of the instrument tackled the tune over the next twenty years: Art Pepper, Zoot Sims, Stan Getz, John Coltrane, Dexter Gordon, Richie Kamuca (with Shelly Manne), Lou Donaldson, Sonny Rollins, Teddy Edwards, and, more recently, Joe Henderson and Lee Konitz. To a lesser degree, trumpeters have also done it—Chet Baker, Joe Gordon (also with Shelly Manne), Miles Davis, and Dizzy Gillespie—as have, as we shall see, plenty of pianists. (The song has also been used as a quote source, as by trombonist Al Grey in the middle of his solo on the 1961 "Home Fries.")

Many of the best jazz interpretations, like those of Bill Evans and Stan Getz, take advantage of how "Summertime" is both an operatic aria and a funky tune with ties to both black religious music and the blues. Getz first came to "Summertime" in 1954 with his "West Coast quintet" of the time, which costarred fellow Woody Herman alums trumpeter Conte Candoli and pianist Lou Levy. He returned to the tune ten years later as a staple of the repertoire of his great quartet of the mid-sixties, which used vibist Gary Burton as the key chordal instrument in place of the customary piano. This group was on the road just as the tenorist's big bossa nova hits were breaking out like crazy in record shops, and Verve Records, Getz's label, seems to have suppressed all of his non-bossa recordings of the period. Thus his major studio treatment of "Summertime" languished in the vaults for thirty years, even though on the road Getz was playing "Summertime" just as frequently as he was "The Girl from Ipanema."

Getz's 1964 studio treatment is nothing short of majestic: he once said that he regarded the standard jazz instrumentation (sax, piano, bass, and drums) as America's equivalent of the string quartet. That's never been more meaningful than it is here, as the semiclassical "Summertime" affords the brilliant Getz the chance to display a virtuosity on his instrument comparable to that of a Heifetz or a Kreisler. Which isn't to say there's anything remotely classical or the least bit unjazzy about the performance; rather, it's a comment on Getz's command of his instrument, in both registers, and even throwing in burplike notes from the lower part of the horn (below low D natural). Getz's tone had gotten even more liquid and translucent in the ten years between his two "Summertime"s, and at thirty-eight, the saxist was in the summertime of his career.

Art Pepper's 1957 reading, done for the Aladdin label, with pianist Russ Freeman, achieves a clarity and a beauty nearly on the same level. Like Getz, Pepper has created a highly personal synthesis of Parker and Young (on alto rather than tenor). And also like Getz, when Pepper plays "Summertime," there's an acid blues quality at work, side by side with the tenderness. Like Getz at his best, Pepper's solos aren't just jamming on the changes but always tell a coherent story, with a beginning, a middle, and an end.

Speaking of West Coast bands and the great saxists therein, there's an arresting twelve-minute treatment by Shelly Manne and His Men, the ensemble that functioned as California's equivalent of Art Blakey and the Jazz Messengers. As with most modern jazz treatments of the tune (except in full-scale big band readings), although there are two horns among the Manne men, those two horns never play the melody together; it's always one and then the other. Perhaps this was just too intimate a melody for more than one voice to sing it at any one time. Trumpeter Joe Gordon, another short-lived martyr of the bop era, takes it first, then tenorist Richie Kamuca, then pianist Victor Feldman; and finally Gordon returns in the last chorus with a prominent obbligato by Kamuca. I haven't encountered a "Summertime" like it elsewhere.

John Coltrane's "Summertime" comes from the same sessions in which he reworked "Body and Soul," an afternoon-and-evening marathon in which he taped enough for two albums. As opposed to Richard Rodgers's "My Favorite Things," which he taped three days earlier, "Summertime" did not become a Trane perennial. Indeed, other than an unissued live tape from three months earlier, this is the only record we have of Coltrane performing the *Porgy and Bess* aria. We could say that in this particular eleven-minute performance Coltrane simply said everything he could possibly say on "Summertime," although that would not be wholly accurate, since one gets the same impression from his original studio treatments of "Favorite Things," "Giant Steps" ("I Got Rhythm"), and other tunes he would play over and over. This "Summertime" is incredibly dense, even by Coltrane's standards, and his "sheets of sound" technique, which stacks one note on top of another with a deep, vertical feeling, has never been more in evidence. Coltrane sails through the melody in less than thirty seconds, barely finishing the first of the two halves of the full thirty-two-bar song before launching into his improvisation. It's not only thick, aggressive, and rhythmically supercharged, it's also probably the scariest lullaby ever recorded.

Coltrane's treatment is *über*-Trane, in the same way Getz's is *ur*-Getz, each bringing the most familiar aspects of his well-known style to bear on the tune. Not so with Sonny Rollins's playing on his 1963 treatment, which finds the no-less-masterly tenorist in transition. For all the usual distinctiveness of Rollins's style, it may take fans or fellow players some time to identify Rollins in this phase of his development. This isn't the case with Sonny's co-tenor here, the father of the instrument, Coleman Hawkins, who uses characteristic phrases and devices (such as his fluttering entrance) that are unmistakably Hawkish (rather than mawkish). Hawkins enters just as Rollins finishes, so even though each of them essentially just plays his solo without interference from the other, there's a feeling of interplay between them. Saxophonic scholar Loren Schoenberg feels that Rollins is paying homage to Coltrane here, and while that may be, he's not specifically recalling Trane's "Summertime," since the Rollins-Hawkins dual version is more melodic in a conventional fashion.

In fact, although many of the most colossal tenors in all jazz have torn into the tune, few have chosen to emphasize its more soothing aspects. Lou Donaldson, like Getz, stresses the funkier side of the song, which perfectly suits the context of Billy Gardner's Hammond organ and which more than pleases the crowd present on this live recording (from his 1965 *Fried Buzzard*). Donaldson opens with a long high note, ever so slightly (and deliberately) on the sharp side, intended to pierce the air and the ear. In his reentrance, he reinforces the notion that Hayward's line about spreading one's wings and flying may be a reference to death by quoting the rather morbid children's rhyme "the worms crawl in, the worms crawl out . . ." and he concludes with another piercing high note before playing the final few notes as a coda. Those worms are going to have to crawl mighty fast if they think they can keep up with this guy.

EVEN MORE THAN MOST other songs, "Summertime" is a tour de force for the human voice as both a pop song and an opera aria. That vocal imperative is readily transferred to such breath-based instruments as the saxophone, but the piano is potentially a different story. Where horns follow the same kind of single lines as singers, pianos traditionally serve as a microcosm of the orchestra, in which it's possible to have several "sections" playing different things simultaneously. Still, pianists have picked up on "Summertime" from the git-go, including such stridemasters as Willie "The Lion" Smith, Earl Hines, and Joe Sullivan.

Coincidentally, the two pianists who have made the most out of "Summertime" happen to be the most extroverted and introverted piano players of the last fifty years—namely, Oscar Peterson and Bill Evans, respectively. Peterson has officially recorded it at least seven times in different settings: on his 1959 Gershwin collection, his *Porgy and Bess* album from the same year, live with his trio in Germany (1968) and Russia (1974), and in duos with trumpeters Roy Eldridge (1974) and Jon Faddis (1975), and guitarist Joe Pass in another whole LP of the *P&B* music from 1976.

Evans did it many times in concert over the years (several of which have been made available commercially), and his most essential version is also live. This is from the single most highly regarded session of the influential pianist's career, his 1962 Village Vanguard date, with his classic trio of bassist Scott LaFaro and drummer Paul Motian. The first time Evans recorded it, however, he didn't get to solo: this was with an all-star orchestra doing a jazz treatment of the whole *Porgy and Bess* score (we'll get to this shortly). Evans's trio rendition of "Summertime" is outgoing by the standards of this generally inner-directed pianist, and it emphasizes the bluesier aspects of the tune.

Apart from Peterson and Evans, there are exotic "Summertime"s, such as a thoroughly Latin arrangement by Wynton Kelly, a less convincingly Africanesque reading by Marcus Roberts from 1994, and a stunning "jungle"-style reading by the Roland Hanna Quartet with Bill Easley on soprano sax. Roughly inspired by Ellington's 1961 trio treatment (about which more later), Hanna's reading is hot and funky in exactly the right way; if Catfish Row had a radio station, this is what they would play.

There are rollicking "Summertime"s, like that of the Erroll Garner Trio, and there are atmospheric ones, like that by the Red Garland Trio. There are low-key "Summertime"s, like the one on *Porgy and Bess: Swingin' Impressions by Hank Jones*. There are authentic "Summertime"s, such as by Al Haig, who comes as close as possible to capturing the feel of the original opera, and lays down a full, two-handed "Summertime" that Gershwin himself might have played. Haig's is an essentially straight reading that only very gradually introduces jazz embellishments. There's also a fine "Summertime" by Hampton Hawes released under Charlie Mingus's name, and, most recently, a grand solo treatment by McCoy Tyner from 2000.

THE MANY JAZZ TREATMENTS of "Summertime" were inspired not only by Charlie Parker, but by a flood of Porgies and Besses in the fifties. In 1951, Goddard Lieberson of Columbia Records produced the first complete recording of the score. The following year saw the first overwhelmingly successful production of the opera, which started by touring the country, then the rest of the Free World, and eventually the not-so-free world behind the Iron Curtain. In 1956, the first major jazz album of a show score, *Shelly Manne and His Friends . . . My Fair Lady* was released, and while not quite as much of a hit as the original-cast album, it nonetheless did well enough to effectively sell the music industry on the concept of the jazz-goes-Broadway album. That same year, the independent label Bethlehem Records released their three-LP box of *George Gershwin's Porgy and Bess*. (This is sometimes cited as only the second complete *P&B* on records and is also certainly one of the earliest, if not the first, jazz treatments of a complete show score predating Shelly Manne and *My Fair Lady*.)

Producer Red Clyde conceived the ambitious idea of using Bethlehem's entire roster of vocal artists (and quite a few of the instrumentalists as well), but then proceeded to do everything wrong. To start with, there was bad casting: Mel Tormé singing the central role of Porgy was just about the best they could do under the circumstances, but it made no sense to cast the sensitive, romantic Johnny Hartman as the villainous Crown. Hiring the deep-voiced nightclub entertainer Frances Faye as Bess was one for Ripley's. (Singer Jack Jones has spoken of getting a kick out of how this particular Bess sang several octaves lower than Porgy, when she even sang in tune at all; I've always felt this production should have been titled *Porgy and Bass*.)

But the very idea of "casting" a jazz *P&B* was a bad one, because to do a plausible jazz treatment of any Broadway score one has to first divorce the music completely from the book and lyrics, which is why the instrumental treatments of show scores succeed more easily. Someday, someone may figure out how to do a jazz treatment of a familiar show in which the story still works, but as of the millennium, no one's achieved it, and they certainly hadn't in 1956. Worst of all is that the Bethlehem treatment tries so hard to make the story work in a jazz setting, even bringing in hipster deejay Al "Jazzbeaux" Collins (who apparently named himself after Heyward's "Jasbo Brown") to read a cheesy narration which, like the rest of the project, can't decide whether it wants to be hip or play it straight.

One participant who supposedly resented the Bethlehem *P&B* was Duke Ellington. A few months earlier, he had recorded two albums for Bethlehem around the same time he was starting a new assocation with Columbia Records. Both Bethlehem projects consisted largely of standard material, one album (*Historically Speaking*) being retreads of Ellington's perennial hits, some inspired ("Midriff"), some less so ("Ko-Ko"), and the other (*Duke Ellington Presents*) Ducal versions of non-Ellington standards. Ellington might have been annoyed had he lived into the early 1980s, when the two sets were reissued as *Duke Ellington: The Bethlehem Years,* Volumes One and Two; it would have struck him as presumptuous of the company to imply that he spent "years" with them, when even "days" was stretching it. His entire association with Bethlehem seems to have been wrapped up in about thirty-six hours. During the course of two sessions on February 7 and 8, 1956, he recorded all twenty-four titles that would be needed for both albums.

Among those pieces, however, was Ellington's major commercial recording of "Summetime." In 1935, he had been slightly critical of the entire *Porgy and Bess* venture, though he was more than willing to concede that the music in and of itself was great. Later in his life, he told Marshall Barer (his lyricist on the 1966 flop show *Pousse-Café*) that he was somewhat suspicious of the song "It Ain't Necessarily So." For writing such an openly sacrilegious song, Ellington maintained, God had punished Gershwin by terminating his life so early. Or so he told Barer, who wasn't sure if the Maestro was kidding or not, especially as there were at least a few commandments that the Duke himself shattered with regularity.

Whatever his feelings regarding the opera, Ellington had been playing "Summertime" since the early forties, usually as a vehicle for vocalist Al Hibbler. The band had also been doing an instrumental version since shortly after Hibbler's departure in the early fifties, but had not recorded it prior to 1956. No one could blame Red Clyde, then, for recycling Ellington's "Summertime" as part of Bethlehem's *Porgy and Bess* project, although, according to Ducal scholar Jerry Valburn, Ellington was not pleased about his inclusion in the project and the implication that he was part of the Bethlehem roster, particularly at the moment he was launching a high-profile relationship with Columbia.

In retrospect, Ellington's "Summertime" seems almost perversely inappropriate to open the opera, since it was a hard and fast treatment spotlighting the eardrum-piercing trumpet of Cat Anderson. Perhaps sensing this, overall musical director for the project, Russ Garcia, amended the Ellington orchestra's version with a brief introduction by "The Bethlehem Orchestra." Garcia's contributions, his backing of vocalists and instrumental selections, were one of the few highlights of the production (in fact, the nicest part of the current CD, from Avenue Jazz, is a newly compiled suite of Garcia's music edited from various cues throughout the original master tapes). Still, one can imagine how Ellington felt about Bethlehem monkeying around with his work.

The Ellington connection on the Bethlehem *P&B* is strengthened by the presence of Betty Roche—a former Ellington band vocalist who recorded an album of her own for the label in April 1956—as Clara. The Bethlehem *P&B* starts with the amalgam of Garcia's introduction and Ellington's "Summertime." Then comes the first part of Jazzbeaux Collins's spoken narration before Roche sings "Summertime" with her customary piercing, somewhat harsh tone (she was always more of a jazz singer than a balladeer). It's a fine performance, but one that belongs on an album of Roche doing jazz standards rather than on a treatment of *P&B* that attempts to address the plot as well as the score. It could be said that she does justice to Gershwin but not to Heyward; this just isn't the way Clara would be singing to her baby.

Given Ellington's long love-hate relationship with the work, he probably never considered doing a full-length *P&B* album. He did, however, come back to "Summertime" on one more occasion. In 1961 and '62, Ellington recorded two albums featuring himself in a piano trio setting: the second, *Money Jungle,* is well known, not least because of the presence of bassist Charles Mingus and drummer Max Roach, and is considered a classic; the first, *Piano in the Foreground,* is just as good if not better, but is known only to Ellington buffs and not available on domestic disc.

It's tempting to speculate that this spiky, angular, nearly atonal, and almost irritating treatment on *Foreground* grew out of Ellington's history with the song and with the opera. It's one of the most avant-garde things he ever recorded; nearly everyone who hears it in a blindfold test automatically assumes it's Cecil Taylor. Critic (and Sun Ra biographer) John Szwed describes it as "letting melodic intervals ring (like Monk) for their own sake, rattling the keys with deep tremolos, and ending with dense clusters and a fist in the bass." Other Ellington works that go this far out, such as the 1949 "Clothed Woman," do so swingingly, even charmingly, whereas this time Ellington seems bent on pushing both the song and the audience way beyond the comfort zone.

Apart from the Duke himself, several longstanding Ellingtonians addressed the *P&B* music. Cat Anderson, who blasted so powerfully on the Bethlehem arrangement, played a bit less abrasively in his own septet version in 1959, with solos by bassist Jimmy Woode and Ray Nance on violin; pianist Leroy Lovett doesn't sound particularly Ellington-like in his own playing, but the voicings in the arrangement, such as it is, are at least kinda Dukish.

Ben Webster turns up on guitarist Mundell Lowe's 1958 treatment of *P&B*, released by RCA on its Camden imprint. This is the ultimate sleeper jazz LP of the opera; it's not even a musicians' and collectors' favorite, the way the Bill Potts United Artists version is. Yet it makes a convincing case for Lowe as an arranger-leader, for he sets the melodies in what might be called a New York version of West Coast cool. Webster is merely the most notable of a starry cast of studio players, including Tony Scott (on baritone sax), Art Farmer, and drummer Ed Shaughnessy of *Tonight Show* fame debuting on vibraphone. Scott's deep bari launches "Summertime," but Webster and Farmer also get a piece of the action. (Webster plays as well on Carmen McRae's version of the song, also from 1958.)

One of the odder entrants in the jazz-*P&B* stakes was *Porgy and Bess Revisited,* a product of two guys named George: namely, George Avakian, who produced the first Miles Davis–Gil Evans album, *Miles Ahead,* but left Columbia (before the collaboration's *P&B*) to run the short-lived jazz division at Warner Brothers Records; and George Simon, more customarily a critic but here serving as producer. Now this was a promising idea: casting the opera *instrumentally,* with a team of black swing soloists playing against an orchestral background. Avakian and Simon wanted to avoid having the musicians merely blow on the melodies and changes, and instead assigned each player a specific role with the appropriate songs: Porgy is trumpeter Cootie Williams, Bess is altoist Hilton Jefferson (Johnny Hodges was unavailable), Sportin' Life is cornetist Rex Stewart, while trombonist Lawrence Brown "sings" the arias associated with both Clara and Serena. (All four of these principals were primarily known for their work with Ellington; Jefferson had logged many more miles with Cab Calloway but did in fact sit in the Hodges chair with the Duke from '53 to '55.) *Porgy and Bess Revisited* is a fascinating concept that never quite gells. Lawrence Brown's treatment of the melody on "Summertime" is exquisite, but the backgrounds are not jazzy enough to be interesting in their own right, nor do they completely suit the soloists. It's easier to describe what they're not: they're not your average jazz-with-strings settings, nor are they elevator music of the kind that Brown recorded with Jackie Gleason. Still, it's a fascinating experiment.

Bethlehem's concept of the jazz-show album lacked a lot of refinement, but Red Clyde still deserves credit for anticipating the trend in the
spring of 1956. The Shelly Manne–André Previn *My Fair Lady* album,
which would put the idea on the map, wouldn't be recorded until a few
months later, in August. Bethlehem was also well in advance of the *Porgy
and Bess* bonanza that would begin in 1958, when it was announced that
Samuel Goldwyn had bought the film rights to the opera and that the
movie was already in production. When the actual picture was released in
1959, the reaction would be decidedly underwhelming. Still, the movie
had already had a positive influence by inspiring a spate of jazz treatments
of *P&B*.

There can be no doubt that the best of all the jazz versions is the classic
Miles Davis–Gil Evans *Porgy and Bess* album of 1958, although the Louis
Armstrong–Ella Fitzgerald recording of a year earlier gives it a run for its
money. (The Bill Potts all-star big band and the Modern Jazz Quartet
fight it out for third place.) Davis later claimed that he got the idea to
record the Gershwin score from his girlfriend and future wife Frances
Taylor, a dancer who was then appearing in a production of *P&B* at New
York's City Center. (The only thing that's suspicious about this account is
that there's little dancing in the opera—in this respect, *P&B* has more in
common with *Il Trovatore* than with *Oklahoma!*)

The Davis-Evans treatment is the most radical of all reimaginings of
the score—although, as Davis biographer Jack Chambers points out,
Gershwin's own instrumental suite of the songs, later titled *Catfish Row*, is
a close contender. The team deemphasizes familiar melodies; "A Woman
Is a Sometime Thing" is gone entirely, and "I Got Plenty o' Nuthin'" is
referred to only very briefly as part of the intro to "It Ain't Necessarily
So." Davis and Evans stress the more obscure items, such as "The Buzzard
Song" and "Prayer (Oh Doctor Jesus)," which are rarely heard apart from
the complete work. They also devote a disproportionate amount of space
to Gershwin's street-vendor chants, "Honeyman," "Crabman," "Straw-
berry Woman." Two religious pieces also rate a lot of attention: Davis
plays the prayer "Oh Doctor Jesus" with the most intensely pious, not to
say anguished, feeling, while the funeral dirge "Gone, Gone, Gone" has
been expanded into two variations: track three, "Gone" (credited to
Evans) features the ensemble playing a fast treatment of the melody spotlighting drummer Philly Joe Jones and kicking Davis into a solo that's as

moving as it is exciting. This leads into the next track, listed as "Gone, Gone, Gone," a more traditional treatment of the dirge in the original tempo.

Which is key to an understanding of the Davis-Evans modus operandi: when they alter a piece that significantly, they feel compelled to change its name. In certain respects, the Davis recording of *P&B* is quite traditional: "Oh Doctor Jesus" is still a prayer, "Bess, You Is My Woman Now" continues to be a love song, and "Summertime" remains a lullaby (unlike, for instance, what happens on the Bill Potts *Jazz Soul of Porgy and Bess,* in which it becomes a flag-waver). The Davis-Evans "Summertime" is close to the original key of the opera, which is in B minor; they take it down just a half-step, to B flat minor. They also retain the concept of the countermelody-vamp, but instead of keeping the original, they come up with their own. This vamp is just a bit more notey than the original, and considerably more rhythmic, and it propels the Davis-Evans treatment just as assuredly as Gershwin's vamp propels his own central melody. (That same Evans vamp appears in recordings by singers Mark Murphy, Helen Merrill, and the vocal group Lambert, Hendricks, and Ross.)

More than anywhere else in the album, "Summertime" is a miracle of Davis's playing: his tightly muted trumpet sounds both passionate and cool at the same time, full of feeling yet laid back and chilled out. "I had to get close to a human voice sound in some places," Davis later wrote, and on "Summertime," he surely achieved it. "That was hard," he continued. "But I did it." It's that vocalized sound, anticipated to a certain extent by several swing trumpeters (particularly in the Ellington band, among them Clark Terry, one of Davis's own inspirations), that sets him apart.

Even by 1958 it was common to dismiss Chet Baker as a mere imitator of Davis—Davis said as much in his autobiography. This seems unfair: Baker was only three years younger than Davis—a product of the same influences—and it's quite likely that he arrived at many of the same conclusions Davis did strictly on his own. While Baker's mature style can be described as roughly in the same ballpark as Davis's, it's hardly mere imitation. At the same time, while Baker never mimicked Davis, he also never strove to cut so deep. Baker's own treatment of "Summertime," recorded in Europe three years before Davis, is pleasant and swinging, and hardly the same kind of high-intensity affair that the Davis-Evans record is. Most important, although Baker sings in his own way on the trumpet, he doesn't attempt to do so in the kind of directly human vocal sound that Davis achieves here: he used his own voice when he wanted to sound like a human voice.

Davis recorded his *Porgy and Bess* album with a studio big band featuring three other members of his regular working sextet: drummer Philly Joe Jones, alto saxist Cannonball Adderley, and bassist Paul Chambers. The trumpeter later said that he didn't want to use either Adderley (who is listed as being in the reed section just the same) or John Coltrane (who would record his own "Summertime," as we have seen, two years later) in the big band's sax section, "because they would have been too dominant. . . . All I wanted was straight tones. Couldn't nobody match their sounds, so I just went with guys who played those plain-Jane sounds for those plain-Jane songs." (Leave it to Miles to find a way to insult musicians who played exactly the way he wanted them to.)

Had there been piano on the *P&B* sessions—and there wasn't—it would have been Davis's current keyboardist Bill Evans. In 1958, the Davis-Coltrane-Adderley-Evans-Chambers-Jones group was well on its way to the perfection of what was later known as "modal jazz," which would reach fruition in early 1959 with the next Davis masterpiece, *Kind of Blue,* the most crucial recording of this particular edition of the Davis group. Pianist Bill Evans encouraged Davis to listen to modern and post-modern classical music, particularly Aram Khachaturian, and Davis was impressed with the Armenian composer's concepts of melody, scales, and harmony. Davis's complaint regarding the bebop, hard bop, and West Coast jazz of the time was that it was becoming too thick with chords, and Khachaturian's work pointed to a way in which modern jazz could be simplified for greater expressiveness. When Nat Hentoff interviewed Davis during the recording of *Porgy and Bess,* the trumpeter directed his attention to a part of "I Loves You, Porgy." "Hear that passage? We only used two chords for all of that. And in 'Summertime' there's a long space where we didn't change the chord at all." (Coincidentally, back in 1934, George Gershwin had already written a modal variation on "I Got Rhythm.")

Davis anticipated modal jazz in "Summertime," perfected it with *Kind of Blue,* and then explored it even more thoroughly with his celebrated quintet of the mid-sixties (featuring Herbie Hancock and Wayne Shorter).

The background riff in "Summertime" may even be looked at as an osti-nato, a repeated figure that's crucial to Davis's concept of modal jazz, although in "Summertime" there is a central melody besides the ostinato. A year later, the Davis-Evans "Summertime" received an unusual tribute from the singing trio of Dave Lambert, Jon Hendricks, and Annie Ross, who translated the orchestration into vocal terms: Hendricks pinned the Heyward lyrics to Davis's interpretation of the melody, while Lambert and Ross sang original words by Hendricks to the background vamp.

Although the masterful Evans-Davis *P&B* is in many ways faithful to the spirit if not the letter of the original, it is a purely jazz reinterpreta-tion. The Louis Armstrong–Ella Fitzgerald double-LP of the *P&B* score achieves a compromise between the dictates of jazz, pop, and Broadway music. It's likely that working in 1957 (a year before Miles Davis), pro-ducer Norman Granz, who masterminded the project, was not directly mindful of the pending release of the Goldwyn film. He later told writer Bill Ruhlmann, "I just wanted to do it because I'm not only a Gershwin fan, but I specifically thought I needed something different."

Although all three of the major participants—Armstrong, Fitzgerald, and arranger-conductor Russ Garcia (the same guy from the Bethlehem *P&B* a year earlier)—were indisputably jazz artists, as Granz, too, was a jazz producer, this project has the touch and feel of a pop album, particu-larly when listened to after the Davis-Evans record, which casts every melody in a startling new light. Granz never mentioned the Bethlehem project, and it could be a total coincidence that he happened to hire Russ Garcia for the same chore on the same score. But Granz didn't make Bethlehem's mistakes—rather than completely "cast" the score with a roster of singers and address the plot, Granz and Garcia divided up the songs between male and female roles and handed them out to his two principals. (Indeed, this is the path that later comparable treatments were to follow, like those by Lena Horne and Harry Belafonte, and Ray Charles and Cleo Laine.)

There were some departures from convention: Garcia starts with an overture of his own devising that sounds more like the big band–influenced Broadway of a later date (like, say, some of Cy Coleman's jazz-ier and more recent scores) than an opera from two decades earlier. Now, "I Wants to Stay Here" (which leads into "I Loves You, Porgy") is a solo for Fitzgerald (she even sings Porgy's comforting words to Bess, which sounds a little strange), whereas "I Got Plenty o' Nuthin' " and "It Ain't Necesarily So" have become duets.

So, for that matter, has "Summertime" (done in the score key, B minor); in fact, Armstrong's trumpet and voice are such commanding and distinct entities that one is tempted to describe this "Summertime" as almost more of a trio than a duo. A description of the outline of their routine can't do it justice: the piece opens with a French horn skimming over the opening three notes before the familiar vamp is heard. Armstrong then plays the first half of the melody, all sixteen bars of it, as an introduction. Fitzgerald finally enters—the first human voice we hear (since "Summertime" comes immediately after the new Garcia overture)—and she starts the piece anew by beginning again with the first sixteen bars. The orchestra modulates down for Armstrong's vocal entrance, and then he sings the last sixteen bars.

The second chorus of lyrics is even stronger: Fitzgerald goes back to the beginning, but this time Armstrong supplies a vocal obbligato, singing an accompaniment to Fitzgerald's main line, thus making the livin' even easier. Unfortunately, they only get through half the song—perhaps Garcia feared that at just under five minutes it was already overlong—and it closes leaving us hungry for the remaining sixteen bars. Armstrong and Fitzgerald are utterly majestic, particularly their final half-chorus together, which ends with Fitzgerald jumping around to E and F sharp rather than simply going to the tonic B as written. Armstrong invented the concept of this particular kind of jazzy obbligato, and anyone else doing this—and there have been many—sounds like a pale imitation. More important, Armstrong knows not to push it too far, and remains in character with the Broadway-classical nature of the performance. Anyone else might have fallen into the realm of empty jive and thereby undercut the credibility of the whole thing.

Following the 1957 P&B album, the song became one of Fitzgerald's theme songs. She recorded it on at least five subsequent occasions, all live concerts: Berlin (1960), Juan-les-Pins (1964), Budapest (1970), and Belgrade and Nice (both 1971). The Berlin (from the famous *Mack the Knife* album) and the Nice recordings are especially winning. Sarah Vaughan also made a career staple out of "Summertime," cutting it for the first time in 1949. There's a Carnegie Hall recording from 1954 with the Basie band, in which she introduces her trio (among them "Little Roy

Haynes") and then zings through a brief, up-tempo reading; a more stately one with Hal Mooney's orchestra from her 1957 *George Gershwin Songbook* (done after Fitzgerald had launched the songbook series on Verve but before La Fitz's 1959 Gershwin spectacular with Nelson Riddle); and a *P&B* live LP from 1982 with Michael Tilson-Thomas conducting the Los Angeles Philharmonic that's as close to pure opera as Vaughan ever got.

Vaughan's first "Summertime," from 1949, and her most intimate reading, done live in Japan in 1973, are the standouts. The '49 is a daring arrangement by Joe Lippman (known for his work with Nat Cole and on *Charlie Parker with Strings*) that starts completely in left field with a most unusual bass vamp before revealing itself to be the latest in a line of alternate "Summertime" countermelodies. The track employs a relatively small orchestra behind Vaughan, while the group on the 1973 live version is smaller still, being just a trio. The band may have diminished, but her voice is so much bigger, and if anyone was predestined to make the most of the song's dual heritage of opera and jazz, it's the Divine Sarah. On the '49, for instance, when we expect her to go to F, approaching the climax on "But till that mornin' " (like the 1958 Miles Davis, she's in B flat minor), she instead goes up a fifth further and lands on C. In both versions, she knows exactly when to push it and when to let it ride, turning the song into an exhibition of contralto pyrotechnics.

But hardly emotionally empty ones. Both Vaughan and Fitzerald are not conventionally lyrics-driven singers in the manner of most cabaret or theater singers. As Jo Stafford once told me, it's not that Fitzgerald didn't know what she was singing about or what the words meant, but rather, "I would say she gave more attention to the music than to the words." Although Fitzgerald and Vaughan rarely invested emotion in specific lyrics the way Rosemary Clooney or Sinatra would, they nonetheless were extremely warm and emotional entertainers, and the glow that emanated from them both, particularly in live performance, was truly something to experience. For whatever reason, both of them did extremely well with the lullaby "Summertime" and were able to put themselves into it in a way that they couldn't always do with more conventional woman-man love songs. Somehow it was easier for them to express maternal love than romantic love.

(Johnny Hartman had the opposite approach, and he sang "Summertime" as if he were singing to a lover rather than an infant. Hartman recorded this arrangement, which utilizes "It Ain't Necessarily So" as a kind of framing device, on two albums, both cut in Japan. In 1972 he cut it in the studio with local players on *Hartman Meets Hino,* and five years later returned to it on *Live at Sometime,* with Roland Hanna and George Mraz. Hartman and Sinatra are among the few male singers to do "Summertime" in slow tempo, as a ballad or lullaby, rather than as a swinger, in the manner of Tormé, Williams, and Murphy.)

Fitzgerald's longtime friend Pheobe Jacobs recalls visiting the singer early in 1995, when she had only a short time left to live and was completely bedridden. A cousin or niece had brought her baby to see "Auntie Ella," and Jacobs remembered Fitzgerald cradling the babe in her arms and softly crooning "Summertime" to it. "It was the most beautiful thing I had ever heard her sing," said Jacobs. "I couldn't stop crying." Magnificent as Fitzgerald's singing always was, it was rare for her to make anyone cry.

AFTER FITZGERALD AND ARMSTRONG, there were still other jazz Porgies and Besses which produced still other great "Summertime"s. If the single best trombone reading is by Lawrence Brown (on *Porgy and Bess Revisited*), Slide Hampton's is also a contender. This comes from an even more obscure *Porgy and Bess* jazz LP, the 1961 *Two Sides of Slide.* The cover, a picture of the leader-arranger reclining on a children's-playground slide while holding his trombone, illustrates two meanings of the word "slide," while the two sides of the LP illustrate two aspects of the creativity of Locksley Wellington "Slide" Hampton. The first side is an original dance suite in four parts; the second consists of Hampton's settings of five *P&B* songs, although, curiously, the words "Porgy and Bess" are nowhere on the cover. Hampton has assembled a powerful octet—including two trombones, two trumpets, two saxes (one played by George Coleman)— that is heard to best advantage on "Summertime." The piece is essentially a solo for the leader's fleet-fingered trombone work, but throughout, his orchestrations are very ambitious, and he achieves big results on a small canvas.

The other two major jazz treatments of *P&B* are those by Bill Potts and the Modern Jazz Quartet. Like Warner Brothers, United Artists, another movie studio getting its feet wet in the record business, commissioned its own jazz version, the assignment going to Potts, who has managed to stake out a career as an arranger, pianist, and conductor while based in Washington, D.C., hardly a center of the music industry.

It's best not to listen to Potts's *The Jazz Soul of Porgy and Bess* immediately after the Miles Davis–Gil Evans masterpiece, yet compared to virtually every other treatment, the Potts all-star big band version can more than hold its own. Whereas the Davis sounds completely unlike any other music ever recorded, even by that particular collaboration, the Potts sounds more like modern-influenced big band music circa 1959—but *brilliant* modern-influenced big band music circa 1959. Yet, while the sonic texture of the Davis-Evans is totally unique, as we've seen, its approach to the melodies is surprisingly faithful. The Potts, on the other hand, sounds considerably less Martian in the voicings of its brass and reed sections, but there are many cases when it does things we wouldn't expect with the tunes themselves: for instance, making "Summertime" into a flag-waver. True, there have been other occasions when Gershwin's lullaby has been reborn as an up-tempo (such as the Chris Connor–Maynard Ferguson combination), but the Potts version, with solos by Sweets Edison and the two-tenor team of Zoot Sims and Al Cohn, is a rare instance in which "Summertime" can be said to kick butt. (Sims recorded it again in 1975, on *Zoot Sims and the Gershwin Brothers,* with Oscar Peterson—the pianist's eighth recording of the song—producing another really aggressive, in-your-face treatment.)

The *Modern Jazz Quartet Plays George Gershwin's Porgy and Bess* is a curiosity on several levels. It was recorded in 1965, long after the movie version had come and gone, and obviously was not made with any coattails motivation in mind. And for some reason, it's not mentioned in the fortieth-anniversary box of highlights from the MJQ's career issued by Atlantic Records; surely the quartet's treatment of "Summertime" ranks as one of those highlights. As with Sarah Vaughan, this score, and this tune in particular, is a natural for the distinguished jazz-chamber foursome; like Vaughan, the MJQ is one of the few performing units equipped to handle both the jazz and the classical side of the *P&B* equation. The piece, which opens the set, is mainly a feature for pianist-arranger John Lewis, who shows that our standard notions of "classical opulence" are completely irrelevant, as he plays with a spareness and economy that would suit Memphis Slim or Champion Jack Dupree as much as Glenn Gould.

Talk about vamps, the MJQ has one of the very best: an engaging little six-note dealie that slowly works its way down the keyboard. Lewis starts with his vamp, then lays down the melody on top of it—or four bars of it—before vibraharpist Milt Jackson enters and begins with the melody again, improvising on the changes while letting us hear a lot of the Gershwin line. This is the Q at its finest, laying down layer upon layer, not only of piano and vibe lines (ably backed by bass and drums), but carefully considering the relationship between melody and variations, the written and the improvised, the background and the foreground. As far as I can tell, neither *The Jazz Soul of Porgy and Bess* nor *The Modern Jazz Quartet Plays George Gershwin's Porgy and Bess* is currently available on compact disc, which is not as it should be. (EMI did issue a CD of *Jazz Soul* very briefly in the early nineties, in an edition that was dubbed from a clean LP because the original master tapes had been lost.)

WHEN THE FILM *Porgy and Bess* was finally released in 1959, the world pretty much agreed with Frank Sinatra's later proclamation that "the opera had been around a billion years" and the movie "shouldn't have been made to begin with." As with many bloodless cinematic musicals, the best thing about it was the score, lavishly orchestrated by André Previn, who opened with a new overture of his own. Of all the principals in the film cast, only pop stars Sammy Davis, Jr. (as Sportin' Life), and Pearl Bailey (Maria) did their own singing. Leading man Sidney Poitier never tried to pass himself off as a singer, and so his dubbing (by the Metropolitan's Robert McFerrin, father of Bobby "Don't Worry, Be Happy" McFerrin) makes perfect sense. The two female leads, Dorothy Dandridge (Bess) and Diahann Carroll (Clara) both had singing careers, yet neither was considered suitably operatic, and so they, too, were dubbed, in the latter's case by Loulie Jean Norman, she of the ethereal vapor voice, one of the most famous of all Hollywood studio vocalists. Around this same time, Diahann Carroll and Previn made their own full-length album of the score; Sammy Davis, Jr., who because he was signed to Decca was contractually prohibited from appearing on the Columbia soundtrack LP (Cab Calloway sang the "Sportin' Life" songs on the album), made his own LP of the music with Carmen McRae guest-starring on two cuts as Bess.

There were also other jazz recordings of the opera: a New Orleans–

flavored treatment done by Bob Crosby (1958), an extended, well-considered dixieland rendition by the Jim Cullum Jazz Band (1986–87), and, most recently, one by the tenor colossus Joe Henderson (1997). A tenorist who combines a big sound with a thoughtful, introspective approach, Henderson offers what in one respect might be considered the most faithful of all treatments, in that he lays the songs out in precise show sequence (delineating them by act and scene) and even restores the deleted "Jasbo Brown Blues." Too much of Henderson's "Summertime" is wasted on Chaka Khan, an R&B vocalist who proves that her genre and jazz are, alas, further apart than a lot of us would like to believe. However, while fuzz-guitarist John Scofield is no less unwelcome than Kahn, Henderson's own playing on this tune and throughout is, typically, beyond reproach. Sadly, this would be Henderson's final recording.

Considering all the outstanding singers around today—including those on the order of Dee Dee Bridgewater, under contract to Henderson's own label, Verve Records—the choice of vocalists for this project is mystifying (as is the use of the British rocker Sting on "It Ain't Necessarily So").

Then, too, Kahn is coming out of a tradition of "Summertime"s from the rock and kiddie-pop arenas. The most infamous of these is the 1967 Janis Joplin reading on her album *Cheap Thrills*. It's done with the blues band Big Brother and the Holding Company, and there's no denying that Joplin's sound is raw and powerful—but, then, the same thing could be said about a sledgehammer. (Of course, taste is taste, and I say the above knowing full well that rock fans could say the same thing about certain artists I happen to like, such as Albert Ayler.) If this is the blues, I'll take vanilla.

Luckily, there were more copasetic treatments in the youth-music sphere—such as that by the great Sam Cooke, who finds the song a perfect embodiment for his aspirations of merging blues, gospel, and traditional pop. Billy Stewart's 1966 top-ten hit with the song is equally untraditional and no less outrageous (the Joplin version doesn't necessarily do anything differently, it just does it all badly). Stewart's single is amazingly entertaining: working with drummer Maurice White, later the founder of the band Earth, Wind, and Fire, Stewart has come up with what could be described as a combination of Otis Redding and Sammy Davis, Jr. On steroids, that is, and perhaps with a touch of Al Hibbler's bizarro humor thrown in. Stewart's lively vocal is further colored by a copious amount of wordless vocalizing—it's not quite scat singing in the traditional sense, but after Sammy Davis, it has the most in common with the unintelligible noises made by Latin singers like Carmen Miranda and Tania Maria. The track exists in two forms, a concise single edit and an extended version. The latter version opens with an a cappella vocalese cadenza that suggests summer in the synagogue and a fine tenor solo, but also, unfortunately, includes an ill-advised yodeling episode. The piece never relaxes in intensity until the ritardando passage that Stewart uses for a closing cadenza. If you listen to a number of Stewart's treatments of standards (such as "Secret Love"), it becomes clear that he was something of a one-trick pony, applying the same technique and effects to everything he sang. But I'll be damned if it isn't entertaining.

Apart from pure jazz and pure rock treatments, there were also pop-jazz and fusion variations on "Summertime": guitarist and singer George Benson did it several times in the mid-seventies, once live with synthe-sized strings and once in the studio. It would be nice to report that the song brought out the best in Benson, but "Summertime" seems only to provide an excuse for him to parade the worst clichés of his pop work, demonstrating why this potentially greatest of all jazz guitarists has been such a disappointment. By contrast, there's Grover Washington; normally a "smooth jazz" headliner, the saxist, here working with guitarist Kenny Burrell, plays in a decidedly more mainstream fashion in a 1985 Town Hall concert. This "Summertime" spotlights the familiar Washington soprano sax sound but with a harder-hitting, more improvisatory bent than we're used to hearing from him. Likewise, Kenny G.'s more recent recording features him sounding at his most Grover Washington–like, which is another way of saying at his best.

Of all the standards discussed in this book, "Summertime" is perhaps the most alive at the millennium. Because of the multi-faceted, poly-generic nature of the piece, it continues to attract interpretations from all corners of the Western musical world. One of the finest of all "legit" ver-sions was done in 1997 by contralto Harolyn Blackwell, with Erich Kun-zel and the Cincinnati Pops, and there's also a country rock version by Willie Nelson and Leon Russell. It's even been translated into the West African language of Fon and sung by the Beninese pop singer Angélique Kidjo, with a steady dance beat and a chanting choir (her own voice over-dubbed) behind her.

Neither of its creators lived to see their opera become a success or their major song collaboration become a standard, but the rest of us can bask forever in the reassuring glow of endless summertime.

BONUS TRACKS

Best Porgy and Bess Album That Never Was

There's no doubt in my mind that Billy Eckstine and Sarah Vaughan would have made the greatest *P&B* teaming on records, even greater than Armstrong and Fitzgerald, and certainly better than any of the other boy-girl versions, Belafonte and Horne, Charles and Laine, Tormé and Fay. We know how Vaughan would have sung "Summertime," and it's not much of a stretch to imagine Eckstine getting big and dramatic on "Bess, Oh Where's My Bess?" and "I'm on My Way," and the two of them turning on the romance and charm for such duets as "I Loves You, Porgy" and "Bess, You Is My Woman Now."

Most Surprising Duets on "Summertime" That Actually Were Made

"Summertime" is Clara's solo in the show, yet in the pop world it's often been sung as a duet, thanks largely to the Ella Fitzgerald and Louis Armstrong tandem treatment of 1957. However, there are earlier boy-girl duet versions of the venerable lullaby, such as one by Dinah Shore and Buddy Clark in 1947. Both were pop singers who made it into the pop mainstream after Crosby but before Sinatra, during the big band era but not quite of it—both sang with the big bands but made their names and their hits as soloists. (Coincidentally, both were Jewish, he from Boston, she from a *shtetl* in Tennessee, though they didn't work together enough to qualify as the Steve and Eydie of the forties.) On other records, Clark occasionally comes off as a little stiff, while Shore wasn't always committed enough to her material, particularly in commercial record sessions (as opposed to radio—in fact, she sang a very credible solo "Summertime" on her *Birdseye Open House* program, circa 1945, which has been released on a collector's-issue CD). The combination of the duet format and the song itself brings out the best in both of them, and their joint "Summertime" is a fine straight-ahead pop treatment. It contains no frills or surprises, but it has absolutely everything that the song needs. In 1949, Peggy Lee guested on Al Jolson's radio show, resulting in a Jewish-Swedish "Summertime." You'd never expect to hear Lee singing "Mammy" or Jolson singing "Fever," yet Norma Egstrom and Asa Yoelson complement each other surprisingly well here.

Least Likely "Summertime" Ever

Ann Sothern, MGM actress and star of a million "Maisie" movies, recorded an album for the Tops label in the late fifties that includes her treatment of "Summertime." Sothern sings it in a low, sultry voice (that bespeaks her admiration for Frances Williams, discussed above, in the "As Time Goes By" chapter) atop a slightly R&B-ish orchestration, with a strong backbeat and countermelody. There's a clarinet obbligato and a flute solo, but what I've never heard before or since is the mystical wail that Sothern uses in place of the customary diva tag at the end.

Most Over-the-Top (in a Good Way) "Summertime"

If pressed to name the most remarkable vocal rendition of "Summertime," though, I wouldn't necessarily choose a jazz version or a classical version. Mae Barnes, like Alberta Hunter and Ethel Waters, could safely be described as either a blues singer or a cabaret singer, depending on who's doing the describing. Barnes's 1958 "Summertime" is one of the very great versions of the song, and, if anything, is even more irreverent, not to mention zany, than Jerry Kreuger's. She starts slow and dramatic, but before too long goes completely bonkers, changing tempos and building up to the line "You're gonna rise up singing" as if it were the punchline for a joke. The first time around, she rises up singing "Wish You Were Here," and the second time, it's "Hound Dog." I've heard few comedy monologues that were funnier, and certainly none with better timing. Just as Barnes is a completely unique and original figure in the annals of American entertainment, her "Summertime" is one for the books.

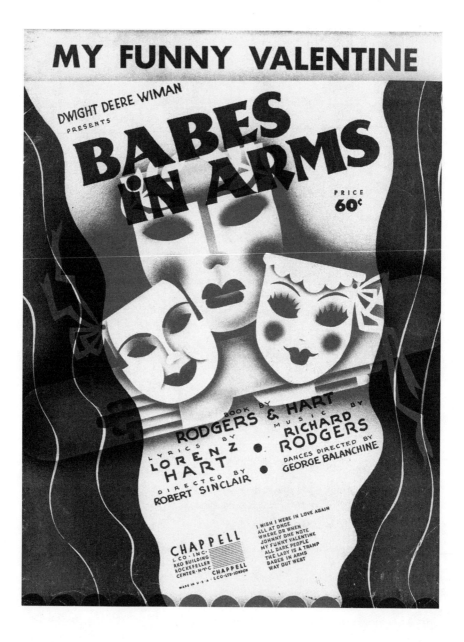

MY FUNNY VALENTINE (1937)

music by Richard Rodgers

words by Lorenz Hart

CABARET STAR MARY CLEERE HARAN has a great take on Richard Rodgers: she grew up, she says, like everyone else in the 1950s, a firm admirer of the classic Rodgers and Hammerstein musicals and the high moral values they exemplified. It wasn't until later in life that Haran learned of Rodgers's earlier career, in which he wrote shows and songs with a brilliant, if self-destructive, iconoclast named Lorenz Hart. "Discovering that Rodgers's first partner was a degenerate," says Haran, "was a bit like learning that Anne Bancroft is married to Mel Brooks."

It's said that later in his life, Richard Rodgers could never understand all the fuss over his old songs, the ones he had written with that first partner, Larry Hart. Why on earth would anybody want to hear those old things when he had moved on and was doing work that satisfied him so much more than that stuff from his salad days. Rodgers had long since left that part of town and couldn't fathom why anyone else would want to pay a visit there.

To Rodgers, his career was a single continuum; what he was doing in the forties and fifties with Oscar Hammerstein simply a better, more polished, closer-to-perfect version of what he had attempted to do in the twenties and thirties with Hart. Hardly anyone else sees it that way. To most of us, there were not one but two Richard Rodgerses, and the composer who wrote with Hart was a completely different animal from the one who worked with Hammerstein. Most people who claim to be able to tell the difference will tell you that they prefer the earlier, Rodgers and Hart, songs, but someone out there must be making Rodgers and Hammerstein the most successful writers of Broadway musicals in history.

We would all do well to remember that these are not only Hart songs or Hammerstein songs but primarily Richard Rodgers songs. "The Gentleman Is a Dope," with its sexual sophistication and casual intimacy, is Hammerstein's most Hart-felt number; it's not hard to imagine Vera Simpson singing it about Joey Evans in *Pal Joey*. In the same way, I can easily hear in my head Dr. Joseph Taylor singing "My Heart Stood Still" to Jenny Brinker in *Allegro*. When Frank Sinatra, in his grandest album, *The Concert Sinatra*, intermingled Hart with Hammerstein (Rodgers composed fully half the tracks), no one complained that "Bewitched," for all its sauciness, didn't belong in the same collection as "I Have Dreamed" and "This Nearly Was Mine," for all their sincerity.

We can debate the differences, but apart from distinctions in content, the central difference between Rodgers and Hart and Rodgers and Hammerstein may be one of packaging: with Rodgers and Hart, we tend to think of songs, with Rodgers and Hammerstein our consciousness centers on entire shows. The technological innovations of the mid-1950s served to swell Rodgers's coffers in several ways: on the one hand, the coming of Cinemascope and Todd-AO helped inspire Hollywood to start filming the major Rodgers and Hammerstein Broadway blockbusters. At the same time, the perfecting of the twelve-inch long-playing album inspired many singers and jazz musicians to start exploring in detail the song catalogues of Rodgers and Hart. Did they film Rodgers and Hart shows or revive them on Broadway? Yeah, a couple of 'em. Did anyone record a *Rodgers and Hammerstein Songbook* album? Sure, once in a while. But generally it was the *individual songs* of Rodgers and Hart that got recorded and the *entire production* of a Rodgers and Hammerstein work that got revived theatrically or filmed.

Rodgers himself never saw it that way. The composer was never trying to write individual songs but complete scores for specific shows with specific characters. (Indeed, "Blue Moon," which existed in several earlier versions, has been widely touted by Mel Tormé among others as the only Rodgers and Hart song *not* written for a show or film—although in fact it wasn't the only one.) The more assimilated Rodgers, unlike such slightly older peers as George Gershwin and Irving Berlin, didn't grow up in a Tin Pan Alley milieu, working as a song-plugging pianist in a publishing house or a singing waiter at "Nigger Mike's." Although no less Jewish, Rodgers, Hart, and Hammerstein were far from first-generation Americans scuffling on the Lower East Side; they came from middle-class professional families, and went to summer camps and college. Unlike Berlin or Gershwin or Arlen, they had little desire to perform in front of audiences and never had an act in vaudeville.

Indeed, Rodgers never wanted to be a *songwriter* per se; from childhood, his goal was to tell coherent stories in music. He had nothing against creating hit songs, but less for the glory of hearing his works performed by America's top singers and bands than for helping to bring crowds into theaters. He came to dislike it intensely when his songs were performed or recorded individually, outside the context he and his partners had carefully crafted for them. By the time *South Pacific* closed in 1954, Rodgers was aware of forty-nine different records of songs from its score—surely a vast underestimate—which he described as "an all time record in vulgarity."

THE FIRST IMPORTANT SHOW that Rodgers and Hart came up with on their own was *Dearest Enemy,* and this was, in fact, a book show. The earlier *Garrick Gaieties* was a revue, but it hadn't even been their idea; it was brought to them by the Theatre Guild. Between the *Gaieties* and *Dearest Enemy,* the pattern was set for future Rodgers and Hart productions: they did write songs for two editions of the *Gaieties,* as well as for some typically twenties slapdash affairs where the book was of no consequence— but these were generally cases when the team was approached by a producer. All the shows that R&H put together on their own—conceived from the ground up, as it were—were thoroughly integrated book shows. *Oklahoma!* and *State Fair* were in fact doing what *A Connecticut Yankee* and *Hallelujah, I'm a Bum* tried to do, only doing it better.

In this context, it may be instructive to consider the relationship of Frank Sinatra and Richard Rodgers, which began in 1943, a banner year for both these iconic figures. Within a few weeks and a few blocks of each other, *Oklahoma!* premiered at the St. James Theatre and Sinatra enjoyed his breakthrough solo engagement at the New York Paramount. In June, their paths crossed: when Sinatra did his first recording session as a solo artist for Columbia Records, among the three tunes laid down that day was "People Will Say We're in Love," the principal love song from *Oklahoma!,* the show that was by then the season's (and the era's) biggest hit. We're told that Rodgers was actually present in the studio when Sinatra recorded his first Richard Rodgers song. (History reports that Rodgers was en route to a dinner party, and thus was formally attired, when he informally dropped in on the Sinatra session; somehow this seems completely apropos.)

Thus began a fruitful relationship that lasted from the time of *Oklahoma!* in 1943 to that of *The King and I,* in 1951. During this time when the early Rodgers and Hammerstein shows were opening, Sinatra, who was primarily recording singles, was more interested in new songs than at any other time in his career, and was very keen to scoop his fellow crooners on the best new showtunes—not only from *Oklahoma!* and *Carousel,* but also from *Brigadoon* and others. It made sense to record these songs as singles when they were new.

But by the mid-fifties, Sinatra and Rodgers and Hammerstein had parted company. By this time, he was primarily recording albums, and it made no sense, by and large, to stick a current showtune in the middle of an album like those two 1955 masterpieces, *In the Wee Small Hours* and *Songs for Swinging Lovers.* Here, the goal was to take individual songs and put them together in such a way that the equivalent of a musical-comedy narrative could be forged out of them; so that they would flow together from song to song and add up to a story, a synthesis, of their own. A song from a contemporary book show such as *The Sound of Music* or *My Fair Lady* wouldn't make sense here, because audiences already identified those tunes with the stories told in the shows they came from; they wouldn't serve the new story Sinatra wanted to tell with them.

Interestingly, the younger Sinatra was better suited to the mature Rodgers (Hammerstein), and the older Sinatra fit more comfortably with the younger Rodgers (Hart). After *The King and I,* Sinatra would never sing a new Rodgers song again. He did, however, continue to sing Rodgers and Hart (and to a lesser extent, older Rodgers and Hammerstein).

It's possible that for all the money Rodgers made from royalties on Sinatra's recordings, he may in fact have resented the singer. For one thing, Sinatra kept alive the song catalogue of Rodgers and Hart at a time when Rodgers wanted to forget about his earlier years. He must have been doubly annoyed when wags expressed the opinion that the Hart songs were better than the Hammerstein ones. Then, too, there was Sinatra's penchant for swinging Rodgers's melodies and playing with Hart's and Hammerstein's words.

In a broader sense, Sinatra, by doing Rodgers's songs in his own way and imbuing them with his own meanings, was threatening to undermine Rodgers's lifelong quest for the perfect song-story integrated book musical. In 1926, Rodgers and Hart cringed when producer Florenz Ziegfeld interpolated Irving Berlin's "Blue Skies" in the middle of their score to *Betsy*, and not only because it bruised their egos and compromised their cash flow. Thus, you can imagine how Rodgers felt when Sinatra, in essence, constructed a new musical work entitled *Frank Sinatra Sings for Only the Lonely*, and used "Spring Is Here" about halfway through the second "act." Now less than ever, no one had a reason to remember that the song had originated with a show (and was dropped from the completely forgettable film) titled *I Married an Angel*. That all–Rodgers and Hart production was to all intents and purposes irrelevant, or, to quote the title of another song on the Sinatra album, "Gone with the Wind." When future generations sang "Spring Is Here," they had invariably learned it from *Only the Lonely*, and they sang it Sinatra's way.

IN A FAMOUS *Babes in Arms* song, Hart and Rodgers offered the following observation: "Hate California, it's cold and it's damp." At one point in our cultural development, it was generally expected of those who wrote about Broadway to dump on Hollywood; yet even those of us who love old movies would have a hard time defending Tinseltown to Rodgers and Hart, whose treatment at the hands of the moguls was nothing less than brutal. The team not only saw individual songs trashed but entire scores reduced to fragments, and in general, the three or four years that the team resided in Los Angeles, working full-time for the studios, can be regarded as the least productive time of their entire career.

So, considering how uneasy the Rodgers-Hart-Hollywood relationship was, it's ironic that the songwriters stumbled across an idea that would turn out to be one of the most employed plot lines in old-moviedom: the "Hey, kids, let's put on a show in the barn" bit. Who would imagine that such a hoary movie cliché could have been dreamed up by such high-minded Broadway sophisticates? The story goes that the partners were walking through Central Park and happened to notice a bunch of children playing. Upon closer inspection, they noted that the kids weren't just playing, they were devising their own games, making up their rules as they went along. "We began talking about kids," Rodgers later wrote, "and what might happen if they were suddenly given adult responsibilities, such as finding ways to earn a living."

From there Rodgers and Hart progressed to talking about a bunch of singing and dancing kids who wanted to take charge of their own showbiz destiny—make up their own productions, even if in a barn. The title *Babes in Arms* was, in one way, a reference to the Jerome Kern and Victor Herbert operettas that Rodgers had grown up on ("Babes in the Wood," *Babes in Toyland*). It also had a nice double meaning: the phrase could refer to infants cuddled in their mother's arms, but it could also mean children empowered with weaponry (as in Danny Kaye's *Up in Arms*). As the title song goes, "They call us babes in arms / But we are babes in armor."

This idea soon turned into the Broadway hit *Babes in Arms* (which opened in April 1937), and that was only the beginning. The property was quickly purchased by their onetime employers Metro-Goldwyn-Mayer at the instigation of Arthur Freed, himself a lyricist, who was in the process of establishing himself as a producer. Freed conceived the idea of building a team out of Judy Garland, who was just finishing her first big starring picture, *The Wizard of Oz,* and Mickey Rooney, who, thanks to the Andy Hardy pictures (some of which featured Garland in a smaller role), was just about the biggest box office attraction in the country. Freed eventually kept Rodgers and Hart's plot but trashed most of their songs. That picture was such a resounding hit (more profitable than *Oz,* which had cost more to make) that it achieved Freed's goal of building Garland and Rooney into a screen team worthy of mention in the same breath as Fred Astaire and Ginger Rogers (who ended their joint run in '39) and Metro's own Nelson Eddy and Jeanette MacDonald.

Freed kept the essential nut of the plot in *Babes in Arms,* but had Kay Van Riper, screenwriter on the *Andy Hardy* series, change things so that the film of *Babes in Arms* came out looking like *Andy Hardy Puts On a Show.* One thing that was changed was the name of the lead character. Rooney's character was named "Mickey Moran," whereas the lead on Broadway had the slightly less all-American name of Val Le Mar, Val being short for "Valentine." (Yes, at one time that was a respectable, albeit obscure, name for a man—think of the screenwriter Valentine Davies.) At some point during the writing of the Broadway version, Rodgers and Hart came up with the song "My Funny Valentine" and decided that it was so strong, it could further tie the plot to the score if the lead character happened to be named Valentine.

There's little evidence that "My Funny Valentine," sung by young leading lady Mitzi Green, was a blockbuster. Competition was fierce: the score also included "Where or When," "I Wish I Were in Love Again," "Johnny One-Note," and "The Lady Is a Tramp," as well as lesser-known gems like "All at Once," "Imagine," and "You Are So Fair"—not to mention the Nicholas Brothers dancing to "All Dark People Are Light on Their Feet" (a title that the man who would later write "You've Got to Be Carefully Taught" must eventually have found embarrassing). No stars of the original cast recorded "Funny Valentine" at the time, although it was cut for Liberty Music Shops by the two-piano team of Edgar Fairchild and Adam Carroll, who played in the *Babes* orchestra pit.

The song is not listed in any of the standard discographies of the period, including *Jazz Records* and *The American Dance Band Discography* by Brian Rust. When in 1940 Lee Wiley recorded her first (and probably the all-time first) album of Rodgers and Hart songs, "My Funny Valentine" was not among them, although she did do the song on her second R&H anthology in 1954. RCA recorded an album of Rodgers and Hart songs in 1946, featuring Vic Damone (virtually his first recording), Marie Greene, Betty Garrett (more about her later), and Milton Berle (yes, Milton Berle), but again "My Funny Valentine" did not make the cut of the most important R&H songs. Columbia also released a 78 album of songs by the team, *Rodgers and Hart Musical Comedy Hits,* which, true to form, does not include "Valentine."

"My Funny Valentine" enjoyed a fleeting glimpse at the hit parade in early 1945, when a dance-band version by Hal McIntyre's orchestra made it to number sixteen on the *Billboard* charts. (McIntyre was better known as the linchpin of the Glenn Miller reed section, and his vocalist was another former Miller-ite, Ruth Gaylor.) The song was kept alive, apparently, by New York cabaret singers like Mabel Mercer, who were, until the arrival of Sinatra, virtually the only artists to keep performing the great songs of the twenties and thirties into the forties and fifties, like monks hiding manuscripts in the Dark Ages.

In 1948, five years after Hart's death, MGM decided to build a movie around the Rodgers and Hart life story and song catalogue. The finished picture, *Words and Music,* could have been titled *Andy Hardy Goes Ballistic,* with Rooney giving one of the performances of his career as the self-destructive Larry Hart (albeit de-Jewished, made considerably more cuddly, and unfalteringly heterosexual). Judy Garland, the other star of Metro's *Babes in Arms,* sang two songs in the picture, both of which were numbers from the Broadway *Babes in Arms* that were not used in the film version nine years earlier: "Johnny One-Note" and "I Wish I Were in Love Again" (the latter a reunion with Rooney). MGM did not, however, include "Funny Valentine," although at one point they considered using it, and had Betty Garrett (just about the closest thing that *Words and Music* had to a leading lady) record it. The Garrett version is short and is one of the few treatments of the song to use the verse. By this time, the song had slowly begun to arrive: Margaret Whiting, in her postwar Capitol album of Rodgers and Hart songs, may have been the first major pop star to record it. (This is virtually the only 78-era collection of R&H songs that actually includes "Valentine.") Then, in 1951, Goddard Lieberson of Columbia Records produced the first full-length recording of the *Babes* score, featuring Mary Martin, and it of course included "Valentine." Still, it was Sinatra who made it into a classic.

IT'S ONLY A SLIGHT EXAGGERATION to say that "My Funny Valentine" was really born when Frank Sinatra recorded it in November 1953. The singer had been singing the song for at least two months by then, as documented at his September 1953 engagement at Bill Miller's Riviera nightclub in Paramus, New Jersey. (In their review of his show, *Variety* mentioned "Valentine" specifically, and it survives in a location recording of truly execrable sound quality.) Both this engagement and the album come from the very dawn of the Sinatra comeback—*From Here to Eternity* was just opening at this time, and a number of early Capitol singles were starting to dent the charts. It was in this context that Sinatra not only recorded "My Funny Valentine" but made it the opening track of his first Capitol album, *Songs for Young Lovers.*

The song is published in E flat (three flats in the key signature), but since so much of the harmony is in minor, many musicians prefer to think of "Valentine" as being in C minor, the relative minor of E flat. The melody, though it begins on C, ends on E flat (hence the justification for deeming the tune to be in that key). The song is essentially in the *A-A-B-A,* thirty-two-bar mold, but with some crucial differences. The melody of the first *A* is indeed repeated in the second *A,* only this time we hear all the notes a third higher; the first *A* starts on C and goes up to E flat and then up to B flat; the second starts on E and goes up to G and then to D. Therefore, the second *A* is more properly described as *A¹* in that it uses different notes, although they have the same relationship to each other and describe the same melody. The final *A* departs even further from the original *A:* we hear the familiar two-bar "My Funny Valentine" "hook" phrase, first going from C to E, as in the first *A,* then going from E to G, as in the *A¹*. The next four bars repeat the hook phrase yet again, this time starting on high C and going up to high E, which is held dramatically for a full two measures. That's eight bars right there; we then get an additional four bars in the form of a concluding tag, ending with a mention of Valentine's Day. As Rodgers's most recent biographer, William G. Hyland, has noted, the composer often liked to end with an additional four bar tag, as he does on "If I Loved You" and "Climb Ev'ry Mountain," in order to make his conclusions even stronger.

From one perspective, the song can sound very rococo. The way that the basic phrase is stated and then reiterated in different registers can be described as in keeping with the classical ideal of theme and variations. The other shoe falls with the verse: there is indeed an eighteen-bar verse at the start of the song, but it is one of the least-heard verses of any standard. Even more than the chorus, the melody of the verse sounds as if it's alluding to musical styles from the eighteenth century or earlier, as if it could be plucked on a harpsichord, a spinet, or a lute. The entire verse has not a single chord: the treble clef contains the melody notes of the vocal line, while the bass clef is completely blank—that is to say, it consists of nothing but whole rests. This lack of chords is a clear allusion to a period in Western music before modern notions of harmony had developed.

Eileen Farrell did Rodgers and Hart one better by eliminating the treble notes as well—in other words, the entire piano accompaniment is gone and she sings a cappella. Paul Desmond's 1961 version with strings is one of the few instrumental jazz treatments to incorporate classical allusions. Although vibraphonist Milt Jackson recorded it with a rhythm section led by pianist Horace Silver, it's a shame that he also didn't cut it with his regular working group, the Modern Jazz Quartet, as that was a group that could really go for baroque. And if the lack of chords isn't enough of a tip-off, the lyrics are a dead giveaway, being full of "thou" and "hast" and "doth" and other archaic usages.

As with many Hart lyrics, it's possible to find autobiographical relevance in the text: Rodgers has stated emphatically that Hart was never
"Glad to Be Unhappy," as the title of one of their best songs went. However, the reference to a "half-pint imitation" in the verse to "Bewitched,
Bothered, and Bewildered" is a far cry from describing the macho Gene
Kelly, who played the protagonist of *Pal Joey,* while it's a perfect description of the diminutive Hart.

"Funny Valentine" is a man's idea of the way he imagines women think
about men. (Although attempts have been made to claim Hart as a gay
martyr, he did have relationships with women—or at least tried to: he
was goofy about leading lady Vivienne Segal, the general inspiration for
the Betty Garrett character in *Words and Music,* but, as in the film, he just
couldn't get started with her.) Just as "Have You Met Miss Jones" (from
I'd Rather Be Right) is a man's song and no amount of pronoun changing
has ever made it suitable for a woman (sorry Anita, Ella, Sarah, but "Sir
Jones" and "Old Jones" just don't cut it), "My Funny Valentine" is essentially a woman's song. That a number of men have sung it successfully—
indeed, it's probably most closely associated with Frank Sinatra and Chet
Baker—is a testament to their abilities as interpreters. It's affectionate
and endearing for a woman to admit that she's in love with a man even if
his "figure" is "less than Greek" (i.e., not the Olympian ideal of masculine
beauty) and his mouth is "a little weak." But a man, especially in old song
lyrics, would never describe a woman in that fashion; when men list their
criteria for feminine loveliness, "strong" would not be the adjective they
would use to describe the lips and mouth of their dream girl. Rule number one, dude, if you're trying to get to first base with a chick, do not,
under any circumstances, refer to her looks as "laughable."

The weak mouth and the less-than-Greek figure are key elements in
the bridge, and that whole eight-bar section is a marvel both of melodic
construction and of what medieval composers referred to as "word paint-
ing," the ideal of matching text to music. The melody of the bridge is
essentially a simple phrase, E♭-E♭-D-E♭ that is heard three times, the climactic note of which gets higher and higher each time it is heard, and is
followed by a rest each time, from a B flat (up an interval of a fifth), to a C
(a sixth), and then a high D (up a seventh). When we go from the high D
down a whole octave to the middle D, the jump occurs on the word
"open," and it goes without saying that this is a very "open" interval

indeed. These jumps back down from the high note to the middle D are punctuated by rests, which give the two notes a sense of openness rhythmically as well as melodically.

The rests can also be considered a further allusion to classical and "formal" music, and in some interpretations give the song something of a waltz feeling. The classic Sinatra performance goes into waltz time for the second part, which is actually a half-chorus that begins with the bridge. The instrumental ensemble is in 3/4 time, although Sinatra himself sings it with a swinging lilt so that the 3/4 feeling is understated. In his live recordings of the piece from his 1962 World Tour, Sinatra seems even less waltzy, although the sextet behind him does go into waltz time. (Sammy Davis, on his Decca version, follows Sinatra's pattern by also going into 3/4 on his second run-through of the bridge.)

Hyland also notes that it was characteristic of Rodgers to start with a comparatively simple melody and then dress it up with a not-so-simple series of chords. This may be one reason why Rodgers's songs are so beloved by jazz singers and instrumentalists—much to the chagrin of the composer. On "My Funny Valentine" the harmony line is so strong it's practically another melody, giving the song an almost classically contrapuntal feeling. Essentially, the harmony line for the central part of the melody is a chromatically descending line. Sinatra's version does not emphasize Rodgers's harmonies, but Sammy Davis's does: behind the singer we hear a series of spare, basic chords in which the notes go down by half-steps, from C to B to B flat to A to A flat. Pianist Horace Silver (sounding curiously like John Lewis) provides a similar effect behind Milt Jackson in the vibraharpist's 1955 Prestige recording: for the first half (four bars) of each of the three A sections, we hear the piano harmony going down from A to F sharp—and for the second half of each A section, the piano pretty much drops out. The three sections are in minor, although Rodgers occasionally will throw in a major chord for the sake of variety, and he also uses diminished chords which, as employed here, are even more minor than minor.

Miles Davis recorded the song several times, including a classic live version from 1958 (on *Jazz at the Plaza*) with his great sextet of the period, featuring John Coltrane, Bill Evans (who also played it with Jim Hall), and Cannonball Adderley. It's the same band that recorded the trumpeter's classic album *Kind Of Blue,* and it's telling that "Valentine" should be one of the major standards in the repertoire of this legendary ensemble. Davis returned to the tune in 1964 on another great live album, this one with his no-less-celebrated unit of the 1960s, spotlighting Wayne Shorter and Herbie Hancock. The *Kind of Blue* band and the sixties band had one major thing in common: these Davis units were among the first ensembles to explore the concept of modal jazz. It seems logical that "Funny Valentine"'s unique harmonic sequence made it attractive to musicians who were thinking along those lines. Rodgers and Hart may have been contemplating the musical past with their allusions to classical, and possibly medieval and Renaissance, techniques, but somehow they wound up looking straight into jazz's future.

Rodgers's harmonic ambiguity is directly reflected in Hart's melancholy, but not bleak, lyric. What makes the whole thing so remarkable is the happy/sad nature of the lyric, brilliantly mirroring the major/minor nature of the music. It's a love song, but far from those "I love you and everything's rosy" tunes so popular in the twenties (vis-à-vis Irving Berlin's "Blue Skies"). It's vaguely optimistic, but it couldn't be described as upbeat. Still, it's far from a downer or a torch song like "Body and Soul." The sheet music instructs pianists to play the somewhat peppier verse "moderato," while the refrain should be rendered "slowly, with much expression." In truth, it is neither glad nor unhappy.

Hart's reputation, especially in his later years (and at forty-two, he was, sad to say, already in his later years) was that he was simply knocking out his lyrics on the backs of envelopes in his increasingly rare moments between drunken debauches. The craftsmanship here, however, is impeccable—as in the famous rhyme of "laughable" and "unphotographable." Tony Bennett, on his 1964 trio version, throws in a mild but effective chuckle on the word "laughable." (Other singers have sung that line even more literally.) Apart from the construction of the individual lines and rhymes, who but Hart would have come up with a musical comedy love song in which the declaration of love is conveyed as a list of the other person's faults? The message is that love doesn't exist *despite* these failings but perhaps *because* of them; these touches of humanity are, in the end, what endear the other to us.

The tonality in the bridge is generally major, although it gets back to minor at the end as we head toward the final *A* section. The words and music never complement each other more perfectly than in that final *A*. In the phrase "Stay, little valentine, stay!" the first "stay" is on a high C supported by a major chord, while the second "stay" is on a higher E flat, this time tellingly backed by a *minor* chord. The dramatic implications are obvious and the shifting between major and minor reflects what has now become the central issue of the lyric: Will he stay or is it a case of "Hello, I must be going"? Importantly, the last line of the lyric is still a little vague. We're told that with this other person here, "Each day is Valentine's Day." Yet that still doesn't tell us whether or not Funny Valentine will stay. The melody gives us more clues: by solidly ending in major on the final four bars, the message is a hopeful, affirmative one.

AS WE'VE SEEN, "My Funny Valentine" was barely recorded at all before Sinatra did it in 1953, but within a few years it become one of the signature songs of the LP era. The industry carefully followed Sinatra's lead in using standard songs, generally from shows that were then ten to thirty years old, as the basic bread and butter of the new medium known as the long-playing record. Very quickly, "Valentine" became one of the most-recorded pieces of music of the 1950s. As early as 1956, the anonymous annotator on June Christy's album *The Misty Miss Christy* (also on Capitol Records) praised Miss Christy's ability to come up with offbeat material; by the same token, he further noted that he had heard of instances of patrons walking into record shops and asking, "Do you have any albums that *don't* have 'My Funny Valentine'?"

Around this time the song was also interpolated into two films, and rendered by two lip-synching leading ladies: Anita Ellis sang it for Jeanne Crain in *Gentlemen Marry Brunettes* in 1955 and Trudy Erwin laid down the vocal track for Kim Novak in *Pal Joey*. "Valentine" was also represented in jazz "cover" albums of the *Pal Joey* movie score (despite the fact that it had originated in *Babes in Arms*), such as that by the Don Elliott Quartet on Design Records. Tops Records, another supermarket label of the era, came out with a "cover" album of the *Joey* score that mimicked both the Nelson Riddle orchestrations and the Sinatra vocals (rendered by a Frank wannabe named Duke Hazlet) as closely as possible. By 1956, when Ella Fitzgerald recorded her double-LP *Rodgers and Hart Songbook*, "Valentine" was inescapable. Fitzgerald and producer-arranger Buddy Bregman (doing some of his best work here) made it a point to include the verse. This served both to make her "Funny Valentine" more faithful to the original and to distinguish her record from most of the other available versions of the song. (She had already recorded a superior live version in Japan, which wouldn't be issued until decades later, with Jazz at the Philharmonic in 1953, that's especially touching, even when she sings "Are you strong?" instead of "Are you smart?")

Fitzgerald and Mary Martin (from her 1951 album of the entire *Babes* score) come closest to capturing that melancholy feel as we imagine the authors wanted it. Fitzgerald and Martin each use the verse to help set the melancholy mood, and it works very well indeed. Martin recorded the song again in an album done in cooperation with Richard Rodgers, who is billed as playing the piano, but what we get is a lushly boring orchestration without a note of piano; it boggles the mind to think that this was the way Rodgers wanted to hear his song.

The verse on the Rodgers-Martin treatment is heard in eighteenth-century fashion; by contrast, the major male versions—Sinatra, Baker, Bennett—capture the mood without using the verse. Indeed, far from having a verse, the classic Sinatra Capitol starts most abruptly: just two brief chords and a few seconds of strings after the needle drops and— boom!—we're up to our armpits in "Funny Valentine." The kickoff of the 1962 live performance from London is even briefer, just one chord, barely a note, and the valentine starts getting funny. Although the Capitol session was conducted by Nelson Riddle, soon to become the most famous of Sinatra's longterm orchestrators, the chart itself is believed to be the work of George Siravo and was certainly written at least a few seasons earlier; where Siravo has an alto sax obbligato, Riddle, at least in his mature work, would have used a flute. In fact, that alto part has been transferred to Harry Klee's flute in the many live 1962 versions. The Capitol has Sinatra holding an especially long fermata to dramatically emphasize the second "stay." "Valentine" remained in Sinatra's working "book" for the remainder of his Capitol Records period (numerous live and television performances were documented in the fifties), making its last important appearance in his life in his 1962 international tour for children's charities.

Or so we thought, until the piece was included on *Duets II,* on which producer Phil Ramone spliced a 1993 studio recording by Sinatra into "How Do You Keep the Music Playing" by country singer Lorrie Morgan. Strange as it sounds, the two songs and the two voices work better together than most of the other efforts on the double-CD *Duets* project.

Yet although Morgan is surprisingly adept at singing this kind of music, one yearns to hear the Sinatra performance unencumbered, especially as he hadn't sung the piece in a studio in forty years. The original 1953 Capitol concludes with an interesting countertheme played on a celeste; it sounds vaguely reminiscent of a phrase from Gershwin's "Bess, You Is My Woman Now." The 1993 orchestration, credited to *Duets* musical director Patrick Williams, extends this into a full-blown coda, in which Sinatra comes right out and sings the appropriate lyrics from *Porgy and Bess,* "Morning time and evening time . . ." It suggests that he had indeed been keeping the song fresh in his mind over the decades.

Tony Bennett recorded three different "Funny Valentine"s, starting with two pianocentric treatments from 1959 and 1964, both featuring his longtime accompanist, Ralph Sharon. The earlier one, from the album *Tony Sings for Two,* is a duet between the two men. With no bass and drums, the piece is slower and more rubato than usual. The printed music shifts from the verse to the chorus on the word "you're," and Bennett's treatment may be the only one that doesn't include the verse but starts "You're my funny valentine . . ." just the same. In this treatment, which is in F major, we expect Bennett to go up to high E on the second "stay"; instead, he surprises us by shooting a third higher and hitting high G. The duet ends with another early-music reference as Sharon detours through a brief quote from "Greensleeves."

Bennett's 1964 treatment was done with a trio, opening with a brief bass intro. This trio track was part of a series of sessions done in New York and Las Vegas that were originally intended for an all-trio album entitled *When Lights Are Low,* some of which were eventually released as part of a mishmash collection of great stuff called *A Time for Love.* This time (in E flat) with bass and drums along, the approach is much jazzier and more relaxed. Bennett doesn't do anything as dramatic as shooting for extra-high notes, but he is much more playful throughout. In 1973, he cut it again, this time at last with a full orchestra, courtesy of Don Costa.

Chet Baker actually began his long association with the song before the Sinatra Capitol, having first cut it while still a member of Gerry Mulligan's classic trumpet-baritone-bass-drums quartet in 1952. That was an instrumental reading, however, and Baker didn't sing it on records for the first time until 1954. Even within Mulligan's group and without a vocal, it was always Baker's feature, the leader very generously allowing the trumpeter to dominate the central melodic statement. Between the 1952 and the 1954 versions, the pattern was set for Baker's many subsequent performances—whether opening with trumpet or vocal, Baker would play it painstakingly slowly and deliberately, almost as if he were plucking out nerve endings. He sings it earnestly, not with a lot of vocal technique but heavy with heartfelt charm. (Mulligan continued playing the tune with later editions of his pianoless quartet, including a live version from Newport in 1957; rather than assigning the melody to valve trombonist Bob Brookmeyer, Baker's approximate brass successor, the leader and bari saxist takes it himself.)

At least a hundred recordings of "Valentine" are listed in Chet Baker's discography, mostly private tapes of live gigs from Europe in the seventies and eighties. The Italian label Philology even released a CD entitled *Seven Faces of Valentine*, which consists of seven different live Baker versions, generally from various venues in Italy between 1975 and 1985. Most use trios and quartets comprised of local musicians, although there is one track from Copenhagen (1983) extracted from a memorable tour that costarred Baker and Stan Getz. There's a trio with bass and French guitarist Philip Catherine (who also cut "Valentine" under his own name and with bassist Niels-Henning Ørsted Pedersen) playing some very Knitting Factory–esque fuzz guitar, two different duos with Euro-pianists (one in which Baker plays muted trumpet, the other in which he scat sings), a quartet with pianist Kenny Drew, and an extra-long treatment with an Italian ensemble of flute, bass, and drums.

No matter what the instrumentation, Baker's tempo is usually rubato. There's an elaborate introduction, which doesn't offer a hint as to what the tune will be, and which is inevitably followed by applause when Baker starts to sing and the crowd recognizes the tune. He usually starts slow and picks up the tempo a bit in the middle, but still keeps everything in what could be considered bebop ballad time. On April 28, 1988, Baker played what is considered his "last concert"—at least the last performance to be officially released—in which he is accompanied at different points by several large German jazz orchestras. And the last tune from that last concert is "My Funny Valentine." (Indeed, the tune could be said to follow Baker from beyond the grave, since it's usually included in memorial tributes to him.)

The Mulligan-Baker treatment, which was the direct inspiration for Anita O'Day's 1958 version, is the first great modern jazz "Funny Valentine." It might be the first great version in any jazz genre, since musicians didn't begin to pick up on it until the modern era. "Valentine" essentially did not exist in the premodern era, and dixieland and swing treatments are comparatively rare—although some were made later on. The big band treatments come not from the swing era but from more modern-tinged jazz ensembles like those of Stan Kenton and Ted Heath. There is a stunning reading from 1954 by Ben Webster and Teddy Wilson, both of whom are *sui generis* players. That June, Artie Shaw cut it as one of his final recordings with a small group costarring Hank Jones. One thinks of Shaw, who stopped playing shortly after these sessions, as a product of the big band and the 78 era; hearing him stretch out on the tune for five minutes, in a high-fidelity recording, makes him sound like a whole new clarinetist, and in his playing here he goes well beyond the traditional boundaries of swing style.

The first generation of musicians to embrace "My Funny Valentine" was, in fact, that of the other modernists. From the 1950s on, the tune was cut by hundreds of such groups, including such bop and postbop colossi as Charlie Parker (who did a fine version live with the Birdland All-Stars at Carnegie Hall in 1954), J. J. Johnson, Art Blakey, Art Farmer, Mal Waldron, Oscar Peterson, Zoot Sims, Don Ellis, Donald Byrd, Charlie Haden, and even experimentalists from beyond the fringe like Archie Shepp and Anthony Braxton. It was lovingly rendered by most of the great romantics of the modern age: Baker, Evans (with Davis, with his own trio, and in a duo with Jim Hall), Stan Getz (most notably with trombonist J. J. Johnson live in 1958, a surprisingly "up," non-ballad treatment), Paul Desmond (as the opening track of *Desmond Blue,* the great altoist's major album with strings, as well as on his 1975 double-LP meeting with a Toronto rhythm section), Art Pepper and Sonny Stitt (together on a brilliant album produced for the Japanese market, not released in the States until 2001 as *Art Peppper: The Hollywood All Star Sessions*). There are noteworthy jazz treatments on guitar (Jim Hall, Philip Catherine, Herb Ellis), violin (Stephane Grappelli with organist Eddy Louiss), vibraphone (Milt Jackson, Red Norvo), and harmonica (Larry Adler with Ellis Larkins, who also cut it with Lee Wiley).

The most enthusiastic instrumentalists to embrace "Funny Valentine," however, were pianists—more of whom have played it than any other song except possibly "Body and Soul." Some piano "Valentines" are merely tinkly (Ahmad Jamal), others are quite ambitious (Hank Jones with string quartet), still others are Latinate (Ronnie Mathews). McCoy Tyner, like Stan Getz and J. J. Johnson, uses it for a kind of jam session with extended solos by his entire quintet. Dorothy Donegan incorporates harplike string plucks. But generally, pianists use the song to get introspective and melancholy: Cedar Walton's 1991 live recording is suitably bittersweet; Mary Lou Williams, who cut it live both at the Cookery in New York (with just Brian Torff on bass) and at Rick's in Chicago (with trio), opens with an abstract vamp and gradually brings in the melody, then plays the tune itself very tenderly; Gene Harris is normally extroverted and bluesy, but on his solo "Valentine" from Maybeck Hall he sounds as if he's moving in on the territory of Bill Evans and Fred Hersch; Marian McPartland lays out the tune with an absolutely crystalline touch, offering a sequence of melodic variations with ever-so-slightly displaced rhythmic accents, again like Evans, in a performance that manages to steadily mount in intensity without ever blowing its cool. Keith Jarrett, who recorded it in 1986 (Munich) and 1996 (Tokyo, in a medley with an original by the pianist simply titled "Song"), seems to be going for the slowest, most ruminative, inwardly directed "Funny Valentine" of all. Jarrett's abstractions of the tune are brilliant (his humming is less so), even if it does seem a little self-indulgent at eleven minutes.

SINGERS, OF BOTH THE "straight" pop and the jazz-influenced-pop variety, especially loved the song. In the first category, there's a characteristically quavering treatment of the verse and chorus by Johnny Mathis from *Open Fire, Two Guitars* (the guitars are audible, the fire is not) and a breathless, sultry version by Julie London (which seems to be the inspiration for the breathless, sultry version by film actress Michelle Pfeiffer in *The Fabulous Baker Boys*). Dinah Shore waxed it with André Previn's piano; she was neither the greatest technician nor the most outstanding dramatic interpreter that the American songbook has known, but on those frequent occasions when Shore put everything she had into a song, she could be quite convincing. This performance is one of her very best, with Previn helping her keep it honest. Likewise, there's a movingly sensitive rendition by Broadway-style belter Gordon MacRae.

Eydie Gorme included it on an album called *Show Stoppers,* opening with a verse that sounds at least vaguely medieval; there's no evidence that "Funny Valentine" actually did stop the show in *Babes in Arms,* but Gorme sings it so superbly that who are we to niggle? In many ways, the best pop version after Sinatra is by his disciple Vic Damone, who success-fully created the illusion that he's completely subjugated his own identity to the song. Indeed, this treatment is pure "Funny Valentine" and, apart from the lovely lilt in his voice, there's virtually no pop-singer personal-ity, nothing whatever to distract from the song's beauty. Another Sinatra student who does well by "Funny Valentine," and vice versa, is Sammy Davis, Jr., who performed it *Live at Town Hall* and who sounds genuinely vulnerable (something he didn't always manage). He ends by entreating, "Please make this Valentine's Day."

Among the more jazz-oriented vocalists, there are generally two vari-eties of "Valentine," sincere and swinging. Perhaps it would be better to divide them into performances that concentrate on the music and those that make more out of the words. Anita O'Day's version (on *Anita Sings the Winners*), for instance, is slow, but more bombastic than romantic; allegedly dedicated to Gerry Mulligan and Chet Baker, this large, brood-ing orchestration has more in common stylistically with Stan Kenton. Carmen McRae, contrastingly, achieved supreme intimacy with her "Valentine," even though she doesn't stick to a slow speed. Instead, she slyly revs up the tempo partway through and slows down again at the end, winding up on a dramatic, ascending pitch. This is a "Valentine" of extra-ordinary beauty, and it appears on a studio album, the rhythm-section-only *Afterglow* (1955), and, two years later, on a live TV broadcast (issued on a Calliope Records LP) on which the high-note ending is even more effective.

Johnny Hartman recorded one of the best purely balladic "Valentine"s in Japan in 1972, an extra-long version costarring local trumpet star Terumasa Hino. When Kevin Mahogany addressed it twenty-three years later, on *You've Got What It Takes,* he was most definitely wearing his Hart-man hat. Chris Connor's 1993 recording, which is done faster than most, conveys a sense of urgency, and shows that even pushing seventy, this "cool"-style singer still has it. Cleo Laine's version is dark, her voice recalling Betty Carter's tightly pinched tone, while her pianist displays a fondness for Beethoven's Moonlight Sonata.

The song doesn't bring out the best in everybody: Connee Boswell, on her Rodgers and Hart album, doesn't quite get the point of it, while Mor-

gana King's 1978 treatment is somehow both minimal and overdone. Yet
some singers respond to "Valentine" in unexpected ways. As noted, Gordon MacRae is far less stentorian than usual, and Sammy Davis, who
doesn't always come off as sincere, sounds very much so on "Valentine."
Likewise, Buddy Greco, who was hardly known for his sensitive ballads,
turns in one of the most romantic performances of his career on it. Best
known for his high-energy, hard-swinging shenanigans and lovable wise-
ass persona, Greco here shows that he could also put over a love song
when the occasion demanded.

Sarah Vaughan came to "Valentine" in her first Mercury session, in
1954, and then returned to it often in the seventies, in five or so documented performances, including two commercially issued live concerts:
in Japan in 1973, and at Ronnie Scott's in London in 1977. As early as
1954, Vaughan's performance, accompanied by a sumptuous string section, combines jazz and pop aspirations, featuring one of the friskiest,
jazziest voices and attitudes there is. The seventies versions have a bigger-
voiced Vaughan demonstrating a sound that's at once more bluesy and
more operatically grand. In London, she focuses on the phrase "a little
weak" as the nexus of her machinations, stretching it out, taking it down
to the ground, then up to the sky, and really running it through the
wringer. She does the same with her voice. Indeed, there's not a part of
her chops—the high notes, the basement notes, the middle register—
that doesn't get a thorough workout.

Knowing Vaughan's tendencies toward operatic grandeur—Martin
Williams called her "an opera singer without an opera"—it's not surprising that her "Funny Valentine" would encompass classical elements. It is
surprising, however, that the considerably more down-to-earth pianist
and singer Matt Dennis would also pursue a classical angle in his "Valentine." Dennis, who made most of his dough as a songwriter ("Violets for
Your Furs," "Everything Happens to Me"), recorded "Valentine" on *Play
Melancholy Baby*. He starts with an exceedingly formal, almost classical
piano intro, which he immediately contrasts with a warm and exceedingly casual vocal delivery. He plays with the meter, for instance, eliminating the pause between "laughable" and "unphotographable," and, on
the whole, keeps finding new ways for us to make sure we keep concentrating on these words that we've already heard a million times before.
Dennis is fresh and vital, and he's emotionally true.

So, too, is Lee Wiley. Wiley, having missed her chance to be the first singer to record "My Funny Valentine" in her 1940 Rodgers and Hart collection, atoned for this lapse by tackling the tune in her 1954 long-playing collection of R&H songs. Wiley is nothing if not direct and believable; there's no artifice whatsoever about the woman or her singing. Few singers are able to use "Valentine" to so vividly describe someone in their life, someone whom they love perhaps in spite of, perhaps because of, his weaknesses. (Incidentally, her two sidemen here, cornetist Ruby Braff and pianist Ellis Larkins, recorded a spectacular instrumental "Valentine" on their own.) As with Billie Holiday or Judy Garland, when Lee Wiley sings, you can really hear the hurt.

HAD LORENZ HART LIVED as long as Ira Gershwin, he would surely have encountered certain lapses in singers that would have given him pause. Just as Ira was annoyed when his slangy "I Got Rhythm" got "corrected" to "I've Got Rhythm," Larry would have cringed when singers change "Don't change *a* hair for me" to "Don't change *your* hair for me." It does make a difference. Rita Reys, the fine Dutch singer who committed this gaffe, is to be forgiven. Although she is certainly the finest European jazz singer of her era, her command of the English language is obviously not on the same level as her dark, sultry, Netherlandic voice and June Christy–like phrasing. Reys cut the disc on her major American release, half of which found her accompanied by Art Blakey and the Jazz Messengers. Individually, both Blakey and Reys returned to the song years later, Reys in a faster tempo and with the offending monosyllable corrected; Blakey with Wynton Marsalis (who also cut it on his own). One wonders what the deep-voiced Arthur Prysock would have offered by way of an excuse for singing "your hair" instead of "a hair"—a screw-up that mars an otherwise fine rendition.

Such changes in the lyric, whether deliberate or unintentional, are plentiful in recordings made by those artists who have sung "My Funny Valentine" but who are far from specialists in the Great American Songbook. For whatever reason, these abound; to a great many soul and R&B performers, "Valentine" seems to represent the whole of the songbook and they take it on primarily to prove that they can handle genres beyond their home turf. There are reasonably good soul and contemporary dance-mix versions by such artists as funk diva Chaka Kahn, soul chanteuse Etta James (with Pat Metheny–like droning guitar and Chet Baker–like trumpet). It was also waxed by two singers who occupy the dividing line between jazz and R&B, or perhaps between smooth jazz and un-smooth jazz, Anita Baker and Rachelle Ferrell. Baker seems to be primarily exploring the sonic stretches of the song and her voice in a manner rather like Sarah Vaughan's (there's yet another Chet-ish trumpet here), while the Ferrell is one of the few tracks by this generally overbaked screaming yenta that I can actually listen to all the way through.

There is also an art-rock treatment by the British group Miranda Sex Garden (from their 1993 *Suspiria*), which features primarily a low-pitched female voice and spare electric keyboard accompaniment, done slowly but with heavy rockish beats, closing with an *Inner Sanctum*-like door sound effect. Elvis Costello, who wrote a song for Chet Baker, included a short, effective, and surprisingly in-tune reading on his album *Taking Liberties* (although with "Valentine" he doesn't). The best of these contempop treatments is by boudoir baritone—and "Godfather of Go-Go"—Chuck Brown, on *Back It On Up*. This six-minute reading spotlights a tight horn section, a full-chorus jazz trombone solo, and a dance beat that suits the tune better than you'd think it would. Mr. Brown introduces all manner of lyric alterations (e.g., "very photographable"), detours into a "Funny Valentine" rap that's quite funny (making it the only performance of a Rodgers and Hart song, I suspect, to include the phrase "tight bikini"), and finds room for a quote from "Honeysuckle Rose."

APART FROM THE Mulligan-Baker axis, the musician most associated with "Valentine" was Miles Davis. (According to Milesian lore, at one point some phone company even ran a magazine ad with reference to the trumpeter playing that song. "I was listening to Miles play 'My Funny Valentine' and I thought about you.") He recorded it on several occasions; among them: for Prestige in 1956 and Columbia (a live version) in 1958. While both these sessions were by the classic Miles Davis Quintet costarring John Coltrane, for some reason the great tenorist sat this tune out on both occasions. The 1958 one spotlights pianist Bill Evans in addition to the leader. Wayne Shorter does take a solo on a 1964 live version, but there's no ensemble playing by the horns, just Davis, Shorter, and pianist Herbie Hancock taking turns individually.

Davis was best known for constantly pushing the jazz envelope, yet the trumpeter could also play a ballad in a traditionally warm, romantic fashion when he chose to, as on his 1961 recording of "Someday My Prince Will Come." However, that's not what he does on his classic live "Valentine" from Philharmonic Hall in 1964. What we hear is far from romantic or lyrical; instead we get an anguished, tormented treatment. Davis opens with a dramatic ascending line, building up to a near-crack, and then throws in a two-note phrase reminiscent of "All the Things You Are." We don't hear anything remotely "Funny" until the bridge, and even then it's not because Davis is actually playing the melody; he's merely hinting at it—slyly dropping it like a name at a Tina Brown cocktail party. From his opening chorus, he drifts stealthily into the improvisation per se, and ends equally unobtrusively. In their solos, Shorter and Hancock are no less probing and angular—although the pianist does take us through some lyrical passages reminiscent of Bill Evans. Even though there's little of Rodgers's melody here (Davis does apparently have a soft spot for the bridge, which he plays more fully at the start of the out-chorus at the windup), Davis elected to honor the tune by releasing this concert album as *Miles Davis: My Funny Valentine Live in Concert.*

It's a near perfect rendition; indeed, it's just about my favorite work of art. Davis had so refined the art of transforming standards and showtunes into his blues-drenched, sometimes modal medium, that in some ways it's not surprising that a few years later he would abandon the Great American Songbook altogether. Apart from the inducement of potentially greater profits to be made with electric music, Davis apparently felt he had done everything there was to do with songs like "My Funny Valentine."

If that indeed was Davis's reasoning, it is patently wrong. As the song's myriad interpreters have shown—not the least of whom was Davis himself—there is no end of new ways to play "My Funny Valentine." As constructed by Rodgers and Hart, it's a road map of infinite possibilities: if there ever was an American *lied,* or art song, this is it. By making both the words and the music so ambiguous, that is to say, so open to interpretation, Rodgers and Hart insured that no one would ever run out of ways to approach "Valentine." It's in major and it's in minor, it's slow and it's fast, it's a romantic song with a comic twist. (When one considers Lorenz Hart's omni-directional sexual preferences and the apparent androgyny of Chet Baker, the artist who sang it most over the years, perhaps we could describe it as sexually ambiguous as well.) Small wonder that Tony

Bennett and Rita Reys could sing it both slow and comparatively fast, and that Chet Baker could go from one tempo to the other in the same performance. The late Mr. Rodgers's own intentions notwithstanding, all interpretations of the song are valid as long as they succeed in making us smile with our hearts.

BONUS TRACKS

How Funny Was My Valentine

It's safe to assume that Hart and Rodgers meant "funny" in the sense of "imperfect," or perhaps "awkward," but, again, the meaning is ambiguous enough to allow interpreters to perform it as "funny" in the Bob Hope sense. Dakota Staton performed the song on her best-remembered album, *The Late, Late Show,* on which she made a point to spice up this otherwise dramatic interpretation with the occasional utterance of "Ha ha!" In 1963, she rerecorded "Valentine" on the album *Live and Swinging,* in which the liner copy describes the new performance as "her classic 'Funny Valentine' in a new arrangement"; indeed, new though it may be, the "ha ha"s are still intact. Still, the funniest of all "Valentine"'s was that rendered in 1986 at a *Highlights in Jazz* concert (held as a memorial for the recently departed baritone saxist Pepper Adams) by an obscure jazz singer named Lodi Carr. When she reached the pause between "laughable" and "unphotographable," Carr emitted the loudest "Ha ha!" I've ever heard, which not only completely demolished the ballad mood she was trying to achieve (up until that point, anyhow) but made Staton's own laughing tradition seem comparatively subtle by comparison. This was a "ha ha" of earth-shattering proportions, made even more memorable, if memory serves, by Carr's decision to mimic the inimitable seal laugh that Desi Arnaz, as Ricky Ricardo, used to perpetrate on the old *I Love Lucy* show. Those fortunate enough to be present at this occurrence looked around at each other, shared the moment, and, realizing that we were experiencing a "Funny Valentine" the likes of which the world would never hear again, got in the proper spirit and chimed in with a few "ha ha"s of our own. In fact, after fifteen years, the memory of that incredible performance still brings a twinkle to my eye and a "ha ha" to my lips.

Most Intense Valentine

Even during periods in her career when her studio recordings were nothing to write home about, Sarah Vaughan could always be depended upon to make a live album guaranteed to blow you away. Her double-length *Live in Japan* (1973) is just about the best, particularly for "The Nearness of You," for which she accompanies herself on piano. Her "Funny Valentine" here is also one for the gods, both in the context of the history of the song and against the larger backdrop of Vaughan's career. The melody of "Valentine" has never received a treatment quite like this, with the ornamentations so ornate, the decorations so decorous. In the first chorus, Vaughan does everything that seems possible to do with "Valentine," but then she flies into a second chorus that's even more elaborate. Never before has Vaughan paraded her multi-octave range so spectacularly, dropping down to basso register on "When you open it to speak" and soaring way above soprano on "Don't change a hair for me." She concludes with a low, low, low tonic—it's the only treatment of "Valentine" that ends on a foghorn.

My Beautiful Valentine

A year after Ellis Larkins and Ruby Braff worked on Lee Wiley's wonderful 1954 Rodgers and Hart collection, the piano player and the cornetist bit off "Funny Valentine" on their own, without any singer at all. Or I should say without a vocalist per se, since Braff sings through his cornet and by any standard is one of the greatest singers of all time. This is an especially lyrical "Valentine," yet a buoyant one that creates a relaxed, romantic atmosphere without resorting to a slow, potentially maudlin tempo. Then as now brilliant storytellers, Braff and Larkins give you the full impact of Hart's meaning without uttering so much as one word of his text.

LUSH LIFE (c. 1938)

words and music by Billy Strayhorn

THE FACTS BEHIND "Lush Life" are no less compelling than the song itself. Billy Strayhorn's best-known ballad is the ultimate in the kind of "sophisticated" love songs favored by café society, an instant favorite of movie stars and jaded roués alike. To most ears, the lyric is thoroughly convincing. Strayhorn writes of a world-weary proto-jetsetter who spends "a week in Paris" in order to distract himself after a love affair gone south, and it never sounds as if he's merely putting on highfalutin airs to give the impression he's more sophisticated than he is. Yet although the song first began to be heard in 1948 and '49, Strayhorn had written it at least ten years earlier, as a precocious teenager who had yet to experience cultures any more sophisticated than those he encountered in Ohio, North Carolina, and western Pennsylvania.

No other song depicts the love styles of the highbrow and sophisticated as movingly as "Lush Life." Before Strayhorn, the best song about the interrelationship of alcohol and love was Gillespie and Coots's brilliant "You Go to My Head," in which the act of getting intoxicated is a metaphor for the giddy feeling of falling in love. By contrast, Strayhorn reveals the dark underbelly of romance as a hangover it would take you oceans of Bloody Marys to shake off. Even Cole Porter, that most directly passionate of Tin Pan Alley craftsmen, tends to view love from a slightly more objective—that is to say, safe—viewpoint. In his saddest of sad songs, "Down in the Depths (on the Ninetieth Floor)," Porter uses irony as a kind of defense mechanism, to insure that the whole thing doesn't get too suicidal. Likewise, Arlen and Mercer's equally alcoholic "One for My Baby" employs a self-deprecating humor that Frank Sinatra exploits to the fullest in his many recorded performances. "Lush Life," though, is witty without being funny—in fact, the song's protagonist can't even manage "to smile in spite of it."

Strayhorn had one thing in common with Richard Rodgers and Jerome Kern: he couldn't stand most of the jazz versions of his song. How can this be, one asks, when Strayhorn is generally considered a jazzman himself and achieved immortality on the payroll of Duke Ellington's orchestra, the greatest jazz organization of them all? Certainly, Strayhorn wrote pieces that were vehicles for jazz orchestra and jazz improvisation (his "Take the A Train" was a jazz conveyance if ever there was one), but with "Lush Life," he had something else in mind entirely.

For this particular piece his inspiration was not Ellington or Fletcher Henderson (who, the composer said, inspired "A Train") but Noel Coward and Cole Porter. Both men, and Coward in particular, wrote all kinds of songs about sophisticated souls who are supposed to be happy and carefree (e.g., Coward's "Parisian Pierrot" and "Poor Little Rich Girl" and Porter's "Down in the Depths") but in reality are not: they harbor a dark secret of past unrequited love. Their outward manifestations of being gay (in more than one sense of the word) party animals are a mere façade; inside lurks a badly broken heart. They drink and play the part of the social butterfly as a way of avoiding their inner pain, but they can't hide their hurt from . . . themselves. The shared sexual preferences of Coward, Porter, and Strayhorn may have something to do with the nature of these unspeakable, inner secrets. Homosexuality was, needless to say, hardly a socially acceptable lifestyle option in the interwar years. "Lush Life's" French references ("*distingué* traces," "a week in Paris") are not so much pretentious allusions to another culture but a road sign to the intercontinental playgrounds of such wealthy songwriting sophisticates as Porter and Coward. No wonder Strayhorn was perturbed when his song became more of a jazz standard than a cabaret or salon anthem, inviting comparisons with Monk and Mingus rather than Noel and Cole.

The tip-off is the fourth line, the one about getting "the feel of life from jazz and cocktails." Strayhorn is deliberately writing about jazz as if he were an outsider. Lyricists in the jazz world would never use the word "jazz" in a song (Bobby Troup's "The Feeling of Jazz" is a notable exception); they might talk about "swinging" or "getting hot," but it would be a foregone conclusion that the only music worth singing about would be jazz. Instead, Strayhorn doesn't want to be a jazz insider, he prefers to be on the outside looking in, as Porter does in "Now You Has Jazz" and "When Love Beckoned on Fifty-second Street," and as Coward does when he writes that the "Songs I used to sing / Now I have to swing" in "Weary of It All," a song clearly meant to be performed with a *distingué* attitude. (And having mentioned *that* word, Strayhorn's sister Lillian claimed to have heard more than one singer turn "*distingué* traces" into "distant gay traces.")

It was all pretty intoxicating stuff for a young man who was barely old enough to drink legally. Yet as David Hajdu showed in his biography of Strayhorn (titled, of course, *Lush Life*), the phrase was more than a song title but virtually a prophecy in which Strayhorn mapped out for himself, very early on, the course of his life, and death.

It seems that Strayhorn could only have created "Lush Life" because of, rather than in spite of, his tender years. Only a precocious eighteen-year-old who hadn't already had his heart run over by a Mack truck a few times would be so naïve as to lay his feelings so totally bare, his soul so completely exposed, such that any passerby could take a shot at it. When Chris Connor sings "Lush Life," one is almost embarrassed to look at her; it's as if she's revealing something so personal that you feel uncomfortable being in the same room with her. Unlike, say, Rosemary Clooney or Mary Cleere Haran, Connor is not especially chatty on the bandstand, with the result that everything she tells us about herself will come from the songs themselves, and in the case of "Lush Life," it's more than enough.

Conductor and Ellington scholar Andrew Homzy has observed that one of the things that makes "Lush Life" so special is the way "the lyrics carry the melody," the implication being that in most pop songs it's the other way around. What makes the music of "Lush Life" so absolutely appropriate for its text is its almost death-defying balancing act. In the first half especially, Strayhorn dictates that the melody line be treated rubato, without ever once moving into a specific tempo. Yet at the same time, there's actually a strong melody that you can follow, pat your paws to, or hum; it's a melody so powerful that it doesn't require a tempo to get through to you.

That "Lush Life" dictates its own tempo and time signature tempts one to label it a "composition" rather than a "song." That is, it's expected that each performer will play it pretty much along the lines of tempo and mood dictated by the composer. Which illustrates one of the ironies of the very concept of jazz composition: tunes from outside the jazz tradition are open to "jazzing" and improvising, while the great works of the jazz canon seem to come with a user's manual. As Lee Konitz has said, he can play a standard any way he chooses, but in tackling a Thelonious Monk tune (referring to modern jazz's most directly post-Ellington composer) he has to play it essentially the way Monk wrote it. Indeed, modern and postmodern pianists like McCoy Tyner and Chick Corea, who might otherwise be tempted to reshape the melodies and alter the harmonies of the standards they play, have recorded comparatively faithful treatments of "Lush Life." Guitarist Bucky Pizzarelli put it nicely when he observed that "Tunes like this are so perfect, they have a sort of sacred quality. You almost have to play them the way they're written."

If you were to take all the major ballads of any of the great songwriters and boil them into a single composition, you might get a song as good as "Lush Life." Which, as it happens, pretty much sums up Billy Strayhorn's career as a writer of love songs. Apart from "Something to Live For," also presented to Ellington in '38, "Lush Life" remains the sole Strayhorn ballad to have entered the standard repertory. And even "Lush Life" came in through the back door. Strayhorn performed it at informal, private appearances, yet neither he nor the Maestro ever regarded it as something the Ellington orchestra should play.

"Lush Life" is key to any discourse on Strayhorn, in terms of both his personal and professional lives. When the young man first met Ellington, in the latter's dressing room backstage at a Pittsburgh theater in 1938, this was one of the compositions he demonstrated for the Maestro. Ellington's decision to hire the young man, who would spend the remaining thirty years of his life as Ellington's composing and arranging partner, was made, one has to assume, partly on the strength of "Lush Life," even if he would never perform it with his orchestra.

There are two points of view regarding that epochful meeting: long-time Ellington associate and literary collaborator Stanley Dance has suggested that "it is quite possible that, but for Ellington, Strayhorn might never have left Pittsburgh." In this very traditional view, Strayhorn is merely an extension of Ellington's talent, brilliantly fulfulling his Ducal duties but with little that was distinctly his own. In short, no one would ever have heard of him had it not been for Ellington. David Hajdu's book, conversely, paints a picture of Strayhorn as an ambitious young musician who, in a sense, regarded Ellington as his ticket to get to the big city and the big time. Although he had the abilities and training, as both pianist and writer, to work in the symphonic genre, he knew that dance bands were a more immediate path to musical success—and to the life he craved. If Ellington hadn't played Pittsburgh that season, might not Strayhorn have hooked up with Count Basie or Jimmie Lunceford, or perhaps even a white band?

In support of his hypothesis, Dance cited how Strayhorn had told him that Ellington's 1934 "Ebony Rhapsody" had made a profound impression on him. Intriguingly, other aspiring jazz orchestrators of the period—such as Andy Gibson and Pittsburgher Billy May—also cited this comparatively minor Ellington disc as a personal influence. The piece does provide a clear illustration of the possibilities open to the jazz arranger: it started life as Liszt's second *Hungarian Rhapsody,* then was transformed into a pop song by Tin Pan Alleyite Sam Coslow, and finally into hot jazz by Ellington. On the other hand, Hajdu has found home-made recordings of early Pittsburgh-based Strayhorn bands that sound a lot more like Benny Goodman than like Ellington.

Nevertheless, the melodies of "Lush Life," to a certain degree, and, to a greater extent, of "Something to Live For," suggest that Strayhorn's decision to bring his wares to Ellington was hardly a random one. While not imitating any specific Ellington song, "Something" is nevertheless very Ducal—like Ellington, Strayhorn uses a lot of accidentals and blue notes, and a kind of rambling, intricate, quirky line that heads off into unexpected places somewhat in the manner of "Sophisticated Lady" or "Reminiscing in Tempo." Harmonically, too, "Lush Life" can be described as kinda Dukish: it begins on the tonic chord (I) and spends much of its time on the I and flatted II chords. Still, there are aspects of "Lush Life" that are distinctly not Ellingtonian. Although the piece sounds spare and open—as we'll see, Strayhorn preferred it to be performed by voice with solo piano, not a full orchestra—the chords change constantly, almost on every note. "Something to Live For," on the other hand, balances consonance and dissonance in a way that made it believable when Ellington's name showed up next to Strayhorn's on the published sheet music, which was not the case when "Lush Life" was finally published.

IT'S HARD TO THINK of another piece of music that has anything at all in common with "Lush Life." The melody is divided into two distinct sections, but unlike what happens in most songs, the first part and the second part are not so easily labeled "verse" and "refrain." Most verses can easily be detached from the rest of the songs that they preface, yet "Lush Life" is almost never performed without its opening section ("I used to visit all the very gay places . . ."). Few performances—Harry James's 1953 instrumental is a rare exception—begin at the halfway point ("Life is lonely again . . ."). The opening section is, however, marked "ad lib," in the manner of most verses (and, like the verse to "Night and Day," for instance, it includes long stretches of repeated notes), while the second section goes into something more like a discernible tempo.

The two sections are constructed very differently: the first, which lasts twenty-eight bars, is hard to map out at all (although the harmonies get somewhat more conventional at the halfway point, at "Then you came along / With your siren song . . ."). The second is thirty-two bars, and can be diagrammed as A-B-A^1-C (the C section begins with "Romance is mush . . ."). The first section is in minor, the second is in major, although many recordings, following the example of Nat King Cole's premiere 1949 single, play both in minor.

All pop music is essentially diatonic. However, the superior composers inevitably succeed in finding enough ins and outs of the system to give the songs variety and freshness. A song like "Star Dust" throws the pattern slightly askew, but there is still some sort of recognizable harmonic trajectory. The chordal pattern of "Lush Life" has little in common with any other piece of music, whether classical, jazz, or popular. The song is published in D flat (five flats, already not one of your easier keys) and is, respectfully, most often heard in that key (as in the Cole and both Coltrane versions). The "verse" spends most of its twenty-eight bars going back and forth between the tonic (D flat) and the VII chord (C flat, or B natural, with a dominant seventh). (Tommy Wolf would employ similar changes some years later in his song "Spring Can Really Hang You Up the Most"). On "*Then* you came along" we get a iii (F minor). In general, the verse features a lot of chromatic movement between major chords. We might choose to think of minor chords as like the night, and major chords as like the day; in which case "Lush Life" has lots of daytime sunshine, but it's less like being at the beach than being in the middle of the desert; it's an arid, harsh, kind of sunshine. There's plenty of sun, but it's not very reassuring or optimistic.

Harmonically speaking, the refrain is fairly unprecedented, there's almost no describing it. Throughout, there is a lot of movement between

D flat (the tonic) and D (which can be described in this case as either a flatted two or really a dominant tritone substitution). Apart from that, the song is pretty much all over the place. Just a few samples: on "Everything seemed *so*," we get a B9 with flatted thirteenth; on "*all* I care" it's a D natural chord; on "*those* who" there's a sharped V (A9+), and on "*strive*" it's a dominant V chord (an A♭13, which means playing the 7 and the 6 at the same time—the chord still has a dominant seventh in it). If you're not totally exhausted as you near the coda, the last two bars will finish you off completely: here the chords change on every single note. And they're not standard chords, either, but funky, difficult chords destined to tie the fingers of even the most daunting keyboardist in a knot. On the last line, "those whose lives are lonely too," the melody moves up chromatically from B natural to F, while the chords move down chromatically, E-E♭-D. The last three words are: "*are*" (G9 with the flatted fifth), "*lonely*" (D♭9, with a dominant seventh), and "*too*" (D♭9, with a major seventh). Kids, don't try this at home! It's complicated just to explain, and murderously tough to play.

Melodically speaking, "Lush Life" is one of the most chromatic songs ever written. From Wagner's "Liebstod" (in *Tristan and Isolde*) to Duke Ellington's "Chromatic Love Affair" (a feature for Harry Carney), a slow melody moving up in half-steps can sound very erotic. Strayhorn achieves that effect here. To achieve it, he needs to use a lot of accidentals: on the word "again," the melody goes from the accidental A natural (on "a-") to the A flat (on "-gain"), as indicated in the key signature, while on "last year" he goes from B natural to B flat, and "*is aw*-ful" the move is from B flat to B natural. In the published music, virtually every note has either a flat or a natural sign in front of it, and the words "*Pa*-ris" and "*bite* of it" are on F sharp—needless to say, it's rare to find a sharp note in a song written in a flat key. (Equally rare, the words "axis *of* the wheel" and "where *they'd* been washed away" are written as B♭♭—that's B double-flat.)

We can take this notion of chromaticism a step further: ordinarily, the key signature will indicate which notes are supposed to be sharpened or flattened. Here, the whole concept of the "key signature" may be irrelevant: there are so many sharps, flats, and naturals in the opening fifteen bars or so of the second section that it doesn't make sense to describe this section as being in D flat, or any other key for that matter. The relation-

ship of one note to the next no longer has anything to do with the key of
D flat, and the whole concept of in-key notes and accidentals seems
beside the point. Strayhorn has written a melody that makes free use of
both the black and white keys on the piano, a tune based only on the chromatic scale.

BY ANY PERSPECTIVE, "Lush Life" is a magnificent song, and it obviously made an impression on Ellington, who hired Strayhorn not only as
his orchestra's other great composer-arranger, but as a lyricist (a function
that he would fill only rarely). As mentioned earlier, Ellington put Strayhorn's "Something to Live For" into his band's repertoire immediately,
while "Lush Life" went into the vault for another ten years. Having
conceived of the tune as a vehicle for voice and piano—and preferably
his own—Strayhorn had no interest in hearing it played by Ellington's
orchestra, or any other. Everything seems to indicate that he wanted to
keep the tune as his own personal property. "It was just something that I
did and I had written that I liked for myself," Strayhorn later remarked,
"and I just did it at parties."

It was at one of those parties that Norman Granz, then a producer for
Mercury Records (Clef, Norgran, and Verve lay in the future), heard
Strayhorn perform the song and immediately decided to record it. The
year was 1948, and Strayhorn consented, probably because it was understood that he would be the one performing it, solo. The cut was sched-
uled to be included in one of Granz's first album projects, an anthology
entitled The Jazz Scene. Although not predominantly an Ellington project,
the album had a certain degree of Ducal content, in the form of a session
produced by Ellington featuring the band's virtuoso baritone saxophonist, Harry Carney, playing against string arrangements by Strayhorn.

The way Strayhorn recalled it, Nat Cole first heard "Lush Life" when
the composer performed it at a recording session for The Jazz Scene. Cole
happened to be in the same studio, and upon hearing the song, Cole asked
what it was. When Strayhorn told him, Cole responded, "Well, I'd like to
do that." Strayhorn apparently thought nothing more of the incident until
the Cole recording came out some months later. There are two things
wrong with that story, however: first, there's no evidence that Strayhorn
or anyone else ever recorded the song at that session (it was not on the

released album, and there's no reference to it in Granz's recording data); second, Cole is not known to have had anything to do with *The Jazz Scene*. However, a recent CD reissue of *The Jazz Scene* includes two previously unissued piano solos that were once thought to be by Strayhorn but which some experts (such as Kenny Washington) now believe to be the work of Nat Cole.

It was around the time of *The Jazz Scene* that Strayhorn decided to present "Lush Life" in concert. Ironically, the first paying audiences in the world to have heard "Lush Life" may have been Parisian. Duke Ellington made a brief European tour in June and July of 1948, but at that time the English musicians' union would not permit any American orchestra to perform in Britain, so, rather than appearing as a bandleader, Ellington was billed as a "variety act"—a piano soloist—and he brought only two performers from the band with him. These were Ray Nance, who played violin and trumpet, sang, and danced—his nickname was "Floorshow"—and Kay Davis, a formally trained singer with a very proper, almost operatic-style voice, who Ellington reasoned, correctly, would appeal to British and Continental audiences.

According to Ellington scholar Jerry Valburn, Ms. Davis, a close friend of Strayhorn's, performed "Lush Life" in Paris on this tour, presumably accompanied by Ellington. Valburn also reports that the French crowd actually jeered when Davis sang the song. We can only assume that they wanted to hear hot black jazz rather than a cabaret song; *their* fantasy was to be transported to jungle nights in Harlem, not a week in Paris.

Undeterred, Ellington included "Lush Life" on his next major event back in the States, which occurred on November 13, 1948, at the last of the orchestra's annual Carnegie Hall concerts. Again, it was Kay Davis singing, and again the orchestra was not employed—the only item on the program presented this way. This time, however, Strayhorn himself played piano, with the benefit of a typically florid and funny spoken introduction by Ellington. This performance, issued semiprivately in the 1990s, must be regarded as being as close as we can come to how Strayhorn heard the tune in his head in those years before the song was commercially recorded.

At that time, Nat Cole was well known in jazz circles as one of the greatest pianists the music had ever known. In the world of black popular music, then known to the record business as "race music," and about to be rechristened "rhythm and blues," Cole was even better known as the singing and playing leader of the King Cole Trio, the most popular small jazz combo of its day. Thanks to frequent radio broadcasts and his long-standing contract with Capitol Records, Cole was also beginning to find a newer and bigger audience in the world of mainstream popular music: he was now no longer restricted to black clubs and theaters but was playing high-profile night spots and even, in 1949, Carnegie Hall. By then, he had also made several records on which his familiar trio was supplemented by a full string section, resulting in such breakthrough hits as "The Christmas Song" and "Nature Boy."

It seems likely that Cole was the one who suggested recording "Lush Life" with a full orchestra, and it was natural that Pete Rugolo be the one to arrange and conduct it. Cole's previous orchestral dates had been one-shot pairings; now he would have a regular musical director to work with, just like Sinatra and Crosby. "I go back with Nat to about 1945, when I first joined Stan [Kenton's orchestra]," Rugolo recalled in 1992. "We did a lot of theaters around together." Cole and Rugolo first encountered each other because the Kenton orchestra and the King Cole Trio shared the same personal manager, Carlos Gastel, who had shepherded his two key clients to Capitol Records. Being similarly affiliated, and appealing to the same audiences, the two groups were a natural combination for the movie-theater vaudeville tours that were still the backbone of showbiz in the mid- to late forties.

Like his ex-boss, Kenton, and like everyone who ever wrote a worthwhile jazz orchestration, Rugolo all but lit candles to both Ellington and Strayhorn. "One day Nat handed 'Lush Life' to me," Rugolo remembered, "and said, 'See what you can do with this.' "

> I'd never heard it before, but I liked it. I just studied the words and I tried to catch all the lyrics in there. I made sort of a tone poem out of it. The verse wasn't written the way we did it—for instance, I added bars at the beginning. Also, on "jazz and cocktails," where I added a few extra bars in between. I thought it turned out really great.

Those familiar with any of the better-known later versions of the song, like the two by John Coltrane (with and without Johnny Hartman), will find Pete Rugolo's orchestral treatment a revelation. Full of Latin percussion, it balances strings and pizzicato harps with bongoed counter-rhythms, underscoring Cole's narrative as if it were the background for a Shakespeare soliloquy. The contrast of light (flute, solo piano) and heavy (brass section) accompaniment points to, and at the same time surpasses, the entire jazz-and-poetry movement of the fifties, even Charlie Mingus's *Scenes in the City* and the Jack Kerouac Zoot-'n'-Al sessions.

"Even after we recorded it," Rugolo continues, "I had no idea what would happen, because Capitol didn't know what to do with it, it was so unusual." Capitol clearly had more faith in two other songs recorded on the same date: "Land of Love," songster-guru Eden Ahbez's sequel to his own "Nature Boy," and a contemporary pop song called "Lillian," dismissed by Rugolo as a "a terrible commercial thing." The label ultimately released "Lush Life" as the B side of "Lillian," an act comparable to releasing the Orson Welles masterpiece *The Magnificent Ambersons* as the bottom half of a double feature with the cheesy B-comedy *Mexican Spitfire Sees a Ghost*. "However, the jockeys started playing it and it sort of caught on," says Rugolo, "When I went to M-G-M Pictures in the fifties, I found out that all the movie stars loved it, especially Ava Gardner. Lana Turner said, 'God, I love that "Lush Life." ' Word about it just went around."

The word about it went around, but the record only circulated to a modest degree. Cole's single, coming from the transitional neither-fish-nor-fowl portion of his career, remained an insider's favorite. Much like Billie Holiday's "Strange Fruit," it was popular with the cognoscenti but hardly known among the masses. For most of its existence, the side was out of print, turning up on a few LPs in either the U.S. or Britain. Which is as Strayhorn would have preferred it: according to the composer's partner, Aaron Bridgers (in an interview with biographer David Hajdu), Strayhorn actually claimed to prefer the flipside, the trite "commercial" tune "Lillian," because it rather goofily rhymed his own full name, William, with that of his mother, Lillian. Championing such a song was merely Strayhorn's way of expressing his dislike for the Cole-Rugolo recording.

"That was the only time I ever, ever heard Billy really upset," said Bridgers. "He was screaming, 'Why the fuck didn't they leave it alone?' " In general, Strayhorn's reaction seems extreme, particularly at a time when most songwriters would have set fire to their pianos just to get Nat

King Cole to so much as notice them. The only one of the composer's complaints that seems valid is that Cole muffed the lyrics in several spots, which indeed he did, most famously mangling "Then you came along / With your siren song" into the nonsensical "siren *of* song." But these were not simple one-time flubs—Cole actually learned the song this way, and reperformed it as such on two further occasions, a concert at the Pasadena Civic Center later in 1949 (with just his trio and no orchestra) and on his stereo remake of the tune on his 1961 autobiographical three-LP package, *The Nat King Cole Story*.

As we've seen, Strayhorn disliked the very idea of doing "Lush Life" with an orchestra, so one can only imagine how he must have felt when Harry James recorded a bravura, swaggering instrumental treatment for Columbia in 1953. It doubtless pleased the composer that, over time, more intimate performances became the rule. In 1954, Chris Connor followed Strayhorn's original road map when she recorded "Lush Life" for Bethlehem, in a minimal treatment using only a rhythm section. Connor's startlingly spare reading became the model for subsequent performances, particularly those of John Coltrane.

In the years 1956–58, possibilities arose for three orchestral-vocal versions of "Lush Life"—by Rosemary Clooney, Ella Fitzgerald, and Frank Sinatra—none of which materialized. In '56, Strayhorn master-minded a collaboration between the Ellington orchestra and Clooney, a pop star then winning her wings as a jazz vocalist, but the composer elected not to include his own "Lush Life" in the program.

In 1958, Frank Sinatra attempted the song via a fresh and original orchestration by Nelson Riddle that combined saloon piano and semiclassical strings. Unfortunately, the singer had bitten off more than he could chew at this particular time, when he was recording his *Only the Lonely* album, and wasn't up to Strayhorn's ambitious art song. "It's a rather complicated song, and I think Frank was momentarily put off by all the changes that had to go on," Riddle later said. "He could not have but admired the song, and that's why he included it in the list, but when it got down to singing it, it was another matter. Not that he couldn't have sung it with ease and beautifully had he tried a couple of more times." On the one circulating partial take of the three allegedly recorded, Sinatra gets through the out-of-tempo "verse" section but breaks down in the refrain. After a characteristic Kingfish impression, he resolves to "put it aside for about a year." According to pianist Bill Miller, Sinatra later said that he'd decided to "leave that one for Nat." Had the Chairman persisted, "Lush Life" might have become his next great saloon song, after "One for My Baby." For that matter, Sinatra would surely have popularized the song among pop singers; as it was, precious few performed it before Coltrane and Hartman put it on the map again. Jack Jones (the youngest of the pop stars who could be said to be part of the Sinatra generation, and who, like Steve Lawrence and Matt Monro, can be considered an honorary Italian) included it on his *Only the Lonely*–inspired LP *Where Our Love Has Gone,* giving us a sampling of how the Strayhorn song might have sounded in Vegas. It's a departure to hear a superior pop singer approach it, personalizing it and bringing it to life while leaving its basic contours intact.

Ella Fitzgerald's 1957 version did ultimately materialize, but not with the orchestral arrangement originally planned. On June 26 of that year, Fitzgerald recorded five tunes, including "Lush Life" with the full Ellington contingent, in an arrangement reportedly by Strayhorn. All four of the other selections made it into the three-LP package *Ella Fitzgerald Sings the Duke Ellington Songbook,* but, again, either Strayhorn or Ellington vetoed the idea of doing "Lush Life" with the full band. What's especially intriguing is that Paul Gonsalves, Ellington's star tenor soloist of the fifties and sixties, was apparently sick on the dates of the Fitzgerald sessions (although illness was often a mere euphemism for his drug problems). It's established that Frank Foster, a fine saxophonist known for his work with Count Basie, replaced Gonsalves on several of the dates, but at least one Ellington discography lists the father of the tenor saxophone, Coleman Hawkins himself, as taking the tenor chair on June 26. The most recent release of *The Duke Ellington Songbook* makes no mention of Hawkins, but the possibility of an Ellington-Fitzgerald-Hawkins foray on "Lush Life" is fascinating.

In October of that year, Fitzgerald returned to the tune, this time accompanied only by Oscar Peterson. It's a lovely performance, one of the best of all "Lush Life"s, and it ranks up there with her voice-and-piano sessions with Ellis Larkins and Paul Smith. Fittingly, she was requested to sing this best-known of all Strayhorn ballads at the composer's funeral, in June 1967, on which occasion Ellington joined her at the piano. The two reprised this duet on Ella Fitzgerald's television special ten months later, in April 1968. The Fitzgerald-Ellington "Lush Life" marks a rare example of Ellington not only playing "Lush Life" but functioning as accompanist to a singer. Fitzgerald also recorded a supremely intimate, slightly-faster-than-usual duo treatment with guitarist Joe Pass in 1973, issued on *Take Love Easy*.

In 1956, two of the great ladies of the jazz-pop pantheon, Carmen McRae (with Jimmy Mundy) and Sarah Vaughan (with Harold Mooney) recorded opulent orchestral treatments (with strings and woodwinds) of "Lush Life" that were obviously inspired by Cole and Rugolo. Although McRae's is more textually sensitive (not always one of Vaughan's strong points), both are outstanding treatments. McRae would also record what might be the definitive treatment of "Something to Live For," accompanied by Strayhorn himself, and one wishes that the two of them had tackled "Lush Life" together in this fashion. In that same year, Chet Baker recorded one of the first great instrumental versions of the song, an intimate quartet number that opens with pianist Russ Freeman playing the "verse" solo and rubato, the trumpeter himself entering in the "chorus."

Was anyone ever to sing the song to Strayhorn's satisfaction? There's only one documented instance of his actually praising a performer for his rendition of "Lush Life." One night in 1960, Billy Eckstine felt two hands on his eyes and heard someone say, "Guess who?" He turned around and there was Strayhorn, an old friend of his from back in the thirties in Pittsburgh. Said Strayhorn to Eckstine, "Thanks, Homie, for doing my song the right way." A few months earlier, Eckstine had included "Lush Life" on his first live album, *No Cover, No Minimum,* on which he introduces the song as the "immortal . . . or should I say *immoral,* 'Lush Life.' " Strayhorn pointed out to Eckstine that he and his musical director, Bobby Tucker, had been the first to do the song as Strayhorn had written it, with the first part in minor and the second in major; all previous versions had used Pete Rugolo's somewhat altered version, with both halves in minor.

However, the most widely heard and influential recordings of "Lush Life," namely the two by John Coltrane, took even greater liberties with Strayhorn's harmonies. On both Coltrane's 1958 instrumental (for Prestige) and his 1963 collaboration with singer Johnny Hartman (on Impulse!), the tenor colossus uses substitute chords throughout. Ellington associate Brooks Kerr remembers that Strayhorn particularly disliked the two Coltrane versions. On both readings, for instance, the chords are supposed to change to B natural in the tag following the penultimate line,

". . . in some small dive," but Coltrane and his pianists (Red Garland on the first, McCoy Tyner on the second) don't go there.

John Coltrane and Johnny Hartman was the tenorist's most accessible album, and as a result the LP triggered a wave of performances in two very different spheres. First, there were modern and postmodern jazzmen who now took up the tune as if it were one of their own, a kind of post-sixties answer to what "Body and Soul" had been in the thirties and forties and "My Funny Valentine" in the fifties. Among Trane's progeny were Rahsaan Roland Kirk, who recorded a moving, comparatively straight-ahead, tenor-only treatment (sans the dozens of saxophonic contraptions he usually sported, generally playing several at once) very much in tribute to Trane, and the "outside" trombonist George Lewis (not the New Orleans clarinetist), in 1979. The other group of performers who took up the tune were jazz singers in search of a strong ballad and pop balladeers who regarded the tune as their passport into the world of jazz.

The Coltrane-Hartman LP was virtually the biggest-selling release of the entire career of one of the biggest names in all of jazz, and its "Lush Life" turned out to be if not the definitive version, then at least the performance that inspired the greatest number of other artists to take up the tune. Strayhorn was the only one who could object to this turn of events: not to take anything away from Cole or Eckstine, but this is a "Lush Life" of rare quality indeed. The eternally underrated Hartman, who never achieved the upper brackets of the jazz world, let alone the larger pop world beyond, seems, in retrospect, one of the greatest voices the music has produced.

Born in 1923, Johnny Hartman made his first records in 1947 as a boy singer with Earl Hines's orchestra, an association that was the start of his being lumped in socially and sonically with the Billy Eckstine–Al Hibbler school of black baritones. Yet for all his respect for Eckstine, it's clear (especially on Hartman's earliest solo recordings) that his primary influence was the young Frank Sinatra. Indeed, Hartman combines Eckstine's rich voice with Sinatra's heightened sensitivity, and the entire Coltrane-Hartman album offers the singer at his absolute best (indeed, "My One and Only Love," the Guy Wood standard introduced by Sinatra, is even better than "Lush Life"). Although the intimate nature of the performance recalls the Chris Connor treatment of a decade earlier, it's fair to say that no singer ever got more mileage out of Strayhorn's words and music than Hartman.

For Coltrane, too, this was an exceptional performance. This was the classic quartet with McCoy Tyner, Jimmy Garrison, and Elvin Jones, the same group that produced such harrowing masterpieces as "Chasin' the Train," "Impressions," "Alabama," "Spiritual"—all pieces that push both human emotion and conventional notions of tonality and harmony to the very edge. Compared to such intense experiences as these (not to mention the extended quartet suite *A Love Supreme*), such albums as *Ballads* and *John Coltrane and Johnny Hartman* offer a very mellow Trane indeed. As far out as he was getting, these sets of standards showed that he was still keeping in touch with the song form and could still put his soul into a ballad. For a mere six glorious songs, the two Johns make one of the great teams in American music. The mystery is not only why they never did it again, but why the jazz world has not witnessed any kind of powerhouse team-up of a great voice and a great horn in the last thirty-five years.

CONSIDERING THAT "LUSH LIFE" spent its first decade barely being heard by anybody and never even received the benefit of an official Elling-ton recording, the song underwent a 180-degree turn in popularity in the jazz world after the Coltrane recordings and Strayhorn's death in 1967. Following Hartman, "Lush Life" was generally performed by jazz singers backed by small groups. It amounted to something of a departure from standard practice for both Anita O'Day and Sheila Jordan. Generally speaking, both of these rather "hardcore" jazz ladies are more interested in playing with the melody and the chords to the songs they sing than they are with making the lyrics come alive à la Mabel Mercer; yet "Lush Life" is a song that brought out their latent dramatic tendencies. Both recorded it in Europe, O'Day in London in 1971, Jordan in Oslo six years later. Jordan recorded hers as a duet with bassist Arild Andersen, and though she's comparatively serious here, she wouldn't be Sheila Jordan if she weren't at least a little bit goofy: hitting bizarre off-pitch notes, pro-nouncing certain words strangely, stopping and starting unexpectedly.

Although the South African vocalist Sathima Bea Benjamin made her first recordings in the company of Ellington and Strayhorn on *A Morning in Paris* in 1963, she did not attempt "Lush Life" on this occasion. Wisely, Benjamin waited until she had a little more experience under her belt before tackling this most difficult of numbers. When she later recorded it—twice, in fact, in 1979 (*Sathima Sings Ellington*) and 1989 (*Southern Touch*)—it turned out to be perfectly suited for her unique combination of African chant and American jazz singing. Mark Murphy, who cut his treatment directly in tribute to Nat Cole in 1983, personalizes it aggressively, bending and stretching words for emphasis, but stopping short of distorting it, and doing most of the piece as a duet with guitarist Joe Lo Duca. Strayhorn would have approved of the singspiel nature of the performance, particularly the way Murphy just flat-out speaks the word "awful." The singer catches us slightly off guard by omitting the last word of the ending ("too"), but this doesn't compromise either the beauty or the effectiveness of the performance.

There have been good orchestral versions, too, even after Coltrane and Hartman reestablished it as a small-group number. One is by Nancy Wilson, who slyly uses "A Train" as a countermelody. Canadian jazz legend Rob McConnell found a new way to play it on his 2001 *Tentet,* opening with trumpet (Guido Bass) and piano, then bringing in the ensemble in the second half, getting into more of a tempo in the second chorus. It was something of a surprise that Sarah Vaughan used a string orchestra, arranged and conducted by Billy Byers, on her 1979 *Duke Ellington Song Book One,* since most of her work in this period was with small groups. It would have been preferable to hear her just with piano on this particular song, but the quality both of Vaughan's voice (no one sings the line "Romance is mush . . ." quite like Vaughan, whose use of a pause after the first word is quite telling) and of Byers's chart make this a worthy sequel to her "pop" version of twenty-three years earlier. Together, Vaughan and Byers created the last of the epic, even heroic, "Lush Life"s.

There are occasions when the singing is great but the orchestration inane, such as the one Joe Williams was subjected to. This starts out like the A minor Grieg piano concerto and gets progressively more off track, particularly when arranger Horace Ott feels compelled to illustrate musically such phrases as "jazz and cocktails" and "tempt me to madness." The piece almost becomes a parody of the Cole-Rugolo classic; they should have taken Hank Jones as a role model for playing a jazz classic, not Spike Jones. On the other hand, there's the Linda Ronstadt–Nelson Riddle recording, in which the orchestration is fine (it makes prominent use of the piano but otherwise has nothing in common with Riddle's aborted 1958 arrangement for Sinatra), but the singer is clearly out of her league. Ronstadt, by the way, is virtually the only female singer who does not change the gender of "The girls I knew . . ." to "The boys" or "The men."

On the whole, the great jazz pianists have an exceptional track record for getting to the heart of this particular composition. Phineas Newborn, who for years was accused of being technically accomplished but emotionally barren—he loves those big breakaway runs that out-Tatum Tatum—came out with a fine, soulful statement on "Lush Life." Newborn is also the only one ever to open Strayhorn's opus with a rather grand introduction based on Maurice Ravel's *Sonatine*. Newborn's is essentially an optimistic "Lush Life," whereas Roland Hanna's is a ruminative tone poem, which also boasts a long, well-constructed intro. Hanna is too much of a professional and a craftsman ever to get self-indulgent, but this is the deepest I've ever heard him dig into his own emotions. Bill Evans never came within shouting distance of "Lush Life," yet perhaps he didn't need to, since he translated so many other ballads into inner explorations in the very manner of Strayhorn's song. McCoy Tyner, the other great romantic pianist of the sixties, recorded "LL" in 1977 with Evans's longtime bassist Eddie Gomez as part of one of his *Supertrios,* and it's everything we would want: florid, expressive, and aggressively lyrical, not to mention rhythmic, all at the same time.

Dick Hyman's solo of the song isn't nearly as personal, but it's still quite nice; he plays it like a piano instrumental and doesn't dwell on the personal aspects of the melody. Bill May's solo version is sufficiently interesting, although it contains no surprises. The Mitchell-Ruff Duo plays it like a classical composition, not in the sense of faux-European filigrees in the Liberace mode (now there's a thought, Liberace playing "Lush Life"), but in overall attitude and in the crispness of its no-nonsense phrasing. As with Hyman, the melody is neither jazzed up nor treated as a springboard for soul-searching.

Two other veteran pianists of the swing-to-bop transition of the forties recorded superior "LL"s, Jimmy Rowles and Al Haig. Rowles's solo is solidly rhythmic, and in a faster tempo than most, yet it's no less personal than any other "Lush Life" I've heard. Al Haig, working in England with a quartet co-led by bassist Jamal Nasser, produced one of the outstanding examples of "Lush Life" being played as just another standard, i.e., a vehicle for a string of solo improvisations. Starting with a pizzicato bass fanfare by Nasser, the melody goes to Art Theman, a fine Manchester-based tenor of Dutch-Carribean descent. At times Theman reminds me of Joe Henderson, at other times of Stan Getz, and always with a touch of a Sonny Rollins calypso edge. Apart from the quality of the individual players, all the solos are very tightly focused, showing that the song can work in still another format far removed from that originally intended by Strayhorn.

The tune is so closely connected with the piano that it brings out the keyboardistic tendencies in players of other instruments. Bucky Pizzarelli and his son, John Pizzarelli, Jr. (in his most significant recordings as an instrumentalist), included the tune in their ongoing series of seven-string guitar duets, thereby proving that their fourteen strings can sound no less melodically and harmonically satisfying than an eighty-eight-key Stein-way. Bobby Hutcherson, the leading vibraphonist of the post–Milt Jack-son era, recorded it as featured soloist in front of a large orchestra, and the combination of his instrument's timbre over that of the various sec-tions of the ensemble often affords a pianistic sound to Hutcherson's instrument.

If "Lush Life" is capable of making guitars and vibraphones sound like pianos, it's also the rare song that can make Maynard Ferguson and Tito Puente sound like balladeers. Although they're normally two of the most exuberant, extroverted players in jazz, this song brings out the rarely revealed sensitive side of these two men. Ferguson's 1983 "LL" (on *Live from San Francisco*), like Chet Baker's 1956 quartet version, uses piano on the first half and mostly trumpet on the second, but it's a well-constructed big band rendition all around, with flutes spelling the trum-pet at what might be considered the equivalent of the bridge in the second half (on the words "A week in Paris . . .").

Puente's treatment (on the 1985 *Mambo Diablo,* which also featured his 4/4 interpretation of "Take Five") has *El Rey del Mambo* taking part one on vibraphone (rather than his customary *timbales*); as in most other ver-sions, part one is rubato, while the Latin beat and the rest of the band come in on part two, as does tenorist Mario Rivera.

If the song represents a departure for Puente and Ferguson, "Lush Life"—indeed the entire Strayhorn song catalogue—is made to order for Joe Henderson. In 1991, the great tenor star recorded *Lush Life,* a Strayhorn collection that launched a series of concept albums for Verve that might be considered the climax of Henderson's productive career. While his tenor tone may stamp him as coming from the Coltrane era, Henderson is one of the most inwardly directed of all modern jazzmen, an extremely introverted, even cerebral player. The thoughtful "Lush Life" is thus ideally suited to him, and he chooses to play it in the most demanding of settings, as an unaccompanied tenor solo. This is not a free improvisation; in fact, he sticks closer to the melody than, say, Coleman Hawkins in his unaccompanied variations on "Body and Soul." Henderson succeeds in completely personalizing the melody, reshaping it in his own image while leaving more than enough of it behind for us to recognize.

There are two treatments by contemporary jazzmen that are very much in that spirit, a full-sounding piano arrangement by Chick Corea on his 1994 *Expressions* and a very Hendersonian tenor and acoustic guitar duo interpretation by Gary Thomas and Pat Metheny on the saxist's 1992 collection of standards, *Till We Have Faces.* One of the best of all nineties "LL"s is the 1992 Harry Allen–Keith Ingham treatment (part one is actually done as a tenor-piano duet), from a two-CD Strayhorn tribute.

As we've seen, except for Ella Fitzgerald's *Duke Ellington Songbook,* the song was never officially accepted into the Ellington canon. Yet Harry Allen's relaxed, breathy treatment gives us an idea of what "Lush Life" would have sounded like emanating from the horn of a classic Ellington tenor like Ben Webster, Al Sears, or Paul Gonsalves. Even when the song caught on in the jazz world, few Ellington-oriented vocalists ever sang it, Joya Sherrill being an exception. Consistent with Sherrill's sunny disposish, hers is the least melancholy of all versions, sung mostly over straight guitar chords and a few piano passages.

Admittedly, "Lush Life" is not a song for everybody—not even for every good singer. As we've seen, Sinatra tried visiting all those very gay places and apparently wasn't happy with what he found there. Tony Bennett sang it on his British TV series circa 1979, a version in which the characteristic Bennett dynamics (the loud louds and the soft softs) almost work against the song. He never returned to it, not even on his 1999 *Hot and Cool: Bennett Sings Ellington.* It also might seem like a sure thing for the prolific voice and piano team of Mel Tormé and George Shearing, but somehow, despite half a dozen albums together, they never got 'round to it. Apparently both Bennett and Tormé agreed with Sinatra that "Lush Life" was better left to Nat, not to mention Eckstine and Hartman, come to think of it. Billy Strayhorn's dearest friend was one of the great pop singers, Lena Horne. Why she never sang "Lush Life" is a secret she'll probably take with her to the grave.

EVENTUALLY STRAYHORN HAD A CHANCE to put his own interpretation down on record. Ole J. Nielson's Ellington discography lists a private "Fraternity Party" at which members of the Ellington orchestra performed in 1951 and at which Strayhorn played and possibly sang "Lush Life"; and although this track presumably exists in private hands on tape, it has never been issued. While Strayhorn was residing in Paris a decade later, he recorded an album of his compositions for producer Alan Douglas entitled *The Peaceful Side,* a very Muzaky conception that combined cocktail piano solos with a wordless vocal choir. In 1964, he performed the tune, in his dry, somewhat nasal (and occasionally flat) voice, during an Ellington appearance at New York's Basin Street East that was, fortunately, broadcast by radio station WNEW. That excerpt from the broadcast was released on CD in 1992 and at last the world had Strayhorn singing his classic statement of loneliness on disc.

It seems inappropriate to complain about too much of a good thing, but for a time in the seventies and eighties, "Lush Life" seemed like the most overdone song that ever was. Just about every jazz vocal performance at every loft in Manhattan in those decades followed the same pattern: the singer would do an hour and half of scatting—that is to say, freely improvising without preset words and music, sometimes without even accompaniment—and then, generally inspired by Coltrane and Hartman, would try to tackle "Lush Life," that most complicated of word-and-music compositions. For a while the song seem divested of both lushness and life. More recently, however, jazz and cabaret singers have begun to explore the totality of the Great American Songbook, and there have been fewer moments when every singer out there seems to be doing the exact same songs. (Even "Peel Me a Grape" and "Never Never Land" were not as overdone in the nineties as "Lush Life" was in the previous twenty years.)

Long after the glasses are empty and the ashtrays are full, "Lush Life" resounds as a quintessential American classic. As Ellington said way back at Carnegie in '48, "I don't know which is better, living a 'Lush Life' or singing about it." I'll drink to that.

BONUS TRACKS

Singing Keyboardists Redux

As we've seen, Strayhorn wrote "Lush Life" as a piece for voice and piano, and it was eventually introduced by Nat King Cole, the greatest singer-pianist in history (no arguments, please). Ironically, however, Cole chose it as one of his breakthrough recordings as a stand-up singer—one of the first recordings to feature him as vocalist accompanied by orchestra rather than his own keyboard. Strayhorn, the reader will recall, was not pleased. Oddly, few of the major pianist-singers have performed the song. I have to think that Strayhorn would have enjoyed such cabareteurs as the veterans Bobby Short, Steve Ross, the late Charles DeForrest, and the contemporary Eric Comstock or Billy Stritch, yet none of these worthy artists has made a point of doing "Lush Life."

Still, two singing keyboardists do come to mind, both of whom would surely have made Strayhorn happy, yet neither strictly qualifies as a piano-vocal recording. Joe Mooney isn't quite a pianist because he spent most of his career playing the instrument formally known as the piano-accordion. On his 1957 recording (originally on Atlantic and now available on a Koch CD entitled *Lush Life*), Mooney jettisons his familiar accordion for a Hammond electric organ, which he makes sound exactly like an accordion. Mooney has a very small voice and absolutely no chops in terms of the ability to hold notes ("I haven't got a voice, just a delivery," he once said), but he has an amazing ability to put a song and a story over. It's particularly instructive to compare his "Lush Life" with Strayhorn's 1964 Basin Street East aircheck. What becomes apparent is that Stayhorn's voice—dry, reedy, and nasal—sounds a lot like Mooney's. One is left with the impression that Mooney sounds exactly the way Strayhorn would have liked to sound himself had he dedicated more of his energies